Human Resource Development

Beyond Training

Seventh e

The Chartered Institute of Personnel and Development is the
leading publisher of books and reports for personnel and training
professionals, students, and all those concerned with the effective
management and development of people at work. For details of all
our titles, please contact the publishing department:
Tel: 020-8263 3387
Fax: 020-8263 3850
E-mail publish@cipd.co.uk
The catalogue of all CIPD titles can be viewed on the CIPD
website:
www.cipd.co.uk/bookstore

Martin Forbes-Young

Human Resource Development

Beyond Training Interventions

Seventh edition

Margaret Anne Reid

Harry Barrington

Mary Brown

Chartered Institute of Personnel and Development

Published by the Chartered Institute of Personnel and Development, CIPD House, Camp Road,
London, SW19 4UX

First published by CIPD as Training Interventions 1986
Second edition published, 1988
Third edition published, 1992
Fourth edition published, 1994
Reprinted, 1995, 1996
Fifth edition published, 1997
Reprinted, 1998
Sixth edition, published, 1999
Reprinted, 2000, 2001
This edition published 2004
Reprinted 2006, 2007, 2008, 2009

Design by Fakenham Photosetting, Fakenham, Norfolk
Typeset by Fakenham Photosetting, Fakenham, Norfolk
Printed in Great Britain by Short Run Press Limited, Exeter

British Library Cataloguing in Publication Data
A catalogue of this publicationl is available from the British Library

ISBN 1843980134

Chartered Institute of Personnel and Development, CIPD House,
Camp Road, London, SW19 4UX
Tel: 020 8971 9000   Fax: 020 8263 3333
Email: cipd@cipd.co.uk   Website: www.cipd.co.uk
Incorporated by Royal Charter   Registered Charity No. 1079797

CONTENTS

FIGURES AND TABLES

Preface

Since its origin in the 1970s this book has been retitled, restructured and rewritten several times in response to the changing training and learning scene. During that time the authors have described and taken part in critical discussion of many major initiatives and ideas in Human Resource Development. Some of these have become dysfunctional as times have changed and some are still a powerful force today. The book has almost been a part of history in the making.

In the UK in 2004, the concept of Human Resource Development in organisations continues to expand and evolve. Online information-gathering and a revolution in telephone texting are promoting new ways of learning and development by individuals and organisations. We now hear continuing support for the concept of 'lifelong learning' and much reference to 'the age of the learner'. But who is the learner? There is no doubt that in early life at least, everyone wants to learn and is capable of learning. We are programmed from birth to learn new skills, and childhood is a series of learning milestones, as Piaget (1969) suggested. This enthusiasm for learning new skills does not always survive into the environments of formal education and of work, and in order for the UK to remain competitive among the knowledge economies of the developed world this needs to change. There has been a constant theme of UK skills shortages since the last edition of the book, and Government-led initiatives have tended to cement the development of centrally directed, qualification-based courses as the main answer.

However, in previous editions of this book, Reid and Barrington have constantly maintained that day-to-day experience is an even more powerful learning tool than formal training or qualifications. Equally, they have stressed that learning is not just something that individuals do – organisations can and do learn to learn. Training in organisations is still vitally important, but it should be part of the process of developing an effective organisational learning environment. A key challenge for Human Resource Development specialists is to develop and promote such environments so that organisation members' enthusiasm for learning is stimulated and effectively rewarded.

The book's new title represents not so much a major shift in emphasis, but reinforcement of the concept that employees are organisational assets whose knowledge and skills are vital to economic survival and progression. I have been asked to update and adapt this book to reflect the increasing challenges that HRD specialists face, although it is clear that Reid and Barrington have already foreseen many of these challenges. In the previous edition of this book, for example, they made the important point that any deliberate training or learning is an intervention into an ongoing process for members of an organisation – hence the need to promote learning in a way tailored for that learning context. In making some cosmetic changes and adaptations to the text, I have always tried to bear this point in mind.

The book is now structured in four parts. Part 1 looks at the context of HRD both in terms of national interventions and theories of how people learn. Part 2 examines the operational arena, from policy development to evaluating the impact of HRD. Part 3 takes two discrete and important groups of employees – new workers and managers – and examines trends in their development. Part 4 looks at the development of learning environments and some predictions for the future. There is also an accompanying website containing many useful online links and information for students and their tutors.

Students and their tutors have always recognised Reid and Barrington's book as a classic. My task has been merely to update and adapt, and any errors or omissions are mine rather than theirs.

Individuals who kindly provided permission for citations for the sixth edition (and whose material I have retained) include:

- Alan Mumford for the material on learning opportunities for managers (chapter 3)
- Peter Honey for permission to reproduce the learning styles descriptions (chapter 3)
- Sylvia Downs for the Four Beliefs about Learning and Ten Principles of Learning (Kogan Page) (chapter 4)
- Department for Education and Skills for reproduction of material in a number of figures and in the text (Crown copyright is reproduced with permission of HM Stationery Office) (passim)
- IiP UK for permission to reproduce the IiP standards (updated) (chapter 2)
- M.Pearn and R Kandola for the material on job learning analysis (chapter 8).

I would like to thank the many writers and thinkers who have inspired the ideas we have described in the book, and specifically:

- David Briggs, Director of HR at Robert Gordon University, for agreeing to share his material on leadership development;
- Cliff Allen, Head of Corporate Development and Learning, Portsmouth City Council for material on developing high fliers;
- Jenny Bell at IDS for permsision to quote IDS Study 753 on Leadership Development;
- Jeff Brooks of ITOL for permission to quote from the ITOL members' site;
- Morag Hamilton and Anne Henderson of Aberdeen Business School for ongoing support;
- David Millar, who as a student of Aberdeen Business School has made some helpful suggestions regarding students' needs from this text.
- I personally would like to thank Ruth Lake and Georgina Mace at CIPD Publishing who have remained calm, confident and helpful throughout this process!

Mary Brown, March 2004

Introduction

In the previous edition of this book, looking forward to the new millennium, we explained that both organisational change and the move in the developed world to service and knowledge-based organisations, away from manufacturing and heavy industry, were creating situations where individuals had to be more comfortable with the idea of multiskilling and increased job mobility. The pace at which change happens now places greater emphasis on self-development and self-managed learning. In the context of the management role, there is now an even greater need for managers to take responsibility for influencing their subordinates' development, and for all employees, managers or not, to be responsible for their own learning. The rapidly changing and highly competitive commercial environment means that they also need to be able to use initiative and engage in discretionary behaviour to cope with sudden new opportunities or emergencies.

How have such changes affected the roles and remits of those who work in the field of training, education and development? Is the change of name from Training and Development, to Learning and Development or Human Resource Development (HRD) simply cosmetic or does it represent a paradigm shift to recognise this new 'Learning Age'? Is it really an issue that interests academics rather than practitioners?

As we suggested in the sixth edition, the word *strategic* is often added to the Human Resource Management (HRM) title, reinforcing the view that the function is an essential element in the process by which an organisation achieves its business objectives. Of course, this does not mean that the 'personnel managers' or 'training managers' of the past were all lacking a strategic overview – many of them were well informed and were effective in translating strategy into action. But, when reflecting on the role of old-style trainers, over the last 10 years or so there has been a change of emphasis in the role from a 'training' to a 'learning' focus. To understand what has happened, we need to be clear about definitions.

SOME STANDARD DEFINITIONS

The three most important concepts covered by HRD are **education**, **training** and **learning**. These terms are not accurately defined in common usage, and it is very difficult to give a precise meaning to any of them that will hold good for every time the word is used. In some instances either or both terms 'training' or learning will do. But there are also instances where we can be specific, such as 'experiential learning', or 'formal training programme'. So it is usually necessary to look at the context of the term to be precise about its meaning. **Learning** is probably the most critical concept. We will explain why shortly, and to indicate how important we believe it is, we shall explore its meanings later in the book (see Chapter 3). There is, of course, no universally accepted theory of learning. Until recently, most writers on the subject thought in terms of the acquisition (usually by some form of teaching process) of new knowledge, which is certainly one acceptable form of learning. But a learner may acquire new knowledge by memorising words that have no meaning for that learner; learning may happen without understanding, or without sufficient understanding to allow the learning to be 'applied'. A person may learn to walk, swim, recognise objects, spot defects or develop any of a wide range of skills without consciously retaining the understanding of what is involved in practising it. It seems to be that 'learning' must involve the ability to do something that was not previously within the learner's capability. Precisely what the new ability is, and whether it has been acquired via a teaching process, and whether the 'learner' is a person or a team or a nation – these things are subordinate to a simple definition of learning as the process by which a new capability is achieved. Later in Chapter 3 we will move into other, more sophisticated definitions that relate to specific aims and interventions, but for the present a simple definition will do.

The central theme of this book is still that an organisation is a learning environment, and membership of an organisation is a continuous learning experience. At the most basic level, people learn from the reactions of others, particularly their managers, and develop attitudes towards them – attitudes that begin to influence the way they do their work. Day-by-day experience is so much more powerful that it tends to overshadow what the individual may learn in other settings. Any deliberate learning or training is an intervention into an ongoing process: the task is to promote learning in the most effective and advantageous way. We are convinced that now more than ever, those responsible for HRD need to have regard to the context when deciding on the way that they assess learning needs and objectives, plan strategies and choose methods to meet those needs.

Training is essentially about 'making learning happen'. This applies to any form of learning, although usually in the service of some work goal or goals. Learning can and does occur naturally as a by-product of everyday experience, but random learning is unpredictable, slow in performance, and may even be counterproductive (a random route to learning that an electric drill is a dangerous instrument may involve a nasty injury). HRD usually involves ways of abandoning random learning routes in favour of more productive, planned routes.

'Education' and 'training' are ways of doing just that – abandoning random learning routes in favour of more productive, planned routes. The (now defunct) Manpower Services Commission's 'Glossary of Training Terms' offered the following definitions in 1981:

Education is defined as 'activities which aim at developing the knowledge, skills, moral values and understanding required in all aspects of life rather than a knowledge and skill relating to only a limited field of activity. The purpose of education is to provide the conditions essential to young people and adults to develop an understanding of the traditions and ideas influencing the society in which they live and to enable them to make a contribution to it. It involves the study of their own cultures and of the laws of nature, as well as the acquisition of linguistic and other skills which are basic to learning, personal development, creativity and communication.'

Training is 'a planned process to modify attitude, knowledge or skill behaviour through learning experience to achieve effective performance in an activity or range of activities. Its purpose, in the work situation, is to develop the abilities of the individual and to satisfy the current and future needs of the organisation.'

Some further comments are required about **knowledge**, **skills** and **attitudes**, all of which are complex, and which are frequently interrelated. **Skills** may be mental or physical; work skills usually combine both, so that a plan to introduce or modify a skill will need to cover both. It is surprising how detailed instruction manuals can ignore the mental aspect. Similarly, skills development inevitably involves knowledge and attitudes; the skill of driving a car, for example, rests on knowledge of the Highway Code, while a cavalier attitude to safety may effectively obliterate the skill. Observers and researchers have in recent years distinguished between types of **knowledge** (explicit or tacit, for example, as Nonaka and Takeuchi (1995) define them and which we explain on page 275), and have explored the realities of knowledge in its corporate as well as individual aspect. **Attitudes** are perhaps the most complex to define and develop, but many training programmes, notably those in leadership and management, include experiences explicitly designed to influence objectives such as confidence building, levels of responsibility, the erosion of discrimination and new ethical standards.

Both education and training happen when conditions are created in which the necessary attitudes, skills and knowledge can be effectively acquired by a learner who, as a result, becomes relatively confident of his or her abilities to apply them. It is important to understand that although confidence is not the only outcome of learning, and not the only generator of the desire to develop further, it is central to the learner's ability to transfer what has been learned to new situations. In a very real sense, it is the learner's confidence that allows the learning to be 'used'.

The underlying philosophy in these definitions is that education gives the general basis for living, and that training modifies and directs people's abilities towards a particular activity or activities. This philosophy assumes that the learner is an individual, and that plans are created by teachers or developers to help, if not guarantee, learners' learning.

Learning, training and development are all part of human resource management and involve the planning and management of people's learning – including ways to help them manage their own – with the aim of making the learning process more effective, increasingly efficient, properly directed and therefore useful. People's learning is typically classified as either education or training; education is 'for life', while training is 'for work'. The reality, of course, is that training and development is a situation-specific art, and must be managed as such. Textbooks traditionally suggest standard approaches and norms, implying that the reader might remember or copy them with confidence. But the student of HRD needs to build and respond to a 'moving dictionary'. A doctrinaire approach is likely to make communication difficult, and the biggest achievements rest with those who can observe, describe and promote change in ways that others find realistic.

Our subject has grown – in importance, and in complexity and purpose – during the past few decades. Education and training are no longer in watertight compartments; individual training is no longer the only aim; national economic health is in the frame alongside individual rewards; teaching is not the only way to ensure that learning happens; learning and development concerns all employees, not just managers, and certainly not just HR or HRD managers. The rate and pace of change have made our subject a fundamental part of work, not just an adjunct to it.

THE NATURE OF HUMAN RESOURCE DEVELOPMENT

There have been many critical appraisals of the move from 'Personnel' to Human Resource Management (HRM) and it is not appropriate to discuss them all here. Armstrong (2003) has a fine review of the whole issue in the ninth edition of his Manual of Human Resource Management. One issue needing briefly to be raised is the belief that the HRM concept might involve treating organisational 'human capital' as expendable (for example, Legge in Storey 1995). This criticism is more difficult to level at HRD. It may well be necessary to develop an organisational culture where learning and 'learning to learn' are secondary to all members for purely pragmatic reasons: knowledge is increasingly an organisation's key asset. But an environment where learning and development are actively encouraged has to be more healthy for employees too, both in increasing their employability and their self-esteem. By increasing the learning capacity of individuals and groups through planned learning experiences, HRD specialists are happily placed to serve the needs of organisations and their members. There is no universally accepted definition of HRD, as is the case for the other terms we considered earlier. Furthermore, the discipline is relatively new and itself developing. However, most definitions attempt to stress the HRD function's aim to enhance learning for individuals, groups and organisations in line with the organisation's business objectives. It does this in a number of different ways, but it is fundamentally concerned with learning and with creating circumstances to encourage learning.

TRAINING TO LEARNING – A SHIFT OF EMPHASIS?

The training manager of fifteen years ago or so would have probably taken a relatively 'pedagogic' view of her job – a rather ugly Greek-derived word for a teacher suggesting training centred on the trainer or educator. It did not mean that trainers were conceited or egocentric – some of them undoubtedly were, and liked the idea of being an impresario or stand-up entertainer, but many more were very concerned to help learners to learn. It did mean, though, more emphasis on the inputs to the process – what training needs are we fulfilling, what course should we offer, what topics will we cover, and how will we do so? There was often recourse to the classic 'tell them what you are going to tell them, tell them, tell them what you have told them' structure. The result was that some delegates came to believe that 'most training is boring, ineffective, or both' (Malcolm 2000) – sending people on a training course will not achieve learning for all delegates, no matter how well we entertain them. Educators and trainers today are increasingly focusing on the learner's own management of learning outcomes. The NVQ competence phenomenon has emphasised this, and in this book we place more stress on 'andragogic' learning – centred on the learner, where learners become the best judge of their own learning.

The impact of this change on the HRD practitioner has been a wonderful release for those of us who were never comfortable with the role of 'trainer as expert', having all the answers at our command. Being only one jump ahead of the learners' own knowledge could be quite frightening. Today, there is much more emphasis on the trainer as a 'Learning Facilitator', not necessarily an expert on every subject, but an expert in the processes of learning and helping learners to learn. This approach is not new – the Greek philosopher Socrates in 400 BC described himself as a 'midwife' to others' learning, in his case by asking them the right questions. In classical Athens, it was possible for Socrates to know just about everything there was to be known at that period. In our era, no-one has a monopoly of knowledge. Information technology has produced new ways of compressing, recording, storing and retrieving information. Complex calculations, comparisons and listings can now often be made instantaneously. 'Knowledge' now includes all forms of 'justified belief', opinions and preferences being as accessible as straightforward data. Lists can be scanned in seconds to reveal nominated groups or divergences. Estimates of the future are equally available by asking the computer to introduce variations into their pictures of today. Meanwhile, researchers into existing and new forms of organisation have defined different types of knowledge, simultaneously suggesting ways of promoting knowledge transfer and 'learning organisations'. Many skills are now defined in detail by specially appointed industry bodies (including one whose remit includes HRD) as 'competences', with added performance criteria and 'range statements' suggesting how and where they should apply. And workplace attitudes can now be better understood as responses to the interplay of socio-technical influences rather than merely individually inherited or developed character traits, offering teams and managers ways of reviewing and adjusting workplace reality.

Most good trainers and educators are people who are passionate about learning. They are now able to develop intriguing new roles as facilitators of learning, helping organisations to develop learning environments, working with individuals or groups to develop their full potential, 'boundary scanning' for the next organisational change that will require a new management approach ... the expertise is not in knowing more about the topic than the learners – but knowing more about learning and how to encourage it. It is also increasingly important for HRD specialists to engage with the organisations in which they find themselves. This may sound obvious, but with the change of emphasis on the HRD practitioner's role to be an internal facilitator or consultant, it is even more important that such people not only understand business decision-making, but are part of it. Cultures where people take responsibility for their own learning, and where the workplace itself becomes a vehicle for positive personal growth, do not 'just happen'. They require a supportive and facilitating management style, and the removal of organisational barriers to learning may be regarded as one of the most important 'training interventions'. Practitioners who really 'know the business' can make these things happen.

It is an exciting time to work in the HRD area, and those who read this book and feel inspired to go out there and get involved will be guaranteed taxing problems and fulfilling challenges. We hope you are able to make use of many of the techniques and insights we have brought together here.

BRAVE NEW WORLD?

Like it or not, countries in the developed world will survive on the basis of their knowledge economies. We now have constantly developing IT networks, which have revolutionised communication: we can 'put a girdle round the earth in 40 minutes', as Puck does in *A Midsummer Night's Dream* – or significantly less. We are gradually ridding ourselves of the command and control approach to leadership, so that decisions are not just cascaded from the top but made after discussion and debate at all levels. Medical advances are helping people live longer and more productive lives, so there is every reason to 'teach an old dog new tricks'.

On the other hand, we also have more and more people at work claiming they are stressed to the point of ill-health, that they cannot trust those set to manage them, and that in spite of all sorts of labour-saving devices they are working longer hours to the extent that family and community life is suffering. Perhaps more fundamentally, many people both in paid work and out of it are complaining of the lack of meaning in their lives. Luddite approaches are short sighted – no-one wants to put back the clock to the Black Death and the landless labourer in order to introduce a few exciting challenges – but we lose sight at our peril to the fact that we are in some way all connected to 'spaceship Earth' and must recognise our need for the aesthetic of nature.

It is not fanciful to suggest that the passionate educator – who will also be a passionate learner – can be a vital contributor to such challenging issues. All learning is fundamentally about change, and we do have the power to change human life on earth for the better if we create genuine learning organisations. Indeed, to survive, the Earth itself needs to be one enormous Learning Planet.

Is this too grandiose a vision? Possibly, but the reality is that all great movements have developed from incremental changes. We can all influence what is going on in our own patch, and we can all develop a learning approach to everything we do. HRD is not just about what goes on in HR departments or in organisations, but how we develop our own lives as learners.

We are sure that you will find a wide range of material in this book to help you, whether you are a student developing a career in HRD or an experienced manager looking to pick up new ideas. We hope you will be able to understand our thought processes; we also hope you will not always agree with us! The intention was to stimulate a learning process that will eventually lead you to acquire a unique and personal view of what learning and development means for you. One of the important issues arising from the change in emphasis from training to learning is that you, the learner, already possess a wealth of knowledge and insights. Do not accept everything we say at face value, but critically evaluate it – you may well have a better answer, and if so we would like to hear about it, perhaps through the website that supports this book.

To assist you to reflect on the issues we believe important, we have included a number of discussion questions interspersed in the main text. You can consider these individually or, even better, in a group. At the end of each chapter is a question to test your understanding of the whole topic, which you could tackle either as a practice examination question, or a group discussion, or a combination of the two. Suggested answers to these questions are available from the book's dedicated website, together with other useful information for tutors and students. The essence of Action Learning, as you will see, is that groups of interested learners are much more likely to develop workable solutions to problems than 'the experts', so . . . over to you!

The Context of Human Resource Development

Part 1 of the book comprises four contextual scene-setting chapters, which review how human resource development (which we will henceforth abbreviate to HRD) in the UK has evolved to its current stage, and examine what is happening when individuals learn, both as individuals and as members of organisations. If you are not a history enthusiast, bear with us, as you will discover that many 'cutting edge' approaches to HRD have actually been around for some time in other guises. HRD practitioners are fond of saying that there is nothing new under the sun. For example, although the development of the Internet has probably not had quite the same impact on ideas and philosophies as the invention of the printing press in the Middle Ages, it has certainly aided the flow of ideas globally as well as influencing significantly the way we learn. However, many of the underpinning philosophies of the World Wide Web have been in circulation for some time. There is little doubt, though, that one of the constant concerns of governments over the last 25 years has been to speed up the process of individual and corporate learning. We will describe some of the key initiatives through which they have attempted to achieve this aim, and some of the institutions set up to carry out government strategy. 'Institution' here is used in its widest sense, and you will discover that some have had a fairly short life, possibly reflecting short-term government time frames.

In Chapters 3 and 4 we move from the nationwide to the individual context and examine how people learn, both as individuals and as corporate members. We suggest that in order for HRD practitioners to be effective both in persuading employers to develop their staff and in designing suitable learning environments, they will find an understanding of key theories of learning can be significantly useful. Part One is set out like this:

Chapter 1 examines **approaches to HRD** in the UK since the 1960s;
Chapter 2 considers the role **and remit of HRD-focused 'institutions'** that have attempted to influence employers and employees to take learning seriously;
Chapter 3 examines some **key theories of how and why learning happens**, and how an understanding of the process can assist the HRD specialist to ensure it is effective;
Chapter 4 looks at the complex relationship between **the learner and the organisation**, suggesting ways in which individual learning may be extended to promote organisational learning.

By the end of Part 1, you should understand what has happened in the past to influence the impact of learning, development and training on individuals and the organisations which employ them. You should also be able to evaluate the success of some of the key learning initiatives introduced by successive governments and their agencies. Did they achieve what they claimed they would? You will discover that since the 1960s there has been a fair number of initiatives designed to raise the profile of learning in the UK but the very fact that there have been so many of them might suggest that they have not always achieved all they claimed. However, learning, development and training are not exact sciences and often it is necessary to look back on a period and its issues before we can pronounce on its lasting learning achievements. At least governments and HRD practitioners agree that action must be taken constantly to improve the knowledge, skills and attitudes of all members of the workforce to ensure the UK's future prosperity. Translating this to the organisational context, we look at the various ways in which individuals learn, and how learning communities may develop from motivated learners within organisations. The Learning Organisation may be a concept which UK organisations have been slow to embrace, but how important is it in meeting government concerns about the skills gap which still exists, despite the warnings of a generation of management commentators?

The Evolution of HRD

CHAPTER 1

In Chapter 1, our key themes will be:

- **The range of approaches to learning and development by educationalists and management specialists over the last hundred years, and how these have tended to reflect government policy on education and skills development;**

- **The implicit underpinning organisational theories and concepts that have influenced organisational learning;**

- **The approaches of the institutions set up to drive the HRD agenda – whose roles will be discussed more fully in Chapter 2;**

- **The response of employers to the need for a skilled workforce.**

In this chapter we will present a brief overview of how and why today's approaches to HRD came about. We will explore the evolution of ideas, of training practices, of employer interest, and of national interventions. Approaches to HRD begin with bureaucracy and instruction, and range through human relations and formal courses, national vocational qualifications, to change management and experiential learning, learning organisations and the Internet. All these developments have conditioned our present scene. Some organisations today may be at the 'cutting edge' of HRD, but this does not apply universally. There will be others where training is at best superficial and at worst non-existent. Overall, we have in the UK a heterogeneous and disparate organisational learning picture.

We refer in this chapter to a number of 'institutions' (the inverted commas are deliberate, as you will discover) with responsibility for promoting the initiatives and approaches to training and learning we describe here. Their roles and remits will be examined in further detail in Chapter 2: here we focus on the approaches to learning and development they have encouraged.

The twentieth century saw dramatic changes within the world of work, and the twenty-first appears to have continued the theme of change. Organisations have evolved in terms of purpose, size, structure, management philosophy and relationships with the outside world. Technological advances have revolutionised all work methods, and for many organisations the operational horizon has moved from a small geographical area to literally the world; for government, 'being competitive' is now a global (as opposed to a selective international) requirement. Everything has speeded up, including the pace of change itself.

It is natural that in a period of change and opportunity, approaches to learning, development and training have grown in importance, broadened in scope, and became more sophisticated in method. Once the object of training would have been the individual employee, and the training method would involve teaching. Now, the picture is much more complex: training may involve any grouping up to and including the nation itself, and even sometimes may have an international dimension. It may also extend to non-employees such as suppliers, customers or outsourcers. Learner-centred activities are becoming just as important as, if not more important than, those that are teacher- or tutor led. Learning is no longer mainly the province of the psychologist or sociologist: researchers in fields such as systems engineering, artificial intelligence, cybernetics, communications technology, management and even biology have extended relevant theory by drawing on their own specialisms, extending and modifying ideas originally geared only to a human dimension. We now think of organisations as well as individuals as being 'able to learn', and indeed of both as being capable of 'learning to learn' – which means much more than acquiring knowledge of how learning happens. We will look at this in more detail in Chapters 4, 12 and 13, when we focus on knowledge creation and Learning Organisations.

> Discussion question: Why do you think some organisations have been able to develop more innovative approaches to learning, while others still regard learning and training of any sort as an 'overhead'?

Three fundamental (and to some extent contrasting) ideas have grown in importance over the last 20 years or so. The first is that the continuously changing environment demands lifelong learning on the part of all – even governments are aware that this is a key to future prosperity, and are attempting to promote it widely. The second is that real-life experience itself offers significant learning opportunities, and that experiences can be designed to stimulate learning – hence more emphasis on the learner than the trainer. The third is that national vocational standards should exist to describe and improve occupational competence, which itself should be recognised by the award of national vocational qualifications.

To understand the reasons for these diverse developments, and how they have gathered momentum in recent years, we will briefly review their evolution, focusing on the key themes that have emerged from almost a hundred years of thinking about learning, and showing how and where these have influenced trainers and educators in achieving their aims.

MECHANISTIC STRUCTURES, BUREAUCRACY AND INSTRUCTION: EARLY TWENTIETH-CENTURY FOCUS ON CONTROL AND HIERARCHY

Early twentieth-century psychologists were fascinated by such matters as perception, memory retention, co-ordination of senses and behaviour conditioning. The last of these initially involved

Table 1.1 *Early twentieth century*

Background ideas on: Organisation/ management	Employer-led/backed training activity	National training interventions
Scientific Management Bureaucracy Hierarchy	'Sitting by Nellie' – new entrants learning from experienced workers Unplanned tuition Craft Apprenticeship Workplace Instruction + College-based education	Vocational education in FE Colleges

experiments to demonstrate that animals could learn regular habits of behaviour by carefully planned stimuli and rewards. Most people have heard of Pavlov and his salivating dogs, for example. The early psychologists developed some new ideas on specific aspects of learning, but their primary aim was to support and improve teaching processes in the world of education. Such ideas of behaviour conditioning fitted well with the classical management theory of that period, which assumed static, mechanistic organisations, led by managers who taught and disciplined workers to conform to imposed routines. F. W. Taylor's principles of 'scientific management' (see Morgan 1997), which had their origins in the US engineering industry, put all the responsibility for the organisation of work into the management role. Management theorists in the UK built on these ideas, creating the hierarchical structures, functional divisions of work and procedural 'rules' that typify the standard 'bureaucratic' model of organisation, still in evidence today especially in large public sector employers such as the NHS or local government .

The early sociologist Max Weber (1864–1920) noted that managing in a bureaucracy involved increasing one's professional superiority by keeping knowledge and aims secret: managers were not expected to enlighten outsiders or subordinates on the reasoning behind decisions, and employees' views were thought irrelevant. In this environment little planned training took place, and new employees were either expected to master their work by copying what they saw established workers doing, or, in the case of complex tasks, from asking their manager to show them. The most visible UK training 'programme' in the first half of the twentieth century was the indentured craft apprenticeship, which offered young (invariably male at this time) school leavers a learning route into 'trades' such as engineering or printing, via some five or six years of 'time-serving'. Instruction typically involved face-to-face instruction 'on the job' by an experienced tradesman who looked after the youth, plus part-time educational study at a local technical college. A similar approach, but without the educational element and invariably implemented with less consistency and commitment, existed in the more labour-intensive manufacturing and packaging fields, where most jobs were not considered 'skilled'.

> Discussion question: Do you think that new entrants to 'the Professions' (Law, Medicine, Architecture etc) have traditionally regarded themselves as 'trainees'? If not, why?

A four-stage approach to instruction was favoured by the few who took enough interest to give advice on the subject. The four stages were: Tell>Show>Do>Review.

The learner was told in detail what must be done and how to do it. Great store was set on splitting the material into short stages, each comprising what could be assimilated and retained. The instructor performed what they had just described; then the learner tried to repeat what had been demonstrated; and, finally, the instructor explained and praised or criticised the learner's performance, leading into a repeat of the cycle or movement to the next stage. There were many assumptions here: the instructor was always right and fully competent in the worker's roles; all learners were equal; training plans were considered unimportant, and certainly not agreed in advance with learners; the learner should copy and should not be invited to innovate; reasons for any given method were not needed; repetition was the way to handle any who did not learn quickly. A common approach involved building up stages: first stage one, then one plus two, then one plus two plus three, and so on. This ensured repetition, which helped memory and cemented routine. Where information (rather than skill) was the subject of instruction, the norm was simply to teach it – ie to present the information in an ordered way, wherever possible with visual aids, the teacher asking questions to ascertain whether the information had been retained and understood.

Table 1.2 *The middle years*

Background ideas on: Organisation/ management	Employer-led/backed training activity	National training interventions
Human Relations	Supervisory training courses Lectures	Training Within Industry (TWI)
Motivation theory	Job enrichment Job rotation Managment courses, seminars, conferences Lectures, visual aids, case studies, discussions Management traineeships	Business Schools
Management by Objectives Organic structures Theory X/Theory Y Participation/consultation	'Systematic Training' Policy, needs identification, appraisal, records Induction Programmes Operational courses (Marketing, Safety)	Industry Training Boards (to 1980s) Open University

Note: Entries in Table 1.1 still apply throughout this period. The precise timing and sequence of new entries should not be assumed from their positions in the chart.

THE MIDDLE YEARS OF THE CENTURY: HUMAN RELATIONS, DYNAMIC ENVIRONMENTS AND TRAINING INTERVENTIONS

The four-stage instruction process was recommended in a 'job instruction' teaching programme drawn up and mounted nationwide by the Ministry of Labour during and after the Second World War – part of a supervisory training package collectively entitled Training Within Industry, or TWI for short. The TWI package was a wholly scripted programme learned verbatim by TWI trainers. In spite of this, trainees could apply it to their own organisations, and the mix of individual presentations, demonstrations and discussion groups was in practice enjoyable for many employees.

The existence of the programme indicates that training was planned nationally during the 1940s, although TWI was aimed only at first-level management. It was nevertheless unusual in focusing on people established in their jobs, and contributed towards the establishment of management training centres by several large employers, to be used primarily as venues for training courses for newly promoted managers or supervisors. Here a standard course menu was a battery of lectures – on the nature of (scientific) management, on the formal organisation chart, on creating job descriptions, on company aims and routines, on cost control and so on. Personnel management was usually included, but concentrated on industrial relations, conditions of employment, discipline procedures and pay negotiation. Training was only rarely covered as a specific subject for a lecture.

Students of organisational behaviour will remember the research of Elton Mayo and colleagues carried out in the 1920s and early 1930s at the Hawthorne plant of the Western Electric Company in Chicago (Mayo, 1933). Initially, the researchers looked into the relationship between workers' physical working conditions and problems of fatigue, sickness and absenteeism; increasingly the spotlight extended into the wider conditions of employment and the less tangible issues of workers' commitment, boredom, aspirations and preoccupations. They concluded that despite the existence of a clearly defined formal organisation, workers collectively colluded in sustaining many unplanned, unauthorised activities to satisfy their social needs, which were at least as important in maintaining morale as their wages. Mayo's research suggested that, in most work organisations, the relationships between people and between management and workers were critical to maintaining interest in work offering in itself no physical or intellectual challenge.

After the Second World War, American psychologists and sociologists continued to research these themes, and developed new theories of motivation. Maslow (1943) defined a 'hierarchy' of needs for the individual in the workplace, at the top of which was an ideal termed 'self-actualisation', which implied both the ability to create and the opportunity to develop. Argyris (1957) explained how workers in authoritarian cultures often worked to the lowest level of their ability, saving their creativity and enthusiasm for periods outside work. Some employees in contemporary organisations argue they are still subject to similar cultural norms. McGregor (1960) contrasted management styles based on 'Theory X' (basically Taylor's scientific management approach) and 'Theory Y' (proposing that workers wanted to contribute to the organisation's objectives). Herzberg et al (1959) proposed 'job enrichment', which involved making work tasks challenging and meaningful for the worker. These 'human relations' ideas began to occupy centre stage in management (and especially personnel management) courses. Training activity was often quoted as evidence of 'human relations in action'.

The world of work in the mid-twentieth century was simultaneously becoming more competitive, more complex, and more innovative. Large organisations adopted new operational functions, such as marketing and sales promotion. Development departments created new products and adapted technical processes. In the finance area, cost accounting joined financial accounting and new management information systems. Short-term project teams, often multidepartmental, sometimes part time, were appointed with special terms of reference. Innovation and change began to be accepted as normal even when it caused problems. Matrix organisation charts began to appear alongside hierarchical charts in basic management textbooks. 'Management by Objectives' was preached by management gurus like Drucker (1964) in the USA and Humble (1967) in the UK; organisations formalised forward plans, short, medium and long term. Today's work started to become a function of a planned future, with past norms downvalued, if not openly criticised.

Discussion question: How do you think an understanding of organisational theory can help the trainer or learning expert to develop an effective learning environment?

UK sociologists and management theorists also considered new types of organisation. Burns and Stalker (1961) looked at a variety of industries and concluded that some organisations could no longer properly be described as 'mechanistic'. 'Organic' was a more appropriate term, as they managed change by minimising formal rules and allowing new tasks and processes to be adopted without regard for past norms. There was no 'one best way' for organisations. Lawrence and Lorsch (1967) went a stage further, explaining that organisations need to cope *internally* with varying needs, and justifying a 'contingency theory' approach, with departments managed variably through time, dependent upon their different degrees of stability or complexity.

In the increasingly dynamic environment, training activity grew and developed within the larger organisations, where employees of most types, and especially those in management grades, attended specially planned courses of many kinds, from marketing appreciation to merchandising techniques, from energy-saving methods to safety legislation. Management traineeships (usually involving specially recruited graduates on 'fast-track' routes to junior, and in some cases higher, management posts) appeared, typically providing planned job experience in several departments before the first management appointment. Newly created business schools offered new business degrees for graduates looking for a fast track into senior management and shorter programmes for young promotable managers. Such programmes usually incorporated lectures on economics, sociology, marketing philosophy, accounting practice and human relations; and much time was given to discussions, often based on real-life case material. Course members might be divided into several syndicates, each of which met to debate a given topic or problem, and then to mount a plenary session at which each group reported its conclusions. The syndicate/plenary approach generated both new joint experience and reflection on it, with decision-making helped by a variety of proposed solutions – all within the 'safe' training conference environment. Believed benefits were found not only in the variety of generated opinions, but also in the cross-functional teambuilding and problem-solving which occurred.

Not all these training interventions involved managers and training methods could vary. Some larger organisations created training units, which developed programmed learning and self-study. Most learners, however, seemed to expect a teacher in front of them: this seemed the only way to answer a learner's questions properly, and equally the only way a learner's doubts, fears and self-imposed distractions could be resolved or diverted. Lectures were still the main vehicle of formal courses, although visual aids in the form of the newly developed overhead projector added some variety of presentation.

Discussion question: How far does the approach described in the previous paragraph still apply, and how far does it derive from formal education? Discuss with reference to organisations with which you are familiar, or have read about.

By the 1960s, in the larger organisations training processes were growing and becoming more sophisticated and trainers were taking over from management some of the latter's communication roles. This trend was accelerated by Industrial Training Boards (ITBs), created by the Industrial Training Act 1964, whose advice was based on large employers' practices. Their somewhat mechanical advice was limited to such things as induction training for new starters and 'systematic' procedures – for example, policy creation, training needs identification, job analysis, appraisal and staff records. Interestingly, the job analyses produced by some of the ITBs had definite resemblances to the functional analyses that are the basis of NVQs. They might also be said to reflect the same advantages and disadvantages (see pages 40, 156).

Even so, the 1960s saw a significant increase within medium-sized organisations (small employers were outside ITB scope) in the number of staff with explicit responsibility for promoting training, and again in the formal identification of training needs, plus their conversion into paper plans. There remained the problem of implementation: plans often remained proposals, with managers uncommitted or just too busy with other priorities to make learning happen. Many HRD practitioners would claim that this is still the case in their organisations today! Certainly, bureaucratic systems did not disappear in this changing world of work. Well-defined structures and procedures continued to be prized by top management. 'Closed-system' assumptions, ignoring the impact of the outside world on internal management decisions, remained the norm, especially in the small enterprise. Again, a significant number of organisations appear to have managed to survive like this up to the present!

Discussion question: How common do you think the standard bureaucratic model is today? Are there specific types of organisation where it is more usual? You may also wish to consider academic organisations such as schools, colleges and universities. How far do they reflect a bureaucratic approach?

Table 1.3 *Later twentieth century*

Background ideas on: Organisation/ management	Employer-led/backed training activity	National training interventions
Socio-technical theory Contingency theory Experiential learning Productivity Management development Oranisational development Change management Barriers to learning Learning styles Strategic management Continuous development	Organisation development Pre-appointment programmes OD seminars Group problem solving/brainstorming New management courses Structured exercises, simulations, discussion Study groups Process review Action learning – 'sets', projects, tutorials Outdoor training	Manpower Services Commission Training Services Agency Youth Training Schemes

Note: A 'carry-over' of relevant entries from Tables 1.1 and 1.2 is assumed. As in Table 1.2, there is no precise timing and sequence of new entries.

THE LATER TWENTIETH CENTURY: TECHNOLOGICAL CHANGE, STRATEGIC CHANGE MANAGEMENT, GROUP DYNAMICS AND EXPERIENTIAL LEARNING

The 1970s and 1980s were decades of relentless change. New products and processes were introduced with increasing frequency with changing internal work methods to reflect this. Bigger organisations began to develop strategic ideas and instruments: mission statements, corporate objectives, medium-term plans and budgets started appearing, initial drafts sometimes being prepared by new forward-planning departments. Personnel issues increasingly merited coverage in such documents. This was also a time of high inflation and low profits, fuelled by hikes in the price of oil and upward pressure from workers on wages. The larger employers quickly attacked overmanning situations and restrictive practices, increasingly negotiating 'productivity deals', revising work schedules, especially where overtime was involved, and reducing numbers in return for improved rewards. A decline in the recruitment of young people alarmed government and led to the creation of a nationwide youth training scheme, which quickly gained employer support while costs were borne by the state but later slumped when it became clear that government aimed to shift the costs on to employers.

The wider world was simultaneously intruding. Competition came from the revitalised continent of Europe, especially Germany, and from the emerging economies of the Far East, where Japan showed near-genius ability in copying Western electronics and automobile technology and then improving creatively on what it copied. Lesser Pacific Rim countries exploited the benefits of cheap labour while developing their own manufacturing operations. Employers were urged – by government, by the CBI, by trade associations and of course by the ITBs – to train for economic reasons.

The London-based Tavistock Institute of Human Relations, with its formidable team of psychologists, psychotherapists and sociologists, developed its own contingency approach (see especially Trist 1981), pioneering theories of open systems (systems open to their environments), and 'socio-technical' systems (systems in which the key management task was continuously to balance the relationships between human and technical elements). Socio-technical theory proposed that a key task for management must be to understand and adjust changing relationships between people, tasks, technology and structure. Worker participation became respectable, together with consultative systems to achieve it.

Contingency theory suggested that, whereas management might be learnt, it could not be taught as a set of rigid constructs. The approach implied that competence as a manager must naturally be learnt 'by experience'. Kolb's (1974) experiential learning theory rapidly gained ground among academics and personnel management in the USA and Britain: it described a four-stage sequential process for learning at work without a teacher or tutor (see page 56). The newly identified critical element was *reflection*, which allows the individual to translate real-life experience into abstract concepts and valued 'lessons', which can be stored in the memory for future use. Kolb stressed the importance to all of 'learning about learning', but did not, however, offer answers to the problems of motivating the experiential learner. In the UK, Honey and Mumford (1986) built on Kolb's theoretical base, defining learning 'styles' and offering ways for learners to understand and work on what they themselves perceive as strengths and weaknesses.

Discussion question: How far do you think is it possible for learners to change their preferred approach to learning? Is it worth it?

In the USA, Argyris and Schon investigated learning and decision-making. In 1978 they publicised characteristics within landmark organisations that they labelled 'defensive routines' – individuals' ways of protecting themselves, deflecting attention from themselves by obscuring issues and problems that might harm their images – and concluded that such behaviour acted as a brake on learning at the levels of both individual and group, and on creativity at the level of the organisation. They presented their 'theory of action perspective', the centrepiece of which was an explanation of how 'unlearning' and 'creative reflection' should take place via what later came to be termed 'double-loop' learning. The key to the double-loop learning process is the questioning of operating norms at the time, or immediately after, information is received. Argyris and Schon suggested that top management should consciously devote time to double-loop learning activity and should require their middle management to do the same in specific cross-functional group discussions.

In the UK, the use of management courses, seminars and conferences continued to increase, many addressing a new central issue of strategic change management, all stressing the critical need to be flexible, and some using new learning methods. 'Organisation development' (OD) consultants were in demand, often introduced to lead internal seminars in which managers reviewed their goals, structures, responsibilities and procedural norms. Enthusiasm for cultural change stimulated interest in brainstorming techniques – typically developed in small, ad hoc groups rather than via individual challenges or departmental edicts. Developments in simulation facilitated the creation of business games, offering competitive experience – usually allied to group decision-making. Externally, consultants such as Adair (1978) and Coverdale (see Taylor, 1979) offered short courses involving structured exercises, allowing managers to practise team leadership in a changing environment and with innovative goals. 'Study groups' offered leaderless group experiences in which members, with the aid of a 'facilitator', could review and reassess their behaviour as team members. 'Action learning' (see Revans, 1980) allowed individual managers to work for sustained periods on significant real-life problems in new organisational surroundings, with tutorial assistance. Outdoor management development (OMD) also became popular, aiming at improving members' understanding of teambuilding and team leadership by group problem-solving in outdoor situations. Management training blossomed at this period, diversifying in many directions and introducing discovery methods alongside the more traditional lecture and syndicate discussion methods.

> Discussion question: In an organisation with which you are familiar, how far are these methods still used as HRD tools? Are they still relevant today? If you are undertaking a college or university programme, does it include any of these methods, and if so, how do they fit with academic study?

Trainers who themselves became experienced in these new forms of training were very different from the typical ITB adviser, and indeed the new breed quickly outstripped the latter as advisers on training methods. The ITBs, as we will see in the next chapter, never overcame their early bureaucratic image, and failed to move from formalised training procedures towards more creative learning practices. With one or two exceptions, the ITBs were abolished early in the 1980s. The new 'professional' trainers, employed mainly within larger organisations, also exerted a wider influence on personnel management through their membership of the relevant professional institute, the then Institute of Personnel Management (IPM), and its innovative national committee for employee development. In the early 1980s, the IPM launched a campaign for 'continuous development' (CD), the main goals of which promoted (a) self-development (meaning learner-centred plans and learner-managed learning) and (b) the integration of learning with work (requiring an ongoing attitude that endless learning opportunities exist at the workplace). CD quickly gained supporters within academic circles and professional bodies, but personnel managers in general were slow to sell the campaign to their line management colleagues. The IPM joined forces with the Institute of Training and Development in the early 1990s to become the Institute of Personnel and Development (IPD); and inherited many training professionals who had developed an interest in new, collective and/or learner-managed forms of learning. Opinion among development professionals is still divided regarding the importance the merged body places on training and learning. In 2000 the Institute of Training and Occupational Learning (ITOL) was formed as an alternative body for development specialists, and has attracted significant interest from these people, although many retain CIPD membership. Personnel management was now dropping its 'human relations' image, actively preaching a 'human resources' philosophy, which put the personnel function into the boardroom and aimed at new strategic rather than traditional negotiation roles. In July 2000 the IPD became the Chartered Institute of Personnel and Development, or CIPD.

END OF A CENTURY: TOWARDS THE LEARNING ORGANISATION, NATIONAL VOCATIONAL QUALIFICATIONS, RISE OF THE INTERNET

In the industrial world of the UK, the 1980s and 1990s were decades when inflation and unemployment steadily diminished, although internal organisational change continued to be

Table 1.4 *End of the century*

Background ideas on: Organisation/ management	Employer-led/backed training activity	National training interventions
Total Quality Management	Youth Training Programmes	
	Guided work experience + college-based education	Training and Enterprise Councils
Information technology	IT training	
	Lectures + simulations + hands-on experience	National Vocational
Competence theory		Qualifications (NVQs/SVQs)
The learning organisation	Teamwork seminars	Industry Training
	Dialoguing	Organisations
Multi-skilling	Job enlargement	National Training Targets
Empowerment/re-engineering		
	Continuing Professional	Investors in People
Knowledge Management	Development	The Internet
Lifelong learning	Self-paced/planned	University for Industry
Organisations as brains	learning	
Neuro Linguistic Programming		

Note: A 'carry-over' of relevant entries from earlier Tables is assumed. As previously, precise timing and sequence of new entries is not implied.

the norm for most large organisations, both from technological advances and downsizing and cultural aims. The IT 'revolution' made communications even more rapid and confirmed the desktop computer as the single most indispensable item of organisational equipment. Both led to redundancies at all levels except the top, with positions amalgamated in reorganisation plans that served immediate, or at least short-term, financial gains. The employment of young people also dwindled; in the engineering industry in particular, the number of apprenticeships quickly dropped in the 1980s (the then government relaunched state-funded youth training programmes). The notion of lifetime service to an organisation accordingly weakened: it gradually became normal for young, capable, ambitious managers (now of both sexes, thanks to equal opportunities and changing lifestyles) to serve their ambitions by becoming mobile and moving between employers. This trend has consequently increased the necessity and value of qualifications. OD programmes disappeared in favour of more prescriptive restructuring plans; the 'pursuit of excellence' often meant a benchmarking operation in which specialists were detailed to find a superior set of procedures that could be copied and internally imposed. In such a climate it was inevitable that sophisticated management development programmes should tend to be reserved for a select minority, and that the specialist post of management development manager, which had blossomed to some extent during the 1970s, should decline. Computer training, usually teacher- or consultant-led, tended for several years to predominate in internal training activities, despite involving much hands-on practice; it predominated especially (but not exclusively) in firms with personnel and training departments.

Academic interest in links between commercial success and internal learning systems nevertheless continued to develop, in several notable instances confirming the relationship between strategic management and employee learning. In the UK, Garratt (2000) and Burgoyne (1995) described organisational patterns that seemed appropriate to generating change on a continuing basis and stressed the critical importance of teams' self-development activity at the workplace. In the USA, Peter Senge became the first director of a Systems Thinking and Organisational Learning programme at Massachusetts Institute of Technology's Sloan School of Management. In 1990 he drew the 'component technologies' of an ideal 'learning organisation', defining requirements for team learning and newly describing the role of leadership to cover above all the management of a corporate learning process – which he claimed could enable an organisation to manage its external environment in its own interest. Senge showed how traditional, 'top-down' management prevents the all-important double-loop learning that is needed for evolution by its insistence on clearly defined and unchallengeable targets. Nonaka and Takeuchi (1995) later described, using Japanese firms as examples, ways whereby a 'knowledge-creating' culture might similarly allow Western firms to dominate their futures; the essence of the culture is a 'middle-up-down' flow of ideas, authority attaching to the ideas rather than any particular position in the organisational hierarchy. The process of exploring and understanding the ideas is seen as the means whereby authority is established. Morgan (1997) has since likened this process to the working of any human brain; he presents a long list of 'critical principles of holographic design' as the basic requirements for organisational learning, among which are the design of networked information systems, the structuring of 'complete-process' work teams, and the habit of double-loop learning. We examine the concept of learning organisations and how they seek to manage knowledge in Chapter 13.

With a few exceptions, UK employers have not yet seriously embraced the concept of the learning organisation. Yesterday's passion for cultural change waned somewhat with the need to improve short-term economic opportunities. Employers concentrated on reducing payrolls, cutting staff levels, increasing contracted-out work, introducing part-time workers and adopting more flexible patterns/hours of work, often with less flexible methods of work. The 1980s brought interest in 'Total Quality Management' (TQM – see Collard, 1989), a set of disciplines that urged formal definition and redefinition of 'high-quality' procedures and routines. The TQM approach openly preached a learning culture, but often assumed that managers should simply establish 'best practice' and teach it. A number of new 'service-industry' organisations (eg McDonald's, an organisation that Morgan describes as 'perfecting' Taylor's principles), which grew rapidly during this period, made it clear that they viewed scientific management principles as the only way to organise. The same emphasis on efficiency, quantification, control, predictability and even de-skilled jobs – sometimes described now as 'McJobs' – can still be seen within hospitals, factories, retail outlets, schools, universities and other institutions that have been forced to rationalise their operations and have known no other way to do it. It is ironic that 'on-the-job' instruction, given to new starters by established workers who make no claim to understanding learning processes, is still the most likely norm in the mass of medium-sized organisations, where training specialists rarely exist and managers usually aim to recruit experienced staff who can quickly commit new routines to memory.

Faced with large employers who seemed to be losing their support for youth training schemes, with small employers who had no training facilities of their own, and with employers of all sizes not recruiting, the UK government stepped up its own national training interventions. Having abolished virtually all the ITBs, government introduced new national programmes for the young and the unemployed run by the (then) Department of Employment (DE) via a new geographical network of employer-led Training and Enterprise Councils (the TECs – known in Scotland as Local Enterprise Companies, or LECs). We discuss these in more detail in Chapter 2. Once these TECs were in place, the DE assumed the lead position in developing a new national vocational system of qualifications (National Vocational Qualifications, or NVQs, in England, and Scottish Vocational Qualifications, or SVQs, north of the border). NVQs are based upon prescribed written standards for specifically named jobs.

NVQs were essentially government's way of updating and upgrading workplace skills via traditional vocational education methods – the classroom and the examination. A sizeable body of literature was produced – by both government departments and by consultants working on government contracts – preaching a new 'competences' approach to skills development. 'Skill' was defined essentially in terms of work outcomes. A body of literature explaining competence theory (see especially Jessup 1991) maintained that learning methods were not critical: the key to competence was seen as its precise definition.

In the early 1990s, the DE was merged with the Department of Education to form the Department for Education and Employment (DfEE). New national training targets were subsequently set primarily in terms of achievements against educational targets, and a new national skills task force was established to co-ordinate the work of the standard-setting bodies. The need for employers to plan and implement training internally was not totally forgotten, however: the TECs were given the right/responsibility to dispense an 'Investor in People' (IiP) award to any work establishment which claimed the award and was able to convince an independent examiner on four counts – commitment to, planning of, action on and evaluation of training (see page 34 for the current IiP standard).

Discussion question: Given that learning from life is often more effective than learning from theory, do you think that it is easier for small organisations to provide employees with development opportunities?

Some TECs managed to forge alliances with their local Chambers of Commerce and pioneered ways of bringing NVQs (and external training resources generally) to the attention of small- and medium-sized employers.

TEC-administered 'Modern Apprenticeships' and 'National Traineeships' were introduced (with a mandatory NVQ study element) in an attempt to improve the eventual flow of technicians. These state moves were further developed by the 1997 Labour government, which introduced a range of 'Welfare to Work' options for young unemployed people.

These government-led moves were criticised for paying more attention to improving the nation's economic health by minimising unemployment statistics than by improving profitability or stimulating growth. Employers did show some interest but, to date (2004), have tended to reduce their recruitment of young people further, effectively leaving the education and training of many to the further education sector. Personnel professionals have also in the main accepted NVQs' national standards in place of more specific definitions of workplace needs. In truth, most had little choice but to accept the national standards – and the (then) IPD, which co-ordinated the creation of NVQs in areas relevant to its own work, led the way by adjusting its membership scheme to accept NVQ routes into membership. Its earlier advocacy of continuous development was transformed into a 'continuing professional development' members' obligation, which required members to keep an ongoing log of learning achievements but made no assumptions about either self-development or learning within work.

Discussion question: Should it be compulsory for existing employees to study for NVQs? If so, which groups do you think could most benefit?

Those who championed learner-centred learning welcomed the rapid international development of the Internet, with its endless reference and forum facilities. Full-time education students also showed enthusiasm for surfing the Net, notably when gathering material for projects. It was promising for educators to find that young people with a wide range of intellectual abilities could enjoy the process of collecting information on the personal-computer screen, although academics take care to warn students that information from Internet sites can vary significantly in accuracy and academic rigour.

Interest in 'lifelong learning' also blossomed in the late 1990s, at least among institutions: the European Commission declared 1996 as their 'Year of Lifelong Learning', spawning a wide variety of initiatives dedicated to stimulating adult learning. Warwick University appointed the first Professor of Lifelong Learning in 1998.

Also in 1998, a consultative Green Paper ('The Learning Age: A Renaissance of a New Britain' DfEE (1)) proposed a number of government-led developments to further the government's view that education and development were key priorities:

- a University for Industry (UfI), using leading technology to make learning available at work, in learning centres or at home. The development was actually announced 'for real' within days of the Green Paper's appearance and the UfI was launched in 1999 to provide a networked system of information and advice on learning opportunities, and a 'brokerage' facility to connect individuals and employers with training providers.

- a freephone 'LearnDirect' helpline on qualifications and courses. This service was launched in 1998.

- 'Individual Learning Accounts'. Treasury money was provided to start these accounts, to which employers and individuals were required to contribute. Course payments can be spread and credit levels secured. These were called in the Green Paper 'the centrepiece of adult learning in the future', but as we shall see, this promise was not delivered.

- more money for higher education (HE) and further education (FE), and again for the Careers Service, including a new learning fund to improve literacy and numeracy among adults.

- a new Institute of Learning and Teaching – to provide courses and qualifications to improve the standard of HE teaching.

- a 'National Grid for Learning', to provide a gateway to educational resources on the Internet, and to develop systems and procedures in educational institutions, libraries, homes and workplaces to support Internet access.

A very ambitious set of proposals was designed to underpin what the government wished to portray as its wholesale commitment to education in all its forms. So, what happened to this ambitious programme as the twentieth century ended and the new millennium began?

Table 1.5 *The new millennium*

Background ideas on: Organisation/ management	Employer-led/backed training activity	National training interventions
Learner focus Skills shortages E Learning Leadership Diversity and widening access to learning 'Emotional intelligence' Knowledge management	Career Counselling Modern Apprenticeships E learning groups Intranets Blended learning Managing diversity Team-based training Project Management training	Individual Learning Accounts Department for Education and Skills Institute for Learning and Teaching in Higher Education (ILTHE) Learning and Skills Councils Sector Skills Development Agency/Sector Skills Councils Connexions LearnDirect, National Grid for Learning

As before, no precise time sequence is implied.

THE NEW MILLENNIUM: A PROLIFERATION OF INITIATIVES AND PROVIDERS

In 2001, following a cabinet reshuffle, the DfEE became the Department of Education and Skills (DfES), ostensibly to concentrate the government's efforts to improve the nation's skills base in one department. The 'employment' part of the DfEE went to the Department of Work and Pensions, with a remit to manage services and benefits for unemployed people (through job centres), retired people, families on low incomes and people with a disability. It covers in essence the whole social security spectrum, with job centres now providing a one-stop shop for claiming benefit and finding new employment.

The initiatives introduced in the 1998 Green Paper had had a mixed rate of success.

Individual Learning Accounts (ILAs) launched with a fanfare in September 2000, gave the first million participants £150 to spend on education provided they spent £25. Training and education providers were not regulated, with the result that fraud proliferated, some providers claiming money for poor quality courses, others even claiming for non-existent training and trainees. By 2002 the initiative had been 'savaged' by government committees, with the Public Accounts Committee in April 2003 suggesting that £97 million of public money had been squandered. 'Failure' and 'fraud' were terms applied by the media, to government embarrassment, although talk of a rebirth of the idea resurfaced in 2003.

The University for Industry (UfI) and its subsequently named service delivery organisation, LearnDirect, have done rather better. Between its launch in 1998 and 2003, LearnDirect received 5 million calls from individuals seeking to gain further qualifications, and 6 million searches were made on its website in two years.

Connexions and the Careers Service. 'Connexions' (the spelling hardly sets a good example of English) was set up as another 'one-stop shop' to provide support and information for young people aged 13–19. Its services include advice on personal relationships, health, housing, training and careers. It has gradually developed on a regional basis and supplements the work done by school and university careers advisers. There is an implicit development aim as well as an aim to widen access to education and development opportunities for young people. In Scotland, Careers Scotland has been set up to replace a plethora of local initiatives.

Institute of Learning and Teaching (ILTHE) was set up in 1999 to develop training for lecturers in Higher Education and to maintain and develop professional standards in the sector. Controversial from its beginnings, and especially unpopular with the 'old' universities, which had tended to focus on research rather than teaching, it nevertheless had signed up nearly 15,000 members by 2003. Initially part funded by government contributions, its aim was to become financially independent through member subscriptions and the accreditation of training courses. It has currently (2004) merged with the Learning and Training Support Network, to form part of a new 'Academy' to oversee standards of teaching in Higher Education.

National Grid for Learning launched as part of the government's strategy to help learners and educators obtain maximum benefit from IT and the Internet, provides a range of links to websites to enhance teaching and learning. Its message has been about promoting web-based education provision and ensuring school leavers are all competent to make use of it (which may be a less onerous task than ensuring older people use the facility; most young people are accustomed to using computers from early school age, although for many homes Internet access is still not available).

The political arena also saw changes in the bodies responsible for driving government initiatives. TECs were abolished in England and Wales in favour of a network of Learning and Skills Councils (LSCs) set up in 2001 with responsibility for funding and planning education and training for all over-16s. At the same time the Sector Skills Development Agency and its network of Sector Skills Councils was created, the latter led by groups of employers in specific industry or business sectors of economic or strategic importance. These bodies, like TECs, have had a mixed reception. They claim to be much more employer led than the earlier National Training Organisations, but the SSDA itself is funded by the Treasury, so there is not complete independence. As will be discussed in Chapter 2, many educators applaud the involvement of industry in bridging the skills gap, yet more bodies with similar areas of interest could be argued to add to the confusion of smaller employers looking for advice on training. There is also the cynic's view that the same individuals who ran the discredited bodies reappear to take the lead roles in the new versions – where then is the real change? It could, however, be said that LSCs have significantly promoted college-based learning for young people by the routing of increased government funding to these institutions, in return for the development of national qualifications. This in turn has tended to hold up the development of work-based learning, now (2004) said to be a priority. The Performance and Innovation Unit of the Cabinet Office, a project management group at the heart of government, was asked in 2001 to set up a 'workforce development project' to fit workforce development into a strategic framework – again, suggesting that there has not been sufficient 'joined up thinking' in the whole area.

A key question for HRD professionals is how far learning methods have really changed in the new century. Online learning continues to be popular but controversial; there have been high drop-out rates and some research has suggested that those learning by traditional methods do better in exams than their e-counterparts. 'Blended learning' involving a number of different approaches, including online learning, might be the answer. Certainly training courses are holding their own, and there has been a growth in coaching and mentoring, as well as a resurgence of interest in methods such as Action Learning. Team-based learning is popular – some trainers see the emphasis on this and mentoring as a means of ensuring best value rather than necessarily improving the learning experience. Particularly 'hot topics' include leadership, project management and diversity training, reflecting the growing organisational interest in these areas. There is a continuing move away from 'Training and Development' to 'Human Resource Development', where training is now far more about facilitating learning processes.

The Learning and Training at Work Survey 2002 carried out for the DfES demonstrated that while only a minority of employers believe that training is not necessary, and most provided learning opportunities, training was happening for more employees but for shorter periods of time. The theme of this look at history has often been one of advances and retreats! The 2003 Government White Paper on the future of Higher Education gave a few clues about new types of qualifications, which are more 'flexible' and responsive to the needs of a more diverse student body, together with the now usual emphasis on developing better links between education and business. It remains to be seen how much of this ambitious programme will be achieved.

Our subject has 'come of age' during the century covered by this chapter. Its scope has extended from a few to virtually all occupations and to all levels of employee. Its application has broadened from the individual to groups and organisations of all kinds, and even to the nation. Its management has produced a large number of new specialist posts, usually (but not always) located within the personnel management sphere, in turn refining earlier views of line management. New approaches have regularly appeared, usually running alongside – as opposed to replacing – existing approaches. New methods, new resources and new technology have similarly extended the range of training opportunities, notably those allowing learner-centred learning alongside simple instruction and teaching.

Our rapid review of history has suggested that any given learning intervention can be reasonably seen as simultaneously contributing towards the improved performance of the individual, the group, the organisation and the nation. But there is no single approach or practice that can exist as a standard discipline to serve the all-time needs of all individuals, all organisations and the nation. Managing learning, like management in general, is a situation-specific art.

The state's own interventions into learning and development over the years have varied dramatically in terms of purpose and method. Employers' preferences have varied and diversified, new technology, new structures and new employment levels yielding training plans that have individually pioneered cultural change. The academic world has similarly been reviewing on a continuing basis the nature of management and organisation within new horizons, producing a stream of new conceptual approaches. Individual learners have, especially since the advent of the personal computer, become much less dependent upon teachers, as we suggested in the Introduction, and many are keen to engage in new learning methods.

The implications for the future are clear and strong. We have a century of empirical evidence why HRD interventions should continue to vary in purpose and design in the future. Although there are many comments to make, many things to criticise and many suggestions to put forward, there is no ground for advocating a return to scientific management principles or a new 'doctrinaire' discipline to be imposed on all. Each individual learning intervention in the future must serve its own up-to-date, realistic appraisal of the twin 'purpose and design' essentials. The most effective HRD interventions will continue to be strategic, relevant and unique.

The mainstream themes of this chapter charted the evolution of what we see as the most important issues in the UK learning and development sphere at the beginning of the new millennium. The central aim has been that of economic progress: training is managed primarily to improve the economic performance of the individual, the employing organisation, and ultimately the nation.

> In this chapter, we have looked at the range of approaches to learning and development by educationalists and management specialists over a century. What key themes strike you as most important over this period? If you were asked by a national quality newspaper to make predictions for the main learning themes to emerge over the next ten years, what would you suggest, and why?

In our next chapter, we will examine some of the institutions, organisations and individuals responsible for achieving the rather daunting aim of improving the economic performance of the nation.

The 'Institutional' Context: National Networks and Their Impact on Learning

CHAPTER 2

In Chapter 2, we will consider:

- **The roles and remits of the variety of institutions set up to deliver the UK's learning and development agenda;**

- **The complexity of the national learning and development network, and its consequent anomalies and challenges;**

- **The diverse roles played by employers, educators and learning and development providers in 'upskilling' the UK;**

- **The problems of the UK 'skills gap' between what people, especially young people, can do, and what the knowledge economy needs them to be able to do;**

- **The impact of 'global perspectives' as exemplified by the Internet, and the role of central government.**

In this chapter we aim to describe and explain the main 'institutions' in the UK learning and development scene at the beginning of the twenty-first century.

As we suggested in Chapter 1, although some of what we had to say about HRD related to what organisations were doing and how they were developing, we also referred to the emergence of a number of 'institutions' dedicated to vocational education and training. We have placed inverted commas around the term 'institution' because we are using it to describe not just organisations, but anything that could be described as exerting a significant influence on those who work with learning and development issues. This may include policies, principles, publications, targets, schemes and even individuals. Many contemporary learning initiatives have in fact themselves created institutions whose essential purpose was to make further or future learning and training interventions.

A NATIONWIDE INSTITUTIONAL NETWORK

Until the 1960s in the UK, there were very few national learning or training initiatives. There were apprenticeships, which in some form had existed since medieval times. In the engineering and printing industries, apprenticeships had long been established as the traditional way of entering craft occupations. After the Second World War, a few large UK employers introduced management training centres, where short-term internal management and supervision courses and conferences were organised, mainly for newly promoted or newly recruited management. Technical Colleges and Colleges of Commerce at this time provided a wide range of vocational courses, attended by employees (usually in their own time and at their own expense) who wanted to acquire qualifications to enhance their job prospects. A very wide range of examining and awarding bodies existed at that time, and colleges often provided their own certificates where national examinations did not exist. The Education Act of 1944 required employers to release young people to attend 'further education and liberal studies' classes in 'County Colleges', which were to be set up throughout England and Wales (the legal obligation was never enforced, and only a few of the colleges were established).

Apart from these limited examples, employee learning, training and development was left as something to be planned or ignored by the employer and/or the adult learner, without any other 'institutions' established at local or regional or national level to help decision-making or to meet specific needs.

The current picture is very different. Over the past few decades, government-led and other nationwide initiatives have reflected the growing beliefs that employee development can and

Discussion question: Have UK employees tended to leave responsibility for their training to others? If so, why might this be?

should make a contribution to solving national economic problems. Lifelong learning is regarded both a natural product and a requirement of continuing change, and there is recognition that a central stimulus is needed to ensure learning goals of a reasonably high standard. The UK now has a national system of vocational qualifications, a national industry-based network of occupational standard-setting Sector Skills Councils (SSCs) under the control of the Sector Skills Development Agency (SSDA), and a network of Learning and Skills Councils (LSCs), responsible for post-16 vocational education. There are also nationally established but locally administered 'modern' apprenticeships and youth traineeships, annual national training awards, national training targets, and easy, open telephone or Internet access to information on training providers and resources.

Figure 2.1 presents the national learning and development scene in the form of a 'network' chart displaying links between the various institutions that are covered in this chapter. Terms and abbreviations appearing in the chart are explained in Appendices 1 and 2. With such a complicated picture it may be helpful to explain one or two points:

- Although the chart names 'institutions' that are responsible for promoting or enhancing employee learning and development in some way, this is not always their main function or concern.
- Each box in the chart represents a mainstream category, as we suggest in the text. 'Institutions' are creations of, or systems managed by, specific organisations.
- Our approach here is selective. Appendix 3 offers a more comprehensive 'quick guide' to training schemes, programmes, initiatives and organisations.
- Dashed lines in the chart do not imply subordinate relationships, but suggest what might be termed 'operational links', suggesting regular direct contact and dialogue.
- Although generally similar, the Scottish and Northern Ireland scenes involve some differently named institutions with slightly different roles. For example, Local Enterprise Companies (LECs) in Scotland carry out many of the functions of LSCs in England.

At the end of each category of 'institution' we have given a few examples of typical HRD interventions that they might engage in.

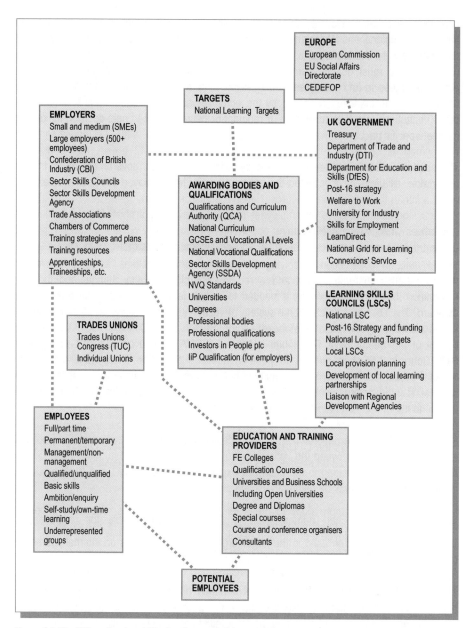

Figure 2.1 *The UK's national post-16 education and training network*

Discussion question: How might government decision-makers simplify the network of learning and training providers? Is it appropriate even to attempt to?

EMPLOYEES

It may seem strange to include employees as 'institutions'. In fact, they remain collectively the keystone to which all learning and training institutions relate, and their behaviour or performance is the target of virtually all learning and training interventions. There have been many sophisticated developments in IT in recent years, but their creative role is limited to their internal programmes, created by individuals. Researchers and observers have explored new meanings for the term 'learning organisation', but they still stress that in the end it is the workforce who must do the learning – using the term 'workforce' to include all who are employed, including (of course) top management.

In 2003, from a total UK population of about 56 million people, approximately 28 million people were in paid employment – somewhat less than half the total. The female share of employment is currently a little below 50 per cent, at nearly 13 million, and is growing steadily, forecast to exceed that of males by the year 2007. Part-time employment, mainly undertaken by women, now accounts for about a third of all work, having increased from about a fifth in the last 20 years (source: National Statistics Online).

Employees who actively seek learning opportunities are probably not the majority. It seems that in the UK we still tend to see learning and development in the mould of formal education – essentially an alternative to work, something to be determined and planned by someone else, something involving dependency, and often something difficult and unpleasant. This attitude has been established during full-time education, which still ends for many at age 16 or so. This means that, apart from induction and safety training activities, training is most likely to be aimed at those employees who were the most successful in full-time education – professional staff, technologists, technicians and management generally, most of whom have successful higher education backgrounds. Some professions – law, architecture, accountancy, human resource management and nursing, for example – now require 'continuing professional development' (CPD) if their members are to retain their professional qualifications.

> Discussion question: Is the CPD concept appropriate for all employees? If not, which jobs do you think should be exempt, and for which jobs is it most necessary?

These employees are more likely to press for learning opportunities, especially if openly linked with professional status and promotional opportunities at work. It is also significant that such employees are often used in the larger organisations as trainers on internal courses – and some see their trainer role as that of lecturer.

The relevant percentage statistics have not changed dramatically in a generation, despite high-level debates on learning and training. Training is disproportionately concentrated on those already in higher level jobs and on those who are already at least partly qualified. A report by the National Institute of Adult Continuing Education (NIACE) in 1998 suggested a 'wide gap between the learning-rich and the learning-poor', stressing the following findings:

- Three in five adults have not participated in learning over the last three years.
- More than half those surveyed had no real intention of taking up learning.
- Three key factors affecting people's decisions not to learn, or causing them to give up early, are 'pressures of work', 'finance' and – for women – 'pressure of family commitments'.

One statistic has changed during the past 40 years. There is little distinction now to be made between the incidence of planned training for female as against male employees, partly, we assume, because of the impact of equal opportunities initiatives and demographic changes.

Typical training interventions that might be made by employees include:

- seeking new or updated knowledge (e.g. asking questions)
- self-study (e.g. reading, personal project activity)
- enrolling as a student on a formal college-based 'own-time' course
- attending branch meetings of a professional body
- joining an Internet-based forum group.

TRADE UNIONS

About a third of all UK employees are members of trade unions. Despite the unions' participation as equal partners in the Industrial Training Boards of the 1960s and 1970s, and perhaps because of their members' relative lack of enthusiasm for learning and training, they have not campaigned hard for employee training rights, limiting their strongest challenges to the training aspects of health and safety. However, the recent developments around union learning representatives have rekindled interest. The 1998 TUC annual conference supported the call for union learning representatives, and this was followed in 2002 by the Employment Act, which allowed paid time off for them. Some unions had already established active training centres, essentially to provide courses for their own shop stewards. The Trades Union Council (TUC) has declared strong commitment to the lifelong learning ideal, and specifically to the University for Industry initiative. Some large employers in both public and private sectors have reported good results from working with Learning Representatives. It appears, not unsurprisingly, that where there have been good employer/union relationships in the past these have promoted effective collaboration on learning.

> Discussion question: Why do you think that the unions are only now beginning to become interested in influencing training provision? What role should they play in an organisation's HRD plan?

EMPLOYERS

The term 'employers' is normally used to mean 'employing organisations', but occasionally it refers to their key decision-makers – the chief executives, managing directors, directors and senior executives who are generally thought to lead organisations. Here we use the term in both ways: where we discuss statistics or practices, we are thinking impersonally, but when we refer to policy, aims or attitudes, we are essentially thinking of the people whose thinking influences these matters.

For a country with a mere 28 million workers, it may seem surprising that the number of enterprises is as many as 3.7 million – and perhaps even more surprising that over 99 per cent of these employ individually fewer than 50 employees. These 'small' employers account collectively for about half of all employment; in contrast, a mere 6,000 organisations employing over 250 (whom we shall call the 'large' employers) account for 40 per cent of the total (see Figure 2.2).

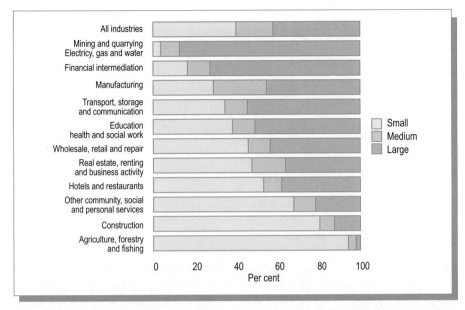

Figure 2.2 *Share of employment by employer size and industry 1996.* Source: 'Promoting learning in small and medium sized enterprises', Maria Hughes and Sue Gray (FEDA) reported in (then) DfEE Skills and Enterprise Executive, November 1998, Crown Copyright.

The low incidence of HRD in organisations which we described earlier is explained partly by the high incidence of small employers (SMEs), few if any of whom employ specialist Human Resource or HRD staff, and few of whom attract young people (except where there is a family connection) direct from full-time education with high qualifications. A Cambridge research study (DfEE (2), 1998), which analysed data covering the years 1987 to 1995 from some 1,640 small firms who had reported in 1991 that they provided formal training for their staff, could find no consistent links between training and growth or profitability, and could find no evidence that the provision of training improved the prospects for survival. There was, however, some evidence that management training in these firms could contribute to growth.

Small employers are often members of their local Chambers of Commerce, which, apart from organising regular meetings offering learning opportunities, maintain links with local educational institutions and are in continuing contact with local training providers, schools, careers advisers and public services generally. However, supply chain pressure is increasingly driving SMEs to develop their employees' skills, particularly in the areas of technology and 'e-business'. Many, not surprisingly, report that the business of dealing with multiple agencies, providers and professional bodies to find suitable training provision is extremely confusing!

Larger employers tend to look at growth differently. They have established markets, suppliers, brands, distribution systems and so on, and seek growth via innovation and 'the competitive edge', ie improved performance, which means being more efficient than the competition, and/or finding new ways to do old things. In these organisations competence may mean something specific to their own unique methods. Tailor-made training may be seen as superior to external courses and even to education aimed at standardised vocational qualifications (a few very large firms now have their own company-based 'masters' degrees and certificates in management, devised and offered in conjunction with academic institutions). In view of this, internal HRD specialists are often employed, centres are built,

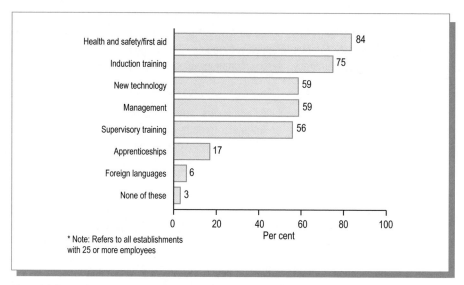

Figure 2.3 *Types of training funded or arranged by employers.* Source: *Skill Needs in Britain,* DfEE, Labour Markets and Skill Trends, 1998/9 Crown Copyright

resources are acquired, and detailed budgets are produced. HRD specialists can be expected to run induction programmes for new staff, to run appraisal systems and collate data on training needs, and even to plan internal courses for established employees, buying in external speakers if necessary but often drawing upon colleagues to provide specialist inputs.

Employers' overall preferences in terms of types of training emerged from a 1997 skill needs survey as heavily weighted towards:

- health and safety training
- induction training
- training linked with new technology
- management and supervisory training.

The percentages in Figure 2.3 summarise employers' own returns and apparently cover only training away from the workplace. They challenge those reported above from employees. The discrepancy is explained partly by the fact that the employers' survey covered a period of three years. Unfortunately, employer involvement in a given type of training does not guarantee its frequency – evidence of a single training event is accepted as evidence of employer involvement throughout the period.

Discussion question: How far do you believe employers are concerned that to invest in training means losing trained staff to competitors? Is this a general problem, and if so, how should it be addressed?

Of course, some large employers provide endless evidence of continuing commitment to a wide variety of types of training. The same employers have usually also been ready to offer facilities for work experience for those not yet in employment. Here again, however, the national picture is very patchy: it remains true to say that most employers are rarely willing to fund training for the non-employed, and hence government has had to accept its responsibility to provide funds to stimulate employers' interest. Generally speaking, employers seem to expect the state to equip unemployed people with the basic skills they look for in a new recruit – primarily numeracy, literacy, communication skills and a clear commitment to work norms.

Employers of all sizes have now installed computers, and in recent years the growing use at the workplace of the Internet, and of 'Intranets' (groups of networked terminals), has been significant, especially in medium and large organisations. Accessing information via the computer is likely to play a large part in employers' future plans and expectations regarding training.

Later in this book (Chapter 12), we will describe a number of learning systems that employers maintain – from an unplanned 'sitting by Nellie' model to firmly designed 'knowledge management' structures. The reality varies considerably between organisations, and we shall also see later that each element in any given model may be managed with widely varying degrees of sophistication. One critical variant lies in the extent to which line management is involved. Where there are no human resource or HRD management and requirements (such as, for example, the identification of learning/training needs and priorities, or the advance budgeting of training costs) must be met, then 'the line' is expected to find the time to do the work. This often reflects an emphasis on informal rather than planned learning, and is true even in many organisations with formal HRD departments.

This means that in such organisations senior management periodically prompts its subordinate management to carry out these responsibilities. And in organisations that see learning and training as key strategic instruments, senior management itself spends time agonising over the organisation's learning goals, the marriage of training with operational imperatives, the adequacy of learning budgets and so on. It cannot be assumed that the existence of HRD specialists implies devolution of responsibility for learning and training from line management. Indeed, the most frequently observed principle in organisations of all shapes and sizes is that management, particularly at middle levels, is expected to carry the prime responsibility for ensuring the continuing competence of subordinates.

One responsibility for specialist Human Resource and HRD management is ongoing contact with local schools, further education colleges, universities and a host of potential training providers. In the largest corporations, managers may become involved with their national trade organisations. Over the past 20 years or so, these have created 'lead bodies', 'industry training organisations', National Training Organisations and latterly Sector Skills Councils (SSCs), responsible for defining industry-wide standards, which are now the basis of approved national vocational qualifications (NVQs). We will explore later the system surrounding these qualifications and their relationship with state-sponsored 'Modern Apprenticeships' and 'National Traineeships'.

Large employers also form the majority of organisations in membership of employer organisations (notably the Confederation of British Industry or CBI) and again of trade associations, which exist in virtually all sectors to promote trade in their specific fields. Because it is a prime aim of any such representative body to promote its members' interests at national level, the trade associations and the CBI can be relied upon to maintain ongoing dialogues with government departments of all kinds, with professional bodies, and indeed with any organisation that might present proposals for nationwide change – and they can be relied upon to present employer views on any and all consultative papers issued. The CBI has perhaps been more proactive than most: it was, for example, initially responsible for suggesting the idea of 'world-class training targets', which government adopted as a main plank of its own strategy. In 1998 it proposed a 'world-class qualifications framework' to bring together all academic, vocational and competence qualifications.

Principles	Indicators	Evidence
Commitment An Investor in People is fully committed to developing its people in order to achieve its aims and objectives	**1 The organisation is committed to supporting the development of its people**	Top management can describe strategies that they have put in place to support the development of people in order to improve the organisation's performance
		Managers can describe specific actions that they have taken and are currently taking to support the development of people
		People can confirm that the specific stategies and actions described by top managment and managers take place
		People believe that the organisation is genuinely committed to supporting their development
	2 People are encouraged to improve their own and other people's performance	People can give examples of how they have been encouraged to improve their own performance
		People can give examples of how they have been encouraged to improve other people's performance
	3 People believe their contribution to the organisation is recognised	People can describe how their contribution to the organisation is recognised
		People believe that their contribution to the organisation is recognised
		People receive appropriate and constructive feedback on a timely and regular basis
	4 The organisation is committed to ensuring equality of opportunity in the development of its people	Top management can describe strategies that they have put in place to ensure equality of opportunity in the development of people
		Managers can describe specific actions that they have taken and are currently taking to ensure quality of opportunity in the development of people
		People confirm that the specific strategies and actions described by top management and managers take place and recognise the needs of different groups
		People believe the organisation is genuinely committed to ensuring equality of opportunity in the development of people
Planning An Investor in People is clear about its objectives and what its people need to do to achieve them	**5 The organisation has a plan with clear aims and objectives which are understood by everyone**	The organisation has a plan with clear aims and objectives

Figure 2.4 *The IiP standard © Investors in People UK 2003*

Principles	Indicators	Evidence
		People can consistently explain the aims and objectives of the organisation at a level appropriate to their role
		Representative groups are consulted about the organisation's aims and objectives
	6 The development of people is in line with the organisation's aims and objectives	The organisation has clear priorities which link the development of people to its aims and objectives at organisation, team and individual level
		People clearly understand what their development activities should achieve, both for them and the organisation
	7 People understand how they contribute to achieving the organisation's aims and objectives	People can explain how they contribute to achieving the organisation's aims and objectives
Action An Investor in People develops its people effectively in order to improve its performance	**8 Managers are effective in supporting the development of people**	The organisation makes sure that managers have the knowledge and skills they need to develop their people
		Managers at all levels understand what they need to do to support the development of people
		People understand what their manager should be doing to support their development
		Managers at all levels can give examples of actions that they have taken and are currently taking to support the development of people
		People can describe how their managers are effective in supporting their development
	9 People learn and develop effectively	People who are new to the organisation, and those new to a job, can confirm that they have received an effective induction
		The organisation can show that people learn and develop effectively
		People understand why they have undertaken development activities and what they are expected to do as a result
		People can give examples of what they have learnt (knowledge, skills and attitude) from development activities
		Development is linked to relevant external qualifications or standards (or both), where appropriate
Evaluation An Investor in People understands the impact of its investment in people on its performance	**10 The development of people improves the performance of the organisation, teams and individuals**	The organisation can show that the development of people has improved the performance of the organisation, teams and individuals
	11 People understand the impact of the development of people on the	Top management understands the overall costs and benefits of the

Figure 2.4 *continued*

performance of the organisation, teams and individuals	development of people and its impact on performance
	People can explain the impact of their development on their performance, and the performance of their team and the organisation as a whole
12 The organisation gets better at developing its people	People can give examples of relevant and timely improvements that have been made to development activities

Nominees from large companies also often sit on their representative bodies' councils and committees; where learning or training committees are concerned, such nominees are, once again, typically HR or HRD managers. The same people may also be asked to sit on governmental bodies, on professional body committees, or further education college boards of governors. If the employer gets a significant track record in the employee development sphere, the nominee may be asked to appear as a speaker at external courses or conferences, or to author articles in the personnel press. In such ways the large employer role expands and extends into the environment.

Since the early 1990s it has been possible for an employer to obtain a training award as an 'Investor in People' (IiP). By May 2003, over 34,000 employers were reported as having achieved these awards. We will explain later how they are administered, but essentially the process involves satisfying independent assessors that the employer matches a number of nationally prescribed standards. The 'national standard' required of, and demonstrated by, an Investor in People is set out in Figure 2.4. The wording in this national standard is carefully chosen and effectively summarises in its principles and statements everything an employer might be expected to do in relation to employee training and development.

More specifically, typical learning or training interventions by employers include:

- sponsoring attendance at external training courses/conferences
- mounting tailor-made internal training courses
- creating or adjusting the internal training needs identification system
- offering 'Modern Apprenticeships', or 'National Traineeships', or engaging one or more unemployed people under the state-sponsored 'New Deal' welfare-to-work scheme
- creating or developing an HRD department
- creating a learning resources unit
- running assessment and development centres, or even in-company 'academies'
- maintaining suitable learning support systems such as appraisal, mentoring and coaching arrangements and career development support
- creating and maintaining Intranet learning systems.

TRAINING AND EDUCATION PROVIDERS

Although learning resources units and specialised learning or training departments seem likely to make employees more learning conscious and employers less dependent upon the outside world for training provision, additional external provision will almost certainly still be sought and used. A glance at the pages of any human resource management journal or at the list of exhibitors at any of the UK's periodic national personnel or training conferences will confirm that the training provision industry is large and buoyant.

Private providers offer everything from consultancy to equipment to film hire to meeting rooms to programmed texts to readymade or newly planned courses – even to services involving expensive technology such as videoconferencing – and a lot more besides. Educational institutions offer even more: they cater extensively not only for their full-time students but also for part-time students from the world of work, preparing them for vocational qualifications. Virtually all universities now have business schools and offer part-time degrees in business as well as professional studies and short management courses. Many have followed the Open University in offering distance learning facilities. Further education colleges provide the educational element in the vast mass of Modern Apprenticeships, National Traineeships and 'welfare-to work' schemes. They also prepare 'released from work' students for a wide range of nationally approved examinations, including many set by professional bodies. Some professional bodies have their own student schemes, these days including distance learning facilities.

> Discussion question: Should private training providers be regulated in some way? If so, how do you think this could be enforced?

Of all these providers, the 400 or more further education colleges are collectively by far the lead provider in post-16 education and training, catering for 4 million students (of whom about half a million are in full-time education), which represents an increase of more than 35 per cent since 1993–4. Since 1994 they have been independent of state and local government, although they still receive the bulk of their income as public funds via the Learning and Skills Council, which 'took over' the earlier Further Education Funding Council. Despite an increase in student numbers, financial pressures on colleges have steadily grown, influencing colleges to negotiate special (sometimes termed 'franchising') arrangements with employers, sometimes in partnership with private training providers; such arrangements now account for about a fifth of all colleges' revenue. (In recent years colleges have often moved into employer premises to take over some of the work-related training alongside the more traditional classroom lectures.)

Each college has its unique internal departmental organisation, each department offering its own range of courses. Subjects such as information technology, motor vehicle maintenance, tourism, design studies and sports studies now draw large enrolments. Over recent years there has been an increasing attempt to address employer concerns that 'basic skills', tuition in number and communication skills, and again in information technology, should be offered as part of the curriculum.

Further education (FE) has been the subject of several major reports in recent years. Two stand out, each identified with the name of the person who chaired the investigating committee, and each gaining widespread support in both political and educational circles. The FEFC's 1996 Tomlinson Report argued forcibly for a new 'inclusive' approach to learning for all FE students, proposing substantial increases in funding to allow students to learn at their own pace and in support of their own objectives – basically suggesting a much more flexible adult learning approach than currently applies. A year later, the Kennedy Report (FEFC, 1997) demanded with equal force that much wider participation in FE be available for all ages. It demanded more money, new technology and new learning 'pathways' – basically a national commitment to promote learning for all with a new system for recognising achievement. The creation of the Learning and Skills Council, bringing together the old TECs and the FEFC, is believed by its advocates to improve the chance of achieving this.

The range of external options for an employee or an employer is enormous. To help navigate the 'learning jungle', a free telephone helpline has been opened nationally under the title 'Learn Direct'. Staffed by experienced careers advisers who have immediate online access to a national 'learning opportunities' database, it offers information and advice on courses and learning facilities throughout the UK.

Typical training interventions by providers are:

- drafting a new course
- liaising with an employer to supply refresher training for established staff
- assisting in reviewing, and where appropriate standardising, staff learning development and training in the wake of mergers and takeovers
- devising new projects and exercises within a course schedule
- supplying customised computer-based training programmes.

THE INTERNET

Of course, the Internet is to a large extent about computer systems. But those of us who may not be in the vanguard of the 'e' revolution sometimes forget that, although it works *through* IT systems, the Internet is fundamentally a way of sharing information over long distances with large numbers of people. It is an international computer network linked through speedy connections. A relevant point, especially when we come to talk about 'Learning Organisations', is that the Internet is probably one of the best examples of a Learning Organisation in practice. No-one really manages it (although it is subject to national and international legal restraints, and there are bodies involved with operational issues around parts of it). It is essentially a network of different networks. The World Wide Web is a method of accessing data stored on these networks. *Intranets* are local internal systems that operate like mini Internets.

There is a significant amount of nonsense on the Net, far too much 'pop up' advertising, where messages appear inviting the searcher to invest in all sorts of IT ephemera, and it can take longer than, say, working through a library of books to extract relevant information. But there is also a plethora of sites devoted to knowledge, like the 'Gutenberg Project', which plans to put all the classic texts on to the Net for readers to download. The better 'search engines', like Google or Alta Vista, will point the searcher to specific sites on production of a key word or words. The disadvantage might well be that the searcher can be sidetracked into irrelevant sites, but for those of us used to working in libraries this has been a perennial problem. If your task is to track down a book on evaluation of training, the obscure text about the influence of classical art on the sculptures of Chartres cathedral always appears equally fascinating! The Internet will point you in the direction of some interesting and relevant Web links, but book lovers will always maintain the superiority of the 'hard copy' text. The reality of course, as sites like Amazon, which sells current and out of print books, realise, is that both are equally valid as educational and learning tools.

AWARDS, QUALIFICATIONS AND THE BODIES THAT REGULATE THEM

Virtually all students attending further education colleges are attempting to obtain a recognised qualification. A large number of organisations, including universities, further education colleges, professional institutes and associations, industry lead bodies, occupational standards councils, training boards and councils, project groups, a variety of examining boards, a national management forum and even the Ministry of Defence, can and do award qualifications. Three bodies in this varied picture are pre-eminent, being more extensively involved and having the longest experience. They are:

■ the *City and Guilds Institute* (CG), whose traditional work was mainly in the fields of engineering and science

■ the *Royal Society of Arts* (RSA), who similarly pioneered qualifications in clerical, secretarial and office work

■ *EDEXCEL*, previously the Business and Technology Education Council (BTEC), offering a mix of business and technician awards.

These three are represented on the nation's Qualifications and Curriculum Authority (QCA, or SQA in Scotland), which oversees all 'officially recognised and approved' academic and vocational programmes and awards.

Discussion question: Qualifications are more and more in demand from employers, and students are today more focused on their future careers. Is extrinsic motivation towards learning (by gaining a qualification) sufficient to retain students' interest?

Employers, employees and even HRD specialists have always had difficulty in charting the vocational qualifications minefield. Since the mid-1980s, however, several developments have combined to make the overall picture easier to understand and to relate its parts more consistently to each other. Acting in line with a central government strategy, industry lead bodies and occupational standards councils have reviewed and newly defined the necessary content of qualifications within their fields of interest, and awarding bodies have revised their syllabuses to match centrally devised 'national vocational qualification' standards. The NVQ system ensures that all such qualifications – also colloquially now known as 'NVQs' – aim at reflecting actual workplace competence and not just relevant knowledge. (Scotland has a similar but technically separate SVQ system; we use the term NVQ throughout this book to relate to both.)

A collective approach to planning future vocational qualifications and a consistent approach to standards-setting was sought during 1998 by transforming the employer-owned, industry-based Industrial Training Organisations, plus state-owned occupational standards councils, into a network of state-funded but employer-driven 'national training organisations', or NTOs. An NTO National Council was intended to develop a collective two-way dialogue with government and to provide services to the NTOs. Unfortunately, by 2001 central government had decided that the NTOs had made insufficient impact on learning and training in organisations, and they were replaced by the Sector Skills Development Agency and its network of Sector Skills Councils, with a remit to:

■ reduce skills gaps and shortages

■ improve productivity, business and public service performance

■ increase opportunities to boost the skills and productivity of everyone in that specific sector's workforce

■ improve learning supply, by developing apprenticeships, higher education and national occupational standards.

One more government initiative had had a short life, to be replaced by another superficially similar body. What were the new one's chances of success? By late 2002, observers had suggested that progress in establishing the SSCs had been slow but steady. Successful SSCs have suggested that a key difference between the old NTOs and the new bodies is that while the latter represented employers, the SSCs are employers. Critics, however, point out that the SSDA is Treasury funded and that its members are ultimately appointed by government. At least there is commitment to get the focus right, but unfortunately governments tend to have a fairly short-term focus, and the trend has been to begin a new body rather than develop an existing one.

The millionth NVQ was awarded in 1995 and the two-millionth in mid-1998, at which time the QCA estimated that some 2.1 million candidates were working towards an NVQ or NVQ units. These qualifications are now the central focus of all government youth training and welfare-to-work schemes; funding arrangements ensure that providers, especially the further education colleges, offer and support NVQs. A sister group named General National Vocational Qualifications (GNVQs), is related less specifically to the workplace but aiming to prepare those still in full-time education – at school or in further education – for work within a particular industry. Although these GNVQs are 'unit-based' (ie a certificate is issued for each unit completed) and based on knowledge rather than workplace competence, they are, like NVQs, approved by the QCA but are exclusively awarded by the 'big three' national awarding bodies – the CG, the RSA and EDEXCEL.

Government funding rules have effectively forced further education institutions to promote NVQs (and GNVQs), and the vast majority of ambitious young employees can now expect an NVQ future. Most young people seem happy with NVQ courses, although some full-time post-16 students who have aimed at both NVQs and A-level examinations seem to have found difficulty in handling two different types of study and assessment simultaneously. College lecturers have also had problems with the need to incorporate workplace realities into their study plans and have complained of the bureaucratic nature of many NVQ standards, but in general they seem to have accepted the competence approach to learning. Small employers – or at least those who patronise further education – seem to be steadily coming to accept the idea of national standards. Some large employers are less sure: their own idea of competence is linked more to their unique needs than to any national denominator, and some have been slow to encourage their established workers to respect the new qualifications.

It is probably true that these large employers will come to accept higher level NVQs for their management as these appear (to date, fewer than 1 per cent of all NVQs are at the highest level). But it is doubtful whether government calls for 'widening participation' or 'lifelong learning' via NVQ enrolments will be supported by large employers unless nationally recognised achievement can somehow be taken to reflect actual workplace performance.

Discussion question: Is it possible or even advisable to 'mix and match' NVQs and academic qualifications?

A less permanent but perhaps more immediately visible opportunity for the employer is the annual presentation of 'National Training Awards' (NTAs), determined by a government committee and ensuring wide coverage in the national and personnel press. NTAs are given in each of several categories, one of which recognises innovative training methods.

We have already mentioned the one nationally recognised employers' training qualification – the Investors in People (IiP) award. This is administered by a private limited company (Investors in People UK), specially set up for the purpose by government. Its positioning in the private sector could indicate an acceptance by government that employers do not welcome the idea of assessment by the public sector. The actual assessment of an employer's application for the IiP award is carried out via arrangements by the local Learning and Skills Council, which we will now consider in more detail.

LEARNING AND SKILLS COUNCILS: BUILDING ON THE TECS OR A REARRANGEMENT OF BUREAUCRACY?

In the later twentieth century, various governments acknowledged the training reputation of some (usually large) firms. Government also capitalised on their readiness to allow their managements to play a community role by liaising with employer representative bodies and inviting their nominees to sit on the 'TECs' or 'LECs' – Training and Enterprise Councils or (in Scotland) Local Enterprise Companies. Set up in 1992, their remit was in part to dispense government money in the locality in support of a number of state-led schemes. Their emphasis was to close the skills gap, by training especially unemployed people to be able to fill jobs where there were skills shortages, such as IT or engineering jobs.

The TECs/LECs, of which there were in all about 100, were geographically sited. They were theoretically independent of government, had their own representative national council, and were free to enter into contractual arrangements with third parties. But like many other institutions established by government, they derived their purpose from government initiatives, their full-time staff were civil servants, and their funds came from the Treasury, with strict conditions as to their use. Basically, they were empowered to use these funds in support of government's published aims – in particular, those aimed at reducing unemployment, especially youth unemployment.

TECs and LECs came in for widespread criticism, not just from political opponents but also from industry and commerce, and in some cases from TEC board members, who also reproached the government for providing insufficient funding and learning resources. Some experts argued that leaving training to the voluntary decisions and exigencies of the business community could not succeed and that compulsion was required. Many organisations, it was argued, would not train enough employees to suit the requirements of the economy, but focus on their own needs. More fundamentally, TECs were accused of being overly bureaucratic and slow to respond to change, rather like their ITB predecessors.

The Labour Government's 1998 'New Deal' welfare-to-work programme for the unemployed 18–24 age group, plus similar 'New Start' projects for the 14–17-year-olds, might have expanded the TECs' role further, but instead the responsibility for this scheme went to the then DfEE. We will discuss these developments later in this chapter when we explore the role of the Department for Education and Skills (DfES). It may conceivably have been a sign that TECs were not trusted to deliver important initiatives; in 2001 TECs were replaced by Learning and Skills Councils (LSCs). In Scotland, Local Enterprise Companies, always believed more effective, were retained. The Learning and Skills Council, like its predecessor, is a national organisation with 47 local councils. Required to work to a three-year plan, its remit is to be responsible for funding and planning all education and training for post 16-year-olds in England. The work, according to the LSC website, covers:

- further education (the old FEFC was subsumed into the new body)
- work-based training for young people
- workforce development
- adult and community learning
- information, advice and guidance for adults
- education business links
- school sixth forms.

In support of LSCs it has been suggested that they state openly that their aim is to improve economic performance. They plan to do so by presenting a unified approach to the challenge of attracting people into learning, improving the quality of provision and raising the skills of the nation. They claim to be concerned with both young people and adults; it is likely that recently proposed legislation regarding ageism in employment (2004) may increase concern about the learning opportunities of the latter group.

The recent (2004) announcement by the government that it is proposing to launch a skills strategy involving DfES, DTI and the Treasury will be a major challenge for the LSC. It will need to show that it can get more value from government training budgets than its predecessors. Critics, however, have suggested that the government has proceeded in the wrong order by setting up a strategy *after* setting up bodies to deliver it! The Engineering Employers Federation commented that there still needed to be 'more coherent working between the various agencies'. Also, we might add that there needs to be recognition, from a nationally established body, of local needs and conditions.

TARGETS

Targets are now a well-established aspect of the UK training scene – the concept of setting performance targets has been a central plank in the government's approach to public service and education. Although there are concerns about the usefulness of statistical 'league tables', at least target-setting may give some indication of the impact of initiatives. National target figures exist for apprenticeships and apprentices, for national traineeships, for 'New Deal employers', for 'employees receiving job-related training', for further education student registrations, and especially for the attainment of vocational qualifications.

A National Advisory Council for Education and Training Targets (NACETT) was established to review continuously both the main targets and achievement against them. These main targets, termed 'National Learning Targets', were revised and expanded in late 1998 to cover – in addition to organisations gaining IiP status – both academic and vocational qualification attainments from age 11 upwards. Table 2.1 presents the targets geared to the year 2002, by which time NACETT had been absorbed into the LSC. In NACETT's 'farewell letter' to the then Secretary of State, David Blunkett, in 2001, it forecast that most of the targets would be met. It recognised, however, that while in England numbers were progressing to university education, the UK still had more people with low-level qualifications than most developed nations. It is this

Table 2.1 *The national learning targets to 2002*

Target	Autumn 2002
11-year-olds	80 per cent reaching the 'expected standard' for their age in literacy, and 75 per cent in numeracy
16-year-olds	50 per cent achieving 5 higher-grade GCSEs 95 per cent achieving at least one GCSE
Young people	85 per cent of 19-year-olds with a Level 2 qualification 60 per cent of 21-year-olds with a Level 3 qualification
Adults	50 per cent with a Level 3 qualification 24 per cent with a Level 4 qualification (a third target – 'Learning Participation' – is promised)
Organisations	45 per cent of medium-sized or large IiP-recognised 10,000 small IiP-recognised

Notes:
- *11-year-olds* 'expected standard' = level 4 in national tests
- *16+* higher-grade GCSEs = GCSEs at Grades A to C equivalent
- *YP* Level 2 = 5 GCSEs at Grades A–C, an NVQ Level 2, an Intermediate GNVQ or equivalent
  Level 3 = 2 A-levels, an NVQ Level 3, an Advanced Level or equivalent
- *Adults* Level 3 = (same as for 19-year-olds)
  Level 4 = NVQ Level 4, ie degree or higher-level vocational award
- *Organisations* medium-sized = 50+ employees; small = 10 to 49 employees.

'underperforming tail' with 'appallingly low achievement' that gives cause for concern (source: tMagazine). Will the LSC make a difference? The evidence is not yet (2004) clear.

> Discussion question: Are targets merely a cynical ploy by government to indicate commitment to learning, or a genuine way to check progress?

CENTRAL GOVERNMENT

The picture concerning learning and training 'institutions' created, funded and managed by the state itself has in recent decades been a highly volatile one. Over the years, successive administrations have created (and abolished, replaced or adjusted) many and varied training 'institutions'. Interventions have been frequent as policies and priorities have changed, Green and White Papers have been issued, special project reports have been completed, and organisational adjustments have been made.

The creation in 2001 of the Department for Education and Skills (DfES) was in some ways a party political move, but may have also reflected the view that government cannot leave employers and employees to provide the skills that the future demands. The DfES's remit was to give new prominence to training and skills, while the Department for Work and Pensions brought together policies and initiatives for unemployed people and their dependants. Problems of unemployment cannot wait for economic growth for their solution. There seems to be a view from central government that education must become more vocational to serve the 'small employer' economy, and that a buoyant qualifications system will serve the country better than imposed levy/grant schemes, pump-priming or simple injunctions to learn.

Old assumptions about lifetime careers within one organisation, and indeed within one occupation, have increasingly been challenged. It is becoming more important now for the individual to have multiple marketable skills, including the ability to learn in changing conditions, than for the employing organisation to create long-term robots. Within this context it is arguable that the central theme of recent UK training interventions has been the creation of versatile individuals who own personal portfolios of experience and portable qualifications. Whatever the intentions of those who might formally be regarded as the leaders of the evolving system, the UK may be moving towards a culture in which individuals manage their own development rather than simply 'join' organisations and rely upon them to look after their learning needs. At the very least, it must be understood that the overall approach of government is moving away from addressing the employing organisation towards serving and influencing the individual – and that corporate-sector institutions are adjusting to promote that move.

Most corporate-sector institutions are now managed as part of the DfES operation, although some are quangos – quasi non-governmental organisations – technically led by people appointed from outside government. Such bodies remain dependent upon the Treasury for their funds, and their day-to-day administrative activities are managed by full-time civil servants in the DfES; their ongoing roles and powers are to a major extent dependent upon Treasury–DfES relations.

We have already noted several of these institutions that are 'of' government but not in it. We have seen how SSCs and LSCs create national training standards and the content of youth training programmes but are financed via the DfES, which effectively imposes a corporate conceptual approach. Similarly, further education colleges are largely funded from a central funding council, which has to date biased its funding tariff in support of government aims, and which also imposes upon each college a periodic inspection routine and makes the resulting reports available to the public. And although LSCs remain independent local bodies, led by local business people, the vast mass of their revenues is tied to government-imposed conditions; as with the further education colleges, private-sector training providers who receive LSC funds are now subject to more stringent inspection, especially after the ILA debacle.

Rather than LSCs, the Department for Work and Pensions currently manages the 'New Deal' programmes. This is a major initiative aimed at improving the employability of unemployed people of all age groups, effectively redirecting national social security funds to serve that purpose.

The management of the nationwide New Deal programme is complex. Intensive help is offered to individuals to update and improve their skills. A critical innovation is the payment of a weekly wage and training subsidy to participating employers. Because options are not equal in kind, and movement between options may happen, and expectations generated at counselling interviews need to be understood by programme providers, the need for efficient administration is great, and communication between participating institutions must be consistently accurate. The delivery of particular elements of the programme is not standardised but varies from area to area, depending upon 'local partnership' arrangements agreed between a variety of bodies involved – government employment offices typically, but not always, co-ordinate the involvement of employers, careers services, training providers, environmental groups and voluntary organisations, in addition to the LSCs.

The Department for Education and Skills is of course a body that drafts consultative papers, commissions surveys, maintains statistical records and above all communicates information on what is available nationally. Its Statistics Unit, linked to the National Statistics Service, publishes definitive figures on employment, unemployment, training outcomes and official estimates of skills shortages; 'special features' address such issues as progress towards learning targets, small-firm training needs and UK links with the EU Commission and the EU's Social Affairs activities, including the distribution of Social Fund monies.

The DfES also accepts a central reference role for people who are seeking learning opportunities and for employers wanting to tap into existing resources. Its 'LearnDirect' telephone operation gives free, confidential helpline advice, including information on existing courses and how they can be accessed. The 'University for Industry' moves a technological step further in pioneering a 'national multimedia network' – which aims eventually to offer self-managed, computer-based learning with the aid of the PC, the Internet, and a battery of online tutors and forums. Similarly, the 'National Grid for Learning' (which provides a fascinating range of educational web links) aims to offer teachers, educators and learners a 'virtual learning resource centre', allowing a forum for the exchange of ideas, a library of documents on learning methods, and resources for teacher/trainer development. The techniques of delivering online learning are still in their infancy. Attempts at dialogue are sometimes ponderous and even information gathering can be relatively slow. But young people in particular are often attracted by these methods, and committed professionals can be expected to devise new ways for networks to work on data, and indeed for the learning and development world to sharpen its awareness of what can be achieved.

THE UK LEARNING SCENE AND ITS EUROPEAN LINKS

Another governmental role involves managing its links with the European Union (EU), and ensuring that the UK observes its responsibilities as a member state.

Employment, learning and training have always been a key aspect of EU social affairs policy. The original Treaty of Rome (1957) included a 'social chapter', which set out the EU's social affairs objectives. The EU's Social Affairs Directorate is responsible for drafting Directives, which are the EU's way of imposing new law. All Directives must be implemented through national law, which means that an employer who complies with national law is also complying with EU law. There is also a social charter, a non-binding declaration of community-wide social aims, which has prompted an action programme driven by the Social Affairs Directorate. And the Commission can itself prompt national action via 'Recommendations', 'Opinions' and 'Communications', all of which member states are obliged to consider.

To date, the only major effect of EU legislation in the learning and training sphere has been related to health and safety, although 1996 was designated as the European Year of Lifelong Learning. This was followed up in 2000 by an EU 'Memorandum on Lifelong Learning', which formally acknowledged that Europe has moved into the knowledge era. The aim has been to begin a European-wide debate on how to implement lifelong learning practices in all the EU states. There is also recognition in the document that a prosperous EU needs to be inclusive, emphasising wider social and political goals. More prosaically, an EU Movement of Workers Directive assumes that work will progress on a common comparison of qualifications – this is a major reason for the DfES's simplification and rationalisation of qualifications. In this development, the DfES has worked with the European Commission's own training agency, the European Centre for Development of Vocational Training (based in Berlin and colloquially known as 'CEDEFOP'), which offers a free information service on all aspects of training throughout the EU, commissions research, publishes monographs, and reports on qualifications systems. The main UK contact point for CEDEFOP is the Chartered Institute of Personnel and Development.

A number of EU training programmes have been promoted, contributing to mainstream objectives such as language training, co-operation between education and industry, and lifelong learning. Specific programmes in this area such as 'Socrates' (European Commission 1995b) or 'Leonardo da Vinci' (European Commission 1995a) have usually involved co-operation across state borders and cross-border exchange of learners; funds and places are (naturally) limited, and the criteria for gaining both are strict. The DfES must be involved in and must support any UK application, and may also require local support (eg from the local LSC) before deciding whether to process an application.

SOME COMPLEX NATIONAL THEMES

Several key themes can still be seen to run through our brief summary of national institutions. First, in the UK the state is now assumed to carry responsibility for preparing people for work and for promoting the employability of unemployed people. Second, employers are assumed responsible for workplace competence, but only a small percentage of employers (although accounting for about half the nation's workforce) are large enough to afford their own professional HR or HRD management and to mount their own training and learning activity. Large employers do generally promote training, especially for management, and all employers regardless of size look to external training providers (of whom the further education colleges are the most visible) for relevant services, which consist primarily of teacher-led courses.

Government, with the aid of the larger employer and awarding bodies, has developed a new system of national vocational qualifications to sit alongside and carry equal status with academic awards. This can be seen as a concentrated and sustained attempt to promote vocational learning during and after full-time education, and recognition that most employers (and employees) relate competence to qualifications. Government funds are now used to promote these qualifications, and government schemes automatically incorporate them. Further state incentives exist in the form of national training targets and national training awards. The system anticipates and meets the probable requirements of any forthcoming EU legislation. Government has also been enthusiastic about EU initiatives in promoting (a) lifelong learning ideals and (b) the development of computer-based learning methods and resources.

Recently (2003) students on a CIPD accredited Diploma in Human Resource Management programme were asked to write a critical evaluation of government learning initiatives in the UK, and to provide for the current DfES a blueprint for future action. Although many were 'native' UK students, some were internationally based, and all were asked to prescribe for the UK as a whole. The general view of the students was that the UK still lags behind many developed countries in economic performance. Although initiatives to tackle skills shortages had aided the government in combating the productivity gap, particularly Investors in People with its emphasis on life-long learning for employees at all levels and stages of career development, more drastic measures were required to secure UK future prosperity.

The students were acutely aware that a modern economy puts a premium on skills, knowledge and understanding, and that people lacking these attributes faced an uncertain future in the jobs market. Higher skills were also seen to lead to higher national productivity, thereby helping the UK to compete successfully in the world economy. They felt that the skills provided by the education system should be the ones that employers and individuals need to make the workplace more productive and innovative. This required the engagement of employers in the education and training system. Strategies for achieving change ranged from statutory paid time off for training for all employees, to a return to tax penalties on those employers who did not provide training. Training of older people was felt to be as important as that provided for young people, and those in low-income brackets were also highlighted for special concern. Apprenticeships were also targeted for development, in conjunction with structured learning and appropriate underpinning NVQ frameworks.

The other finding, confirmed by editorial research to update this latest edition of the text, was the sheer complexity of bodies involved nationally, and the sheer rate of change of their remits and responsibilities. This can be confusing even for those who work in the business of education – how much more so from the point of view of an individual employer or employee seeking advice. The students, and the editor, report masses of available information, especially on the Internet, but difficulty in obtaining specific answers.

Although the students were imaginative and innovative with their proposals for improvement, they were also realistic enough to appreciate that the problem was a complex one, and that there was in consequence no simple solution. As potential future HR managers and CIPD members, these students could play a significant role in the process of addressing the skills problem. Almost exclusively, though, the view was that learning should be applied rather than pursued for its own sake. The current Minister for Education and Skills, Charles Clarke, has also endorsed this view, to the annoyance of traditional academics in the 'old' universities. Will it prevail into the future, and is it possible to develop the two learning approaches side by side? Given the historical complexities of the national skills debate, it is not easy to make any predictions.

> In this chapter we have described a complex network of organisations and individuals with a role in promoting learning and development. If you were an HRD consultant, and were approached by a local small business providing IT services and expertise, which was keen to improve its overall skills base but had a limited budget, which national initiatives might you suggest it could investigate further, and why?

In the next chapter, we will move beyond institutions and examine how people learn. Would an understanding of learning theories and models assist those responsible for promoting learning within UK organisations to be taken more seriously? By the end of the next chapter you may feel better equipped to decide..

How We Learn – Theories of Learning Explored

In Chapter 3, we will consider:

- **What we mean when we talk about learning**

- **Some of the key learning theories and their use for the HRD practitioner, with the proviso that no one theory is universally applicable**

- **Mental processes, memory and techniques to improve learning skill**

- **The wide range of individual learning styles, which should be taken into account in the design of learning interventions.**

Learning theory really deserves a detailed study in its own right, and that is beyond the scope of this book. If you do want to read more, we give some ideas for you in the suggested reading list in Appendix 1. Most good organisational behaviour or introductory psychology books have an overview of the topic. Of course, as educators, we have a particular interest in this area as it helps to inform the way that we help people to learn. But we also want to encourage you to seek out more specialised texts by demonstrating some of the ways in which learning theory can be related to learning and training techniques and to some of the learning strategies that will be found in Appendix 4.

We will outline six main groups or sets of learning theory:

- reinforcement theories
- cybernetic and information theories
- cognitive theories and problem-solving
- experiential learning theories
- learning to learn and self-development
- mental processes.

The chapter ends with two examples of the ways in which HRD practitioners may build upon research to develop their learning strategies.

To begin, we would like you to think of two or three recent occasions when you think you learned something.

Does reflection on what happened help you to describe what learning is?

How did your learning take place?

Was it the same kind of learning in each case?

WHAT DO WE UNDERSTAND ABOUT LEARNING?

Think about these examples:

1   Mary is a trainee in the sales department. Her first boss never seemed to notice or praise her when she attracted new business, so she concentrated on looking after her 'regulars'. She now has a new boss, who makes a point of congratulating her immediately she gains a new customer, and if a large order is placed she is given a bonus straightaway. Mary has now set herself a monthly target of new customers and has brought considerable business to her company.

2   A child picking flowers innocently grasps a nettle and stings his fingers and cries. After having made the same mistake two or three times he recognises the nettle and avoids it.

3   The experienced car driver has learned to recognise the condition of the road surface and potential hazards and monitors her speed accordingly, especially when driving in wet or foggy conditions.

4   While sitting in his bath, the Greek scientist Archimedes suddenly shouted out 'Eureka!' (I have found the answer), when he had a flash of inspiration that enabled him to formulate his famous principle. (If you don't remember school physics, the principle is that a body displaces its own weight of water!)

5   Martin was sitting at a computer logged on to the Internet. He was one of a group of sixth-form pupils trying to find information about the oldest rock formations in the north-west of Scotland as part of an assessed group project. He found hundreds of entries under 'rock' and did not know which to choose, but was fascinated by one relating to a personal contribution from a climber in the Himalayas and also started to pursue another relating to rock music and its development. The rest of the group became frustrated that he was not finding out information they could use in their project, and one of the others demanded to take over the computer to find something more relevant. The next day, Martin logged on to the Internet by himself and spent an hour following up the entries on the Himalayas and rock music. He subsequently bought a book about the Himalayas, and started a computer dialogue with the author of the personal contribution on the Internet.

These examples have at least one common factor: they all involve a change in behaviour. How did your own examples compare? Did they support the definition given by Bass and Vaughan (1966) that learning is 'a relatively permanent change in behaviour that occurs as a result of practice or experience'? This appears to be a very simple definition. How we interpret 'behaviour' is an important point, because learning has been said to consist of knowledge, skills and attitudes. If the learning relates to attitudes and/or knowledge, the behaviour may involve only showing interest in a particular topic, such as an open style of management, because the learner may not have the skills to change his or her behaviour. There may be a considerable time lag between the learning taking place and the opportunity to display behaviour change.

To give a comprehensive definition of learning would be neither short nor simple. This did not discourage a group of well-known 'authorities' on learning who met to see 'how far they could agree upon statements about learning that would be of benefit to policy makers and leaders in organisations and to promote discussion. The result was not a definition but a two-page 'declaration on learning', which appeared in *People Management* (Honey et al 1998) and caused a vast amount of comment and correspondence. Often, of course, it is easier to criticise someone else's version than to produce one yourself!

> Discussion question: Why do you think Honey et al believed it necessary to publish a 'declaration on learning'?

The Bass and Vaughan (1966) definition is helpful in distinguishing two different aspects of learning: 'practice', which tends to be related to events that are deliberately planned, and 'experience', which may have been intentionally arranged (such as a short secondment to another organisation/department) or may have occurred spontaneously in the natural course of events. People cannot be brought together in an organisation to achieve any kind of common purpose without this 'spontaneous' learning taking place. As a result they will change their behaviour in various ways. At the simplest level, they learn each others' names, technical terms and the location of equipment. At a more sophisticated level, they learn about the behaviour of their colleagues, supervisors and management, and from what they learn they develop attitudes that can have complex effects on their behaviour. This in turn will confirm or alter the manager's attitude towards the subordinate. The process is interactive, both learning about each other and modifying their behaviour accordingly. People learn by imitating others (modelling), by perceiving and interpreting what happens in the organisation and by the cumulative experience of trial and error. In this sense, therefore, learning is an inevitable organisational activity. Later in this chapter we shall show that many of the learning opportunities presented by the organisation pass by untapped because they are unrecognised, and we shall suggest that the ability to identify them is the 'take-off runway' for the process of 'learning to learn'.

In managing the HRD function we are continually attempting to decide whether some kind of deliberate learning or training intervention needs to be inserted into the natural learning process. If we decide that it does, the next question is what specific form the intervention might take. We first examine some of the ways in which the intervention might reflect the HRD specialist's assumptions about how people learn. These assumptions may be well informed an considered, or they may be implicit, the trainer or learner relying solely on intuition or anecdotes. Anyone responsible for HRD should have a working knowledge of the processes involved in learning before committing an organisation to considerable expenditure, and a sensible organisational management will make sure this happens.

> Discussion question: What assumptions have you made about individuals and their ability to learn? Were these correct or not? Have you ever assumed you were not capable of learning a skill that you subsequently mastered (driving a car, or understanding statistics for example)? What can you remember of the experience?

This brings us to the third of our questions above. Was the learning the same in each of the cases? Even the few examples we quoted show that there is a variety of different kinds of learning. The range of human abilities is extremely wide, from *psychomotor skills*, such as operating a keyboard or styling a client's hair, to the *negotiating skills* of an industrial relations expert, the *symbolic skills* of a computer programmer, or the *decision-making skills* of a finance expert. The HRD specialist searching for one set of simple rules that adequately covers such varied activity is going to be disappointed. Researchers have concentrated on different aspects of this complex process and have been able to demonstrate certain principles, but no one theory can claim to cover all eventualities. We have selected four main types of theory for you to consider.

REINFORCEMENT THEORIES

On a television programme, a volunteer was told to watch the numbers moving round on a counter on the wall. He was promised £20 every time the counter moved to a new number. He was not told what caused the counter to move, but it actually did so every time he blinked his eyes. The camera showed a rapidly increasing rate of blinking as the counter moved around. After a few minutes, he was asked if he could explain what caused the counter to turn or if he could suggest how his behaviour had changed since the beginning of the programme. You probably won't be surprised that he did not know.

A very basic concept in learning is that of 'conditioning' or 'shaping' behaviour, the main enthusiast for this being Skinner (1965), who tested his theory by carrying out many experiments, the most famous of which concerned pigeons. By rewarding his experimental subjects with corn every time they made an appropriate movement, he was able to teach them many things, even including how to play 'ping pong' with each other. Although behaviour in animal experiments can never be an accurate reflection of complicated and sophisticated human conduct, it has been claimed that conditioning is an essential ingredient in many types of learning. In fact, the first of our examples (about Mary and her new customers) may be seen to incorporate this type of learning. Praise or reinforcing feedback from her new boss engenders confidence, which acts as a strong motivator for her to continue and extend the desired behaviour. Parents of young children will perhaps be attempting 'positive reinforcement' advised by childcare experts by, for example, praising them when they do make the bed as opposed to complaining when they don't!

Another instance is provided by techniques of programmed learning and its current, more sophisticated development into computer-assisted learning. The assumption is that receiving a 'reward' (which might be feedback in the form of learners being told that they have answered correctly or 'done well') gives positive reinforcement to that response and so motivates them to continue and develop their learning.

CONDITIONING APPLIED TO SOCIAL SYSTEMS

Skinner (1976) extended the application of his theory from experimenter and subject (trainer and learner) to the whole area of the structure of social systems. In his novel, *Walden Two*, he developed the concept of an entire society based on the use of positive reinforcement. In other words, the citizens were not controlled by law but by the way in which the environment was designed. A visit to the Internet discovered that the novel has triggered a number of utopian communities based on the story and an equal number of criticisms of what has been considered totalitarian propaganda. Other writers, eg Nord (1969), have attempted to apply Skinner's ideas to management through positive reinforcement, in job design, compensation and rewards, organisational design and change. The reinforcement must take place in such a way that the link between the behaviour and the reward is clear. For instance, Nord suggests that annual merit interviews and salary increments are very inefficient development techniques, because the rewards are so delayed that they have little feedback value.

Discussion question: Is there a place today for Skinner's ideas, or was he naive in assuming that society may be controlled by positive reinforcement?

Training is an intervention into an ongoing learning process; the culture, philosophy, policies and procedures of the organisation form a very powerful learning environment, which must be taken into consideration. On a note of caution, however, Skinnerian theory goes only a limited way towards assisting understanding of the process by which human beings acquire a whole range of knowledge and skills. His concept of 'social engineering' by the provision of positive reinforcement is now regarded as too simplistic, but it constitutes an important reminder of the need to consider the organisation's culture and to provide feedback or knowledge of results, without which planned learning is unlikely to be effective.

PUNISHMENT

Now consider our second example, of the child and the nettle. In this case a particular action (grabbing a nettle) was discouraged, not promoted. Some researchers, eg Estes (1970), have investigated the effect of punishment in suppressing an inappropriate response. His experiments (which mainly involved giving mild electric shocks to rats) demonstrated the principle that punishment may temporarily suppress a response but will not extinguish it. After having been 'punished' for pressing a bar, the rats made fewer trials, but later, after the punishment was withdrawn, they resumed their original behaviour patterns. The same caveat regarding the difference between animal and human behaviour also applies here.

Although positive feedback can bring about a relatively permanent learning outcome, negative feedback or harsh criticism may be effective only as long as some threat appears imminent. There are implications for safety training, where it might be said that the learner is being taught to avoid possible punishment (in the form of accident or injury). The nettle stung the child every time it was touched and would always do so even if the child made further attempts to touch it. Accidents, however, are different. They have been described as chains of events when a number of different conditions all coincide at one, sometimes fatal moment. Because these events do not normally all happen together, the threat does not continuously appear imminent. It may be possible to ignore certain safety features for a considerable time without necessarily meeting with an accident, and therefore on occasions malpractices go 'unpunished'. If safety equipment is uncomfortable, and a worker has managed to do without it and no accident has occurred, the habit of neglect will be reinforced as thoughts of danger recede. Car seatbelts are a good example of this. Until the law demanded it, many people refused to wear seatbelts largely because the habit of ignoring them had been reinforced. It was not until the threat of prosecution became constantly imminent that most people began using them consistently. Now, in the unlikely event that the law was changed back, most people would probably still wear seatbelts, as the mental link between safety and wearing them has been well established.

This is thought to be one of the major reasons why safety training is often ineffective, and you might like to think of ways in which the imminence or possibility of danger can be constantly emphasised. For instance, in some countries there is a practice of leaving a wrecked car at the side of a road, to emphasise particularly dangerous hairpin bends. In Scotland, notices were put up counting the number of accidents on a particular stretch of road in a year, but were taken down after it was suggested that drivers trying to read the notices might cause more accidents! We shall return to the question of making safety training more effective later in the chapter.

Discussion question: How might you discourage children and young people from smoking, when evidence suggests that attempts to portray smoking as dangerous to health simply do not have an impact?

CYBERNETIC AND INFORMATION THEORIES

A trainee sewing machinist finds that she is unable to concentrate on controlling the foot treadle and at the same time guide the material correctly through the machine. After special exercises in machine control and demonstrations and supervised practice in handling the material, she gradually becomes proficient and is able to increase the speed and quality of her performance.

Cybernetic theories concentrate on how information is received and monitored. People who have learned to drive on an automatic car with no gear shift often need a good deal of practice to co-ordinate the clutch pedal and accelerator. Stammers and Patrick (1975) and Duncan and Kelly (1983) liken the way in which feedback can control human performance to the manner in which a thermostat controls a heating system. The temperature is monitored and regulated because information fed back from the thermostat determines the level of power input to the system. See Figure 3.1, which is based on Stammers and Patrick's model.

This monitoring is a constant process in all activities. For example, someone who is profoundly deaf will have to develop a different way of knowing when to change gear while driving. A deaf colleague explained that she takes her cue not from the engine sound but the speed and rev. counters. The motorist in our third example was receiving 'stimuli' from the environment, by which she monitored and regulated her performance or, in other words, her input to the system. She received these stimuli through the senses – touch, sight, hearing, kinaesthesis (the sense of muscular effort or the 'feel' that one's limbs are in the correct position) and balance. For instance, the machinist above might interpret the sound of the machine, the pressure required by her foot to operate at the correct speed and the appearance of the work in the machine. Similarly, a cook or a wine taster might be relying on her sense of smell and taste to monitor performance.

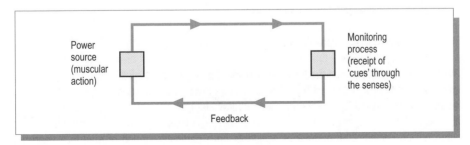

Figure 3.1 *The monitoring and regulating process*

In a training situation the most usual form of feedback is provided by comments from an instructor, but sometimes it can be given by simulators which act as artificial 'thermostats' and help the trainee monitor her performance.

An important part of skills analysis (see Chapter 8) is to determine by which 'cues' or 'stimuli' an experienced worker is being guided and by which of the senses they are being received. Probably the best-known example is to be found in the job of a word processor. Observation of a skilled performer reveals heavy reliance on kinaesthesis, or the 'feel' and positioning of the fingers on the keyboard. Left to her own devices, it is likely that a beginner will rely upon sight, looking intensely at the keyboard and using what has been described as the 'hunt and peck' method. Anyone who has taught themselves to type in this way finds it difficult to learn to touch type because they have to unlearn all their bad habits. A skills analysis, which includes not only a record of exactly what is done but also the details of exactly what 'cues' or stimuli are being used to monitor performance and trigger action, can provide the basis for an efficient learning programme for many psychomotor jobs. The training time can be shortened by providing practice in recognising and reacting to the stimuli used by those with experience, rather than allowing the learner to work unsupervised and thereby reinforcing less efficient habits, such as the 'hunt and peck' method.

> Discussion question: How far do you think it is helpful for learners to know about theories of learning to be successful in learning new skills?

Since recognising stimuli is central to learning, it is helpful for a trainer to understand the process of perception. For instance, training for inspection tasks is largely a matter of organising the perception to highlight certain stimuli or details and ignore others. During the learning process the 'selectivity' of stimuli becomes increasingly automatic, and the experienced worker stops thinking consciously about it (in other words 'sheds the perceptual load'). Think of a learner car driver, who has first to concentrate hard on braking, accelerating and changing gear. After sufficient practice these operations become second nature and are carried out almost without thought. Similarly, when you are learning to ski, you have to concentrate hard on cues to assist your balance, the correct position of your body in relation to the skis, how to traverse, how to turn or stop. After a number of painful experiences, you may look wistfully at the experienced performer, who seems to carry out all these operations naturally and apparently without thought, although possibly observing other matters such as the texture of the snow or the position of other skiers on the piste. In other words, certain of the experienced skier's actions have been 'pre-programmed'.

We can now have another attempt at answering the question posed earlier in this chapter:

How can safety training be made more efficient?

Far more effective than the threat of punishment to persuade people to avoid accidents is the positive aspect of ensuring that from the beginning the trainee will always perform in a safe manner (compare the example above of the use of car seatbelts). Developing safe working methods and habits must be the prime concern and will help to ensure that, even when the perceptual load is 'shed', the safe way has become automatic.

Kay (1983) gives a useful explanation of accidents as enforced changes from programmed to unprogrammed activity. For example, someone walking along a pavement is carrying out an activity that has been programmed since childhood; she therefore does not need to think consciously about it. If, however, her foot slips on a banana skin, the programmed activity is not enough and she has to concentrate rapidly on new-style evasive action. Injury may result if she cannot think out and effect this action in time. Someone trained in the art of falling, such as an ice-skater, could probably manage this because her mind is preprogrammed to do so, but the rest of us would most likely fail!

An important part of safety training, then, is to preprogramme trainees for possible hazardous situations (eg training vehicle drivers on a skid pan) so that they can more rapidly recognise and interpret the stimuli they receive in the monitoring process (eg the first feel of the vehicle's wheels sliding). Because an appropriate response pattern has been preprogrammed, the trainees have a much improved chance of avoiding an accident. This theory has a further implication for safety: because learners have to concentrate on many items at once and cannot shed the perceptual load, they have less ability to anticipate potential hazards and are thus more prone to accidents. Trainers need to pay special attention to this fact, particularly when dealing with young employees and students and schoolchildren on work experience. In these examples, the learner is not only attempting to cope with cues and signals from the job itself but also has to become acclimatised to a whole new work environment, as opposed to the familiar background of school or college.

COGNITIVE THEORIES AND PROBLEM-SOLVING

> Craft apprentices are confronted with a model of a live electrical wiring system. By operating levers and watching the results, they can work out the principles of electricity for themselves and apply them to their work.

In direct contrast to reinforcement theories, which are concerned with the establishment of particular behaviour patterns, cognitive theories draw attention to behaviour that we might describe as 'insight'. They reflect the way in which we learn to recognise and define problems or experiment to find solutions, whether by trial and error, by reasoning from first principles, by seeking information and help or by a combination of all three. We see the situation as a whole and begin to organise it. Eventually we conceptualise or 'internalise' the solution and methodology, so that we are able to extend their use and adapt them to future situations. Sometimes the solution comes by sudden insight, as in the case of Archimedes above.

These theories are not new. In 1925, Kohler (1973) observed captive apes using primitive tools to reach fruit beyond their grasp. These techniques have also been observed in the wild and there are several examples of animals developing strategies to assist them. Even a thrush that looks for a hard stone to smash a snail's shell could be said to use a primitive insight, albeit one inherited by some genetic memory. There is a close relationship between cognitive theories and the training technique called discovery learning. In this technique the trainee is given tasks that require him or her to search for and select stimuli or 'clues' on how to proceed. The aim is to provide a means of unassisted learning and appropriate experience to develop insights into key relationships. The success of this method obviously depends upon the effectiveness of the task design.

The craft apprentices in our example learn with the aid of a practical working model, but the technique is very versatile. For instance, depending upon the method of presentation, a case study, a project or assigned task can provide discovery learning. This training technique has the advantage of assisting transfer of learning to the job because, as the learner has found an answer for him- or herself, it becomes internalised. However, this method requires the trainer to be very sensitive in structuring the situation to the learner's needs, because vain pursuit of a solution that is well beyond current capability can prove an extremely frustrating and demotivating experience. In these circumstances, anger and irritation are likely to be turned upon the trainer who has misjudged the ability of the trainee to assimilate the required information. As we have seen from reinforcement theory, however, finding the solution acts as a well-earned reward to reinforce the learning. Obviously it is usually quicker to tell learners than to let them find out for themselves, and therefore discovery learning sessions tend to be time-consuming, although by providing better learning transfer they are likely to be more effective in the long term.

EXPERIENTIAL LEARNING

A human resource manager conducts a disciplinary interview, and when writing up the results for her records discovers that she does not really know enough about the offender's side of the story. On reflection, she realises that she did not give him the opportunity to explain, most of her questions having required a 'yes' or 'no' answer. It occurs to her that, when she needs to obtain information in an interview, she should ask at least some questions that are open ended to encourage the interviewee to talk. She tries out this idea at the next interview and discovers that it works, and so resolves to do this in future interviews.

We can see that there are really four stages here: the experience; observation and reflection; theorising and conceptualisation; and testing and experimentation. To be effective, the learner correspondingly needs four different but complementary kinds of abilities. This is how Kolb (1974) conceived the learning process, which he illustrated in the model in Figure 3.2.

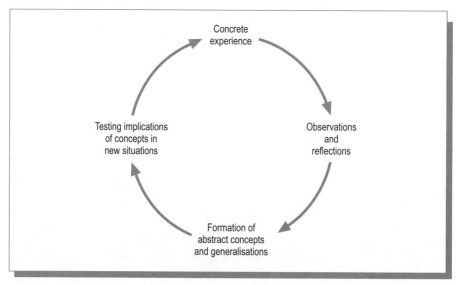

Figure 3.2 *The Kolb learning cycle,* adapted from Kolb P, Osland J, and Rubin L. *Organisational Behaviour: an experiential approach, 6th edition.* New Jersey: Prentice Hill 1995

Kolb suggests that this learning ideal is difficult to achieve and argues that in fact the required abilities might even be in conflict. He claims that:

> as a result of our hereditary equipment, our particular life experience, and the demands of our present environment, most people develop learning styles that emphasise some learning abilities over others.

In other words, most people are better at, and prefer, some of the four stages rather than others. For instance, a mathematician might give preference to abstract conceptualisation and active experimentation, whereas a manager may have greater concern for concrete experience and the active application of ideas.

Building on Kolb's theoretical base, Honey and Mumford (1986, 1992) defined four major categories of learning styles: activist, reflector, theorist, and pragmatist. These correspond with the four stages in the Kolb cycle, viz. concrete experience; observations and reflections; formation of abstract concepts and generalisations; and testing implications of concepts in new situations. Honey and Mumford have kindly given us permission to reproduce in full their descriptions of people strong in each of their four styles:

Activists

They involve themselves fully and without bias in new experiences. They enjoy the here and now and are happy to be dominated by immediate experiences. They are open-minded, not sceptical, and this tends to make them enthusiastic about anything new. Their philosophy is 'I'll try anything once.' They tend to act first and consider the consequences afterwards. Their days are filled with activity. They tackle problems by brainstorming. As soon as the excitement from one activity has died down they are busy looking for the next. They tend to thrive on the challenge of new experiences but are bored with implementation and longer-term consolidation. They are gregarious people constantly involving themselves with others but, in doing so, they seek to centre all activities on themselves.

Reflectors

They like to stand back to ponder experiences and observe them from many different perspectives. They collect data, both first hand and from others, and prefer to think about it thoroughly before coming to any conclusion. The thorough collection and analysis of data about experiences and events is what counts, so they tend to postpone reaching definitive conclusions for as long as possible. Their philosophy is to be cautious. They are thoughtful people who like to consider all possible angles and implications before making a move. They prefer to take a back seat in meetings and discussions. They enjoy observing other people in action. They listen to others and get the drift of the discussion before making their own points. They tend to adopt a low profile and have a slightly distant, tolerant, unruffled air about them. When they act it is part of a wider picture that includes the past as well as the present and others' observations as well as their own.

Theorists

They adapt and integrate observations into complex but logically sound theories. They think problems through in a vertical, step-by-step, logical way. They assimilate disparate facts into coherent theories. They tend to be perfectionists who will not rest easy until things are tidy and fit into a rational scheme. They like to analyse and synthesise. They are keen on basic assumptions, principles, theories, models and systems thinking. Their philosophy prizes rationality and logic. 'If it's logical it's good.' Questions they frequently ask are: 'Does it make sense?' 'How does this fit in with that?' 'What are the basic assumptions?' They tend to be detached, analytical and dedicated to rational objectivity rather than anything subjective or ambiguous. Their approach to problems is consistently logical. This is their 'mental set' and they rigidly reject anything that does not fit with it. They prefer to maximise certainty and feel uncomfortable with subjective judgements, lateral thinking and anything flippant.

Pragmatists

They are keen on trying out ideas, theories and techniques to see if they work in practice. They positively search out new ideas and take the first opportunity to experiment with applications. They are the sort of people who return from management courses brimming with new ideas that they want to try out in practice. They like to get on with things and act quickly and confidently on ideas that attract them. They tend to be impatient with ruminating and open-ended discussions. They are essentially practical, down-to-earth people who like making practical decisions and solving problems. They respond to problems and opportunities 'as a challenge'. Their philosophy is: 'There is always a better way' and 'If it works it's good.'

> Discussion question: Is there a 'one best style'? Defend your own preferred style to a colleague with a different one.

The concept of learning styles is an important development because it helps to throw light on how people learn from experience. It indicates first that a variety of learning/training methods might be planned in sequence. In the example of the interview situation on page 56, immediate experience requires a practical interview session (either 'for real' as part of the learner's daily work, or as a simulated exercise in a classroom situation). Observing and reflecting might take place by individual thought or by discussion with a coach or mentor, or observer and tutor in the case of the classroom exercise. Generalising and theorising might involve the learner in comparing her findings with relevant literature and formulating and re-examining her own principles and guidelines on, for example, the use of specific techniques and strategies. The next stage would be testing out these perceptions in a new situation and so back to experience. This example demonstrates the need for all four stages. However, when planning specific learning programmes or selecting participants for external courses, good trainers will allow for the fact that some people learn better by one style than another and some may reject certain styles altogether. So, programmes will ideally be planned with knowledge of learners' own preferences, and diagnostic activity will be built into the early stages of (flexible) plans.

It is also important for HRD practitioners to realise their natural learning/teaching style and that in choosing appropriate techniques they should consider the trainees' preferred or desired learning style as well as their own wherever practical. An 'Activist' trainer, for example, who plans lots of role play and discussion groups for her largely reflector delegates might be disappointed by their lack of enthusiasm, while they sit silent and worried that they might have to engage with an activity they find acutely embarrassing.

A rich menu is on offer to those who can take advantage of all four learning styles. For instance, consider in how many ways we can learn a sport such as tennis or golf. Your list is likely to include methods such as practising, experimenting, coaching, reading, watching others, watching oneself on video, talking to other people, thinking about one's game and, of course, playing. Each of these methods involves one or more of the four learning styles and, taken collectively, they encompass the whole of the experiential learning cycle. The successful professional will ideally take advantage of them all.

Similarly, many learning opportunities are available to managers. Mumford (1989) points out that learning opportunities do not have to be manufactured: they already exist in the real environment. Many of them pass unnoticed and unused, and managers need help in learning to recognise and take advantage of them. Table 3.1 lists examples of situations that may provide these opportunities within organisations and in leisure time. The right-hand column lists the processes by which managers can learn, and again it will be seen that taken together they embrace all four learning styles. Managers who rely on only one learning style are restricting themselves unnecessarily to just one course on the menu. In Chapter 11 we revisit this idea when we talk about ways to develop managers as learners and as 'modellers of good practice' in the organisation's learning strategy.

Considerable developmental work on learning styles has already taken place and there is

Table 3.1 *Learning opportunities*

Situations within the organisation	
Meetings	Modelling
Task – familiar	Problem-solving
– unfamiliar	Observing
Task force	Questioning
Customer visit	Reading
Visit to plant/office	Negotiating
Managing a change	Mentoring
Social occasions	Public speaking
Foreign travel	Reviewing/auditing
Acquisitions/mergers	Clarifying responsibilities
Closing something down	Walking the floor
	Visioning
Situations outside your organisation	Strategic planning
Charity	Problem diagnosis
Domestic life	Decision-making
Industry committee	Selling
Professional meetings	
Sports club	**People**
	Boss
Processes	Mentor
Coaching	Network contacts
Counselling	Peers
Listening	Consultants
	Subordinates

The opportunities identified here are not necessarily separate. You may, for example, think of something first in terms of something happening at a meeting – or you may think of the way in which one of your colleagues achieved success at a meeting.

Source: *Management Development: Strategies for action* (IPM, 1989). Reproduced by kind permission of Alan Mumford.

now a wide range of literature. For example, Richardson and Bennett (1984) have examined the structural and cultural barriers to behaviour at each of the stages in the experiential learning cycle. They suggest that it is possible to think of the organisation itself as having a preferred learning style, which influences those within it. As we suggested earlier, it is important for L&D practitioners to realise that their own natural training style may be at variance with the culture of their organisation and with that of the learners. The question then is how flexible they might be in developing their less preferred styles to ensure a better 'fit'.

Another traditional difficulty of group training activities is the effect of the composition or 'chemistry' of the group and the influence it can have on individual learning. Although the concept of learning styles does not produce instant answers to this problem, it does provide a potential explanation, and may help to promote useful discussion and understanding within the group. During the course of their research, Honey and Mumford (1986, 1992) developed a Learning Styles Questionnaire based on self-description and established norms for different types of manager, such as those engaged in research and development, production or finance. The questionnaire can be a useful measuring instrument for the trainer and could provide data relating to the influence of different learning styles on group activity. It can provide a valuable guide in, for instance, deciding on an optimum composition of learning groups. For the individual it provides a tool for self-diagnosis as a guide to building on strengths (best learning styles) and overcoming weaknesses (least favoured learning styles), leading to the use of a richer variety of methods. Honey and Mumford (1986) give advice on making the best use of your learning strengths and how to improve and practise each of the four styles.

Research studies (Allinson and Hayes 1988, 1990) suggest that the Honey and Mumford LSQ may be preferable to Kolb's own Learning Styles Inventory, on account of the distribution of its score, its temporal stability, construct and face validity. However, the researchers sound a note of caution as to its predictive validity, and raise the possibility that the questionnaire measures two general constructs of cognitive style (Action and Analysis) rather than the four dimensions of learning style relating to each of the stages of Kolb's learning cycle.

LEARNING TO LEARN AND SELF-DEVELOPMENT

In 1979, Kenney, Donnelly and Reid wrote: 'Our cyclical economy and the speed of technical change suggest that "learning to learn" is the central training problem of our time.' At the time we suggested the need for further research in this area, and the issue if anything has become even more important with the advent of 'knowledge economies'. Attention has been gradually focused on the activities of learners and the means of equipping them with strategies and a range of styles that are not only appropriate for present learning but will transfer to future situations and enable learning from experience to take place. The emphasis has moved from activities largely controlled by the trainer to the learning process and, where possible, to self-directed and self-managed learning. New technology such as computer-assisted programmes is used frequently to support this process, but less 'state of the art' methods such as reading and discussion with other people can be equally effective.

In 1981 a report 'How do I Learn?' was produced for the Further Education Unit (FEU) by a team from the then Industrial Training Research Unit (ITRU); the team had been asked to look into what the FEU called 'doing' learning (as opposed to 'memory' and 'understanding' learning). The team made two important points:

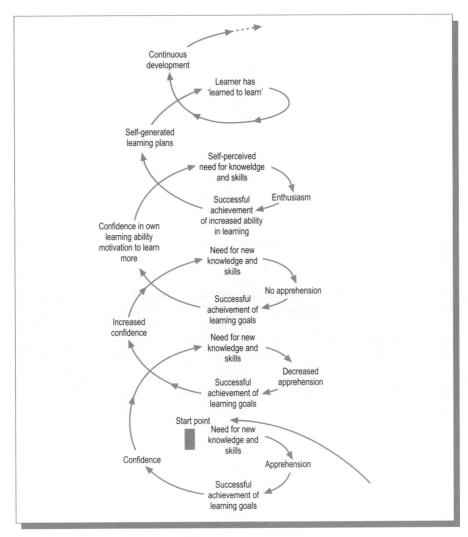

Figure 3.3 *The continuous development spiral*

- learning is something one does for oneself.
- the most effective ways of learning involve conscious mental activities such as checking, self-testing and questioning.

These points emphasise the fact that, whatever the activities of a trainer, the ability of the learner to manage learning is the key to making learning effective.

Learning theory in the past assumed that learning objectives represent a static work state. In this case, competence depends largely upon memory and the acquisition of basic skills, which ought to last a lifetime. Knowing 'what' and 'how' and 'when' is a matter of remembering what the manual (or textbook) says; and/or what worked last time. But memory cannot always be relied on if the content, and the context, of work is constantly changing. For example, if manual bookkeeping changes to computerised book-keeping, the individual's memory of mental arithmetic won't be enough: the computer now performs this task. Confidence in the relevance of the bookkeeper's knowledge base is dented, and must be replaced by some new knowledge (eg how to make the computer perform calculations), plus keyboard skills. The whole process is illustrated in Figure 3.3.

There are, of course, both positive and negative factors affecting attitudes. Apprehension about ability to learn and fear of change can be followed by confidence and sense of achievement in attaining competence, and this acts as a motivator to further learning. This is reinforcement theory in action. In ideal circumstances, the desire to learn can be self-generating, the sense of achievement from successful learning giving rise to confidence in one's ability as a learner and reinforcing the desire for further learning. The learner remains competent and 'learns to learn'. This enables her eventually to create new 'improved performance' objectives and to manage the learning process required to realise those objectives. This is the essence of self-development in action.

Discussion question: What negative factors do you feel have influenced your own learning experience? Compare with colleagues and/or fellow students. How might you overcome your feelings?

Curiosity is a strong motivator. Learning is like opening a door in a corridor that gives a view into a room beyond. The room has other doors that had not previously been in view, and when we open these doors further doors appear. This phenomenon becomes very apparent to users of the Internet, where the skill often lies not in finding a door, but in choosing which one to open and which corridor to enter, as Martin's experience in the fifth example at the beginning of this chapter shows. The Internet is full of fascinating 'learning blind alleys'! As the Internet becomes universally available it will be an increasingly important tool for self-development. There may be conflict between a highly structured learning style of formulating and pursuing precise objectives, and one that is more open, creative and exploratory when the user is confronted with the dilemma of sticking to what appears to be totally relevant material at the expense of missing something that could lead to exciting and unpredictable learning outcomes. Sometimes the latter might well be the more rewarding in the long term by opening up new perspectives that might otherwise never have been contemplated – at least that is what 'divergent' thinkers, who like to follow their learning noses, maintain.

Discussion question: Which of the Honey and Mumford learning styles is more likely to follow the unpredictable route?

Although an important tool for self-development, the Internet offers a lot more than the opportunity for the learner to obtain almost unlimited information by means of a computer. It can provide continuous learning in the form of contact and exchange of views and information with people with similar interests and problems throughout the world. However, to access and use the information they have gained, users need to develop specific and sophisticated skills such as reading, editing and drafting, those of research (eg posing the right questions, evaluating the data, evaluating the search, selecting, storing and saving information) as well as co-operation and collaboration with other users internationally. Research into the impact of online learning suggests that the process can be made more effective through discussion groups and group projects.

The Internet isn't just a medium for the solitary user, because it can be an invaluable vehicle for a collaborative and co-operation learning environment, such as that described in the fifth example (Martin and the 'rock' research). This is particularly likely to happen in schools, where it is increasingly being used to enable small groups of pupils to take part in investigations for themselves and negotiate how to progress. Discussion is taking place in many parts of the world to identify the issues that arise from use of the Internet, and to explore the implications for those involved in teaching and learning.

There can of course be a number of barriers to learning. Fear of failure, inability or unwillingness to expend the time and effort, and lack of positive feedback from tutors in the past can all hinder the learner. In a rapidly changing environment it is not enough to acquire the standard knowledge and skills. The process has to be constant. The successful organisation will pay attention to minimising the demotivating factors by creating a supportive climate and by developing employees' confidence in their ability to tackle and overcome barriers to learning. This is a genuine learning organisation, which fosters and encourages the natural self-generating learning process. This is a critical aim. Learners who have grown to believe that they are competent as learners take the lead in managing change and develop themselves in the process. Writers such as Hayes, Anderson and Fonda (1984) have stressed that interest in continuous development is one of the main features that distinguishes workforces in countries such as Japan and the USA from those in the UK, where the training emphasis tends to be placed more upon short-term considerations. The concept of continuous development is discussed more fully in chapter 13. There is a need not only for learning organisations but also for individuals who can readily move from organisation to organisation, or even take part in several 'virtual organisations' at once. As we saw in Chapter 1, awareness is growing of the economic necessity for continuous self-development, as security lies increasingly in marketable skills rather than in a 'safe' job, and learning is seen as an important part of the total employment contract.

MENTAL PROCESSES

We would like now to discuss the concept of memory, and the dual memory theory, which has important implications for HRD specialists. Some exciting discoveries about learning may lie in extending our knowledge of the way the brain works, sometimes linking with the study of the effect of brain damage on the brain's functions. New technology, particularly the use of sophisticated scanners, has helped scientists and researchers understand more about the functioning of various areas of the brain. Here we give a brief outline of the activities of the right and left hemispheres of the brain, followed by examples of the ways in which educationalists and trainers claim to have built upon research findings.

Memory

The average number of discrete items that the human mind can comfortably take in at one time is seven. We can remember much more if we combine small items into larger 'bits'. For instance, it is only possible to remember about seven random letters of the alphabet, but if we combine them into meaningful words or sentences we can remember many more. The implication for the trainer is that meaning assists memory. It is very difficult and time-consuming to remember something we do not understand. Because Latin and Greek have very complex grammatical forms, it is easier for students to remember particular phrases. Julius Caesar's 'Veni, vidi, vici' (I came, I saw, I conquered) is very useful for remembering the Latin first person perfect tense!

Retention

The two factors of long-term and short-term memory have serious implications for trainers and indeed academics who set exams. Any matters that learners cannot recall shortly after a training session are unlikely to have entered into long-term memory: such matters will therefore 'decay' and not be retained. There are four important issues here:

- memory decay – the rate of decay slows down with time, so prompt reinforcement of what has been learned is an advantage;
- interference – learning one piece of material or skill can hinder learning another;
- levelling – after a time-lapse, the material is remembered in very general terms, and much of the detail is glossed over;
- sharpening – certain items and details are remembered for their peculiarity or particular interest (although they may not necessarily be the most important items of content). Jokes or amusing stories may be remembered long after the serious content of a presentation has been forgotten and care should be taken to ensure that it is the important items that are 'sharpened' in the learners' minds. Lecturers are often dismayed to find their 'funny' stories quoted back at them in student exam answers at the expense of the important point they were trying to make!

The implications are that a trainer should present material logically, ensure that every point is clear and easily understood, and summarise the main points succinctly at the end. Other ways of assisting retention are mental imagery (see the example of electrical coding in Chapter 9), appealing to more than one sense (for example, the use of slides in a presentation involves sight as well as hearing and helps to 'sharpen' the main points), and finally, overlearning (see page 79).

The right and left hemispheres of the brain

Researchers have found that the two hemispheres of the brain have very different ways of processing information. The connecting network that sends messages from one side of the brain to the other is called the 'corpus collosum'. When this is undamaged the two hemispheres are effectively integrated, but studies of patients in whom the 'corpus collosum' has been severed have indicated separate awareness in right and left halves of the visual field and for objects in the right and left hands. For instance, it has been found that such patients cannot match an object felt in the left hand out of sight with the same kind of object felt separately and unseen in the right hand. By studying these patients, researchers have been able to demonstrate that each side of the brain appears to have its own specialisations. The left hemisphere appears to be analytical, logical, associated with spoken language skills, number and scientific skills, and reasoning. The right hemisphere is related to art, three-dimensional forms, music awareness, imagination, creativity, insight and holistic perception. The right side also has a visual learning capability. There are still many questions to be answered concerning these complementary abilities and the way in which the two hemispheres are co-ordinated. It must be emphasised that neither has a complete monopoly of its particular cognitive style. The specialisms of the two hemispheres are now regarded as a matter of degree rather than as an absolute. Studies have shown that individuals vary greatly in the ways in which the hemispheres are habitually activated, and such factors as sex, age, left or right hand preference, education and special training appear to have an effect.

New technology has enabled more extensive and accurate research in scanning the brain and measuring its electrical activity while the individual is exposed to different kinds of stimuli such as a conversation, a piece of music or synchronised words and music. Researchers claim that by this means they have obtained scans showing the particular areas of the brain that are activated by these different stimuli (see Rose 1991).

Johnson and Indvik (1991) consider the implications of this research in relation to the job of a manager. Not surprisingly, for those who have attempted the role, they suggest that the integration and synthesis of both the analytical left- and the intuitive right-brain activity are critical. For instance, too heavy reliance on the analytical left can result in loss of intuitive powers on the right side of the brain. They indicate that left-brain-oriented managers pursue rational and logical reasoning and work in a highly structured way, but may dismiss imaginative ideas generated by more intuitive right-brain-oriented colleagues. It is suggested that, where policy issues are complex, right-hemisphere and integrative skills are needed more than purely left-hemisphere skills, because the complete data on which to base a totally calculated and logical decision is not always available. It has been suggested that advances in computer technology will diminish the need for managers possessing left-hemisphere analytical skills, while the demand for those with creativity, imagination and the ability to take a holistic perspective will increase.

Discussion question: Do you agree with the suggestion that right-brained managers will be more in demand than their left-brained equivalents? If not, why?

What, then, are the implications for HRD practitioners? First, employees might find it very useful to be aware of the functioning of the two hemispheres and of their own particular dominant skills, as well as of the effect they might have on colleagues and subordinates. There are computer programs designed to help you discover your dominant skill. Johnson and Indvik (1991) suggest that this knowledge might be used in career management, to ensure that people are placed in jobs appropriate to their particular mental strengths. They indicate that the advantage possessed by 'great minds' lies in the inclination to use both hemispheres effectively and they suggest exercises to enhance brain interaction.

From an HRD perspective, it would seem sensible to attempt to involve both hemispheres in any structured learning activities. For instance, learning that relies upon logical interpretation appeals to the left hemisphere and can be effectively reinforced by the use of visual aids, imagery or sensory stimuli relating to the right side of the brain.

From work with patients who have suffered brain damage, researchers have discovered that certain mental functions appear to be associated with particular areas of the brain. These discoveries have led to theories that types of mental processes may be discrete activities, and to the hypothesis that ability (whether learned or innate) in one activity does not necessarily transfer to another activity. These theories obviously have important implications for learning transfer.

However, despite this functional characteristic, researchers (eg Jensen 1995) have pointed out that the brain works holistically and by parallel processing. It does not function in a discrete manner, concentrating on one thing at a time, but has the capacity simultaneously to take in and interpret many things while also controlling subconscious activities such as breathing, digesting etc. It is multifunctional, operating on many levels of consciousness at once, observing the world around, selecting what appears to be important and matching and comparing it with past experience. And, as Jensen points out, 'In addition, the brain is attaching emotions to each event and thought, forming patterns of meaning to construct the larger picture and inferring conclusions about the information acquired.' The exponents of 'Accelerated Learning' (see below) suggest that the ability and capacity of the brain is massive but greatly underutilised, and that by exploiting the phenomenon of parallel processing and emotional aspects, learning can be greatly enhanced.

Multiple intelligences?

Gardner (1987) proposes a modular view of intellect, suggesting that there are seven different 'intelligences': linguistic, logical mathematical, musical, spatial, bodily kinaesthetic, interpersonal and intrapersonal ('an effective working model of oneself and the ability to use that model effectively in the light of desires, needs, wishes, fears and skills'). Gardner's theory suggests that principles of learning, perception and memory can vary according to the seven types of intelligence, so that each type has its own set of learning principles. So in the case of memory, the way in which a dancer remembers a dance step is different from the way the same person remembers a phrase in a foreign language. This has value for the HRD specialist, for it suggests, if we accept Gardner's reasoning, that learning and development in one intelligence is unlikely to affect another.

OTHER HORIZONS

Trainers and educationalists have attempted to devise techniques based on the interpretation and application of research findings such as those we describe above. We don't have space in this book to describe any of these in detail, but we end this chapter with a brief outline of two examples.

Accelerated Learning

Enthusiasts for Accelerated Learning have developed methods for which they claim spectacular results. These are described in detail by Rose (1991), who suggests that the average human uses only 4 per cent of his or her potential brain power. He suggests that we have a cultural legacy of self-imposed limitation, produced in part by the way in which we are taught to learn at school. Rose claims that most schools relegate right-brain activities to two or three hours a week, the main emphasis being on the left-brain functions required by verbal and deductive subject matter. As a society we also tend to value logical and analytical thinking more highly than artistic or intuitive ability, and in the main we do not reward independence of thought or creativity. This is the basis for the theologian Matthew Fox's concept of 'creation theology' (Fox 1996), which focuses on the belief that creation and creativity are divine gifts. It has been suggested that our focus on reason at the expense of creativity starves the right hemisphere of development and can systematically damage the brain. Accelerated Learning methods stimulate the whole brain, not just one hemisphere, and emphasise the role played by emotional content in learning because it effects a higher state of arousal, thereby making the learning more likely to be retained. If the whole brain is to be used there is a need for imagery as well as logical thought, and visual association may well assist memory.

An innovative feature of Accelerated Learning is the use of music as part of the learning event because it is claimed to stimulate right-brain functioning. In particular, it is suggested that the Baroque composers produced exactly the right frequency and sound to harmonise with the rhythm of the brain, thereby inducing a state of relaxed alertness and calm conducive to learning.

Accelerated Learning enthusiasts maintain that in every learning activity there is a focused and central component, but also an area of peripheral activity, in which the brain subconsciously processes more than the learner realises (peripheral, subconscious and paraconscious often being used interchangeably). Peripheral learning contributes strongly to what is retained, so Accelerated Learning builds in techniques that appeal to the subconscious. These include visual presentations that take into account peripheral vision; the use of posters and cards arranged around the room; materials directed to visual, auditory and, where possible, kinaesthetic channels; games and role-playing, which distract the attention and allow information to be subconsciously assimilated.

It is not possible here to give more than this brief summary of the underlying concept of Accelerated Learning, but a much fuller account will be found in Rose (1991).

Neuro Linguistic Programming

Neuro Linguistic Programming (NLP) was developed from research in the USA in the early 1970s by John Grinder, a professor of linguistics, and Richard Bandler, a mathematician. They selected three communicators (all of whom were therapists renowned for their excellence) and studied them at work with their clients. The purpose of the research was to identify the precise behaviours that contributed to this excellence, and to produce a framework or model of excellence in one-to-one communication that could be used by others. By combining the skills of linguistic analysis and mathematical notation, they were able to organise their data into a set of hypothetical 'rules' that could be used by other therapists, who thereby improved their performance (see Bandler and Grinder 1976).

Since this original work, practitioners have applied the use of NLP to education, learning, training and development. Although the original work related to self-management and one-to-one communication, later work extended the scope to leadership and management of groups and organisations. The exponents of NLP suggest that each person's concept of reality is actually his or her subjective interpretation, because the mind is a filtering mechanism. The interpretations made by each individual are influenced by their experiences and attitudes relating to other people and the world around. From birth onwards, individuals learn to programme their reactions and develop strategies, which are then likely to become automatic or unconscious. These strategies are of two kinds: those involving language, and those relating to body movements and physical reactions. From their studies of the strategies used by 'excellent performers', the researchers developed a framework that can be used to help an individual identify his or her own strategies and those of others. Having been made consciously aware of his or her own strategies, the individual can begin to have choice and control by adjusting what would previously have been 'automatic' responses and behaviour.

Routledge (1995) used NLP methodology to investigate the critical behaviours and strategies used by effective learners on an interpersonal skills programme. The model was based on the assumption that, consciously or unconsciously, we set goals and develop a test to indicate to ourselves whether the goal has been achieved. If it has not been reached we change and do something to get closer to it. This process was the basis of the data collection, and it was found that effective learners had the following characteristics.

- realisation that interpersonal skills are useful not only at work but also in a number of aspects of their lives
- validation of the learning process took place outside the formal class – effective learners felt that the true test of the course was whether the skills could be used successfully in the work/social environment

■ use of visual and kinaesthetic senses – effective learners could 'go inside themselves' and visualise occasions when they would be able to use the skill

■ judgement of success was not a matter of pass/fail, but of moving towards ideal performance, or an opportunity for feedback on how to improve

■ natural inclination to plan – effective learners were outcome oriented (set themselves targets), conscious of what they were trying to achieve and of the level of skill required

■ motivation to develop themselves personally.

NLP embraces many different techniques and approaches, for which there is no room to describe more fully, but you may wish to follow them up if you are interested, for example from the NLP Academy website: www.nlpacademy.co.uk. Some of them relate to self-management, an example being 'outcome thinking' – thinking of the positive outcome required in a particular situation, and rehearsing it by imagining it through as many senses (sight, sound, feeling etc) as possible. The next stage is to identify the personal resources (eg confidence) needed to bring about that outcome, and to summon those resources using stimulus/response technique, which require the individual to think of a time when he possessed the particular resource, to relive how it felt and to recall how he reached that state, in order to help himself recreate it. The final stage is to rehearse the use of that resource in the new situation in order to bring about a positive outcome. Other skills are concerned with the micro-skills of communication, to enable the individual to become aware of how he or she is progressing towards the desired outcome, and to help him acquire the flexibility to adapt as necessary. For fuller accounts see Johnson (1991) and Kamp (1991).

We hope it has become clear to you that no one theory explains the complex processes of learning in all situations. This chapter was intended to provide a background to help you to choose and devise appropriate learning and training strategies, which will be discussed in more detail in Chapter 9.

By now you should have realised the importance of feedback (or knowledge of results) in the learning process. We will continue this theme in the next chapter, when we discuss its role in guiding the learner towards certain behaviours and in gradually enabling self-monitoring to take place. In preparation for this, you might like to think of as many ways as you can in which feedback, both positive and negative, occurs in your organisation. Is it always positive and constructive, or are there too many examples of the 'blame culture' where feedback is only given, negatively, when something goes wrong?

> This chapter has introduced you to a range of theories of how people learn. No one theory is universally applicable, but which of the theories you have read about most appeals to you as an explanation of how learning takes place? How might you use it to assist you in the role of an HRD practitioner?

In the next chapter we will examine learners in organisations and the challenges they face.

Learners and Their Organisations

CHAPTER 4

In Chapter 4, we will consider:

- **Learners at work and the factors that can influence their successful learning;**

- **Transfer of learning from the learning programme to the workplace;**

- **The organisation as a learning environment, and some important considerations for those managing learning;**

- **Organisational practices to nurture learning, and assist the creation of an organisation capable of learning to learn.**

We stress throughout this book that learners do not exist in a vacuum. They live and work in an environment that influences the behaviour and learning of its inhabitants, and which is in turn influenced and shaped by them. We will discuss this interaction in the first two sections of this chapter. The first section looks at contextual factors that might affect individuals and their motivation to learn. In the second section we examine the organisation as a learning environment. In the third section we discuss the concept of double-loop learning, popular with exponents of the learning organisation idea, and the way in which the organisation can learn to learn.

THE LEARNERS: INFLUENTIAL FACTORS FOR SUCCESS?

We have looked in Chapter 3 at some of the issues that might affect people's ability to learn. Now we will highlight some key factors that can positively or negatively affect success in learning. These are:

- motivation
- knowledge of results (or feedback)
- attitude formation and change
- the age factor
- learning transfer.

Motivation

A group of students all assured their tutor that they were undertaking their degree course because it would open doors to a 'better', ie more highly paid, job. The tutor who had asked them about motives assumed that the students were all 'extrinsically' motivated, that is, motivated by what the course might do for them, rather than 'intrinsically' by genuine interest in the topic. She was heard to complain that this lack of interest was 'typical of young people today'. In reality, as the tutor later discovered when she got to know the students better, they had not been sure what answer was the 'right' one, they were intimidated by the idea of answering direct questions like 'what do you expect to get from this course?' and were worried about how they were going to cope with the demands of the course. Later they were much more thoughtful – 'I'm the first person in my family to go to university and I want them to be proud of me', 'I want to travel and work in other countries', 'I'm the one my friends ask to help them solve computer problems and I want to start my own business doing that work' and so on.

Motivation is a complex concept and it is most important to recognise that, as the example shows, people are multimotivated and that they can be motivated towards or against specific behaviours. So there is no easy answer to what motivates people.

Discussion question: The website 'Friends Reunited', which puts old schoolmates back in touch, has been in trouble because of potentially libellous insults posted about ex-teachers who were loathed by their students. Which teachers at school motivated you to learn and why? Which made you feel negative towards learning?

Otto and Glaser (1970) suggest a useful classification of motivational factors based on the kind of rewards that are involved in learning:

- achievement motivation, for which the reward is success
- anxiety, for which the reward is the avoidance of failure
- approval motivation, for which the reward is approval in its many forms
- curiosity, for which the reward is to explore the environment and be exposed to novel stimuli
- acquisitiveness, for which the reward is something tangible, such as money or material benefits.

None of these classification groups should be regarded as excluding the other: for instance, both achievement and anxiety motivation are possible in the same person at the same time. This is what the lecturer in the example had forgotten. All the factors are influenced by the immediate experiences of the learner, and as motivation is a personal matter, the case for careful discussion of individual programmes is obvious. Frequently, though, a variety of people are undertaking the same programme and it is necessary to bear all the general motivational factors in mind. For instance, achievement motivation requires that learning should be a successful experience. This has implications for the size of the learning 'steps' in relation to the target population, for timing, for the provision of ample knowledge of results or feedback to learner and trainer, and for assistance in case of difficulty. If the programme is long and involved, and possibly daunting, the setting of intermediate targets can be a useful means of effecting a sense of achievement, as can the introduction of a competitive element for some learners, although older learners (and possibly women, who tend to be more collaborative), tend to react unfavourably to that type of atmosphere. Approval is also concerned with knowledge of results, and psychological theory suggests that it is more effective to approve, and so reinforce, correct actions, than to punish and ridicule incorrect ones, as we saw from Skinner and his followers (p 51).

> Discussion question: What factors for you ensure a higher level of motivation to learn? Discuss these with colleagues or fellow students – are there any common themes?

There is probably an optimum level of motivation. Learners who are too eager can suffer from excessive anxiety, which may inhibit learning. This can apply particularly to older workers, who may be anxious for financial reasons, for prestige, or because of domestic problems; a good trainer should be prepared for this and allay any fears. It should be understood that 'sending on a course' should *not* be seen or intended as a punishment for failure – unfortunately training is still used by some organisations in this way. It is always useful to help the trainee to face the cause of the anxiety and so overcome it. If this does not happen, the learner either wastes time worrying about failure or practises very hard. This is beneficial if he or she is practising an effective method but, if not, he or she may be reinforcing errors that may be difficult to eradicate. It is not always true that 'practice makes perfect'. Think of the earlier example of the bad typist who looks at the keys (p 54).

> An office supervisor took delivery of a new piece of technical equipment, which he wanted all staff to learn to use. He left it covered up in the office and claimed that within two weeks every member of staff had found out what it was and how to use it, so illustrating the importance of curiosity as a motivator for learning.

Curiosity can be a very powerful motivator, as experience with small children and kittens shows, discovery methods of learning (see page 62) are often very effective. This is why young children have no fear of 'breaking the computer' and adults are more circumspect, as fear has replaced curiosity. Curiosity is one of the trainer's most powerful allies and should be encouraged by building on the learners' interests whenever practicable rather than destroying them by a rigorous insistence on logicality. It is essential, especially in induction training, to consider curiosity and anxiety when timing learning events so that as far as possible they occur at the most appropriate point for the learner.

> Discussion question: How might a trainer make use of delegates' curiosity to make an induction course more interesting?

There can be difficulties in establishing a direct link between the acquisitive instinct and successful completion of a learning programme. The relationship is probably at its most obvious in the field of operator training for pieceworkers, where a resultant increase in output will be reflected in a higher overall wage. In management development, however, the outcome is likely to be less clear; the relationship is more likely to be indirect, in that if the training leads to better performance, an increase of salary or promotion may result, but as many factors contribute to improved managerial achievement, it can be extremely difficult to attribute cause and effect. The students who really wanted a degree to obtain a better job might find that soon after graduating they were not earning much more than a school leaver. And of course, now that there is so much emphasis on learning for life, they could not rest on their laurels without further development.

Knowledge of results

Knowledge of results

This is a form of reinforcement, and without it, it is difficult for learning to be retained and applied. It has important implications for the way learning situations are structured. The more prompt and specific the reinforcement, the more effective it is likely to be. For instance, in the case of learning the piano it is more effective to hear a wrong note at the time of hitting the key than for someone to tell you of your error three weeks later. In the case of development where results are longer term (such as certain managerial skills) it is useful to set criteria for adequate performance to act as subgoals to final achievement. There are also obvious relationships with continuous assessment of progress, behavioural objectives, target setting or goals in managerial jobs.

Extrinsic knowledge of results

This is provided artificially, for example, by comment from the manager, trainer or fellow trainees, or by information derived from a simulator such as a monitoring screen in simulated pilot training.

Intrinsic knowledge of results

This relates to the monitoring and guidance the learner is able to gain from cues within the job itself. Unless learners can internalise knowledge of results, ie convert it from extrinsic to intrinsic, and know themselves whether they are performing well or badly, the effects may not last after removal of the extrinsic provision and may not transfer to the working situation. Success depends upon drawing attention to the intrinsic cues so that the trainee recognises them. For example, a learner driver may initially look at the speedometer to decide when to change gear but, with trainer help and experience, will learn to know instantly from the feel and sound of the engine.

A good tutor or a manager well trained in coaching skills will help to convert extrinsic knowledge of results to intrinsic by the manner in which feedback is given to her subordinate.

Frank sent for his subordinate, Jim, and told him that the job he had completed was unsatisfactory and that he must do better with the current one or he would have to go. Jane, however, opened a discussion with Peter, her assistant, by asking him how he thought his latest job had turned out. Together they identified and agreed the criteria for success, how far they had been met, and what Peter should have been watching and monitoring during the course of the job. This enabled Peter to estimate the quality of his work through Jane's eyes, and when doing a similar job on future occasions he could monitor for himself how well it was going and decide what corrective action he should be taking. Poor Jim might well have been so anxious to improve that he made an even worse job of his tasks, and in some organisations his continued poor performance could result in dismissal.

In Peter's case the criteria could be related to predetermined goals, and obviously the more explicit the objectives and related feedback, the better the subordinate can learn to monitor his own performance.

> Discussion question: Suggest ways in which line managers might give positive feedback to assist their subordinates' learning.

Learning curves

These indicate the rate at which learning takes place, providing knowledge of results to trainer and trainee. Progress is plotted on a graph, with the vertical axis representing a measure of achievement, such as output per hour, and the horizontal axis denoting the time period or number of attempts made (see Figure 4.1).

The curvature can be described by the way the gains vary from trial to trial – in the case of sensorimotor skill the curves are most often of decreasing gains (the change in performance from the current trial to the next is frequently less than the change that took place on the previous trial): this is one reason why the learning of a skill is often discouraging. We may be progressing from 'unconscious incompetence' to 'conscious incompetence'. Young cricketers who are trying to improve their batting technique may have this problem. Coaches find that trying to correct errors may initially cause the player to be out more often! Sometimes it is practicable for trainees to plot their own learning curves, and seeing their own progress can act as a motivator.

Fleishman and Hempel (1955) have suggested that as the attainment of skill level in a task increases, the importance of certain ability dimensions can vary. For instance, having gained more competence in the task, the learner's further progress may be affected by his or her reaction time and rate of movement, while other abilities, such as spatial relations, may have a decreasing influence on performance improvement. The learning curve may therefore not be measuring the acquisition of one skill but of different skills, which are called in to use as the learning progresses. This may be one cause of a plateau of learning.

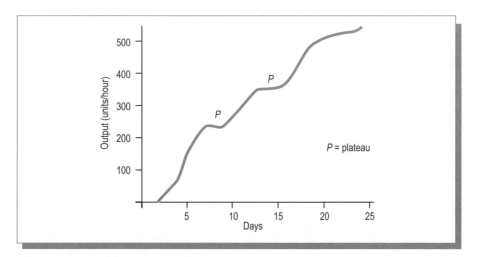

Figure 4.1 *A learning curve*

Plateaux of learning

These are periods of no improvement. They can sometimes be explained by a shift from a lower order of learning to a higher order (eg from letter habit in typing to word habit, ie learning to type familiar words as a single unit rather than concentrating on one letter at a time). A plateau is often followed by a rapid burst of progress. The trainer should attempt to discover the causes of plateaux, particularly those occurring regularly, in order to assist the learners to overcome them. For instance, there may be certain stages when learners become demotivated, indicating an alteration should be made to the programme. They may need to concentrate more on one aspect – perhaps, in the example above, in learning to type particular combinations of letters where errors are most frequently made or, as Fleishman and Hempel (1955) maintain, they may have reached a stage when they are dependent on a different type of ability that has not yet been adequately developed.

> Discussion question: How would you attempt to motivate a colleague who is struggling to make sense of a topic they find difficult (statistics for example)?

Attitude formation and change

Attitudinal aspects of training are extremely important because they predispose learners to action. The relationship between attitudes and action is, however, by no means a simple one. Attitudes are formed through our relationships with other people and are notoriously difficult to change. The concept of cognitive dissonance (Festinger 1957) provides an explanation based on the premise that we normally like our attitudes to be in harmony with each other. Admiring a superior who actively supports an organisational practice of which I strongly disapprove, eg promoting on the basis of length of service rather than merit, I am left in an uncomfortable and dissonant state of internal inconsistency, in that someone whom I admire is supporting something I dislike. The problem can be resolved by modifying my attitude about my superior, or about the organisational practice or by a decision that the practice is not very important anyway. Whatever the outcome, I shall have altered my attitude in some way. If I cannot alter my attitude, the state of cognitive dissonance may be so uncomfortable that I may decide to leave that organisation. In a training situation, cognitive dissonance can occur in role-playing where, while acting to a brief, I may be required to give a convincing argument from a standpoint other than my own (such as that of a subordinate). If this is done in public, I am left with an uncomfortable state of dissonance and may begin to move slightly nearer my subordinate's viewpoint. In other circumstances, however, it may cause me to reject new learning as unimportant, possibly even subconsciously, because it is inconsistent with my other firmly held attitudes. A useful discussion of this phenomenon in relation to management development is given by Mumford (1980).

Group discussion has been found to be one of the effective ways of attempting to modify attitudes. Examples may be found in study groups, and other forms of social skills and leadership training. We will examine this in more detail in Chapter 11.

Another method of attitude change is by providing new information. For instance, people's attitudes towards certain medicinal drugs can change radically when they learn of research that indicates harmful consequences. With smoking, unfortunately, cognitive dissonance might cause the smoker to consider these unimportant (or, 'it won't happen to me!'). This fact is particularly important in training as preparation for organisational change. If little or no information is given on important issues, people may develop attitudes to the change that may harden and be difficult to alter. When a particular attitude has been adopted, the natural tendency is to seek confirmation that reinforces it, unless there is extremely strong evidence to the contrary.

Discussion question: What attitudes do you feel you possess that could inhibit your learning? How might you overcome them?

The age factor

The climate and the approach to teaching in schools are usually different from that in commercial organisations, and school leavers can experience considerable difficulty in adjusting to a different kind of learning situation. Trainers must take this into account when designing programmes if young people's natural enthusiasm is to be channelled in the right direction. Young learners usually react favourably to intergroup competition and appreciate variety in their programmes. They often prefer to keep within their original training groups, membership of which gives them confidence. Leaving school and looking for work is a big and worrying step for many young people and self-destructive behaviour, such as overconfidence or shyness, often results from a feeling of insecurity. This can be hard for a trainer to remember when faced with an aggressive young person determined to cause trouble, but it frequently happens. A patient and supportive trainer can do a great deal to help; this is particularly true with those taking part in temporary work experience, who may be discouraged if they see little hope of obtaining a permanent job. A perceived and desired outcome is an essential motivator, and it is important that learners are consulted about their programmes and are thus participating in training that is seen by them as interesting and relevant.

Research on the effect of ageing on learning shows the interplay of a number of factors, and happily that the effect is by no means totally adverse. Gradually, as we become older, the reproduction of new cells to replace those that die slows down and those which continue to reproduce start yielding a higher proportion of unhealthy offspring. The result is that speed of performance can decline. For example, as they grow older the majority of people will perform less well on a timed test. Welford (1962) found that the process of ageing impairs the central decision processes. This affects the time taken to reorganise information, monitor movements and deal with a number of matters at one time. We looked in Chapter 3 at the effect of memory on learning. Short-term memory deteriorates with age, resulting in time increase and errors in complex cognitive tasks. On tasks involving number matrices, Welford's older subjects were unable to cope with a large amount of information arranged according to different criteria. This involved not only short-term memory but the reorganisation of behaviour to shift from one aspect of the task to another. This appears to emphasise the potential value to the older worker of certain types of modern computer software such as spreadsheets. Certain tests, such as those of vocabulary and comprehension, demonstrated an improvement with age, but reasoning and numerical sections of intelligence tests showed a decline for older people and therefore, although they were able to score as well as (or possibly even better than) in their youth, the marks were obtained in different ways. Of course, the rapid pace of change and growth of technology in recent times has had a radical impact on lifestyles and consequent learning experiences, so that if something like Welford's research were conducted today, different tests might be needed. Many older people nowadays are much more confident about beginning new activities than their parents were.

It is generally agreed that a number of factors are likely to affect achievement in later years and that age is by no means the sole determinant. The first of these is the original level of intelligence. Vernon (1960) gives evidence that the rate of decline is slowest among those whose original score was high. There is therefore an accentuation of individual differences.

The second factor is stimulation. A number of studies suggest a slow decline among those who make the greatest use of their intellectual ability and a more rapid decline in intelligence among those who do not. 'Use it or lose it' in other words. There is also evidence that stimulation can increase mental ability and may have physical consequences for the brain. Evidence from animal studies shows that the weight of cerebral cortex is affected by stimulation from the environment (Bromley 1990). Evidence was found by Vogt (1951) of slower deterioration in brain cells of those whose level of intellectual activity had been high. A third factor is education and training. Welford (1962) suggests that the manipulative, occupational, mental and social skills acquired through experience help to offset a decline in abilities as a result of the ageing process. Other important factors are state of health and motivation. One also may speculate that factors such as improved nutrition, coupled with more aspirant attitudes, have made the 'baby boomers' born soon after the Second World War less inclined to accept artificial age restrictions.

For information on designing training programmes for older people, see Plett and Lester (1991).

Our knowledge of the ageing process is imperfect, but there are a number of important implications for the trainer. Demographic trends indicate the availability of fewer young people in the workforce and an increasing dependence upon the services of older people. There may have been a time when people of 50 and over were deemed to be unsuitable for job change and retraining but organisations of the future are unlikely to be able to take this view. In fact one supermarket has opened a store staffed entirely by people over 50, as there is evidence that employees in their late 40s and early 50s tend to stay with an organisation much longer than those in their early 20s, that they have lower absenteeism and accident rates, often have greater spirit and reliability, and may already possess useful skills (Worsley 1996). Fear of difficulties in training should not therefore be used as a barrier or discriminatory factor in recruiting more mature workers. The government is (2004) putting together a package of legislation to make discrimination on the grounds of age illegal in the same way as disability, sex and race discrimination. It would be nice to regard this as driven by ethics – that older workers should not be deprived of the chance to contribute to society – but it is also likely that economic factors have been the motivator, as increasing life expectancy means people are living on pensions for much longer and thus costing the economy more.

> Discussion question: What is your opinion of the above discussion? Do you agree that ability to learn changes with age and if so, how?

If people are at their most receptive to learning in youth, and in later years draw upon their attainments, it is essential that the young are given every opportunity to learn. If those with lower cognitive ability are likely to show greater deterioration than those with above-average potential, it is extremely important that a broadly based training is given to young people so that through vertical transfer (see below) they may find it easier to learn a variety of skills when they are older. These arguments also provide a strong case for national traineeships and supply a justification for the prevention, although at a high cost in financial terms, of a young unemployed workforce.

Learning transfer

Having learned to drive a particular model of car, we expect to be able to drive different models. Although some of the controls may be different – usually reverse gear in many cars – we can adjust ourselves to them without having to repeat the entire learning process. This is because of positive learning transfer, which is said to occur when learning that has already taken place on one task assists later learning on another. Positive transfer can be either vertical or lateral. We shall discuss each type in turn.

Vertical transfer occurs when one subject area acts as a basis for another. For example, a basic knowledge of mathematics can transfer vertically to make it easier to learn statistics. The justification for starting many training schemes with a basic foundation course before allowing the learner to move on to specific modules is that, as well as providing an overview, the content will transfer vertically in a number of different ways. This is also the rationale of providing a broader general education in schools. In a rapidly changing environment, pupils can make better use of vertical transfer to assist in the acquisition of a wider range of knowledge and skills later in life.

Lateral transfer occurs when the same type of stimulus requires the same response. Training simulators are devices for teaching a skill that will transfer, usually laterally, to the real task. For example, a trainee pilot can practise in a 'safe' situation provided by a computer-controlled flight simulator that imitates the effect of using different controls. Care is required, however, in the provision of simulators, because the extent of transfer obtained by their use is complex (see Annett 1974).

On- and off-the-job learning/training

At one time there was a tendency to regard learning and training off-the-job more highly than that which took place on-the-job, or 'sitting with Nellie' as it was sometimes called. This was because 'Nellie' was often paid mainly for doing her own job, not for training others, and the trainee was left to watch and pick up the skills as best he or she could. In addition, Nellie might have had little or no training in the skills of tuition. Gradually, however, attention has been paid to the training of trainers and instructors and to the coaching skills of managers. On-the-job training has the advantage that the question of learning transfer to the actual job and the working environment does not arise, and, if properly planned and carried out by well-trained people in a safe environment, it can be very effective for some jobs. The emphasis on experiential learning, based on the work of Kolb and Honey and Mumford (see pages 56–8) is enabling managers to 'learn how to learn' from their experience at work, and it is also seen that there can be much advantage in arranging special assignments at work as an integral part of individual management development. The concept of 'cascading' has devolved more responsibility to managers for training their subordinates and given some impetus to coaching on-the-job. We will look at this in more detail in Chapter 11 when we discuss management and leadership development. Learning organisations and continuous development necessitate the integration of learning with work and, although not precluding opportunities for learning off-the-job, place a high premium on self-development by learning from working experience. This capability is increasingly important as the pace of change accelerates. The organisation itself is a powerful learning environment, and although there are many extremely valuable forms of off-the-job training, the advantage of the learning opportunities on-the-job cannot be underestimated. Very often the ideal is a combination of both.

Discussion question: What would you recommend to a trainer to assist transfer of learning from a formal off-the-job training event to a work situation?

Off-the-job training relies upon lateral transfer to the working situation. It can have many obvious advantages, including the provision of conditions conducive to learning away from the noisy rush of the workplace, properly trained instructors, planned training methods, a carefully prepared programme at a pace governed by the trainees' needs, the creation of safe and inexpensive situations in which to try out and practise newly acquired skills and techniques, use of a greater variety of training techniques (eg discovery learning, case studies, films, closed circuit television, simulators and interactive computer programs) and the opportunity to emphasise all four stages of the Kolb learning cycle, particularly observation and conceptualisation.

On the negative side, learning undertaken in a specialised environment may hinder the learner's ability to cope with the actual situation. For example, case studies are useful in the consideration of a variety of possible courses of action, and of principles and concepts, but they can be criticised on the grounds that in the 'real' world we frequently have to decide on one best course of action and undertake personal responsibility for the results. Of course, in the real world, unlike training course exercises, we can ask for help for colleagues. What is learned during a leisurely contemplation of alternatives may not transfer to a stress situation. If the on-the-job climate is not supportive of what has been learned in the training situation, it is unlikely to be transferred.

Although it is generally agreed that off-the-job training can often be helpful, it is necessary to introduce factors from the 'real' world (eg workplace jargon) and on-the-job experience when it becomes appropriate. There has been a progressive increase in the number of 'organisational placement periods' as an essential part of educational courses, and a significant increase in the on-the-job element of teacher training. The NVQ requirement that training shall be carried out and tested to workplace standards emphasises the importance of obtaining learning transfer.

Negative transfer

Sometimes, however, old learning or past experience can hinder performance on a new task, that is when the same stimulus requires a different response. For instance, having learned to drive on one side of the road can make it difficult to drive on the other side when touring abroad. The EU opening up more trade between the UK and mainland Europe has meant more lorry drivers coming over from France, and frequent accidents around Dover or Portsmouth. Literature suggests that although negative transfer can interfere, it quickly gives way to positive transfer and may actually result in more flexible performance in the long term (see Duncan and Kelly 1983).

In matters relating to safety, as in our driving example above, or where dangerous or expensive material may be involved, it is necessary to overcome negative effects immediately. Duncan and Kelly (1983) indicate that the more similar the responses required in the two tasks, the greater is the likelihood of negative transfer: it increases with response similarity until the point is reached where the required responses are identical and transfer becomes positive. There is no guaranteed method of overcoming the problem; one precaution is to check the learner's previous experience of similar tasks and carefully point out the differences and possible consequences of negative transfer. It is worth noting that it is most likely to occur when the learner's attention is distracted by, for example, situational factors or new elements of the task, such as approaching a roundabout when driving abroad, as in the example above.

Factors that assist transfer

Transfer of knowledge and skills to new situations is essential for continuing development and the attainment of flexibility. It is a complex area and there is no one set of infallible rules but the following points may be helpful:

Understanding of general principles: Transfer occurs through the understanding of general principles and concepts rather than by concentration on one narrow application. It can be facilitated by discovery learning. It is necessary both to understand the general principle and to be able to apply it under different conditions. For example, knowledge of employment law is less likely to transfer to the working situation if the learner has had no practice in applying it to the actual procedures in an organisation. Examples of training methods that might assist this process are discovery learning, case studies and histories, structured exercises, assignments and projects. Group discussions and any means of associating and integrating new learning with existing knowledge help too. You might also like to consider the relationship of learning transfer with the reflection and conceptualisation stages of the Kolb learning cycle described above.

Overlearning: (ie practising beyond the level of minimum competence) In situations where confusion could be caused by the acquisition of several similar skills, minimum negative transfer will occur if the learner obtains a really good grasp of the first step before proceeding to the others. Systematic rehearsal and mental practice assist in the maintenance of skills already acquired.

Association factors: The transfer of learning will be assisted if the trainee can associate and integrate new learning with other learning that has already taken place. Any structured exercises that help to achieve this aim are very useful.

Discussion question: Do universities and colleges adequately consider how academic learning can be transferred to the organisations where students work or will work in future? If not, how would you improve things?

THE ORGANISATION AS A LEARNING ENVIRONMENT

If we accept the link between experience and learning in Bass and Vaughan's (1966) definition of learning (quoted on page 49) and consider Nord's (1969) application of Skinnerian theory of reinforcement to organisations, we find a number of important implications for the HRD manager.

A continuous learning process

The first implication is that the HRD manager is really intervening in a continuous learning process, and therefore requires diagnostic and analytical skills of a far higher order than is commonly realised. People learn by example and reinforcement, and the influence of a superior upon his or her subordinate is very powerful. It is particularly strong when the superior holds the key to what may be termed the rewards and punishments of the organisation. Consequently successful training requires active management support – ideally it should start at the top and filter down through the organisation, each superior being involved in the training of her subordinate. McGregor (1960) maintains that:

> every encounter between a superior and subordinate involves learning of some kind for the subordinate (and should for the superior too). The attitudes, habits and expectations of the subordinate will be reinforced or modified to some degree as a result of every encounter with the boss ... Day by day experience is so much more powerful that it tends to overshadow what the individual may learn in other settings.

In other words, there's no point in introducing teambuilding and development in an organisation that rewards individual effort and discourages a team culture.

Range of learning/training interventions

The term 'training intervention' embraces much more than the provision of courses and off-the-job training: it includes any activity initiated by an HRD specialist, owner/line manager, or the learner. Such activities range widely and include: short periods of work in different organisations, jobs or roles; problem-solving discussion groups; projects; action learning sets; giving advice; feedback on performance; coaching; and mentoring. Measures to remove barriers to learning constitute important interventions and can include attempts to overcome attitudinal and cultural constraints, as well as practical assistance such as the granting of day release to attend classes or the provision of open learning facilities. A highly skilled HRD manager can act as facilitator and consultant, helping the whole organisation to learn more effectively.

> Discussion question: List the barriers to learning you have discovered on an individual and organisational basis. Which can you do something about? Will the same barriers affect a new entrant to your organisation? What can be done about these?

Influence of organisational culture

Off-the-job learning/training requires reinforcement at the workplace: the attitude of the superior and the culture of the organisation are both powerful influences in determining whether learning is likely to be transferred to the working situation. For instance, as we suggested earlier, it is difficult for a manager to put into practice what has just been learned about the adoption of a participative and democratic style if the organisational structure and atmosphere is autocratic.

Everyone in the organisation, not least management, already has, and is constantly formulating, attitudes towards learning. Views do not have to be expressed, and often remain hidden within assumptions that are themselves accepted uncritically by those whose own views are unclear or equivocal. These attitudes and assumptions are perhaps the most important factor within the working environment. Many observers have suggested that cultural variations explain the differences in organisations' ability to innovate; others have criticised the existence in UK organisations of 'anti-development' assumptions, which threaten developmental forms of organisation through discrediting new ideas before they have a chance to take hold. Dore and Sako (1989) wrote:

If we were to single out just one salient point ... the one for a British audience would probably be this: by such criteria as training expenditure and man-hours in off-the-job training, Japanese firms would come rather badly out of any international comparison. Where they do seem to be distinctive is in the way they motivate ... to learn in order to gain in competence.

In other words, Japanese attitudes naturally promote workplace learning, whereas British attitudes often block it. All the political parties and social partners involved with the German economy give frequent vocal support to Germany's 'dual' training system, which combines on-the-job training and vocational education, and French society appears strongly committed to its educational framework, currently fairly centralised and strongly focused on vocational or academic education. In contrast, UK attitudes still seem much less certain about the value of spending time and money on planned training once full-time education has ended.

One person who spent a considerable portion of her working life in the now-defunct Industrial Training Research Unit (ITRU) at Cambridge presented her 'collective' views on how to remove or diminish the blockages and stimulate learning activity at work. Downs (1995) sets out four basic 'beliefs about learning' and follows them up with 10 'principles of learning'; her interest throughout is cultural – that is, she is more interested in what the workplace might offer to help learning than in how an individual learner should set about the learning process. However, her conclusions are essentially related to the way people think and are not geared to specific procedures.

Downs' four 'beliefs about learning' maintain that:

- Learning at work is largely a social activity. In other words, the competitive bases of full-time education (eg tests, grades, pressures to succeed) should give way to collaborative learning activity. Comparisons between adults' achievements tend to prevent development.
- Everyone has a role to play in helping people to learn. Checking people have understood is as important as instructing; giving feedback and encouragement are as important as answering questions. Keeping knowledge to oneself is at best unproductive, at worst, sabotage.
- Everyone has something to contribute and something to gain when learning. It is an error to assume that others have no previous experience or relevant knowledge. Interactive learning processes are more effective than passive ones.
- Colleagues, trainers, parents and teachers sometimes unwittingly prevent people from learning. Making instructions or lectures difficult, laughing at others' mistakes, viewing questions as disruptions – these and many other responses kill learner motivation.

(Downs' 10 Principles of Learning (see page 85) are each linked to long lists of 'pitfalls' and 'remedies'.)

If we accept that these beliefs are not unconsciously promoted by the majority of employees, and are not likely to be presented strongly by an organisation's top management, it follows that one of the HRD manager's key operational aims should be to find ways of developing and maintaining them. This, as we suggested, moves the skills set of the job to a much higher strategic level (and arguably makes it much more fulfilling for the job-holder).

Unexpected repercussions

The fourth implication is that training may be compared with a game of skittles where aiming at one target may have repercussions in a variety of other areas. The 'skittle effect' suggests that it may be impossible to train one group of people effectively without changing the behaviour of another group. Apparent inefficiencies on the part of one section of employees may in reality be caused by poorly maintained equipment or defective materials, indicating training needs for a totally different section of the workforce. Training of one group of people can sometimes act as a catalyst in triggering change in other parts of the organisation, and may have unexpected consequences: in one instance, a complete redefinition and reappraisal of the organisational structure resulted from an in-house training course for managers.

Attitudes influence political decisions

Positive management attitudes are particularly important in influencing political decisions about training. The advantages of planned learning/training have to be 'sold' and clearly demonstrated. The ability to do this is the first requirement of a HRD manager; it may be no easy task, and there is no one recipe for success. Deciding where in the organisation to start can be a critical decision and, although straightforward discussion and debate might be the obvious first route, and a convincing and detailed demonstration of the cost benefits might be all-important, ultimately minds are likely to be swayed by successful results. This means that decisions on where and how to train must at least be influenced by estimates of likely success and of attitudinal outcomes. The logical starting place is at the top, so that learning can 'cascade' down the organisation; during courses for supervisors a common cry is, 'It's our managers you ought to have here.' Notwithstanding its obvious advantages, depending upon the attitude of management, such a simple recommendation might not always be practicable or culturally profitable. In such a case, it might be more worthwhile to start where success in demonstrating financial return appears the most likely, or where an acute organisational problem might be solved, with the aim of creating a more favourable climate.

Necessity for commitment

McGregor (1960) suggests that:

> knowledge cannot be pumped into human beings the way grease is forced into a machine. The individual may learn; he is not taught. Programmes do not produce managers; we cannot produce managers as we do products – we can only grow them.

We will look at growing managers in more detail in Chapter 11.

Skill and knowledge are required in the design of learning/training programmes to meet specific needs, but the most difficult task is often that of gaining enthusiasm and whole-hearted co-operation, because people will normally learn only if they want to do so. It is all too easy to pay lip service to learning and training. We could extend McGregor's horticultural analogy a little further and suggest that a gardener will succeed in cultivating a delicate plant if he or she starts by allowing it to grow in appropriate conditions and encourages and feeds it to help it bloom. We must never lose sight of the fact that commitment comes from involvement, and if we involve people we must attempt to use their suggestions, even if they do not necessarily accord with neat and tidy models of systematic learning. It is necessary for an HRD manager to be fully conversant with planned methods but the skill of adapting them to specific situations is paramount. 'Learning outcomes' are all well and good, and useful in measuring success but we shouldn't ignore learning 'serendipity'.

Discussion question: How do you feel about training courses going 'off the point'? Have you attended a training event or lecture where you learned something different from your expectations? Was this experience positive or not?

THE ORGANISATION CAN LEARN AND LEARN TO LEARN

The final implication is that, while the organisation is a learning environment for the people within it, they, collectively, constitute an entity that itself can learn, and learn to learn, the collective experience of the whole being greater than that of any of its members. To consider one of the ways in which this learning takes place we turn back to cybernetic and information theories in Chapter 3 and the example of the thermostat. If this model were applied to an organisation and its controls, such as performance indicators and budgets, it would ensure that any deviation from operating norms was discovered and adjusted. Many organisations have become good at devising and monitoring controls that do this effectively. However, this is a description of a system to maintain the status quo, and is described by Argyris (1977) as single-loop learning. Figure 4.2 illustrates this three-stage process.

Double-loop learning involves questioning the relevance of the specified operating norms. In the case of the thermostat, these questions might refer to whether the temperature at which it was set was the most efficient and economical for the purpose, or even whether the thermostat was placed in the right location to be typical of the environment. See Figure 4.3.

In other words, single-loop learning occurs when addressing the surface symptoms of a problem and double-loop learning occurs when we ask why the problem arose. It is much more difficult to introduce double-loop learning into organisations and only a very small proportion of them have managed to achieve it. People's behaviour tends to be determined primarily by previous events and experience, and there are many barriers, such as inertia, bureaucracy, defensive routines (some of which are described by Argyris as 'the organisational games that inhibit learning'), the inability to see beyond the status quo and/or vested interest in maintaining it. Argyris later cites the US space shuttle *Challenger* disaster of January 1986 as an example, where serious problems with the O-ring seals were buried by the desire to conform with plans and launch on time. In some types of organisation, controls

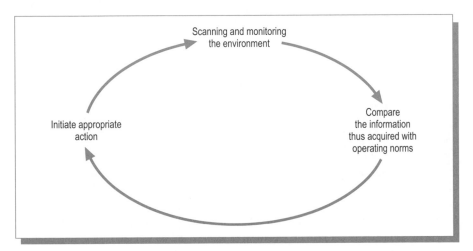

Figure 4.2 *Single-loop learning*

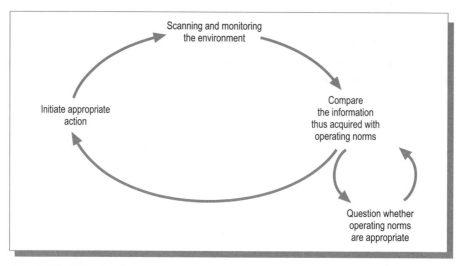

Figure 4.3 *Double-loop learning*

and procedures can be sources of managerial power and there may be strong resistance to anyone who questions them or suggests changes. It may take a serious disaster such as the one above, a 'revolution' from within (new management) or without (political interference or takeover) to trigger an effective 'rethink'. In the oil industry, the *Piper Alpha* disaster triggered a completely new approach to safety training after the Cullen Report (1990).

> We have, however, seen double-loop learning come about in a small owner-managed company that had been run the same way for years. The staff all knew their jobs and there did not appear to be any learning needs. The owner-manager attended an external training programme and, beginning to see the potential of his company in a different light, he started to question the operating norms. The staff had to acquire new skills, began to query their own procedures, and a new organisation structure emerged. Learning needs thus became apparent at the second level and the whole operation changed from a relatively static to a dynamic process. It was the beginning of a learning culture, and the company started to learn to learn.

In this chapter we have given a few ideas about how HRD practitioners might take concepts like learning organisation and start to apply them. You should be able to draw upon the concepts, ideas and examples, to apply them to the design of situation-specific training/learning programmes and opportunities and to be able to relate them to the concept of the 'Learning Organisation'. Below we give Downs' (1995) '10 Principles of Learning'. You might want to consider them and, for each one, list any organisational or training features that might constitute barriers to learning, and any features that would be helpful and promote learning. You may use your own organisation or one with which you are familiar as a reference point.

01 Learners need to know where they are going and have a sense of progress towards their objectives.

02 The learning environment has to be one of trust, respect, openness and acceptance of differences.

03 Being aware of and owning the responsibility for learning lies with the learner. Others can only give information and support, and provide feedback.

04 Learners need to participate actively in the learning process.

05 Learning should be related to and use the learner's experience and knowledge.

06 Learning is not only a basic capability but also a group of skills that can be developed/learned.

07 Facts, concepts and skills are learned in different ways.

08 Getting ideas wrong can be a valuable aid to developing understanding.

09 For learning to be processed and assimilated, time must be allowed for reflection.

10 Effective learning depends on realistic, objective and constructive feedback.

(Reproduced with kind permission from Sylvia Downs, *Learning at Work*, Kogan Page, London, 1995.)

In this chapter we have described the ways in which organisations can become learning environments. We have concentrated on organisations as employers; can you think of other organisations with which you are familiar that could also develop environments to encourage learning? Schools and colleges of course are learning providers, but does this automatically mean that they have 'learned to learn'? What might inhibit them in this process?

The Operational Arena: From Organisational Policies to Analysis and Meeting of Learning Needs

Part 2 of the book is about the policies, strategies and procedures needed to underpin effective HRD in organisations. We examine the ways in which organisations might position the HRD function so that it both helps to determine business policy and ensure that policy is reflected in the organisation's HRD plan. We describe the ways in which HRD practitioners may usefully investigate learning needs at individual and organisational levels, recognising that it can sometimes be necessary to adapt and amend complex procedures in the interest of holding senior management's attention. We look at the range of strategies available to fulfil learning needs, and how to plan effective HRD interventions. Finally, we examine an issue that is sometimes unjustly neglected by HRD practitioners. Evaluation of HRD interventions is not, as we show, just a simple case of return on investment, but can be a fascinating process of investigating cause and effect, which, if done properly, can add significant weight to the HRD specialist's role in their organisation.

Chapter 5 examines the relationship between **the organisation's vision and aims, and its strategy for learning**. We give some advice on developing HRD policies to put the organisation's future aims for learning as far as possible on the management agenda.

Chapter 6 examines the options available to organisations to **position the HRD function**, recognising that for smaller employers this can be a case of making the most of scarce resources rather than staffing large strategic departments.

Chapter 7 looks at **strategies available** for examining **organisation-wide HRD needs**. We give some advice about suitable procedures for conducting reviews, while recognising that resource needs may sometimes require more streamlined approaches in today's turbulent environments.

Chapter 8 examines **learning and training needs for individual employees**. We examine suitable analytical tools and suggest ways in which line managers can assist their staff to establish their own needs and seek ways of meeting them.

Chapter 9 looks not only at the development of **techniques and methods** available to the practitioner to meet learning and training needs, but also raises the question of how to **evaluate their effectiveness**. Often HRD practitioners are unenthusiastic about researching the impact of their work, but we aim to show that effective evaluation can be both stimulating to carry out and useful in raising the profile of the HRD function.

By the end of Part 2, you should have a complete picture of the operational context of HRD, and be able to explain its role in supporting organisational business strategy and policy.

Corporate Matters: Mission, Strategy, Policy and Resources to Align Learning with the Organisation's Business Plan

CHAPTER 5

In Chapter 5, we will consider:

- **The development of organisational vision, its translation into strategy and how its scope may influence HRD policy and strategy;**

- **The need to align effectively the organisation's HRD strategy with its business strategy and plans;**

- **How policies on HRD may give rise to corporate plans that themselves require budgets: the content of an HRD plan and the typical resources that can help to implement it;**

- **Learning costs, and the kinds of decisions that may have to be made in allocating the HRD budget, including cost/benefit analysis and the requirement to be creative in resourcing HRD initiatives.**

FORMAL APPROACHES TO STRATEGY DEVELOPMENT

During the late twentieth and early twenty-first century, many larger UK organisations have adopted a more formal approach to their forward planning, and written documents have increasingly appeared describing aims, objectives, targets and strategic operational priorities. Within or alongside such documents, complementary HRD goals, strategies and plans have been formalised.

The trend reflects the growing awareness that change is a normal part of working life, and that setting strategic objectives is preferable to reacting to environmental challenges. The introduction of dedicated HRD strategies may also reflect the increasing spread of Investors in People, the award of which requires written statements of the organisation's goals and targets, together with the organisation's 'training and development needs', specifying actions taken to meet them. This assumes that learning activity should serve operational ends, and that planned HRD should stem from defined corporate aims. In this chapter, we will expand on this concept to consider the relationship between an organisation's philosophy and policies and its (written or unwritten) HRD policy. We will look at business strategy development, and the trend for it to include human resource goals. We will then look at the concept of a corporate HRD plan that is regularly renewed and influences key management priorities, as well as any dedicated HRD function responsible for defining detailed needs and activities.

As we discuss policy development and its uses, you might like to think of organisations you know, and try to gauge what their approach might be. Do they have a vision statement or a policy? If so, how formal is it? Not all organisations have written statements, of course. The examples we give in this chapter are from large organisations or those that have achieved IiP standard. Should all organisations have formal statements? Many smaller organisations might argue that their lack of written statements about business or learning strategy does not mean that these concepts are ignored in a more informal way. If an organisation does not possess such written documents, should the HRD specialist formulate them for his or her own unit? By the end of this chapter you should be in a position to debate these ideas and suggest some possible answers.

ORGANISATION VISION AND AIMS

If you want to achieve anything you must have a vision of where you are going. It is easy to think of sports people who have trained with the utmost dedication because they have had their eyes firmly fixed on 'going for gold'. Sports psychologists sometimes suggest that it is helpful to visualise exactly how you will feel when you reach the finish line or throw the javelin out of the circle! The same principle of knowing where you are going applies to organisations, and the standard set by IiP is a very sensible one. Organisations should:

> develop and communicate to all employees a vision of where the organisation is going and the contribution employees will make to its success, involving employee representatives as appropriate.

The vision statement describes what the top executives think the organisation can achieve and how they would like to see it develop. It is a step in ensuring that everyone is working towards the same ends. Top management's decisions are likely to be more effective if those concerned can understand how they fit into the total picture. To be effective the vision statement is usually ambitious, providing a stimulus to innovation and entrepreneurship, and may be encapsulated in a short challenging sentence. Here are some examples:

> To become the world's leading music company (EMI 1998)

> To lead in the development of new methods of teaching, learning and research (University Library)

> I have a dream ... (Martin Luther King's famous speech, which was a real vision of hope for the future)

Such a statement is really an expressed wish. It expresses, all things considered, where it is that the organisation (or nation in King's vision) wants to be in the future when everything has been achieved. It is insufficient to be used on its own for planning, and many organisations produce a mission statement elaborating what this means in more detail. If the vision is the destination, the mission statement is the vehicle. It represents more about what the organisation currently represents, and what it is trying to achieve to reach its vision. 'We will re-energise tired and stressed people by providing a relaxing stay in a peaceful location with healthy food and exercise' is an example from the Chartered Institute of Marketing's advice on developing a 'mission or vision' statement – note that the terms are interchangeable (www.cim.com). An example of a mission statement will be found in the extract from the CIPD Code of Professional Conduct & Disciplinary Procedures (available from the CIPD website). Some organisations produce a statement of their overall aim. For example:

To contribute to high levels of employment and growth, and to individuals leading rewarding working lives, by helping people without a job to find work and employers to fill their vacancies.
Employment Service (1997–1998)

Not all organisations use these terms in precisely the same way. For instance, some do not produce a mission statement, and some combine it with their vision statement, or a statement of values. There is a tendency for the terms vision and mission to be used interchangeably. The important thing is that they should define the way ahead in a form that employees and all stakeholders, such as shareholders, customers and suppliers, can understand. It is also important to remember that organisation visions and values may extend much wider than the 'bottom line'. Some corporate aims may have a bearing on all other aims, including the 'bottom line'. For example, 'to become the lead employer within the (specific) industry', or to 'pioneer research into new resource applications and bring into existence new product concepts' will condition all emerging plans and budgets. Some organisations have created 'charters', which present future goals and marketing aims in priority order. Theoretically this leaves managers no choice but to use limited resources in this direction. However, a mission can be easy to follow when operations are going smoothly but might have to be suspended if a short-term crisis erupts. Unfortunately training activities have suffered badly in organisations that have declared a commitment to HRD but have suddenly hit financial problems. Some of us have worked in organisations that have declared 'learning and development is not a bolt-on issue', only to 'unbolt' the HRD budget when times are hard.

> Discussion question: Consider the vision or mission statement of an organisation with which you are familiar. Is it meaningful? How might you improve its relevance?

CORPORATE STRATEGY

Many organisational writers have described forms of corporate strategy. Both diagnostic and prescriptive models have been developed to suggest how an organisation might assess its present reality, how it might plan its future, how it might relate to its environment, how it might adapt to change, how it might maintain 'healthy' employee relations policies and procedures or how it might succeed financially, and how it might translate its findings into operational plans. None of the proposed models are 'right' but will be conditioned by the operational situation as interpreted by the organisation's key opinion-former(s).

Morgan (1997) suggests the following as areas for diagnosis:

- the environment (stable or turbulent, simple or complex)
- current strategy (proactive or defensive, undefined or clear)
- technology (rigid or flexible, established or developing)
- culture (closed or open, conservative or innovative)
- structure (bureaucratic or organic, condensed or dispersed)
- management (authoritarian or democratic, prescriptive or consulting).

The alternatives are not mutually exclusive but are better seen as standpoints from which to consider the organisation. The list could be extended to include other areas such as the historical dimension, while operational results also give indicators of success.

It is not too ambitious to claim that any change stemming from the strategic review will justify a more detailed review of employee learning in that area. The greater the change, the more necessary will be a specific learning strategy. In Chapter 7 we will examine in more detail the central task of identifying HRD needs, which ultimately govern learning and development activities. We should distinguish between corporate strategy, which deals outside and beyond the HRD function, and defines the organisation's main goals, and the operational HRD strategy, which determines learning and development activities.

HRD strategies and systems

As any planned change in a corporate strategy may impact on learning, anyone accountable for HRD (the HRD practitioner if the organisation employs a dedicated one) must think through the impact on operational work systems, whether employee-led or relying on condition learning activities. Some work systems serve a clear HR purpose, such as appraisal; others might serve a variety of ends, for example financial conventions or implicit changes to human behaviour. So, many systems can be seen as supporting organisational learning, and system development arising from corporate strategy is likely to affect its HRD version. The following are probably the most relevant to the task of developing HRD strategy:

- Appraisal
- Benchmarking
- Career development
- Communications
- Formal assessment
- IT systems
- Meetings
- Mentoring
- Networking
- Performance-related pay
- Project management
- Promotion
- Quality control
- Questionnaires
- Target setting
- Work scheduling.

Any of these systems could be relevant to, and feature in, the organisation's HRD policy statement. Corporate strategy can be seen to adjust corporate policy implicitly, and so any systems changes should be the subject of management briefing.

An organisation's corporate HRD strategy may or may not move into specific learning events. But it should describe the factors that arise from the environment and goals of the organisation that will affect learning and development activities. Figure 5.1 indicates the more significant ones.

You will see that the organisation's HRD strategy will move some steps beyond its corporate operational objectives, and so could justify a document in its own right.

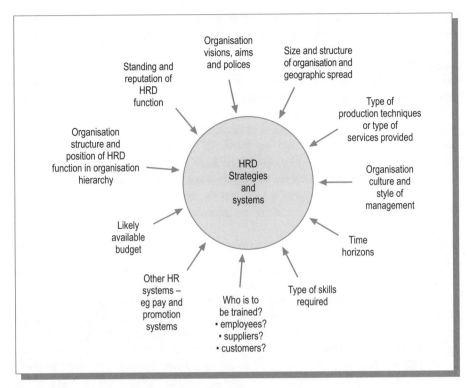

Figure 5.1 *Factors influencing HRD strategies and systems*

We have suggested so far that the process of developing a corporate HRD plan ideally requires:

- An environmental review
- The creation of a corporate mission statement
- The creation or updating of a corporate strategy document
- Appreciation, after management discussion, of the factors in that document that impact on learning systems and strategies.

This is a major task, and it is understandable that many smaller organisations do not complete it. Most small organisations do not prepare formal documents to cover these things, although IiP gives a helpful shorthand approach that has been streamlined with these smaller organisations in mind. In reality, HRD strategy usually follows corporate strategy, the requirements of which it is produced to satisfy.

We would stress that an essential of effective business strategy development is an integrated Human Resource Management strategy, which in turn is aligned with organisation vision and objectives. Imagine an organisation with a vision of leading the world in innovative design, whose product depends essentially upon teamwork. The long-established remuneration system allows for large bonuses awarded in a highly individualistic way, which puts employees in competition with one another. The recruitment policy is to engage personnel at low levels and promote from within. There is, however, no complementary HRD policy to prepare employees to climb the career ladder. When stated in simple terms this case sounds ridiculous, yet in how many organisations do supervisors find themselves promoted to manager overnight without any attention being paid to the competences they require? You may well be aware of an organisation like this – most people have at least one on their CV! As a further example, coaching from a superior is one of the most valuable methods of management development, yet managers are seldom awarded any recognition, let alone tangible reward, for excelling in this. On the contrary, they can actually suffer in consequence either by frequently losing highly promotable subordinates, or in some instances, being replaced by the younger protégé they have coached so well! Our philosophy is that the organisation is a learning environment, and ideally the messages that come across from all aspects of that environment should be consistent and in harmony. Although a careful examination of learning and development needs is an important step in the right direction, complete integration of policies cannot be brought about by HRD specialists alone. Directors and senior executives need to take the lead, and be seen to be doing so. Unfortunately this does not always happen.

HRD POLICY

Which should come first, policy or strategy? We discuss policy second, because in spite of its philosophical standpoint, it tends, in practice, to be influenced by strategic decisions. An organisation's philosophy towards the learning and development of employees is reflected in its policy: this governs the priorities, standards and scope of its HRD activities. All organisations have an HRD policy, which may be explicit or implicit. Some policies are the outcome of a planned human resource management approach; others are reactive responses to requests and problems. Some are written; others are not. Some are regarded as being semi-confidential, others are readily available to all staff. Some, where there is no organisational support for HRD, are by implication negative; some apply only to certain job categories – others concern all employees; some are enforced – others seem to pop up only when they are broken by employees ignorant of their existence.

In addition to the statutory requirement for health and safety training, organisations develop HRD policies for four main reasons:

- to define the relationship between the organisation's objectives and its commitment to the HRD function;
- to provide operational guidelines for management – for example, to state management's responsibilities for planning and implementing learning and development, and, in particular, to ensure that resources are allocated to priority and statutory requirements;
- to provide information for employees, for example, to stress the performance standards expected, to indicate the organisation's commitment to HRD and to inform employees of opportunities for learning and training activities (including willingness to grant time off, and/or payment of fees for external courses);
- to enhance public relations – for example, to help attract high-calibre recruits, to reassure clients and the public about the quality of the products (eg in pharmaceutical and food companies) or services (an airline's safety standards), or to protect an image as a caring and progressive employer by taking part in government-sponsored 'social' training programmes.

These four purposes overlap and are expressed in policy statements, in the organisation's plans for HRD and in the rules and procedures that govern development access and implementation.

A corporate policy statement that aims to influence the outside world tends to be expressed in such broad terms as 'We offer learning and development as part of our equal opportunities programme.' Corporate policy that regulates internal action may be published as a 'free-standing' policy document or included in the organisation's HRD plan. Both typically include general statements of intent to set the corporate frame of reference for HRD activities: 'The Council will provide appropriate development opportunities for all its employees'; and specific statements that define the organisation's current priorities for training: 'All managers and supervisors will attend a seminar on the company's industrial relations procedures.' The policy should also clarify who is responsible, or who shares responsibility for different aspects of the HRD function and decision-making activities, such as assessing needs, allocating resources, determining strategies or providing training.

Discussion question: What are the main problems of translating corporate objectives into HRD objectives and plans? How might they be tackled successfully?

Now think about the situation of the HRD director of an electricity company. During the reorganisation that followed privatisation, the HRD department was designated a profit centre, selling its services and advice to management on request, in competition with external providers. When this change first took place, staff were extremely concerned because they felt that the new system might not allow them to discharge their responsibilities of adequately meeting all learning and development needs. A policy statement was issued, which included a requirement that, in general, the onus for ensuring that employees were given access to sufficient training was upon line management, not the HRD department, but that to ensure uniformity, some areas, such as certain aspects of health and safety and induction training, would remain that department's responsibility.

Without this statement, there would have been confusion about accountability, and the HRD staff would have been in a very difficult position, not knowing where their responsibilities lay.

Corporate policy at departmental level shapes the line manager's action plan by specifying what learning and development will be provided for which staff, when it will take place and who will be responsible for ensuring its implementation. It is at this level that policy can play the important role of helping to ensure equality of opportunity between employees working in different parts of the organisation. For example, published policy such as 'Junior administration staff should be encouraged to attend day-release further education courses', or 'All employees within two years of retirement are entitled to attend pre-retirement courses', will limit the discretion that a manager might otherwise apply unfairly.

POLICY DEVELOPMENT

An organisation's policy for HRD is influenced by a number of variables, such as:

- aims and strategic objectives of the organisation
- size, traditions and prevailing culture
- products and services

- economic and social objectives
- recruitment policy
- the labour market and the alternative means of acquiring skilled and qualified staff
- obligations to provide professional updating (continuing) training, eg for nurses
- top management's views on the value of learning and training
- availability of information about the organisation's learning and training needs
- past and current HRD policies and practices
- learning and experience of its managers
- calibre of its specialist HRD staff
- resources that can be allocated to the function
- expectations of employees and their representatives
- legislation, eg disability issues, health and safety, and government-funded schemes.

HRD policies are consequently unique, varying with the approach and requirement of different organisations. They are more often determined by the prevailing interest than principle, and tend to be impermanent and susceptible to change. This applies whether or not an organisation has adopted a planned approach. If this is the case, top management decide what contribution they want the HRD function to make in the achievement of the organisation's objectives. Their decision provides the framework within which the policy and plans are determined, but effectiveness is likely to be increased if that decision has been reached after consultation at all levels.

In organisations without a planned approach, policy for HRD results from the unsystematic growth of decisions, rules and procedures introduced to deal with particular problems. These decisions are typically made on a piecemeal basis and, with the passage of time, may be accepted as precedents and become 'policy'. Ad hoc policy development of this kind might be sufficient for a time, but it can also give rise to inappropriate emphases and inconsistencies in application in different parts of the same organisation, particularly if changes in demand for skill and professional competences occur over short periods. A regular review of an organisation's HRD policy is essential to assess the relevance of existing priorities, rules and procedures in relation to current objectives. These policies, of course, must be well integrated with all other organisation policies, and the regular review should take this into account. There are other reasons that can prompt an organisation to review its policy regularly, including:

- national developments, eg NVQs
- the availability of new methods of delivering training
- unexpected demand for learning and development caused, for example, by mergers or restructuring to a flatter organisation
- the need for retraining or retrenchment stemming from fluctuations in trading, eg through recession or international developments.

The following is an extract from a company's policy statement:

The directors recognise the important contribution which HRD makes to the company's continuing efficiency and profitability. They further recognise that the prime responsibility for staff learning, training and development rests with management. The Company HRD

Manager is accountable to the Managing Director and is responsible for submitting an annual assessment of organisational training needs, as well as advising and assisting all managers on HRD matters and providing the necessary training services. The annual HRD budget is approved by the Board and managed by the Company HRD Manager.

This company's HRD policy refers to all employees and aims to:

- provide induction training for all new staff and for those transferred to new departments;
- provide day-release facilities at the discretion of the appropriate departmental manager in consultation with the company HRD manager;
- ensure that appropriate learning and development is available to enable individuals to reach and, through updating training, maintain satisfactory performance in their jobs;
- provide the learning and development required by those selected for promotion so that they are appropriately prepared for their new responsibilities;
- provide information, instruction and training to ensure the health and safety of all employees.

There are a number of advantages to be gained from making the HRD policy widely known in the organisation. This approach:

- clarifies the purpose of HRD and communicates top management's intentions;
- defines the organisation's responsibility for the development of the individual employee;
- helps those responsible for implementing training;
- clarifies the role and function of the HRD specialist;
- states in general terms the training opportunities available to employees;
- may indicate priorities.

If the contents are progressive, publication enhances employer–employee relationships, but the success of a HRD policy is likely to be affected negatively if the 'public relations' element is overplayed or if the employees' expectations are not met. Employee resentment and, as a consequence, the possibility of other more difficult problems can result if an organisation fails to honour the development opportunities promised in published policy statements.

> Discussion question: How far is the HRD policy 'visible' in an organisation with which you are familiar? How do you think organisations might effectively communicate their HRD policies to employees?

Writing a HRD policy is a task that requires good writing skill and attention to detail. The starting point is to clarify the reasons for introducing the policy and the objectives that it is designed to achieve. It is important that the staff categories to which the policy will apply are clearly stated. Account should be taken of any contingent precedents that may have been established, either in a formal way or by custom and practice. Discussion with representatives of those who will be affected is an essential part of the process of drafting a policy statement. It is important that the policy is written in an acceptable style, that the statement is positive (avoids using negatives) and that it contains no ambiguities.

CORPORATE HRD PLAN

An organisation's HRD plan should be a detailed and authoritative statement of the learning, development and training that will take place over a given period. The plan results from a reconciliation of priority HRD needs, policy for HRD and available resources, particularly budgets.

A range of requirements for learning and development is identified prior to the preparation of the annual budget and/or from a detailed investigation of the kind described in Chapter 7. These learning needs should then be appraised against the criteria contained in the existing HRD policy statements – a process that may eliminate some requirements from the proposed plans. For example, a proposal from one department head for certain managers to attend a day-release MBA course would not be included in the plan if there are to be no exemptions from a company's policy that staff over the age of 21 are not granted day release. In other cases it is the policy that has to be changed to meet new conditions. Finally, HRD priorities have to be established by ranking, in order of importance, all the requests received. As an organisation never has enough funds to meet all requests in full, it is important to remember that resources for learning, development and training are likely to be in competition with provision for other purposes and that decisions about respective allocations may well be highly political. Obviously, requests that appear most closely related to the organisation's strategic objectives are the most likely to be successful. For instance, the board of a company that has limited resources and is introducing an important new range of products in the coming year is more likely to allocate money to provide product training for its salesforce than to what appears to be less urgent training in other fields, particularly if the latter can be postponed without serious repercussions.

The HRD plan should be drawn up with great care and political acumen, always a useful competence area for HRD specialists if one is established within the organisation. A typical plan would contain the following elements:

- details on a calendar basis (monthly, quarterly, half-yearly) of each department's learning and development requirements by job classification and by number of employees involved, eg Accounts department, four clerical staff and two supervisory staff (NVQ junior management course); Laboratory, one technician (attachment to raw material supplier); Production department, an estimated 25 operatives (induction and initial training) and four managers (computer applications course);
- details on a monthly, quarterly, half-yearly, etc basis of the projected training for categories of staff not permanently allocated to a department, eg three graduate trainee managers);
- specification, against each item of learning, development or training, of the standard to be achieved, the person responsible for seeing that it is implemented, the strategy to be used (eg self-development, on-the-job coaching, internal or external course), how much the intervention will cost, its duration, when it will take place and its target completion date;
- a summary of the organisation's and each department's budget allocation for training: this may be divided into training that is continuing and to which the organisation is already committed, for example, craft trainees who are part of the way through their apprenticeships, and other training;
- possibly a sum set aside for additions to the company learning resource centre, or for the development of material to be used over the organisation intranet.

It should be noted that similar data could be collected and used to develop plans of longer duration, such as two- or three-year rolling plans.

There is a large organisation with branches throughout the country that produces such an annual document with 14 sections, starting with a business review and followed by a section dealing with a projection of costs and of activities in each important aspect of the company's operation in the forthcoming year, thus linking all functions closely with corporate objectives. The following extract is the section that deals with HRD. This is a real case, altered only to conceal the identity of the company, and is, of course, backed up by a more detailed plan (too long to reproduce here), which provides a blueprint for the work of the HRD department.

The main thrust of our efforts during this year and next will be to achieve cost-effective and more sharply focused training covering a wider group of people. Examples of current initiatives, actions and plans include:

Development of the Senior Management Team
A series of short lunchtime workshops has been arranged for all Directors and Department Heads. The programme of monthly sessions extending to the end of the year covers all aspects of the organisation under the headings Managing the Business, Managing Others and Managing Ourselves. Material from the Group Learning Resource Centre will be used as a basis for the sessions.

Development of Supervisors
A series of training courses for first line supervisors has been launched. Subject areas include: an examination of their role; personal organisation and prioritising; effective delegation; use of branch diary; safety, etc. Use of existing materials, including company guidebooks and the Learning Resource Centre will be encouraged.

Development of Trainers
Greater emphasis is to be given to the use of senior/more experienced staff to provide guidance and training both on the job and during more formal courses.

Performance Review
Training sessions will be held to emphasise the importance of the review in the overall management and improvement of the business. The review is to be extended to include hourly paid supervision.

Trainees Under Contract
Improved monitoring of training will be achieved next year and more of these trainees will be involved in the business review groups set up under the Total Quality Initiative.

External Learning and Development Professional Bodies
We continue to be involved in a wide variety of external committees and advisory groups covering professional bodies, local institutions of Further and Higher Education, Learning and Skills Councils and Sector Skills Councils. The involvement allows us to influence the shape of future learning and training within the industry and to draw on best practice from other industries/companies.

> *Personal Effectiveness Programmes*
> Selected senior management (including Directors) are undergoing individual programmes of guidance on personal effectiveness. This is leading to performance improvements.

At the beginning of this chapter, we pointed out that not all organisations possess written HRD strategies, plans and policies, but that some have plans on a less formal basis. This may be because of the factors illustrated by the Warwick University research described on page 140, which make it impossible for some small to medium enterprises to make forward plans with any degree of certainty. It could also be that in times of rapidly developing technology and economic change, or recession, larger organisations no longer experience their former stability, and their managements, too, may be constrained from committing themselves to longer-term planning and adopt an ad hoc approach. In this case, plans may well be discussed with managers and constantly reviewed to ensure that most urgent problems are addressed. Alternatively, the development may be phased – the precise pattern and content of each phase depending upon the outcome of those preceding it. In certain types of organisation, action learning groups or project teams may draw up their own learning plans. The optimum approach to planning may therefore have to be decided according to the context in which the organisation is operating. Whatever approach is used, however, it is useful if decisions are recorded (however briefly) in writing with a proposed date for revision, and circulated to all concerned. Such documents can then act as a blueprint against which to monitor progress and evaluate what has been achieved.

> Discussion question: What arrangements would you recommend in an organisation to ensure that departmental learning plans reflect the corporate HRD strategy?

HRD RESOURCES

When an HRD practitioner recommends or chooses a strategy to meet an identified need, he or she strives to achieve the 'best fit' consistent with the learning objectives, the organisation's policy, the learner's preferences and the resources available. HRD resources are the input required to enable a HRD plan to be implemented. The range of resources that can be drawn upon are considered later in this chapter and include people (eg the practitioner), and facilities (eg the self-learning packages, a 'walk-in' open access resource centre, a training room) and money (ie the HRD budget). However, it is often not so much the resources themselves that achieve results as the skill with which they are managed. We will look in Chapter 6 at a variety of ways of organising the HRD function to meet the needs of specific organisations. Whatever the function's structure, there are certain areas in which those responsible for HRD need to exhibit competence.

Central to the success of an individual responsible for managing HRD is the function as a manager of learning resources. Credibility and influence are enhanced when she is accepted as:

- the focal point in the organisation for advice and information about all learning and development activities (both internal and external);
- the source of specialist knowledge and experience about learning in a work context, as the co-ordinator and monitor of the organisation's HRD policy, plans and budgets;

- a competent trainer, and as a successful (line) manager of the HRD department, its staff, the learning centre and learning aids, if any or all of these exist. It is through contacts with top managers that he or she benefits from the key resource of 'political' support for his or her activities;

- a facilitator, with relevant skills such as listening, encouraging people to question existing ways of doing things, assisting appropriate learning to develop from planned and unplanned interventions.

During the last 20 years or so, the work of many HRD managers, or training managers as they would have been, has been dominated by organising and contributing to in-house courses and arranging attendance at external courses. The resources at their command were those required to carry out this restricted function, for instance a limited training budget and a training room or area. In recent years, however, the benefits of structured on-the-job learning have gradually become more recognised. This recognition has extended both to the techniques and, through the greater involvement of line managers, the range of resources that an organisation can apply to planned learning. Work-based projects, job rotation and coaching are all examples of activities that can result in effective learning of a kind that, by itself, classroom-based training cannot achieve.

The recognition that successful learning does not have to take place in a training centre has been powerfully reinforced by the application to learning and development of the new technologies. These technologies are having three main effects:

First, computers, video recorders, compact discs, interactive video systems, access to computerised data bases, intranets and the Internet have greatly increased the choice and flexibility of learning systems available. Wherever there is a computer terminal there is a potential learning resource.

Secondly, these applications of the new technologies are changing the perceptions of learning and training. As a result, and as we have argued, effective training is no longer so widely perceived to be primarily a classroom-based activity and few would now hold the simplistic view that, to be trained, employees had to attend an in-house course. However, in the right circumstances, the 'course strategy' remains a very important method of achieving learning objectives.

Thirdly, new opportunities are being opened up for employees who have in the past been 'disenfranchised' from HRD programmes because they worked shifts (ie could not attend 'normal' courses on a regular basis), worked part time, worked in dispersed units or in small organisations, could not be released for training, or lived in an area without a local college or university.

The new technologies have enabled the creation of sophisticated 'online learning' systems, which make it possible for employees (and employers) to study at home, at work (even in the car on their way to and from work!) or wherever they wish; to begin their studies when it is suitable for them (as opposed to the fixed enrolment date of some educational institutions); to have access to a very wide range of courses, irrespective of where the learner happens to live; and to construct their own learning environment without having to cope with the 'going back to school' anxiety.

There has been a trend to reduce what have come to be accepted as 'artificial' admission barriers to vocational educational courses (for example, traditional and notional minimum or maximum age regulations). There is also increasing recognition that in some circumstances adults' 'life experience' and high motivation to learn can more than offset the lack of paper qualifications. This has opened up learning and development opportunities for the 'unqualified' person. This characteristic of online learning is of particular importance in helping less well-qualified technical personnel to acquire improved qualifications in the context of serious shortages of skills in the new technology industries, and in allowing employees in all industries to update their skills and receive certification for units of NVQs. A number of large organisations now have their own open access learning centres, where employees can use technology-assisted instruction at times to suit themselves, and many organisations have designed their own learning packages, which can be used by employees across a wide geographical area either as distance learning or as open access material supported by tutoring from local managers.

Clearly, the role and expertise of the HRD manager in influencing and evaluating these approaches to planned leaning and training are very different from those required for traditional in-house training activities. For example, the explosive increase in the number and variety of online learning programmes becoming available presents a major challenge for the HRD practitioner to give advice on which is the most appropriate programme for a particular employee.

All learning resources ultimately cost money, and the HRD manager is responsible for advising on the best use of the available resources to facilitate learning. To do this he or she requires an up-to-date knowledge of the resources on which to draw and how they can best be employed. We now describe the three major categories of HRD resources: people, internal and external facilities and money.

People as a learning resource

Line managers

Many organisational HRD policies clarify that the learning of their staff is ultimately a line management responsibility, and indeed most learning takes place in the day-to-day work situation. Managers can act as coaches, mentors, appraisers and role models for their subordinates, as well as helping them to identify and use the many learning opportunities that occur in the course of normal work, and the *Learning Organisation* concept places increasing emphasis on these aspects. In addition, successful off-the-job training relies heavily upon the trainees' receiving suitable briefing by their managers prior to the training and being given support to transfer their learning to their work. Line managers' commitment to HRD is crucial not only to maximising the benefits of formal course training, but also a powerful factor in creating and developing a climate that expects and supports learning and training interventions as a normal part of organisational life. At an operational level, line managers, especially if they are good trainers and coaches, are an important source of lecturers for induction and other in-house programmes.

HRD specialists

An experienced HRD specialist is potentially one of the major contributors to an organisation's HRD operation. The extent to which his or her knowledge and skills are put to profitable use depends in practice upon many variables, in particular upon her credibility, technical competence and the degree of co-operation received from fellow managers.

Trainers

Trainers act as the essential link between the learner and the training plan and may include managers (when coaching their own staff), company tutors overseeing trainee technologists, craft trainee supervisors and operator instructors.

Former trainees

Satisfied 'customers' are the best ambassadors in helping to create informed opinion about the HRD function. They can also be of great assistance in getting a new form of training accepted, such as outdoor training sponsored by an organisation. Again, because of their experience of a former programme and its subsequent value to them in their work, past trainees can often make helpful contributions as speakers or syndicate leaders.

> Discussion question: Imagine you, as a former trainee on a junior management development programme, have been asked back as an external speaker on the course. How would you structure your talk?

Internal learning facilities

These can range from residential management centres, off-the-job training rooms (some equipped with simulators), to learning resource centres containing hardware and software of many kinds. With the development of many forms of online learning, the Internet and organisational intranets are making the boundaries between work and learning even more flexible. Staff can come in first thing and get through an hour or so of self-study before beginning operational tasks – or do the same in the early evening if they are not 'morning' people. Alternatively, many people now have PCs with Internet access at home and might avoid rush-hour traffic by organising their learning period at peak times. Some organisations derive an income from hiring out their learning and training facilities to other less-well-equipped organisations, thus providing a welcome addition to their budgets. The availability of general organisation resources such as desktop PCs, videoconferencing systems, a corporate intranet and/or access to the Internet facilitate a wide choice of methodology and delivery. Consultants and external training providers have not been slow to anticipate a considerable potential market, and it appears to be becoming more frequent for organisations to commission templates they can adapt for themselves, or custom-made software for use with the latest technology. Records, such as job descriptions, training undertaken, competences achieved, can also be a useful internal resource, as they can save much time searching through information. Some of the software mentioned above is designed to record automatically for each employee such information as programmes undertaken and standards and competences attained.

External training facilities

For the purpose of this chapter, such facilities can be grouped under six headings:

1   private-sector courses and consultants
2   group training schemes
3   professional associations
4   public-sector education and training services

5 programmes under the auspices of the LSCs, LECs and the Department for Education and Skills

6 courses run by trade unions.

Private-sector courses and consultants

Numerous organisations offer a wide and, at times, bewildering variety of courses on almost every aspect of training. Reduction in the number and size of HRD departments and the sophistication of new methods of delivery have resulted in an increased demand for outsourcing and for external courses. Selecting the right course is a difficult but important task if the company is to benefit from what can be a very considerable cost.

Consultants are a valuable source of expertise and organisations considering employing them should apply similar criteria to those used in selecting courses. An external consultant can often achieve results that would not be possible by using internal staff. It is not only the wider expertise that a consultant is likely to bring, but also the advantage of being unaffected by internal politics and value systems (although the best consultants will be astute enough to pick up an organisation's cultural 'nuances' without being sidetracked by them). Techniques such as videoconferencing and multimedia-based online learning can require expensive equipment, and specialist skills that may not be available in-house.

Group learning, development and training schemes

These are formed by a group of employers, often in a similar field or sector, who establish joint facilities that, individually, they would be unable to afford. These schemes normally offer employers, particularly small employers, the facilities of a HRD specialist, instructors and an off-the-job training centre. Traditionally, group schemes were concentrated in the craft training area, particularly for the first-year off-the-job training, and the decline in numbers of craft trainees has affected group training schemes. The more farsighted schemes, such as that of the Engineering Employers' Federation, now cover the whole spectrum of training and development, and can also assist with employee selection and assessment centre work.

Professional associations

The growth in professionalism in many fields of employment in recent years has led to new professional bodies being formed. The HRD specialist needs to be familiar with those professional associations relevant to her organisation. They can supply detailed information on various courses and programmes that lead to membership qualifications, and of post-qualification short courses to assist their members to keep up to date in specialist fields – courses an organisation could not normally afford to run internally.

Public-sector education and training services

Universities and institutions of further and higher education offer vocational courses in a wide variety of subjects and skills. Many of these courses are geared to national examination syllabuses, but there is a trend for colleges to provide courses to meet specialised regional demands and the specific requirements of individual organisations. Some of these courses can, if required, lead to certificates that can be accumulated for NVQs. The availability of courses tailor-made to meet an organisation's specific requirements is a well-established feature in management development, where it is closely associated with consultancy. In addition to their more traditional role as providers of standard courses, colleges and universities are increasingly regarded by industry and the public sector employees as 'resource centres' from which they can commission research and consultancy and obtain guest lecturers. The Open University, which pioneered 'open' learning, the 'LearnDirect' Internet resource and the University for Industry (see Chapter 1) might also be considered.

Programmes under the auspices of the LSCs/LECs and the Department for Education and Skills

As well as controlling the local funding for a number of national schemes, LSCs (LECs in Scotland) offer a variety of different services to assist organisations to develop an HRD strategy linked to their needs and objectives, as well as measures designed to help overcome perceived local needs. Such provisions will obviously vary from time to time and from locality to locality, and HRD managers should, therefore, be thoroughly aware of the activities of their local LSC and ensure that they are kept completely up to date with funding available. They should also be aware of local link arrangements and consortia involved with initiatives such as those under the 'New Deal'.

Trade unions

Employers are not always aware that trade unions run a wide diversity of training courses for shop stewards and union officials. Some of these courses are sponsored jointly by employers' associations and trade unions, and are usually oriented towards a particular industry: most, however, are arranged by the TUC or by a trade union, sometimes in conjunction with colleges. Since the Employment Act 2002 put Trade Union Learning Reps on a statutory footing, the TUC has been enthusiastic in promoting the role. There is a particularly useful TUC Internet site, www.learningservices.org.uk, which offers a comprehensive overview of national training initiatives and sources of funding.

Identifying costs and benefits

Organisations claiming that learning from haphazard or unplanned experience 'on the job' does not incur costs are usually deluding themselves. The costs that are incurred in this way are normally termed *learning* costs. The usual approach to costing planned training is to consider the various learning costs and then to determine how these can be minimised or even replaced by new earnings through expenditure on training. A list of examples of learning costs is given below:

- payments to employees when learning on the job;
- the costs of materials wasted, sales lost or incorrect decisions made by employees who are less than competent;
- supervision/management cost in dealing with incompetence problems;
- costs of reduced output/sales caused by the damaging effect on an established team of having members who are less than competent;
- cost attributable to accidents caused by lack of 'know-how' (these can be very significant in human terms when considering injury or even occasionally death caused by ignorance of safety training);
- cost resulting from employees leaving – either because they find the work too difficult, resent the lack of planned learning or feel they have no prospects of further development.

'Training' costs are those deliberately incurred to facilitate learning and with the intention of reducing learning costs. Some of these costs might be aimed not at planned training per se but at the learning system: for example, a training intervention might involve investing in appraisal procedures in order to get better data on learning needs, and the act of clarifying learning objectives might in itself generate some learning. But most training costs are more directly related to planned training itself. There are two kinds: fixed costs, which are not expected to change with the amount of training that takes place (eg salaries of permanent staff) and variable costs, which must vary directly with the training (eg materials used, or college fees paid).

Here are some examples of training costs.

'People' costs

- wages, salaries of trainers and instructors
- managers'/supervisors' salaries while training/coaching
- fees to external training providers
- fees to external assessors
- fees to assessing bodies for in-house courses
- travel and subsistence of trainees and trainers.

'Equipment' costs

- training equipment and aids
- depreciation of training, buildings and equipment.

Administrative costs

- wages/salaries of administration staff
- telephone, email, fax and postage
- office consumables
- systems and procedures (eg post-training questionnaires)
- hire of rooms.

'Materials' costs

- films and tapes
- IT packages
- distance-learning packages
- materials used in practice sessions
- protective clothing
- books and journals.

Large-scale initial costs relating to buildings or major items of training equipment (eg a simulator) will normally be 'capitalised' – that is, they represent a transfer of liquid funds into 'fixed assets', the costs of which are spread over a long term via the annual 'depreciation' item. Additionally, the upkeep of a learning/training centre (ie a purpose-maintained building) will incur all the normal costs usually associated with buildings: community charge, insurance, cleaning, heating, lighting, decorating and general maintenance. HRD departments will also usually be required to carry a proportion of the organisation's overheads.

Ideally, the relationship between learning costs and training costs should be such that both are minimised, because any expense is justified only if it reduces the costs of unplanned learning. As always in an area seen as more art than science, the degree of certainty attached to any estimates will vary, and decisions usually have to be made on incomplete information. This demands that an organisation must set an upper limit in advance on what can be spent in a given period (usually a year).

HRD BUDGET

Exactly how the budget is compiled will depend upon the following two key factors:

- the organisational structure, which affects the way in which the HRD department or function relates to the rest of the organisation. For instance, some departments can be designated as profit centres, supplying services to line managers on request and charging accordingly, and sometimes contracting their services and resources (premises, equipment) to external clients for a fee. Such departments are expected to pay their way, costing their services and overheads to determine the prices charged and operating a profit and loss account. In other organisations, the HRD department is regarded as an overhead, and allocated a budget.

- the financial systems and controls that operate throughout the organisation. For instance, zero-based budgeting assumes starting with a blank sheet and receiving an allocation justified by the estimated cost of carrying out the HRD plan, and possibly limited to agreed priorities. More usual is the annual budget allocation, the content and size of which depends on many factors. Of particular significance are the importance given to the HRD function, the level of its activity, and (not least, we feel), the HRD manager's tenacity and professionalism in 'fighting his or her corner' when the budgets are being finalised! The size of the budget is likely to vary from year to year depending on the profitability of the company, or in a public-sector organisation, on government policy. This is an added challenge because training or retraining needs can be greatest when financial resources are at a premium. It is always necessary to plan well ahead and to assess the probable future requirements carefully so that whatever finance is available goes to the real, and acceptable, priorities. Regular monitoring of expenditure is essential, so that any discrepancies are noticed at an early stage, and corrective action taken before the situation becomes out of hand.

Whether the budget consists only of amounts earmarked for specific purposes is likely to depend on the organisation's accounting norms. Most 'active' HRD budgets now contain contingency sums which are not so earmarked and which can therefore fund unanticipated costs. Where contingency sums are included there may be a temptation to create or 'find' ways of spending them: unspent budgets may be thought to promote future budget reductions. It is risky to let those who control the budgets find evidence that money for learning and development is being spent on interventions that do not show a worthwhile return. Like all management decisions, HRD decisions involve the allocation of limited resources to alternative uses, and contingency sums that are wasted are, of course, less likely to be renewed than those that are saved.

> Discussion question: How might you review the total learning needs of an organisation for next year, as part of a 'zero-based' budgeting exercise? Which areas would be priority and why?

Although budgets vary from one organisation to another, all need suitable systems of forecasting the financial resources required and of controlling the money that is allocated. Singer (1977) has specified certain main requirements of a budget and budgetary control in the HRD function:

- an adequate HRD plan must be created (which sounds obvious but it is surprising how often this is not thought through!);

- the expenses incurred in achieving the HRD plan must have been identified and estimated (as above, this sounds simple but does not always happen);

- the responsibility for items of expenditure must have been allocated between HRD specialists and other managers;

- account classification must have been made so that expenditure can be allocated to specific cost areas;

- cost information must be recorded accurately and a mechanism for feeding back the collated information must be present so that individuals can take corrective action when required. Sometimes a simple spreadsheet is enough to show that continuing an expensive development programme could result in an overspend – there will then be time to propose an action plan depending on the success of the programme so far.

Cost–benefit analysis

A full-scale cost–benefit analysis, in which all the results of the learning intervention are systematically quantified and compared with all the learning and training costs, is rarely possible or economic. The management of learning interventions remains a situation-specific art. This in turn means an organisation-specific art: the extent to which costs and benefits are assessed will often be determined by organisational norms. If periodic budgeting operations happen, they may need some sort of cost–benefit support for new items, for items over a certain sum, for capital proposals, for 'earmarked' items – or again budgets may be decided solely on the basis of comparison with past actuals or by allocating a new finite sum to a variety of uses in a prescribed way. New, unbudgeted proposals may similarly require detailed supporting evidence and face-to-face 'selling' – or they may naturally follow from a committee minute. A simple rule might be 'the bigger and more innovative the proposal, the more a cost–benefit spotlight will be expected and is in fact needed'.

The growth in importance attaching to learning and development initiatives makes it desirable for practitioners and their organisations to improve their ability to judge specific proposals in cost–benefit terms. In most organisations with a recognisable HRD function, however disparate it may be, the days are long gone when approaches to learning and training involve no more than allocating expected costs to an insignificant budget, and assuming as an act of faith that hoped-for benefits must follow.

Cost–benefit judgements might be best made in league with accountants: it is popularly believed by some HR people that accountants are 'the enemy', expecting short-term results and only understanding simplistic comparisons. However, this is a stereotype and in our experience many accountants are very sympathetic to HRD initiatives, not least because the accountancy professional institutions strongly advise CPD and self-development. Accountants will, in any organisation, have 'conventions' and 'norms' that they use in other fields to give money-values to things that do not obviously have a monetary value. They also tend to appreciate readily the consequences of decisions. For example, cutting production times can also cut overtime payments; adding competence can lead to wage claims, resignations and recruitment; and improving the image of staff who have consumer contacts can dramatically improve the frequency of those contacts. But regardless of whether help is available from accountants or others, the cost of HRD must be compared in some way with what it is expected to achieve. The more explicitly it can be demonstrated and quantified (and, usually, the more sophisticated the accompanying detail – although here it may be necessary to judge the requirements of those whose approval the HRD specialist is seeking), the easier the task will be of persuading the organisation to 'buy' a proposal, and the more convincing the result.

Comprehensive coverage of cost–benefit analysis in relation to learning and training has been offered by Talbot and Ellis (1969) and by Pepper (1984). More recently, an American professor (Campbell 1994, 1995) offered a variety of simple cost–benefit methods. We now describe three of these methods, and then illustrate them with a fictional case study (although based on a real-life situation) of our own. We have omitted here all the relevant money figures from the case, because they may tend to distract from our main purpose, which is to emphasise the ideas and attitudes in a cost–benefit approach. The three methods are 'payback', 'cost–benefit ratio' and 'return on investment'.

Cost–benefit method 1: 'payback'
A 'payback' judgement involves asking the question, 'How long will it take for HRD to pay for itself?' The implication is that from a break-even time that can be calculated, savings and/or new income will be realised. The simple formula to define the 'payback period' is:

$$\frac{\text{Full cost of learning/training intervention}}{\text{Annual operational savings and/or new income}}$$

In Campbell's words, 'payback' offers 'a quick initial look at a potential investment'. The shorter the payback period, the stronger the case for training – provided the annual improvement can be expected to last.

Cost–benefit method 2: The cost–benefit ratio
This method projects the ratio between total learning/training cost and total estimated benefits. It is especially useful where benefits are difficult to quantify, not least because it forces judgements on those benefits and their monetary values. Its formula immediately shows whether expenditure is likely to pay for itself of not. The formula is:

$$\frac{\text{Projected full cost of learning/training intervention}}{\text{Predicted total operational benefits}}$$

If the resulting ratio is less than one (1.0, or 100 per cent), training clearly looks 'profitable' – provided the prediction of operational benefits can be trusted. This latter point is critical, however. To begin with, what is the assumed time frame? Unlike payback, a cost–benefit ratio does not of itself indicate how soon results will accrue – an issue our accountant colleagues like to know about. Are the benefits expected to appear in a matter of weeks, months or years? And will other factors soon intervene to change the details of the operation? Equally significant, all assumptions must be rigorously vetted, and estimates used that are both realistic and prudent. Finally, it must be remembered that costs and benefits tend to be multidimensional – that is, a saving in one area may affect another, which itself may involve both costs and savings – and hence an attempt must be made to estimate and include any knock-on effects.

Cost–benefit method 3: Return on investment
This is perhaps the most used method within the private sector, where a saving or a surplus

is likely to be judged against others in relative rather than absolute terms, and a specific yield is often required to match or better another that uses and 'ties up' the same amount of cash. ROI is usually calculated as a 'per annum' percentage:

$$\frac{\text{Operational savings each year} + \text{increases in annual income}}{\text{Total costs}}$$

This is the cost–benefit ratio in reverse – or rather, upside-down. Here a high resulting percentage ensures further consideration. As such, it still demands great care with its assumptions. If the expected yield is higher than that from using the money in another way, there is a prima facie case for transferring the money to this purpose. If not, or if there is no prospect of such a transfer, but the yield is still higher than the cost of borrowing, then organising a loan immediately looks a worthwhile option.

The contemporary ROI 'guru', Jack Phillips, suggested recently that ROI should not necessarily be carried out on every training programme because the process is resource

Our specific case study involves a further education college with a complement of 350 staff and over 5,000 students, whose main 10-storey building is now over 25 years old. The building still uses its original three lifts, which serve all floors. During the last 10 years the cost of keeping these lifts running has itself increased significantly, involving both consultancy and breakdown maintenance – but they are not yet fully depreciated, and the college governors do not see any possibility of replacing the lifts for at least another decade.

The running of the building, including the lifts, is the responsibility of the estate manager supported by an assistant at manager level; neither has any real knowledge of lifts management. The estates manager is due to retire in some five years' time when, it is hoped, his highly committed and enthusiastic assistant will succeed him. All lifts maintenance is currently handled by an outside firm, which operates an annual planned maintenance schedule and is called in whenever a breakdown occurs. The estate manager has several electricians and mechanical fitters on his team, but they are not multiskilled and do not work on the lifts.

Jane Simpson is the head of adult training. She has also been made responsible (part time) for college-wide staff development. She reflects on the lifts problem when she reads annual appraisal reports on the estate manager and his assistant, both of which refer to the issue without allocating criticism to the appraisees. It occurs to Jane that a training intervention might be a cost-effective option. How about upgrading the estate manager's – or his assistant's – technical knowledge of lifts and lifts management?

Jane talks with the lifts manufacturers and learns that they themselves run an expensive residential course in lifts management, which should go a long way to making anyone who attends something of a consultant. They are also developing their own training operations and plan multiskilling courses for groups of qualified engineering staff, although again at fairly high cost – but that cost can be almost halved if team training can be mounted on an operator's own premises. Jane's HRD budget can cover the estate manager or assistant attending the residential course, but she has no budget for the engineering staff and multiskilling; such training would have to be specially funded by moving money from a non-training college use.

Jane and the college accountant look at the options from the points of view of (a) payback, (b) cost–benefit ratio (C–B) and (c) return on investment (ROI). The following chart summarises their discussion:

		Payback	C–B	ROI
1	Estate manager	Quick – but not lasting	C>B	Minus qty
2	Assistant	Quick and lasting	Some extra costs in year 1	Minus in year 1
			B>C from year 2	OK year 2
				Good year 3 onwards
3	Multiskilling – away from base	Two years minimum – but probably lasting from then onwards	Knock-on costs years 1 and 2	High once training completed
			Probably B>C from year 3 or 4	
4	Multiskilling on premises	Quick and lasting	Few knock-on costs if mounted during college vacation	High once training completed
			B>C from year 2	

It is not difficult to establish a preference for both items 2 and 4. The discussion uncovers a clear link in operational terms between the two training proposals – the value of the manager acquiring lifts management skills is improved by his having a team of trained engineers at his disposal, and the team training is more valuable if the team works for and with an informed specialist in lifts management. Jane and the college accountant can easily 'sell' to governors the unbudgeted investment – largely on the ground that the ROI is unusually high and the annual saving can be earmarked for lifts replacement, allowing replacement well before 10 years.

intensive and expensive. Quality rather than quantity counts and 5–10 per cent of an overall training programme should be sufficient (http://www.itol.co.uk/cgi-local/dcforum/dcextra.cgi).

Our brief case study has ignored reality in some respects. We have assumed constant money values, and in the summary chart we have not offered quantified conclusions where some would have existed. The case remains fictional, although some aspects of it are taken from real life, and its key assumptions are, we believe, realistic.

The three cost–benefit methods outlined above are by no means the only ones available, nor do they adequately explain all the issues that might be addressed when judging viability, choosing between alternatives or evaluating past or present norms. Here are some other relevant issues and approaches – some of which involve complex-sounding terms to summarise what are essentially simple concepts!

- **inevitability**: Must the training intervention be carried out regardless of cost or benefit? Examples include legal directives, safety imperatives, and – more simply – new equipment or systems that can be used only if new learning takes place.

- **'waiting cost'**: The estimated cost of waiting (ie not training until a specified future date), compared with the cost and benefits of moving ahead without delay. This highlights the issue of timing (especially if the intervention is not already backed by a budget): when is the best time? The calculation may need to include any costs of specially raised finance, but also any expected operational benefits from the time the training is completed. An inflation element may be applied to either, but not simultaneously to both.

- **'opportunity cost'**: What is the value of any alternative activity that must be given up if the training intervention goes ahead? What alternative activity benefits (eg work output) will be lost? What alternative activity costs (eg work materials) will be saved – or (eg overtime payments) incurred? Care should be taken to estimate both within the context of the specific training plan: for example, the estimates will differ widely if the training intervention is planned to take place during or outside normal working hours.

- **'interference cost'**: What is the cost of interfering with 'normal' work routines? This cost can be wide-ranging, extending beyond the immediate workplace to sales figures, and/or to other intermediary functions that depend on the output for their own work.

- **'establishment cost'**: What part of the organisation's standard HRD overheads (eg full-time training, staff training centre running charges) should be included, if any? Will establishment resources actually be involved – as planners, trainers, space providers, etc? (See 'Cost–benefit ratio' on page 109 above.)

- **'marginal cost'**: What additional (ie over and above any 'interference cost' and 'establishment cost') money must be spent to carry out the training activity? This can reflect a long list of items, including course fees, travel, accommodation, allowances and backup administration.

- **'work benefits'**: How are trained employees expected to influence work – in terms of such things as output, worktime per unit produced, utilisation of equipment, efficiencies, tolerances, raw material wastages, 'rejects', system improvements – even morale, absenteeism, accident histories? As with 'interference cost', can benefits be expected beyond the immediate workplace? Will trained employees release others for different work? Might any such benefits be offset by any possible adverse effects?

- **'employee benefits'**: Will employees become more skilled, more versatile, more motivated, more knowledgeable of related activities, more committed to a new or revised work system, more contented? Are these benefits likely to be offset by new fears, hopes, ambitions? Might employees be likely to look for new rewards, new equipment, new – maybe external – opportunities? Will they need or want more or different information in the future?

Clearly many of the elements included within the issues listed above contain qualitative elements that cannot easily be transformed into monetary or numerical values readily agreed by everyone. Four related points are worth remembering. First, an overall approach that builds contingency sums into HRD budgets will make 'unproven' decisions easier to take. Second, the ultimate results of a learning/training intervention will be in part a reflection of the degree of commitment behind the decision. Third, if trainees' learning is monitored as training proceeds, the training process can itself be adjusted with greater chance of success. And fourth, trainees themselves might sometimes with advantage be helped, urged or allowed to share the responsibility for both the decision to train and for managing training's 'bottom line' as the training evolves. A decision to move ahead with a training intervention is not an end in itself, but the prelude to activity that must still be managed, and in many cases the person in the best position to justify the training intervention is the one who trains.

Discussion question: Now, have a go at drafting a policy statement for an organisation that does not currently have one, making sure you include identification of learning and training needs, performance appraisal, work experience, role of line management and specialists, paid leave and release for training.

CONCLUSIONS

So what have we established in this chapter about the links between organisational policies, strategies and plans?

- All managers need to understand mainstream operational goals and priorities, and to seek ways whereby HRD can contribute towards them.
- The HRD policy not only clarifies the purpose of learning, training and development, but also defines responsibilities and provides guidelines for decision-making.
- It should be frequently reviewed.
- The HRD plan translates the policy into learning/training events to meet specific situations.
- Large organisations with a stable bureaucratic culture and planned training programmes for different categories of staff are more likely to have long-term HRD plans.
- Rapidly developing organisations have the most difficulty in producing detailed learning plans and may be constrained to operate on an ad hoc basis. In any organisation, however, written policy statements and plans are extremely useful documents.
- The HRD budget may be drawn up in one of several ways, usually depending upon the financial systems and controls in the rest of the organisation.
- Because the budget is likely to be a fixed amount, it may affect the details of the plan, and the HRD practitioner may have to prioritise.
- As learning needs unfold progressively, budgets should be constantly reviewed.
- HRD almost always involves both costs and benefits, although a clear-cut reliable

This chapter looked at a number of ways in which the HRD function may be financed in an organisation. Think of your own organisation, one you know well, or have read about. Does it operate as a profit centre or a cost centre? Does it have a budget? What system is used? Work out the costs of any one learning or training intervention in this organisation. When you have done this, try to work out a cost–benefit analysis on any training intervention in which you have been involved, using the most appropriate of the three methods above.

quantifiable cost–benefit calculation may be impossible, but HRD specialists should be able to think in cost–benefit terms.

■ HRD practitioners can add value to their own roles by discussing needs, options, priorities, methods and follow-up with other operating managers, not least line management and accountants.

The next chapter describes a variety of ways of positioning the HRD function in organisations to take forward organisational strategies and policies. As you will see, the function may be a large department or an individual with other accountabilities. Either can be successful in their context.

The HRD Function – Roles and Responsibilities for Specialists and Line Management

CHAPTER 6

In Chapter 6, we will consider:

- **The formal organisation of HRD activities;**

- **Roles and responsibilities of HRD specialists, functional HRD staff such as technical trainers and instructors, and line managers;**

- **The complex process of resourcing HRD to align with organisational culture, structure and operational norms, recognising that HRD functions can effectively support business strategy, but too often are relatively mechanistic and lacking strategic influence;**

- **Establishing and resourcing dedicated learning and training units;**

- **The need for HRD specialists to achieve credibility through ethical standards and political acumen.**

In the previous chapter we looked at HRD strategies in organisations, and how these can effectively support business strategy. In many smaller organisations, there may be limited resources to allow for a dedicated HRD department, and activities may be carried out by a range of different people with other dedicated roles. Alternatively, in large prosperous organisations we may be talking about significant numbers of specialist staff. This chapter explains who is who, and why, in the HRD function. We will discuss the responsibilities of line management, and the justification for, and establishment of, dedicated HRD units – including their structure, positioning, role definitions and organisation. We stress that we are not suggesting a standard form of operating organisation, nor a logically consistent approach to learning. We believe quite strongly that management is an art, and a situation-specific one at that. It serves but is also served by the environment in which it takes place. This means that an organisation's approach to learning has to be appropriate for its cultural realities and normal operating procedures.

Think of any organisation with which you are in regular contact – for example, your local bank, health centre, supermarket, cinema or leisure centre. Do you know if learning and training activities take place in that organisation? If so, who makes (or should make) these happen? Perhaps you don't know. Perhaps they are not managed formally at all. Perhaps you assume they happen, especially when the bank is closed until 9.30 'because of staff training', but you are never able to observe. Now assume that you are responsible for advising any of these organisations on their whole operation. Do you want any learning or training activities to happen? Do you want these activities formally defined? Do you want anyone to be formally identified as responsible for making them happen? If the answer to any of these questions is 'Yes', try adding the detail to each – and then think about how these things might fit into a chart or map or picture that describes the organisation as a whole.

THE HRD FUNCTION

The word 'function' comes from a Latin verb meaning 'to perform or to act', suggesting that any 'function' should do things not just talk about them! We have used the different terms HRD and 'Training' function advisedly, in that, as we suggested in the introduction, they represent in effect specific ways of looking at the concept of learning, one emphasising externally managed activities, and the other learner-centred control. Of course, many organisations will use the terms interchangeably. An early definition of the training function (based on that contained in the former Manpower Services Commission's Glossary of Training Terms 1981) is:

> the purposes, structure and specialised activity of training and its relationships with other activities within a working organisation.

Donnelly (1984), in his review of the evolution of training as a specialist function, drew attention to the fact that, prior to the 1960s, training activities were very restricted and diffused within organisations. Not surprisingly, at that time there was an almost complete absence of any objective analysis of dedicated training and development jobs and (in the minds of top management) the nature of company training activities rarely justified the status of a 'business function'.

So, we are dealing with what is a relatively recent feature of organisational life and, one that, often from a zero base, has enjoyed a spectacular but ephemeral growth.

Although a number of large companies (eg Ford, Lever, Cadbury, Pilkington) had training units in operation even before the Second World War, training departments first appeared in quantity during the late 1960s – in the form of off-site course centres or wings of existing personnel departments, and occasionally as mere one-person administrative units. There was no general pattern of organisation; nor was a standard pattern advised by the 1964 Act or the Industrial Training Boards, which were the main stimulus for the development. In later years, when the legislative and hence financial support was withdrawn, many of these training departments failed to consolidate their position. As might be expected, there were great variations in the ways in which training units evolved, in their perceived purposes and achievements, and in the extent to which they were accepted and valued within their organisations. At one end of the spectrum, they existed simply as a token presence to satisfy minimal internal needs, and perhaps also to justify (often non-existent) ITB grants. At the other extreme, training units were developed that enjoyed a high status and influence, and came to be embedded in the mainstream activities of the organisation.

Bearing in mind the very limited amount of training expertise that was then available, the inexperienced staff sometimes appointed to the training positions and the limited training they were given themselves, the expectations that organisations had of their training departments at that time were often unrealistically high. A warning note about the range of activities of training officers was sounded by Rodger, Morgan and Guest (1971). In their study, carried out in the mid-1960s, they sought to clarify the function of the training officer and the limits of the function, and they commented that:

> Training is a means of making better use of human resources in the organisation by developing people to meet the requirements of the job to be done ... Any attempts to extend the expertise of training officers into broader human resource specialist roles is

to change the trainer into … a more exotic role that would be beyond the aspiration of all but a minority of training officers.
A Study of the Work of Industrial Training Officers, 1971

The writers use the term 'HR specialist' as far back as the late 1960s/early 1970s, although the sense of HR at this period was of an administrative or negotiating function not concerned with development.

The quotation does not of course mean that the authors thought training had no part in organisational change and the creation of a flexible workforce. We know that it can be a primary strategy in these developments. But their achievement demands the exercise of a high order of training expertise, and this tended to be in short supply at that time.

The economic recessions of the 1970s and 1980s provided the *coup de grâce* for many weak training departments, especially those in small organisations, typically resulting in the end of planned training activities in the host organisation. In more robust organisations, some training departments lost their independent functional status, and the responsibility for the activities that survived cost-cutting was dispersed to other functions. In many small and medium-sized organisations the training function that had enjoyed a departmental state in its own right regressed to its pre-1964 state.

But the seed had germinated. Some organisations, particularly those with buoyant personnel departments, had increasingly appointed good-quality human resources to their employee development positions. They found during the 1980s (for many reasons) that employee relations problems were less in evidence. Consequently employee development could justify more resource time from the personnel professional. The economic recovery of the 1980s, coupled with the success of government's Youth Training programmes, further renewed many organisations' involvement with employee development, and although the recession of the late 1980s and early 1990s hit companies hard, the tendency to ignore the training function has not been so evident. Indeed, by 1990 some commentators were coming to describe the function as critical for forward growth.

> Discussion question: What is the structure of the HRD/training and development function in your organisation, or an organisation with which you are familiar? How long has it existed in this form? Could it be more effective in another one?

Rodger et al (1971) noted a wide variety of activities in response to variables such as:

- the status and importance of the function as expressed by top management's interest and support
- the extent to which there is a need and demand for training within the organisation
- the natural development of training in the firm
- the managerial calibre of those in specialist training and development posts.

Similar data emerges again from studies 20 years later. Strategic, political and organisational constraints still influence, if not mould, the function, and the emergence of 'knowledge management' systems is at the same time sophisticating the concept of a learning function and making it more generalised in its application. It is, though, still possible to suggest three main conditions that must be satisfied if the HRD function is to achieve a secure status in the organisation:

1 Line management should accept responsibility for the learning and training of their staff.

2 The function should be appropriately structured within the organisation – with roles that are perceived as relevant to such aspects as boundary management, organisational culture, operational strategy, management style and the organisation's geography.

3 Specialist HRD staff should be seen as professionals – trained, with clearly defined roles.

We will now consider these primary indicators for success.

LINE MANAGEMENT'S RESPONSIBILITY FOR HRD

Although there are different types of managerial responsibility for learning, development and training, we would suggest forcefully that all managers, without exception, ought to accept personal responsibility for the learning and training of their own staff. This involves taking an active interest in their careers, providing opportunities to improve and extend their abilities, especially by using day-to-day work tasks, and, above all, by encouraging them to continue learning (Singer, 1979). An organisation should ensure that each of its managers accepts the importance of this particular role when contributing to the corporate learning effort and that their success in exercising this responsibility will have a bearing on their own career prospects. Unlike other HRD responsibilities, this cannot be delegated.

These recommendations for good practice, however, are sadly not universally accepted by managers. 'More urgent tasks have to be given priority' and 'general pressure of work' are the usual reasons given by managers for not being involved in HRD. Although not discounting these reasons (and all managers have expressed them at some time, as all parents have said 'because I say so!') a critical aspect of the management process is concerned with identifying and dealing with priority tasks, and, for many managers, employee learning and training is simply not seen as a priority. We have drawn four conclusions from numerous discussions we have had with senior, middle and junior managers attending management development programmes:

■ A significant obstacle to progress in exercising this responsibility is that, for many, the task is regarded as too difficult – and is consequently avoided.

■ It is unusual (perhaps for the same reason) for managers to be assessed rigorously on this aspect of their work (in appraising managers and determining their own learning needs, much more emphasis should be placed on expertise – or the lack of it – in this sphere).

■ Many learning and training activities (especially those linked with determining training needs – which we shall explore more fully in Chapters 7 and 8) demand a heavy and sustained allocation of a manager's time.

■ It seems that many managers have negative feelings about learning which stem from their own early experiences of formal education – feelings that are both uncomfortable and unpleasant, and that they hoped to leave behind when they entered adulthood. We referred to this phenomenon when we talked about motivation to learn (page 70). Such feelings act as powerful anti-development influences, and ensure that trainer-training for managers is itself a complex and lengthy process.

The nature of the responsibility for learning and training, and how it is exercised, varies with the level of management. Very senior managers should have four main responsibilities:

- They bear the main responsibility for creating and sustaining a positive attitude to HRD in all its forms.
- They make decisions about the organisation's HRD policies and the level of resources to be allocated in support of them.
- Their personal involvement in decisions about learning and training, in formal training events and their own self-development practices, offers an example to ambitious subordinates.
- Their HRD interventions (not least via critical comments on what they observe) provide a quality control service for the HRD function.

Middle and junior managers are responsible for implementing the organisation's HRD policy within their own spheres of influence. They must themselves communicate information linked with work plans, for example, new work schedules or new output targets. They must ensure workplace competence despite such hazards as raw material variances, machine breakdowns, variable hours of work, sudden workforce sickness and frequently changing specifications – all of which require a flexible workforce with trained backup available at short notice. They must honour conditions of employment – for example, those allowing leave of absence to attend external courses. Above all, they must encourage subordinates' learning on a continuous basis, to ensure that all these other operational learning processes can flow smoothly. As with their own top management superiors, their own learning decisions, their involvement in discussions, their self-development and their training interventions give to their subordinates an ongoing justification for learning. In one editor's experience as an academic, bringing back ex-students who have reached senior organisational positions to talk to current students can be very beneficial in stressing the importance of life-long learning; thankfully, most speakers are enthusiastic about their commitment to learning, rarely claiming to have reached their current senior positions without it.

> Discussion question: As a HRD director of a large organisation, how would you encourage managers to take more responsibility for developing their subordinates?

SPECIALIST HRD RESOURCES

Paradoxically, an increasing commitment by line management is often the strongest influence leading to the use of specialist, 'dedicated' HRD people and units.

It is important, though, for employees in different departments to be treated equally and consistently. The potential problem grows if employees move across organisational boundaries to learn. Imagine your own reactions if, as a management trainee on a roving familiarisation programme, you are welcomed in one unit by senior management, given access to strategic material, and regularly allowed to attend management meetings, while in the next unit these opportunities are missing. Imagine the effect of the sales department allowing you to draw sales expenses on sales attachments, while a distant research laboratory provides none. The aftermath of your critical questions at head office is likely to be a standard ruling – which in turn may involve a central budget of some kind, clearly defined within a named manager's span of control.

Results of this kind are confined neither to management traineeships, nor to large organisations. Any activity that serves, or is commissioned by, a department other than that in which the activity happens, demands a focal point to which problems can be referred for decisions. In a small or medium-sized organisation, this may well be the senior executive him- or herself, or at least a senior manager, who of course has only limited time and specialised knowledge, and is likely to delegate the task if the need recurs regularly. And the need may be for regular action, not just ad hoc decisions. This is not to say that wherever learning and training activity grows, full-time HRD specialists and specific departments must appear. Those taking on the new responsibilities may well combine them with more visible existing responsibilities: a safety officer may be asked to handle the ongoing training of safety stewards, an accountant may be asked to coach newly appointed supervisors on cost-effectiveness, and so on. The 'HRD' tag may not appear in their job titles, and the time to be spent on this aspect of their jobs may remain unspecified.

Nevertheless, many HRD roles, and especially those serving more than a single purpose, are often delegated to a 'dedicated' unit or person. A 'dedicated' induction unit, for example, might be created to ensure recruits are consistently and properly introduced to a company. Again, if 'diagnostic instruction' is needed on several jobs prior to a decision on initial placement, a 'dedicated' technical training unit might handle this. These units usually do have 'training', or 'learning' in their title, as it is their main task. And if their work spans departments, we may find them placed in a central Human Resource department, since HRD roles often link with, and in some cases overlap, HR management roles.

The picture in large, multidepartmental and multisite organisations is more complex, but the organisational issues are basically the same, especially if organisational change happens frequently, which it does in most complex organisations. Even if specialist HRD roles already exist, decisions on whether line management roles should be changed (and specialist roles decentralised or redrawn or abandoned) are periodically needed. The need can be crucial, as is clear in this example:

A well-known multinational corporation originally organised its operations in one product sphere in separate manufacturing and selling operations. Six manufacturing companies (each comprising one site) existed, each with its own head office. Each of three sales companies had its own regional office and nationwide sales force. All nine companies had central training units, working from and within their central personnel departments. Competition forced a series of major reorganisations: a new marketing-oriented company took over the entire operation, manufacturing being concentrated over several years on three sites, and a new head office, with a newly created marketing department, focusing a single, combined salesforce. There were of course many redundancies, but none among training staff, whose workload grew enormously. Extensive training was envisaged over a number of years to train the remaining factory employees to handle newly moved equipment and processes, to retrain sales reps used to 'old' routines, to brief newly recruited marketing staff, and to generate a single corporate identity.

To achieve these objectives, (a) the three factory sites were each given an enlarged training unit, housed within the site HR department, which itself reported to the site general manager; (b) the sales department was given both a central training unit (reporting to a sales controller in head office) and a 'regional personnel and training manager' in each regional office (reporting to the regional manager, and independent of the central sales training unit); and (c) a 'company training manager', working from head office and responsible to the new company's newly appointed personnel director, took over management and management trainee training. The key point here is that operational decisions forced existing specialists to relocate at new bases – manufacturing organised geographically, sales geographically and functionally, and head office on the basis of management grade. But some key line management responsibilities also changed in the process.

Further changes evolved during the next few years. In one of the factories, a technical training unit was established within the main production unit, managed by a full-time technical manager who reported to the production manager. A 'head office training and development manager' post was newly established, responsible for 'determining and where appropriate implementing training plans' for the marketing, commercial and HR departments in head office; for convenience this new post reported to the company training development manager, but most of the appointee's time was spent in discussions with line management in the three mainstream departments. The salesforce introduced 'cycle days' at the end of each four-weekly sales cycle, when reps came together with their area managers; half of each cycle day was given over to training led by the area manager, but uniquely scripted by the regional personnel and training manager in discussion with the regional and area managers concerned. To ensure some overall co-ordination of expense, the company training and development manager was given the added responsibility of advising annually on all training budgets, of creating a corporate 'annual training review' document, and again of commenting quarterly on actual company-wide training expenditures. The company training and development manager chaired and controlled the agenda for a new 'training and development committee', which met quarterly and subsequently reported to the board of directors via a written document and a board meeting agenda discussion. Attendance at this board meeting varied, dependent upon the Chief Executive's view of what should be discussed, but the company training and development manager was always present.

Later again, the title of the company training and development manager was extended to become 'company training and management development manager', and he was given responsibility for liaising with directors in maintaining ongoing development programmes for specifically listed promotable managers. His first act was to carry through amendments to the formal appraisal processes to ensure that promotability ratings were determined and agreed annually with the directors concerned. A small technical instruction unit was established in the head office to train audio typist and administrative assistant recruits who, when trained, worked in central pools; this unit was led by an instructor reporting to the office manager, but it was also required to handle all administration relating to external training arranged within head office.

This case example shows the potential complexity of organisational decisions regarding HRD, taken to complement operational change. Roles and reporting responsibilities must be newly clarified, new base points determined and even new co-ordination methods arranged. There is no single model to be followed: a new, unique model must be created, and operational and political influences are usually the strongest determinants of specific decisions. Nevertheless, the example does suggest a number of critical lessons:

- Where widespread change is extensive – we have seen that few organisations today are 'immune' from change – and the organisation is large, dedicated learning and training responsibilities are usually justified. A worthwhile 'rule' might be that 'in turbulent operating conditions, the responsibility (or responsibilities) for HRD must be formally and clearly outlined, and must be both understood and acknowledged by all levels of management'.

- In a large organisation, spread over geographical and functional boundaries, it is unlikely that a single unit or department can adequately handle the wide variety of learning and training responsibilities that top management will want or need to see managed, and managed professionally, and hence need to delegate.

- The creation of one or more 'dedicated' HRD units or departments does not necessarily involve the total delegation of the function to those units and departments.

- While the HRD function might appear to fit naturally within the HR function, there are often major reasons why formal HRD units are better placed close to the line management who still carry the prime responsibility for operational results and attempts to improve them.

- Technical instruction (including in this instance training in such skills as IT operations and administration) demands technical know-how, and can reasonably be considered part of technical operations, so run by technical staff.

- Sales training can involve special geographical problems, and hence often justifies unique arrangements.

- Training administration can be handled anywhere, and will ideally be managed by people who are used to managing logistics.

- Management development (by which we here mean preparation for future promotional moves, and the forward organisational planning that may be dovetailed with them) requires support and commitment from the very top, and a degree of confidentiality that justifies direct links between the specialist and top management, often bypassing middle management in the process. We look in more detail at this complex area in Chapter 11.

> Discussion question: What are the pluses and minuses of placing the HRD function in the HR department?

Perhaps the main lesson in the last case example relates to the endless ongoing need for liaison between HRD professionals and line management. A technical training unit may be given sole and complete responsibility for instruction activities, especially where new recruits are concerned. A central induction programme may be installed without reference to future bosses; a management development manager may work directly with top management. But normally, an HRD department established with no more than a generalised responsibility to determine the ongoing learning needs in a geographical or functional area of the business, and to see these are met as well as possible, does not take over sole and unique responsibility for the function. In these circumstances, which are usual in most medium-sized and large organisations with dedicated and formalised learning units, the overall responsibility remains shared with line management.

It is simply not possible for job descriptions to divide and prescribe detailed task responsibilities on a permanent basis. What is needed instead is a mutual appreciation of roles, or more precisely, role expectations – that is, who is expected to carry the prime responsibility, and indeed to make the first moves, for and in specific areas of the function. (We shall look much more closely at the definition of roles later in this chapter.) What this means is that, over time, following some initial structuring of roles, and as a result of an ongoing interplay between the line and the 'professionals', a working relationship between the two evolves. The positioning within the organisation chart of the dedicated unit or units, person or persons, team or teams, is important, but it must also be reviewed regularly. This positioning can promote or hinder the evolutionary process that is so important for operational results.

POSITIONING AND DEFINING DEDICATED UNITS
Arranging the structure

As we have already noted, the need to structure the HRD function 'appropriately' within the organisation is easy to prescribe and difficult to describe. There is no one correct way of 'positioning' the department within organisations that vary in such respects as employee numbers, employee types, geographical sites, organisation charts, historical tradition and culture, and management style.

In a very large number of small organisations, and a minute proportion of large ones, the function is not itself detailed at all. Responsibility is held to rest with line supervision and management, and corporate decisions are taken by the owner, managing director or whoever else is the senior executive. In the 1990s some organisations 'outsourced' provision of HRD, leaving small 'client' teams to purchase HRD expertise. Others came up with a frequently half-hearted alternative, setting up an internal HRD function as a business unit responsible for earning its practitioners' salaries while competing with external providers – not always a very successful compromise. In organisations that number more than 100 but fewer than 250 employees, it is often the case that a Human Resource function (or department or unit) exists, and the HR function is taken to cover that of HRD. In many organisations like this, the HR manager is unlikely to be supported by substantial resources, and he or she will not be able to spend a large proportion of working hours on these matters. Typically, the department will arrange for external training activity (eg vocational courses at local colleges) to be taken up. Some small companies meet their needs and obtain much valued resources by joining group training schemes or consortia, which plan and manage learning and training for specific categories of staff, or use an external HRD consultant/adviser on a permanent contract.

But the majority of middle- to large-sized organisations, both public and private, do now formally describe and place the function in their charts. Role designations vary considerably, as can be seen from the following list of existing titles (which is by no means exhaustive):

- Personnel director
- Personnel controller
- Human resources director

- Human resources controller
- Human resource development manager
- Personnel development manager
- Personnel operations manager
- Group training director
- Group training manager
- Group training officer
- Group employee development manager
- Company training manager
- Company training and development manager
- Training manager
- Learning and development manager.

Some of these positions might be 'part-time' posts in specific organisations, or perhaps held in conjunction with other positions (eg the company secretary may also handle the management development role; a regional sales manager may also be the sales training manager).

The essential need for a suitable infrastructure is not met simply by choosing titles for those carrying responsibilities. The function must attempt to 'fit' all those strategic, political and cultural issues already discussed. Above all, it must be integrated with the overall HR management function and, equally importantly, with other operating functions. Here are a few examples of this sort of integration:

Example A is a smallish company that operates on only one site, apart from a small field salesforce, and it does not itself run training events of any kind. Its basic approach to learning is a mixture of 'sitting by Nellie' and 'competences' systems. Learning and training needs have always been satisfied by sending young entrants on part-time courses at the local college or (in the case of supervisors and managers) to selected short external courses run by various providers such as the local university. The function is not itself to be seen in the formal company organisation chart: it is in fact carried out by the HR department, headed by an HR manager

Induction courses are run about once every two months by either of the two HR officers, who draw on others (eg the safety officer) to handle individual sessions. The administration manager keeps information on external courses, makes all bookings and arranges for the fees to be paid and also records course attendances on personal files. He issues blank appraisal report forms (covering only management grades) and reports incorporate salary recommendations, but not training needs. Line management and supervision decide who attends what courses and when.

This is an authoritarian, tight-knit organisation run by management who believe in helping young people to acquire formal qualifications but who have no current belief in the need to plan learning on a continuing basis and do not aspire to any sophisticated employee development plans.

Example B is somewhat larger than A in number of employees, although it also operates from a single site and it does have a specialist training centre run by an HRD manager. That unit is responsible directly to the MD, who is an enthusiastic supporter of youth and management training but believes the company should manage these issues internally, to ensure learning is geared to the actual workplace. The training centre comprises a youth training workshop (covering engineering and administrative skills) and a residential building in which management courses are run. Induction courses are also held in the training centre.

In this example, learning and training serves the organisation and has been 'designed', but it is becoming more evolutionary and less prescriptive. In recent years the MD has insisted that his HRD manager develops (mainly by buying in appropriate hardware and software) a range of self-study facilities, with the result that the training centre is now called a 'learning resources centre'. Employees can apply to attend and have access to audiovisual and computer-based programmes. Now that the majority of staff have Internet access, a range of online learning programmes is being developed in conjunction with the local university and there are plans to develop an organisation-specific management NVQ.

Example C is a small provincial building society, which has 35 branch offices all within about 40 miles of the company's head office. The company is diversifying into a wide range of new customer services; these developments are led by a marketing department, staffed by so-called marketing development managers. Branch offices are closed to the public until 11 am each Tuesday. This time is 'operational training time', and is used both to train people in new procedures and to discuss problems with office staff. Branch office managers lead the Tuesday morning training sessions, but their formal content is agreed in advance with the relevant development manager, who often attends and indeed sometimes operates as an instructor.

This is clearly a 'problem-centred' system. The HR director, the company HR manager and a management development officer all operate from head office. They handle all other employee development activities, including central induction, further education regulations, liaison with outside training providers, attendance at management courses and conferences, management trainee programmes and 'one-off' programmes created for managers before or on promotion. Line directors have a major role to play in the management development system, maintaining succession plans and mounting periodic interviews with all who are on promotion lists.

Example D is a supermarket chain, with many branches and an annual intake of around 350 retail management trainees, whose recruitment is a major annual operation and whose later development has justified the emergence of a large central training unit. This unit reports to a member of the board known as the human resource director; a number of managers are responsible to her, including a career development controller and several training officers.

Apart from engaging in the annual recruitment 'milkround' and running specific management courses and conferences, the main role of the central training department has been to manage the management training system and its outputs. This involves endless discussions – with trainees and with regional and district HR office staff – about the objectives and methods in individual programmes. The system is moving towards becoming a competences system. The department has detailed some 40 'areas of competence' (eg stock control, running wines and spirits, opening new stores) that must be mastered by a trainee before an initial management appointment; specific plans are worked out for each individual, the vast mass of actual learning being completed in real-life shop circumstances. The final say on what is included in a personal plan rests with the central career development controller; but, in practice, decisions are invariably jointly taken, regional HR officers handling the liaison with supermarket management (who themselves take on the day-to-day training and instructor roles).

Example E is a large company with several thousand employees (including several hundred managers) and operations involving a head office, two manufacturing sites and a regionally organised national salesforce. The company has a long history of learning and training – applied to all departments and all levels of employee. Full-time training managers exist in each functional department (technical department has one in each factory). Company and departmental learning plans are created every six months.

In this company, a matrix arrangement ensures that responsibilities are often shared, but one person will always carry prime responsibility for training within each site or department, or for training applied to a specific category, or for a given training task.

Example F is a medium-sized company that during the past five years has doubled its turnover, trebled its profit and reduced by 40 per cent the number of employees on its payroll. The reduction in employees is perhaps more apparent than real: an outsourcing policy has led it to negotiate the transfer of some of its staff to outside companies who have been given rolling three-year contracts to supply services, and again to establish others as self-employed specialists whose fee earnings are underwritten provided they spend a third of their time working for their former employer. In this way, market research, product research, advertising, selling, distribution, engineering maintenance, catering, public relations, advice on quality and even the implementation of learning and training have been 'outsourced', as discussed above. The policy owes its origin to the 'flexible firm' model put forward during the 1980s following research by the then Institute of Manpower Studies: workers are organised as 'core' (full-time employees), 'peripheral' (part-time, self-employed individuals) and 'external' (employed by contractors and agencies, but working full- or part-time within the company). Forward strategy gives a high value to maintaining control over peripheral and external workers via ongoing learning and training. As part of their agreements, outside companies and specialists are committed to spending the equivalent of at least two days per month in training activity prescribed by the main company. The traditional hierarchical organisation chart is inappropriate, being replaced by a 'doughnut' (see Figure 6.1).

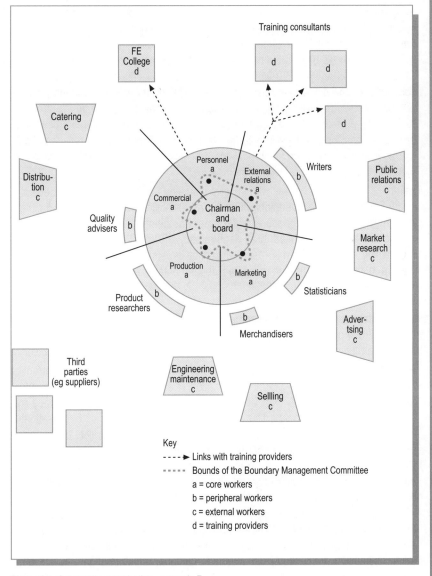

Figure 6.1 *Outsourcing organisation – example F*

External learning and training facilities are used: three firms of outside consultants are employed and the local college provides formal courses. There are no formally designated learning/training staff: training of core staff is the responsibility of line management, whose departmental budgets include training budgets. The training of peripheral and external staff is concerned mainly with (a) identifying needs, (b) deciding priorities and (c) briefing/negotiating methods with the training providers. Training costs in these areas are centrally paid for from the HR budget.

The Managing Director chairs a 'boundary management' committee, meeting every two months to review non-core operational (which in practice means mainly briefing or training) needs. The committee comprises a senior manager from each main department, including those responsible for managing links with peripheral and external groups, plus the HR manager. The secretary of this committee is the external relations manager. Once needs and priorities are determined and budgeted funds are confirmed, the external relations manager and the HR manager jointly establish the detail of what is required, together with how/by whom it should be carried out, plus any funding limits. The dialogue with outside providers is usually conducted by the external relations manager, although the HR department handles college course administration requirements. Over the past three years the practice has grown of monthly 'briefing meetings' for non-core staff held on company premises and organised and run by the training consultants, with inputs from line management. A consequence has been the growth of similar internal meetings mounted and run by line managers themselves.

It can be seen that 'outsourcing', although removing names from the payroll, does not necessarily reduce learning or training activity. Indeed, it arguably increases the need for regular, period learning to be managed. In this example, the importance attached to managing outsourcing, plus the decision not to delegate learning and training roles to full-time trainers employed as core staff, has led to increased attention to training by line management, even if the words 'learning' or 'training' are not used.

Example G is at the cutting edge of organisational structures. It reflects the currently developing concept of the 'virtual organisation' – a term borrowed from computer terminology, where it is defined as 'not physically existing as such, but made by software to appear to do so'. This is not easy to translate into an organisational model, but might typically describe an operational set-up that is project-based, new projects appearing frequently and project teams endlessly re-forming to tackle them. Each change brings with it new roles, new relationships and (most importantly) new and unique information needs. These information needs are satisfied by access to a networked intranet – which, married to simulation methods, provides new knowledge and suggests how it might be used. It even offers a forward view of what the results of adopting the information will be. In our example, project teams are formed and re-formed by the project leaders, who also operate as team members but carry the prime responsibility for resolving detailed day-to-day problems in the ongoing management of each project; team members access the databases using their own computers and telephones. Project work moves forward as members, operating in 'chains' or networks, feed their personal findings to colleagues via unique processes, which are regularly reviewed at team meetings. HRD interventions are frequent and commonplace but the word 'training' is rarely used, as the learning system is effectively integrated with the project work. Everyone nevertheless has a 'training function' and a contribution to make to the corporate learning system, even if in most cases they are serving temporary ends. Two key roles exist, however – that of the IT specialists who maintain and develop the information system, and that of the process consultant/s whose job is to understand and help project leaders and team members to understand their own process reality. There is no specific HRD practitioner. HR officers handle induction training as part of the induction process, and provide the process review expertise.

Discussion question: How do you think HRD is best 'embedded' in a virtual environment?

You will probably appreciate from your own experience at work, college or university that advanced information technology is a major influence promoting new 'knowledge management' systems. As well as being likely to promote flatter and more flexible organisations, it also tends to merge learning with work and to make the individual the master of his or her unique learning process. An article in the *Independent on Sunday* (6 March 1994) discussed work by the well-known organisational commentator Tom Peters. This drew a picture of an environment in which 'independent contractors such as freelance journalists, software programmers and gardeners wake up knowing that before sunset they must (i) prove themselves again with their clients and (ii) learn a new wrinkle to improve their odds of survival'. The article then went on to suggest that everyone in salaried employment might need to achieve this same attitude. Charles Handy, the British management guru, was suggesting at the same time (*The Empty Raincoat* 1994) that the changing models of organisations might be influenced positively by the less structured non-profit organisations. It is interesting to speculate, a decade later, how far this picture has developed. The answer is probably not sufficiently to herald a new 'learning age'! The key point for HRD specialists is that in such 'free form' organisations the training function effectively becomes a learning function and it is organised as part of work processes, not as an extra.

These seven examples underline the wide variety of possible ways of organising employee development activity in organisations. There is no one model that can be suggested as appropriate for any given size of unit, category of work or type of worker: each organisation must develop its own, aiming to 'fit' dedicated training and development units into its operational activities in line with its policy, its purpose, its environmental constraints and opportunities and the imagination of its personnel and training staff. The nature of this 'fit' is an important determinant in the selection of the most appropriate HRD approach and methodology.

DEFINING DEDICATED HRD ROLES

For the previous edition of this book, we used the Employment National Training Organisation's (ENTO's) national standards to set out a 'standardised' version of the work of the dedicated HRD specialist. The ENTO has since made revisions to its standards, incorporating further roles that apply mainly to full-time FE teaching staff, which makes them less useful for our purposes. The earlier version, though, remains a useful summary of what dedicated HRD functions might involve. It follows the 'training process' system (to be examined in more detail in Chapter 12 when we look at organisational systems and environments), which in essence follows the approach of 'plan-organise-do-review' advocated by the ITBs in the 1960s and 1970s, when it was known as 'systematic training'.

A single statement of purpose was first developed, using 'functional analysis' (see page 155): 'To develop human potential to assist organisations and individuals to achieve their objectives.' This was broken down into functional areas and sub-areas, then into units and elements of competence – the latter being described in terms of what people in relevant positions are expected to be able to do at the workplace. The eventual result was a detailed 'mountain' of statements comprising:

- one statement of purpose
- five areas of competence
- 14 sub-areas of competence
- 56 units of competence, including 11 'management' and six 'personnel management' units
- over 100 elements of competence, each carrying up to eight performance criteria, plus range statements and 'evidence required' lists.

The core framework describing these functions is reproduced here as Figure 6.2.

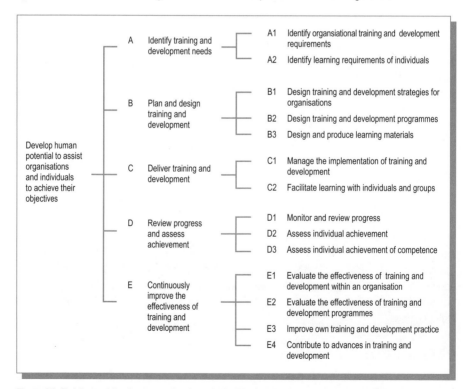

Figure 6.2 *Training and development national standards: The main functional areas and sub-areas*

Operational indicators

Practitioners must be able to:

1. Co-operate with learning and development stakeholders in learning and development policy, strategy and plans, in order to integrate learning and development activity with wider personnel and business policy.
2. Advise on how to achieve a well-managed, appropriately staffed and value-adding learning and development function.
3. Contribute to learning and development that will aid the processes of recruitment and performance management.
4. Contribute to learning and development that will help the organisation retain the people it needs for the future.
5. Contribute to learning and development that will expand the organisation's overall capacity and competence, and will help to introduce and embed organisational change.
6. Promote learning that will stimulate strategic awareness, and will develop and help to disseminate organisationally valuable knowledge.
7. Contribute to the design and provision of effective learning processes and activity, using new technology as appropriate.
8. Evaluate learning outcomes, and help to assess the returns on the organisation's past and planned investment in learning and development.
9. Identify and promote learning and development processes and practices that meet or exceed legal, mandatory and ethical requirements.
10. Continuously develop their own expertise, professionalism and credibility in the learning and development field.

Knowledge indicators

Practitioners must understand and be able to explain:

1 The integration of learning and development activity and organisational needs, with special reference to:
1. The organisation's business environment and internal context.
2. The goals of the stakeholders in learning and development, and the building and sustaining of partnerships that will produce and communicate effective learning and development processes and initiatives.
3. The formulation of the organisation's learning and development goals and strategy, and their implementation at different organisational levels.

2 The provision of a value-adding learning and development function
1. How the learning and development process adds value for the organisation and the individual.
2. The organisation, management and evaluation of the learning and development function and roles.
3. The delivery of organisationally focused projects to time, cost and quality.
4. Aids and barriers to effective performance as a learning and development consultant.

3 Learning and development's contribution to the recruitment and performance management processes
1. Induction, basic skills training and continuous improvement that will motivate learners, achieve competent performance, and build commitment to organisational goals and values.

4 Learning and development's contribution to employee retention
1. Career and management development processes that help identify, develop and use people's potential and adaptability and aid their continued employability.

5 Learning and development's contribution to building organisational capacity and facilitating change
1. The skills and attitudes needed to work effectively in changed/changing organisational roles, structures and working environments, and how they can be developed.
2. Learning and development strategies for organisational culture change.

6 The stimulation of strategic awareness and the development of knowledge
1. Learning and development initiatives and processes to stimulate strategic awareness, creativity and innovation.
2. Learning strategies and processes to develop, share and disseminate knowledge that is valuable to the organisation.

7 The design and delivery of learning and development processes and activities
1. The planning, design and delivery of learning processes and activity that will add value for the organisation and for individuals.
2. The appropriate application of new technology to training and learning.

8 The evaluation and assessment of learning and development outcomes and investment
1. Methods and models for:
   - evaluating the outcomes of learning and development processes and activity
   - evaluating the organisation's past learning and development investment.
2. The identification and assessment of learning and development processes and activity that will benefit the organisation in the short- and longer-term future.

9 The role and tasks of the ethical practitioner
1. The impact on, and implications of, diversity of people, style, and employment contracts for Learning and Development policies and practice and organisational learning strategies.
2. The information and actions needed to identify and achieve legally compliant and ethical Learning and Development practices and processes.

10 The importance of continuing professional self-development
1. Methods and processes of continuing personal and professional development, including coaching, counselling and mentoring.
2. Databases and information sources that provide up-to-date information about current and emergent theory, practice and issues in the field.

Figure 6.3 *CIPD professional standards: learning and development*

A different and equally complex collection of HRD roles exists in the CIPD's 'professional standards' (see Figure 6.3). The most usual route into CIPD membership, as you may be aware, involves examinations that include HRD topics. Two of these (Learning and Development, and Managing the Training [sic] and Development Function) overlap and use varied language. Copies of all the CIPD professional standards are available from their website www.cipd.co.uk. They comprise lists of what the job-holder 'must be able to do', and 'must understand and be able to explain' – the operational and knowledge indicators. We reproduce the operational and knowledge indicators here.

The complexities of these two approaches from ENTO and CIPD make it hard to compare and contrast them. But if we look carefully we can see a substantial, even dramatic, variation in approach. The ENTO functionally analysed model is essentially mechanistic, assuming a static process and job-holders who take and implement decisions on their own behalf. The CIPD version actively promotes change, linking the HRD function to the organisation's plans and objectives, and building in the continuing development of the function itself and the self-development of the specialists within it. CIPD's emphasis on knowledge indicators recognises that the HRD specialist must collaborate with stakeholders in advising and explaining before determining activities. This implies that the function must operate via the efforts of line managers. A performance indicator to which we will return refers to the need to 'be able to [promote] practices that meet or exceed ethical requirements'. The picture that emerges of the HRD function suggests collaboration and leadership, added value and creativity.

Decisions on these issues should be important when a new HRD unit is established or an existing one reviewed. Will it have defined guidelines and set operational goals, or will it have its own vision and purpose? If so, will that vision be sanctioned by top management and appear in strategic documents? These are complex questions, but it is clear that defining the unit's roles must be done uniquely with regard to organisational culture and norms.

Sadly, recent (2004) research suggests that few HRD units have clearly defined roles, and the norm remains mechanistic. Authority is generally top down and if there is a HRD specialist that individual will report to the Head of HR. Major changes require external approval, and in practice despite its name change, many units will still deal with permanent 'training' arrangements such as induction, appraisal and the like. There are honourable exceptions, of which you may be aware or may be lucky enough to work in, but we would suggest that in this era of change, especially change of emphasis from 'training' to 'learning', the case for reviewing purpose and roles is a strong one. Obtaining a set of the ENTO and CIPD standards and reviewing your own organisation against them would be a mammoth task, but would achieve significant understanding of what is in place and what is missing.

POLITICAL AND ETHICAL ROLES

The ENTO national standards make one point that seems surprising, to say the least. 'Comply with professional and ethical requirements' is mentioned as a 'core' unit only at the top level, and it is not even given optional status elsewhere. The issue here is an important one, especially in view of the CIPD's stress on ethical requirements for members at all levels 'to be able to [promote] practices that meet or exceed ethical requirements' (see CIPD's website for details).

If we temporarily translate the term 'professional' into 'political', we can reasonably argue that all HRD management roles must be exercised with both political and ethical judgement, and that a person who has neither is unlikely to be viewed as competent by superiors or colleagues. Our multinational organisation case study showed how important the links are between line management and any specialist HRD function. Put simply, the 'health' of those links goes a long way to determining the strength of the function, conditioning in turn its structure and position. Two important criteria in establishing the priorities of learning or training interventions are (a) whether they appear likely to be successful, and (b) whether they will actually yield their 'promised' returns – which, because interventions always involve discussions on plans, effectively means whether line management, and especially the key decision makers, trust and know they can trust what the specialist suggests.

One way towards this is to know about and be able to discuss the cost/benefits of 'unplanned learning' against those of planned learning, not least with accountants and senior management. It is also critical to 'market' HRD, which of course means that specialists must have a clear understanding of business as a whole, and be up to date on all organisation matters. Most important of all, they must become 'involved' in all mainstream activities: those who confine themselves to their own units are unlikely to exert the necessary degree of influence, however good the interventions they might plan.

Ethical standards are, of course, as important as technical competence, and in real life cannot properly be left out from role definition. In the early twenty-first century, ethics in organisations have become prominent – several well-publicised organisational scandals have emphasised the lack of ethical as well as financial accountability in large companies. Of course, personal standards and behaviour of managers can greatly affect credibility both among top management and the shop floor. In the case of HRD specialists, learners are unlikely to seek advice or guidance from an unsympathetic trainer, or explore blockages with a trainer who seems self-satisfied, biased or critical of others' failings. What this all means is that training is about relationships as well as decisions, about example as well as comparison. Moral dilemmas can and do arise, of course, in the application of any management role (see Marchington and Wilkinson 2002). Realistically, loyalty to one's organisation is a prime reason for accepting its salary, and most HRD practitioners would be too pragmatic to attempt to 'reform' their organisations by campaigning for personal causes. Sometimes, however, the cognitive dissonance (p 74) felt by those in organisations with suspect ethical standards might be too much to contend with and the out-of-step individual has no choice but to leave. This is rare (at least, we hope it is) but it is not unusual for HRD specialists to encounter some ethical dilemmas.

Institutional sexism, racism and bullying of those who are 'different' unfortunately still exists, if only covertly in some organisations. In the learning field, as elsewhere, there will be examples of organisations not practising what they preach. There are examples of people with disabilities of from minority ethnic groups being sidelined with no training on offer, or part-time staff, usually women, being left out of training events because they cannot organise child or dependant care. In an increasingly litigious environment, claims of unfair discrimination can be pursued and, very occasionally, complainants win large amounts of compensation. More usually, their claims fail and they may be branded as trouble-makers by potential new employers – so no-one really succeeds.

The CIPD has, of course, a code of professional conduct (available from CIPD website), and we would strongly suggest that it is much better to challenge unfair or bad practice from a position of strength, especially from the 'moral high ground'. It is not, for example, easy to complain about lack of development opportunities for women if, as a woman manager, you have not tried to develop your own subordinates. The message of treating others as we ourselves would want to be treated may appear simplistic, but it does work. Consequently it forms the basis of many organisations' equity and diversity policies. We will look further at practising what we preach, or modelling appropriate management behaviours, when we look at management and leadership development.

> Discussion question: How can HRD practitioners alert their organisations in 'ethical' ways to their lack of commitment to training?

DEDICATED UNITS OR FUNCTIONAL ROLES?

The national standards assume a coherent, autonomous, 'watertight' function. Where the dedicated HRD unit serves a wider operational purpose, the function will always be bigger than the unit, and it is desirable that the overall organisational design provides for this. Especially important is to ensure that all line management who head major mainstream departments appreciate and accept their own HRD roles, and indeed see them as a branch of their ongoing responsibility for improving performance; one way of achieving this is the establishment of standing committees on HRD, which typically are chaired and attended by non-specialists while being serviced by professionals. The quality of the interplay between the dedicated HRD staff and their line colleagues is the central influence in determining whether the overall function is managed competently or not, a result that no formal definition of specialist roles can independently guarantee.

> **This chapter has focused on the need for HRD specialists to be aware of the complex nature of organisational cultures, structures and operating norms in which their function exists, in order to align HR practices with business objectives. If you were appointed as HRD manager with a small specialist team in an organisation that had never had a dedicated function before, what sort of Strengths, Weaknesses, Opportunities and Threats (SWOT) analysis would you consider to assist you? How might you 'sell' your services to busy managers who might see your function simply as an overhead?**
>
> The next three chapters will examine some of the key ways in which HRD practitioners can 'add value' to the business; analysing organisational and individual learning and training needs and meeting those needs with appropriate learning and training strategies that are professionally evaluated.

Learning and Training Needs for the Organisation: Strategies and Methods

In Chapter 7, we will consider:

- **Tools and strategies for reviewing organisational learning;**

- **Reasons for learning needs reviews that influence whole organisations;**

- **Different types of organisational review and the reasons for them;**

- **The requirement for awareness of learning needs at different organisational levels;**

- **External influences on organisations' learning needs, such as legal and statutory requirements that may result in a need for review of organisational learning;**

- **The need for appropriate diagnostic skills by the HRD specialist to understand the implications of organisational change on learning.**

Members of the Training Institute, ITOL, recently debated a news item in *Personnel Today*, which suggested that six out of ten HR and financial directors have little or no idea what return they get on their company's investment in training. Over a third of the respondents, directors at 40 of the UK's largest companies with an average training spend of £1.5m per year, claimed that they saw business benefits arising from their investment. Further questioning, however, revealed that many were basing their views on an inherent belief that training produced business benefit. Few had implemented mechanisms to produce real evidence of training benefit, with most citing evaluation forms as their only measure (source: http://www.itol.co.uk/cgi-local/dcforum/dcboard.cgi).

So where are organisations going wrong, in our view?

- HRD is not an end in itself. It should be an essential element of the strategic process by which an organisation achieves its objectives.

- In order to fulfil its strategic role, HRD should be based on an insightful analysis of the organisation's present and future needs.

- Providing learning and development that is not directed at the most important needs can be counterproductive and can tarnish the HRD function's own image. It is demoralising for employees to be sent on unnecessary training courses while being unable to obtain help in acquiring the skills they need for the job, particularly when lack of these skills has a wide organisational impact. Providing training that does not

Note: At appropriate points in the chapter, we have retained the term 'Training Needs Analysis' (TNA), as this is a technical term widely used by HRD practitioners. However, strictly speaking, a more accurate term should perhaps be 'Learning Needs Analysis' to discover needs for learning and development that can be met by specific HRD interventions.

work costs money and wastes time that could more profitably be channelled elsewhere.

■ Identifying these needs and illustrating the possible consequences of failing to meet them is a persuasive way of gaining support and resources from top management.

■ Failure to develop an appropriately trained workforce is likely to cause problems such as lack of efficiency, costly complaints and poor image, which can affect the whole organisation.

■ HRD is an important facilitator in organisation change – in a way, all learning is about change and is therefore future oriented, another factor which practitioners can use to underline its importance.

THE LEVELS OF TRAINING NEEDS

In Scotland in August 2003, the Scottish Executive announced a widespread training needs analysis of all NHS staff in the area of public involvement, with the aim of providing a more patient-focused service which recognises patient diversity (source: http://www.rcgp-scotland.org.uk/news/html/view_news.asp?N). This case illustrates that training needs may occur at a number of levels:

■ at the organisational level – for example, to ensure a supply of individuals with the skills necessary for promotion and transfer, and a culture which would enable NHS staff to see the bigger picture

■ at the occupational level – for example, developing nurses as managers as well as carers

■ at the individual level – for example, remedying skill gaps identified during individual appraisal sessions and recognising skills already possessed.

Of course, it is important to realise from the outset that the needs at the different levels can sometimes conflict. School-leavers need training to stand them in good stead for future promotion or job-seeking elsewhere. The short-term organisational need, however, may be very narrow and specific. If there are insufficient promotion prospects or opportunities for wider experience, the long-term development of the employee may be sacrificed to the specific requirements of business objectives. Although management may be aware of the need for new experience and fresh challenges, it is not always possible to provide them at the right moment, particularly in times of recession or fierce competition when budgets are reduced. Enthusiastic staff may become frustrated, especially if they do not know why they are being, as they see it, held back from progressing. The current trend towards flatter organisational structures (where the tiers of the hierarchy are reduced and more staff require a broader base of skills, reward often being based on output and value-added contribution rather than status) should encourage learning contracts and help towards providing wider experience, as may the use of project teams. We have looked in Chapters 1 and 2 at how NVQ programmes, both external and in-company, can offer a framework for career progression, providing recognised and 'portable' qualifications for the individual and, possibly, at the same time meeting organisational needs.

In this chapter we are concerned with reviewing the organisation's needs within the HRD sphere. These requirements may be expressed in terms of systems, procedures, priorities and the like, as well as explicit statements of 'training need', which may themselves be linked with specific sites or departments or operations, but not with individual employees. (We shall deal with the individual level in Chapter 8.) Before attempting an organisational review of needs, it would obviously be necessary to be familiar with the overall objectives and goals of the organisation, described in the previous chapter, as this would influence the depth of enquiry in specific areas, and highlight 'priority problems'.

> Discussion question: What are the main strategic HRD issues facing 'leaner', flatter and more competitive organisations?

We referred earlier in Chapters 1 and 2, to the national 'Investors in People' award, which is based on a defined set of national standards governing what might be termed an organisation's internal training and development systems. The standards are set in terms of outcomes, not processes: they do not, for example, assume that dedicated training staff must exist, nor that specific documents should be created. They do, however, require:

- a written but flexible plan of business goals and targets
- recorded learning and development needs
- clear training plans to meet those needs
- ongoing evaluation of learning and development activity.

An organisation needs to meet these basic standards before it can monitor the extent to which its current training and development activity is adequate for good operational health. Different organisations have carried out the task of claiming (or more accurately ensuring they can justify claiming) the IiP award in different ways. For example, Kingston College set up a small working party comprising the principal, the quality assurance manager, the head of personnel, the head of adult education and the head of staff development; this group reviewed what they already had, and proposed developments that were carried into effect before the claim was made (Elms 1998). At Sinai Warren Holiday Village, where the training and development system was less firmly established, a consultant was appointed to oversee the early stages of the project, and to identify key innovative developments. Ten members of staff, including chefs, housekeepers and entertainers, then volunteered to form a working group to keep records of each department's progress towards the establishment of these developments (Merrick 1998).

These cases demonstrate that any decision to claim, or move towards claiming, the IiP award will require an organisation-wide review of the existing HRD system, They also provide the opportunity to develop it further as a worthwhile exercise in its own right. The IiP exercise nevertheless remains a one-off project. Regular, periodic, operational reviews are additionally needed (and ideally will be demonstrated as 'standard' activities within the IiP claim) to ensure that the system itself continues to develop, and – most importantly – that the prime link between HRD activities and organisation results is being maintained.

> Discussion question: As a provider of HRD, your local university has asked how your organisation's needs in this area are expected to change and develop over the next five years. You have been asked to construct an appropriate response. How would you set about establishing the facts and drafting a suitable reply?

TYPES OF ORGANISATIONAL REVIEW

There are many different 'organisational learning systems', as we will see in Chapter 12, and a variety of approaches towards HRD interventions. This diversity can present us with difficulties in dealing with the operational practicalities. We do not intend to be prescriptive or uncritical. We believe that each of the methodologies we describe is valuable in the right circumstances. We do not suggest that any one of them is intrinsically 'better'. On the contrary, a combination of several methods is often more useful.

We outline below four different (although not necessarily mutually exclusive) types of organisation review activity. Of course, any review of organisational training needs is likely to highlight problems with no training solution. In a production process the cause may be faulty material or inadequate or outdated machinery; in managerial spheres problems may be caused by a wide range of factors such as fluctuations in rates of exchange or government policy. It may be that recruitment and selection procedures are not bringing in the right people in the first place. The purpose of the review is to identify the situations where learning and development, as opposed to other types of management intervention, could make an important contribution.

'Global' review

This starts with an examination of the organisation's short-term and long-term objectives. After that, each job category is analysed, its overall purpose is reviewed in the light of organisation objectives, and the necessary knowledge and skills are identified. Each employee is then assessed against the appropriate specification, and training and development provided where a shortfall is identified. In its extreme form this is a very time-consuming exercise, and assumes a certain degree of organisational stability. Most contemporary organisations exist in rapidly changing markets where speedy adjustment is required and they may require other techniques. This approach can, however, be used differentially, that is, applied in a very detailed way in some specific departments where there may be justification.

An approach like this, based on the accumulated analyses of jobs within the organisation, may seem deceptively straightforward, even if time-consuming. In some of the more recently developed types of organisational structure, such as the 'virtual organisation' or the 'outsourcing organisation', the first stage would be to answer such questions as 'who is an employee?' and 'where does the boundary of the organisation begin and end?' In a fiercely competitive environment, it may be necessary for an organisation (which may be only one link in a chain) to provide some types of learning intervention for its clients or customers, or even its suppliers.

In a 'Matrix Organisation', how do individual needs apply to the teamwork required? An analytical global approach assumes that assessing the skills of individuals and adding them up tells us how good an organisation will be at achieving its goals. For a deeper discussion of this see Hirsh and Reilly (1998), who question this assumption and suggest that organisations are more than the sum of their individuals. They ask how, 'even if you measure skills and add them up, you know whether the "quantity" of skill is enough for your future needs?' We suggest that although a mechanistic analytical approach can be extremely useful in some types of organisation, it possibly needs to be supplemented and supported by other methods. It may also need to be speeded up significantly, especially in organisations operating in fast-moving environments.

Competence and performance management approaches

A well-known contract catering group announced a few years ago that they had taken a major step from old-style 'systematic' training to a 'performance management' approach. They 'cascaded' the whole philosophy of training throughout the organisation, bringing the improvement of standards down to 'unit level'. Managers were required to draw up job descriptions for every member of staff, specifying competences against which performance was to be reviewed. Line managers accepted that training was an integral part of their management role, and they were expected to possess or acquire the necessary skills. They then had to put together a systematic training programme for new staff, which provided a framework that could be related to NVQs.

This is a form of global review using competence assessment and key areas as a means of aligning training and development to the achievement of organisation objectives. In many organisations, competency studies have almost become synonymous with training needs analysis. The current QCA approach requires a specification of competences and standards that could provide a ready-made basis for a review of this type. It must be borne in mind that the analyses made by the NTOs and latterly SSCs require adaptation and further detail to be useful for individual organisations. If responsibility for preparing the competency standards is 'cascaded' down the hierarchy in this way, HRD becomes an integral part of the managerial responsibility. It also becomes compatible with the concept of Total Quality Management, and linked with continuous development of staff. The role of the HRD specialist then becomes one of process consultant providing expert skills and advice.

Although it is still subject to the limitations of the global review, this type of approach can appear attractive in that it is firmly related to outcomes and provides a potential basis for performance-related pay. An increasing number of companies are using competences as a way of determining pay levels, and the trend is continuing despite criticisms of performance-related pay. This provides a good example of coherent and integrated HRM procedures, always the aim for the HR function. Such schemes may involve much detail, and computerised systems can be a great advantage. Several specialist consultant organisations have prepared computer software that includes templates providing a structure and headings for NVQ-type analyses and assessments, to assist large or global organisations to standardise their procedures. As the incidence of organisation-based NVQ programmes, with their emphasis on workplace assessment, increases, this may become a common approach. The IiP standard stipulates that targets and standards should be linked, where appropriate, to the achievement of NVQs, although for a variety of good reasons (not least of which is cost), not all organisations using this method of analysis have embarked on NVQ programmes.

> Discussion question: Has your organisation, or one with which you are familiar, considered competence programmes linked to NVQ/SVQ? As an HRD manager in an organisation that has not considered NVQs, how might you go about introducing or developing such an approach?

Critical incident or 'priority problem' analysis

A retailing company suffered bad publicity owing to press and TV coverage of unfortunate incidents in some of its branches. In a number of cases the company's employees were alleged to have had a very poor attitude towards customers' requests for after-sales service. Unfortunately this problem is not uncommon in the competitive environment for selling electronic equipment, for example. The chairman called for an urgent investigation. The subsequent report accepted the criticism but showed that in almost every case the employees were competent in selling. However, because of work pressure in the branches and management emphasis on high sales targets, insufficient attention had been paid to the importance of after-sales service.

The report insisted that this weakness must, as a matter of priority, be addressed both by management directives and training, and the HRD manager was instructed to take immediate action. She worked with line management in reviewing and amending the job specifications of both managers and staff, and then provided training for those employees whose assessment showed they required it.

In this model the objective is not to produce a comprehensive list of every possible HRD need but to identify and prioritise the main problems of the organisation that appear to have a learning solution. Notice in the case above is that it was not only the sales staff who needed training to higher quality standards but also their managers. They needed an awareness of the concept of total quality management and the ability to design appropriate procedures. This is an example of the 'skittle' effect described on page 82, where, to achieve the desired result, it may be necessary to include other targets before tackling the one that appears to be the most obvious. Priority or problem areas therefore require careful examination to determine the real source of the difficulty, and whether the solution also necessitates learning interventions for levels of staff who did not at first appear to be involved. This approach is extremely important, as the main message must be to decide which areas are vital to the strategic objectives, or possibly even the survival, of the organisation, and to concentrate the main effort on them.

Critical incident analysis is a strategy that is likely to be suitable for small- to medium-sized enterprises (SMEs), particularly at an early stage in their development. A study by Warwick University's Centre for Corporate Strategy and Change (1991) suggested that in an SME, particularly in its early stages, when markets are evolving, goods or services are being refined and the customer base broadened, training needs unfold rapidly and an ad hoc approach is required in order to maintain current viability. Flexibility and adaptability are more important than systematic across-the-board analyses of training needs based on job descriptions and specifications. After five to seven years, when the organisation has become more complex, and the numbers of staff have increased, new problems can arise, indicating the need for a different approach. For instance, people have not had time to develop their skills and keep up to date, or they have continued to learn on the job as the complexity has increased and there are difficulties in training new inexperienced staff to replace them. The findings suggest that 'there may be a natural life cycle of training, which matches the intake and progression of employees', the precise nature of the cycle differing in different organisations.

Discussion question: The theme of change appears throughout this book. Identify the four or five major changes that you expect will affect your organisation, or one with which you are familiar, over the next two years. What might the HRD requirements be and how would you attempt to manage these?

Learner-centred analysis

We have suggested that these types of analysis require the intervention of an HRD specialist or consultant. Some readers may be members of an organisation-based action learning set with important company goals to achieve. If circumstances require it, your 'set adviser' might, if reluctantly, act at an appropriate time as a catalyst, but an important part of your 'set's functioning is to work out for yourselves how to determine what learning and development you need in order to achieve your objectives, and to take steps (possibly assisted by the 'set adviser') to acquire it. Your learning in the 'set' is essentially targeted directly at organisational needs, because it is encapsulated in the action itself. At the same time it is highly developmental and an embodiment of 'learning to learn'. It brings together the needs of the organisation and those of the individual. The whole process is an important part of your learning experience, and unless an intervening HRD specialist approached his or her task in a highly participative and democratic manner, the culture and norms gradually developed by your 'set' might cause you to resent the 'external' person probing into your training needs.

Similarly, in a 'task' culture (see Handy 1985), where knowledge and skill requirements might vary from one project group to another, the first, most important group task might be to determine its own learning needs in order to complete the project. Quality circles are likely to display the same characteristic. The uninvited intervention of an HRD manager might well be regarded as interference, unless he or she was asked for specific advice. The approach to identifying training needs and the manner in which the task is carried out will therefore be influenced by the organisational culture. A mechanistic form of global analysis is likely to be most suitable for a 'role culture' or 'training process', where the content of jobs can be specified in detail, and is likely to remain constant for long enough to make all the necessary analytical work worthwhile. The number of organisations in which this is possible is limited. Current trends, particularly those relating to NVQs, are analytical; but is there a contradiction here? The pace of change is accelerating and, in such a climate, will top managers not tend to assign the key problems of the company to project teams, whose responsibility it will be to determine their own needs and possibly those of others whose jobs impinge upon the task in hand? Perhaps the question we should be asking is, 'How can we develop people to develop themselves?' Training needs are never static: they unfold as situations develop, even more so in a changing environment. Although it is logical and necessary to produce an overall assessment as a basis for a company training plan targeted at organisational objectives and for boardroom justification of the budget, such a document rarely offers more than a snapshot in time. Most senior managers, of course, want immediate results rather than lengthy processes. So any review that can provide a snapshot would be welcome!

BEFORE STARTING A REVIEW

You might be the HRD specialist of a large national building society that has decided to instigate a formal training review to be carried out every three years. Imagine you have been asked to draft proposals for its content and process and to create an appropriate statement for discussion at a future top management meeting. What would your first considerations be? How would you set about your task? Would it be different from that of an owner manager of a building company who was at the same time undertaking a training review of all aspects of the business?

It would be a good idea if your first query concerned the purpose of the review! This would determine whether it would require an audit of current skills, and possibly an evaluation of existing training, or an investigation into current and/or future learning and training needs. It would also help to establish whether the review should be total or partial, as well as who might attend the top management meeting and the items on the agenda on which decisions need to be taken. Every review, of course, should relate to the strategic objectives of the organisation, but these are likely to be much wider than the all-important one of achieving profit targets. Most organisations also have objectives relating to public image (the public are usually customers!) and to compliance with the law (on matters such as health and safety and equal opportunities). Adapting to national and international developments, such as EU regulations, increasingly impacting on the UK, or coping with government economic policy may well be reasons for companies to consider their learning needs. A partial review may relate to one of these or a variety of other objectives. In an industrial relations audit the questions that would arise and the composition of the meeting would probably be different from that convened to discuss a learning and training needs review for Total Quality Management. This obvious example emphasises the fact that the first step must be to make sure of your objectives, because it is all too easy to waste time in irrelevant discussion and information-gathering.

REASONS FOR AN ORGANISATIONAL REVIEW

There may be apparent contradictions between analytical, problem-centred and learner-centred approaches, but there are circumstances, such as those we describe below, when a review might be necessary in any organisation, regardless of its culture.

Corporate planning and longer-term development needs

Organisations monitor trends in the demand for their goods or services and attempt to forecast possible threats and opportunities that would affect their survival or growth. These forecasts should take account of critical factors such as economic conditions, government policies (including possible legislation or entry into the European Monetary Union (see Welch 1998)), financial constraints, expected market changes, competitors' activities, technological developments, investment programmes, new products or services planned and personnel issues. A useful technique you may have used is that of SWOT analysis, which involves identifying organisational strengths and weaknesses (internal factors), and opportunities and threats (external factors).

Data from these sources is used to construct possible future operating scenarios, which top management evaluate, in deciding the organisation's future policies and strategies. Human resource planning should of course play an important part in these processes.

Human resource specialists can help to develop the scenarios and offer advice to top management when the strategies are being formulated, and later translate the staffing implications of the agreed strategies into operational plans. The organisation's expected staffing profile, expressed in numbers by occupational category and competences required, is then compared with the existing workforce and, after making adjustments for retirement and other expected staff losses, surpluses and shortages of staff are identified and succession plans are drawn up. This is the first step in developing a comprehensive human resource plan for the organisation which, by co-ordinating recruitment and training, retraining, career development and other personnel responsibilities, will help to ensure that appropriately trained and experienced staff are available when required. For a detailed discussion of human resource planning see Bramham (1994) and also Bennison and Carson (1984). The important issue for HRD specialists to consider is that all learning needs to be future oriented in order to be future proof!

Discussion question: What are the essentials of a succession planning system? Who should the key contributors be, and how should their work be linked?

The preparation of a HRD budget and plan

The organisation's HRD requirements may be reviewed annually in order to prepare budget and training plans for the following year. These result in a statement of intent, which shows how the specific HRD objectives required by the company's staffing plan will be met. The draft will specify what has to be achieved, how it will be done, whom it will affect, what benefits will accrue to whom, and what financial expenditure will be required. Of course, the criteria for the Investors in People standards include a written but flexible business plan in which the resources for HRD should be clearly indicated.

A major change in an organisation's activities

HRD plays a major organisational role in preparing people to be readier to accept change and, when necessary, in equipping the staff concerned with the expertise they need to do the new work expected of them.

Imagine you are employed by an airline that has just decided to buy a new type of aircraft, and consider the range of training that will be required. New skills and knowledge will be needed by some of the pilots, navigators, maintenance engineers, marketing and sales staff and, in varying degrees, by other employees. Even the cabin crew will need to become familiar with the plane's new features and change their safety routines to take account of this. The successful introduction of the new aircraft will partly depend on all the staff concerned being trained to undertake the new tasks required of them. The training implications must be identified if the changeover problems are to be minimised and the benefits gained at the earliest possible stage. As the learning specialist, you would rightly want to be involved from the very beginning. Policies, priorities, costs and schedules of training must be determined and co-ordinated at an organisational level and, eventually, detailed training programmes prepared. Working with and using data obtained from planning and senior line management, the HRD specialist examines in turn the list of activities to be undertaken by each function, how each function will interact with other parts of the airline (the boundaries of the subsystems) and with the external environment. It is then possible to clarify the specific and general training that will be needed and prepare a schedule of priorities, sequences of training programmes, and costings.

Significant changes or discontinuities that affect the whole of an organisation present big challenges to the HRD function, as in the case of the privatisation of a nationalised industry. For instance, one of the water boards in the 1990s carried out a major review of operations following privatisation. This resulted in an extensive 'upskilling' programme involving the then BTEC national certificate in water and water-waste operations for the incumbents of about 700 new operations controller posts. A lower order but still powerful challenge is presented by a major change in the way part of an organisation operates, for example when a decentralised computer-based management information system is introduced. This type of change can be deceptive in that it may ultimately result in a new style of management, requiring totally different abilities. Many companies are turning to the 'flat organisation', which needs staff with a broader base of skills, thus eliminating the need for many specialisms; traditional boundaries and practices change. New management and leadership skills are needed by complex organisations. Organisational restructuring could begin with a skills audit and sufficient financial resources to pay for its recommendations. In an organisation undergoing cultural change, particular attention should be paid to team-building skills. Development activity should be linked to the achievement of change; people should be encouraged to identify their own qualities and strengths and relate them to the organisation's objectives; employees should take responsibility for their own learning; the focus should be on learning rather than teaching; flexibility is required to cater for the needs of individuals. You will probably see later that these are all characteristics of learning organisations!

> Discussion question: Some researchers have suggested there is no link between organisations' investment in management training and their commercial results. You have been asked to organise a CIPD branch discussion on this topic. What would your aims be for the meeting and how might you organise it?

Mergers and takeovers

Usually these require considerable culture and organisation change, and HRD programmes may be crucial in achieving a smooth transition. Where mergers and takeovers are on an international basis, the problems can be even more complex, with each national unit having objectives of its own.

We have known examples of merged companies which years after the original merger still regard themselves as employees of company x or y. An early appreciation of the HRD needs associated with sensitive issues like mergers could have prevented the entrenchment of attitudes.

Requests from management

These might indicate the lack of a more systematic approach. On the other hand, learning needs can arise suddenly, particularly in small organisations, and may not occur at the time of regular audits. Such requests may have political significance in encouraging line managers to accept responsibility for defining training needs, and in demonstrating that the HRD department can play a useful role in helping to achieve organisational objectives.

Incorrectly identified training needs

It is necessary to approach an assessment objectively and with an open mind, without being unduly influenced by the assumptions that management and others may make about the cause of a problem and how it should be solved. Sometimes a difficulty is in fact not a learning problem, even though that is how it has been presented. For example, the HRD specialist in a civil engineering company was asked to prepare a training programme for supervisors in the subcontracting department. On investigation she found that the supervisors' apparently inadequate performance was caused by the irregular flow of work into the company and therefore into the department. The problem was an organisational one and could not be solved by supervisory training.

> Discussion question: While conducting a HRD audit in your company, you discover that high turnover in one department appears to be linked with the bullying style of its manager. How might you tackle this problem diplomatically?

Partial learning needs

Help may be sought from HRD specialists in tackling such problems as removing bottlenecks in a production department, the assumption being that the shopfloor workers concerned have not been trained to do their jobs correctly. Although this might be the case, an investigation might also show that inadequate operator-training is only partly responsible for the poor quality of the work or slow working: the major causes may be poor supervision or machine maintenance, discontent over pay or recruitment of unsuitable employees. HRD specialists need to be effective at distinguishing between those problems that are wholly or partly due to ineffective training, and are therefore likely to have training solutions, and those that result from non-training factors, for which there are other answers.

'Displaced' learning or training needs

Often problems can escape the notice of the HRD department because they are not recognised by management as learning needs. Look at this example:

An investigation into the backlog of work in the accounts department of a rapidly expanding company showed that the root of the trouble was not, as the chief accountant had claimed, a shortage of staff but a deterioration in the calibre of the accounts clerks employed by the company. Previously the recruitment position in the area had been favourable and new employees had not needed formal training. We might imagine that the company also 'poached' trained staff from other organisations. When the labour market was tighter, less able or experienced staff were recruited and still no attempt was made to train them. The newcomers were eventually able to learn how to do the work (without training) but this obviously took time and in the process they made many more mistakes than their predecessors.

The HRD specialist has to be well in touch with the organisation's mainstream activity, to be aware of such problems and be prepared to offer assistance when the time seems right.

Skills audits for specific purposes

An audit of existing staff's competence in a particular facet of their work is another example of an organisation-wide training needs analysis. Such an analysis may be undertaken for a variety of reasons, such as an industrial relations audit (Jennings and Undy 1984), an Equal Opportunities discrimination audit or an audit of needs relating to membership of the EU.

Benchmarking

This is the search for the best practices that should lead to best performance, and has been used with such aims as improving total quality, product reliability and customer satisfaction. Increasingly it is being applied to the HRD function. It is a conscious and systematic attempt to compare one's own current reality with what is believed to be 'best practice' somewhere else – leading to judgements on whether to bridge the gap and, if so, how. The two main types of comparison are:

■ external – against other organisations, where the choice is wide but is usually confined to those considered similar in some way (by type of work, size etc)
■ internal – against other parts of one's own organisation.

Comparisons can be made in terms of what is done or (more usually) where the home organisation already has some expertise in how it is done. Both can result in decisions on whether and how to bridge a gap, which will usually involve some new learning on the part of the home organisation. The main stages of a planned benchmarking process are likely to be:

1   initial decisions on the process – who will conduct it, what aspects of performance are to be studied and how to define them, where 'best practice' is to be found (an interesting issue in itself), how data will be collected and reported

2   production of performance indicators, preferably relating to 'output' rather than 'input'

3   data collection – by reading, arranged visits, attendance at conferences, correspondence, arranged discussions

4   analysis – in which initial comparisons with the home reality are made, and possible new practices, activities or behaviours emerge, to be rejected, modified or confirmed

5   planning (perhaps including a brainstorming element) the route towards what are now confirmed as 'priority needs'

6   implementing any desired new processes.

In a 'continuous development culture', 'review and replan' stages might be added.

Benchmarking was widely promoted during the early 1990s – to the point where some enthusiasts argued for joint benchmarking practice, in which two or more organisations could share information and influence each other towards improvements. The underlying philosophy was that no organisation has a monopoly of best practice and hence a joint review is likely to benefit all who participate. In a competitive environment some organisations are worried about openness, but others argue that rivals benchmarking 'against' them actually bring in new insight into their own strengths, allowing them to advance further before the rivals have caught up. There is a hint of the 'action learning' philosophy of Reg Revans (1983) here. The benchmarking activity can be more than the identification of needs, offering a natural, if rather undefined, learning opportunity in its own right.

It is probably better, though, to see benchmarking as an operational 'trigger' rather than a straight training needs assessment tool. There is no real guarantee that by adapting the best HRD practices in other successful companies, organisational effectiveness or benefits to the bottom line will necessarily result. Training effectiveness is situational and we may not be comparing like with like in all respects. Benchmarking will provide indications and ideas for improvement, which must be well thought out and tested before implementation. The right reason for introducing a development procedure or technique is that the organisation needs it and will benefit from it, not purely because it is fashionable or that other companies do it. Joint benchmarking practice involving discussion and sharing of information is more likely to overcome this difficulty.

Discussion question: What do you consider to be the advantages and disadvantages of benchmarking? If you are currently attached to an organisation, with which organisation(s) might you wish to be benchmarked and why?

Total quality management

The decision to develop total quality management and/or the attempt to reach the ISO standards series requires a careful audit of learning and training needs throughout the organisation. Every facet of work must be performed to the highest standard, and quality targets must be defined and met. This requires not only initial training to make staff aware of the targets and to assist them to attain the necessary competence, but also continuous monitoring to ensure that standards are not allowed to slip and are kept up to date, taking into account the implications of any organisational changes. Procedures for continuing professional updating and 'upskilling' are also required.

Ensuring that statutory requirements are met

Organisations, their executives and employees are all affected by both new and long-standing statutory obligations. Ignorance of the law is sadly no defence for failure to comply with it. Nor will an organisation's legal obligations usually be met by a once and for all training intervention. Laws can be amended, and it is helpful to study the outcomes and implications for the organisation of current cases and High Court rulings. The HRD function has a continuing role to play in helping to ensure improved compliance with legislation, and this can be achieved by the maintenance of a checklist of statutory responsibilities to use in reviewing training needs for a department or for the organisation as a whole. Such a list would include the following areas: health and safety; industrial relations; race relations; sex discrimination; disability discrimination; and working time regulations.

Health and safety

The Health and Safety at Work Act 1974 requires every employer to provide:

> *such information, instruction, training and supervision as necessary to ensure, as far as reasonably practicable, the health and safety at work of his employees.* (Part 1 Section 2)

Subsequent sections of the Act are concerned with a written statement of policy on health and safety and the 'arrangements' (which presumably include training) for its implementation, together with the appointment in 'prescribed cases' of safety representatives and safety committees. The philosophy of the Act is clearly supportive of employee participation and consultation, and this has training implications. It will also be necessary for employers to be aware of any complementary legislation adopted by the UK in connection with membership of the EU.

Note that Part 1 Section 2 of this Act (quoted above) mentions the provision of supervision. It is generally recognised that safety training must be an integral part of a company's training schemes and must be included in programmes for supervisors and managers as well as in induction courses and in operator training. School-leavers and 'work experience' assignees are particularly at risk because of their inexperience, and require special attention.

The infamous High Court ruling (Walker v Northumberland County Council) illustrates the need for all managers and supervisors to realise the implications not just of bare legal requirements but also of relevant court cases and judgments. Under the 'Walker' ruling, a social worker received £175,000 in damages, based on loss of salary, after successfully proving that two nervous breakdowns had been caused by the stress of his impossible workload (See Welch 1996). Unless regular training programmes are provided so that supervisory staff realise their responsibilities to their subordinates, an organisation could find itself required to pay out large sums of money for matters of which top management were previously totally unaware. The Walker case paved the way for a significant number of similar claims. Although legal and HR specialists claim the 'peak' of such cases has now happened, this is by no means certain. The Health and Safety Executive is currently (2004) looking at fine-tuning its stress management standards based on six causes of stress at work: demand, control, support, relationships, role and change, and shows no signs of lowering the profile given to stress management in its work with organisations.

> Discussion question: What advice would you give to an organisation that wants to react proactively to the proposed stress guidelines? How can a HRD specialist assist?

Industrial relations

Of course, the inept handling of what appear to be relatively minor problems by supervisors and managers unaware of the law can lead to major industrial relations issues. Furthermore, if a case is brought against an organisation at an employment tribunal, it is extremely damaging if senior managers cannot support the actions of their subordinates. In cases of unfair dismissal because of incompetence, one of the first questions that arises at a tribunal concerns the amount and quality of the training and counselling provided and whether sufficient warnings were given. In addition to knowledge of the relevant law, skill in devising the procedures necessary to comply with it, and training in company policies and practices, as well as in union agreements, are necessities.

The Trade Union and Labour Relations Consolidation Act (1992, section 168) puts an employer under a legal responsibility to allow trade union officers time off with pay during working hours to take part in industrial relations training relevant to their duties.

Race relations

Training alone will not solve problems of race relations or diversity management, but it has a contribution to make. Awareness of the special needs of particular groups of workers is likely to be achieved most effectively when included as an integral part of the organisation's training plans for managers, supervisors and other employees. There are obvious needs relating to job-centred training. The Race Relations Act 1976 (as amended in 2000) encourages positive action to promote entry of racial groups into new areas of work by stipulating that the employer or trade union can provide training facilities exclusively for members of a particular racial group to fit them for work in which they are underrepresented. For examples of positive action in this field see Prashar (1983). Another important aspect is induction to the organisation and to the trade union, including knowledge of all relevant procedures. This training can help to prevent the painful consequences that may otherwise arise from later misunderstandings. Language teaching may be necessary (although it should not be assumed that people from minority ethnic groups are not native English speakers). Race relations audits have shown that people from ethnic minority groups tend to be underrepresented in more senior posts and point to the necessity for improved opportunities and training for career development, as well as effective training in selection procedures for those involved in appointment and promotion.

Advice on problems, ranging from provision of language training to courses for managers and shop stewards can be obtained from the Commission for Racial Equality.

Sex discrimination

Organisations have a legal responsibility to comply with the requirements of the Sex Discrimination Act 1975. As in the case of the race relations legislation, an organisation should ensure that its managers and supervisors understand their obligations in this field and, where necessary, they should ensure that appropriate training is provided for their subordinates. Appropriate management development including advice and, where appropriate, mentoring should be available to assist women to progress up the career ladder. As the number of school-leavers declines, women employees are going to constitute an increasing proportion of the workforce, and special measures may be even more important to ensure that they are adequately represented in the upper levels of management. Special training arrangements during career breaks, as well as for those returning to work after a number of years' absence, are likely to become more commonplace (see Chapter 9).

Disability discrimination

The Disability Discrimination Act 1995 relates to many aspects of employment, including recruitment and selection, terms and conditions, opportunities and benefits, dismissal and any other detriment. It imposes a legal responsibility upon employers not to treat a disabled person, for a reason relating to their disability, any less favourably than they treat, or would treat, others to whom that reason does not apply. It is the employer's duty to take reasonable steps to modify or remove any arrangements or physical features of the premises that place a disabled person at a substantial disadvantage. It is important that all employees, but particularly supervisors and managers, have a good knowledge of the provisions of the Act and their implication for the organisation. Some examples are provided of the steps an employer may have to take in relation to a disabled person. These include such matters as making adjustments to the premises, allocating some duties to another person, allowing time off during working hours for rehabilitation or treatment, or providing a reader or interpreter. Of particular interest to trainers is the inclusion of the following:

- giving her, or arranging for her to be given, training
- acquiring or modifying equipment
- modifying instructions or reference manuals
- modifying procedures for testing or assessment.

To help to ensure that disabled pupils receive the best possible education prior to seeking work, the Act amends the Education Act 1993 to the effect that the annual reports of all county, voluntary or grant-aided schools must contain information pertaining to the arrangements for the admission of disabled pupils, facilities to assist their access, and the steps taken to ensure that they do not receive less favourable treatment than other pupils.

The Disability Rights Commission advises government on the operation of the Act and specifically on ways of reducing, and eventually eliminating, discrimination. The setting up of this body in 1999 should also strengthen the rights of people bringing cases under the Act.

Discrimination and language

It is possibly a small point, but HRD specialists might benefit from occasionally reviewing their language in the light of diversity. We have tried to use both 'him' and 'her' in our text; early efforts at redressing the gender balance often claimed that 'for he read also she', but rightly it was pointed out that managers and the like have been assumed to be 'he' for many years, so some positive action was required. The other linguistic infelicity thankfully not so evident today is referring to minority groups as 'the': the disabled, the unemployed, or ethnic minorities, suggesting that all individuals in this group are somehow homogeneous. Using the terms 'people with a disability', 'unemployed people', 'people from minority ethnic groups' might sound long winded but at least is an attempt to treat those people with respect. Phrases like 'wheelchair user' instead of 'wheelchair bound' are also polite – after all no one wants to be 'bound to a wheelchair'. Language is a very powerful tool to bring people together or drive them apart, and as such it is not just 'politically correct' to seek the appropriate terminology.

Discussion question: How would you respond to a traditionalist manager who suggests that this language issue is 'overstating political correctness'?

Working Time Regulations 1998 (amended in 2000)

Traditionally there has been very little statutory control of working time in the UK and employers, managers and supervisors will not be accustomed to taking this into account when planning their work schedules. Although large companies may have a central department making company regulations to ensure compliance, any member of staff who authorises working hours will need to be made aware of the statutory regulations, and of the consequences of non-adherence. In smaller organisations, it will be particularly important for managers to know the different types of agreement that may be used to supplement or modify the regulations, as well as exactly what constitutes 'working time' and the definition of 'worker'. Such knowledge may be particularly important to those drawing up schedules in certain industries, for instance where unexpected delays could cause expensive disruption to schedules, or where workers may be 'on call'. It may also be particularly necessary for shift supervisors to be knowledgeable about the statutory regulations, if there is any possibility that they might have to make on the spot decisions about individual workers without the advantage of any advice.

After reading this chapter, you should by now be fully aware that:

1 **The HRD effort must be directed to the most important organisational objectives**. A survey of organisational needs or key areas is a logical step to ensure this. How it is carried out, and to what extent, will depend upon a number of factors, such as the culture or the stage of development of the organisation. It is also the basis for the learning and development plan and budget. Without any investigation into real needs, large sums of money might be invested with little positive result. If large capital sums were to be spent on the purchase of an IT system, a detailed investigation into the need for it and its use and advantage to the company would be undertaken. The same discipline should be exercised in expenditure on learning and development.

2   There are a number of approaches to identifying organisational needs, none of which is inherently 'good' for all situations; there is seldom likely to be one 'right' answer. Identifying 'own training needs' is an important part of some types of organisational activity, such as project groups. In these organisations the design and conduct of any review must take this into consideration.

3   The 'best' answer is likely to be that which appears to offer the 'best fit' in all the circumstances. To determine this may well involve the consideration of a number of different variables.

4   As well as being skilled in a range of learning techniques, the HRD practitioner needs diagnostic skills of a very high order.

Discussion question: Do you know of any organisation that completes a systematic analysis of learning/training needs? Can you contrast it with one you know that does not? Why do you think this difference exists? And can you identify any effects of the two approaches?

We have presented here a detailed account of examining HRD needs in the organisational context. We have, since the last edition of our book, reduced the complexity of our account, as there is evidence to suggest that most organisations do not have the resources to conduct organisation-wide learning and training needs analyses. We have focused instead on less time- and resource-intensive strategies. In practice it is possible to adapt the techniques we have described for use on a small scale, and it can be endlessly fascinating to look at an organisation's future challenges to interpret the learning needs they will give rise to. Sometimes this can be as simple as a quick SWOT analysis or brainstorming session, and all that is needed is imagination. If you are a student looking for suitable areas to research for a management report or dissertation, an organisational training needs analysis is often an excellent project that covers many areas of organisational interest.

The chapter has shown many ways in which the HRD practitioner has to be both a detective and a prophet to be able to see into the organisation's future learning and development needs. From what you have read, what do you think will be the key external influences on organisations' needs for HRD in the next two years or so?

In the next chapter, we will consider how needs at the individual level may be met, and how employees may be encouraged to take responsibility for their own learning needs.

The Individual and the Job – from Job Analysis to Discretionary Behaviour

CHAPTER 8

In Chapter 8, we will consider:

- How to identify the requirements of a particular job or task;

- The wide range of tools and techniques available to the job analyst and the necessity of choosing one appropriate to fast-moving environments;

- How to assess the existing competence and potential of the employee against these requirements;

- The importance of effective organisational systems and procedures, such as appraisal, to support learning analyses;

- How individuals can assess themselves and how their managers can assist them with this;

- The need for 'discretionary behaviour' in developing thinking performers who take responsibility for their own learning.

In practice jobs are varied and have many facets. Some consist of a few tasks, others of many. A few are relatively static, but most are subject to frequent changes. Some need a high degree of discretion, whereas others are mainly prescribed. Additional complications arise from the range of social and physical environments in which they are carried out.

A wide variety of skills and knowledge may need to be analysed. For example, job skills may be manual, diagnostic, interpersonal or decision-making. The knowledge component is particularly important in contemporary organisations, and may be technical, at the 'cutting edge', procedural or concerned with the operations of the company – or even its competitors. Jobs also vary widely in the range, variety and degree of skills and knowledge needed to perform them. With many different combinations of these components in jobs, different analytical approaches and techniques are needed.

Let us look at the first aim of this chapter – identifying the requirements of a job or task – by considering some of the different ways of analysing jobs for training purposes. We will also describe some of the techniques that HRD specialists use. Then we will look at the second question, of how an individual's performance may be assessed. Of course, the situation is not always quite so clear-cut, because changes in organisations, such as the trend towards flatter structures, or matrices of project teams, may mean assessing the capability and potential of the team rather than the individual. In fact, individual needs may vary according to the team mix. Of equal importance as technical expertise may be the role each person plays as a team member, and this may have to be assessed during the process of the teamwork itself. Theories of experiential learning tell us that we need to reflect on what has happened, assess our own performance, then determine how to improve and what help we need. This process is an essential part of the learning itself.

GAINING THE CO-OPERATION OF ALL CONCERNED

Before carrying out any of the methods we will describe, it is essential that the analyst informs everyone of the purpose and process of the investigation, or suspicions may be aroused when he or she starts asking questions. Consulting and involving people from the start also ensures a better chance of obtaining commitment to any resulting training programme, and constitutes the first step in a learning intervention.

> Discussion question: You have been asked to conduct a programme of individual job analysis in your organisation. Draft a suitable e-mail to employees in explaining what you are planning to do and why.

METHODS OF ANALYSING JOBS

'Traditional' job training analysis

The old style training boards required job analysis to give rise to certain documents, the main ones being a job description, job specification and a training specification. A very detailed examination was then required, resulting in a minute definition of the 'knowledge, skills and attitudes' needed by any job-holder. In the relatively stable background of those days, the expenditure of time and effort was justified, but in these times of rapid change a process known as functional analysis has evolved. This is the approach we will describe. In many organisations, the job specification has been replaced, at least in part, by the standards and performance criteria defined during the process of functional analysis. We think, though, that it is important to distinguish between knowledge, skills and attitudes, because they require different learning methods. Also it is useful to give details of all three documents, because even in 'turbulent' environments they can still be useful.

Job description

It is likely that this is already in existence, but it is still useful to check its accuracy. It might also contain extra details like the job-holder's hours of work, which might be helpful to know when arranging HRD programmes. It is also vital to include the date, especially as jobs are constantly evolving, and it is also helpful to note the people and departments with whom the job-holder liaises. This can be charted diagrammatically (see the section on Role Analysis below).

> Discussion question: What do you consider to be the strengths and weaknesses of traditional job descriptions?

Job specification

'A detailed statement, derived from the job analysis of the knowledge and the physical and mental activities involved in the job, and of the environment within which the job is performed' (MSC 1981). These activities are normally classified under the two headings of 'knowledge' and 'skill', and sometimes a third heading, 'attitudes', is added. In the case of an Administrative Assistant's job, two of the tasks in the job description might be typing letters and answering the telephone. Associated physical and mental activities might be the interpersonal skills required in dealing with irate customers on the telephone, or knowledge of organisation style and format of letters.

Training specification

'A detailed statement of what a trainee needs to learn, based on a comparison between the job specification and the individual's present level of competence' (MSC, 1981). Methods of determining competence may be by comparison with experienced workers' standard in the case of an operator or, in the case of a more technical role, by an appraisal system.

COMPETENCE AND COMPETENCES

The concept of competence has evolved over the last two decades or so, originally in relation to management development, and received a further impetus when researchers were trying to find ways in which trainees could be provided with learning experiences in one organisation that would also help them in a subsequent one. The original solution was to identify number of 'Occupational Training Families', 'Key Competences' and 'Transfer Learning Objectives' (Hayes et al 1983). Later, the Management Charter Initiative (see page 233) adopted the competence approach and a national framework of management competences was devised. Over the course of time, a number of different methodologies has been used to identify desirable competences. We look at two below.

'Input' approaches

There have been many studies of what it is that effective managers contribute to the job, some of which we describe in Chapter 11. Mintzberg (1975) identified eight basic groups of management skills, but possibly the most comprehensive study involved 2,000 US managers and was carried out in 1979/80 by the American Management Association and documented by Boyatzis (1982). The researchers were trying to answer the question, 'What are the characteristics that distinguish superior performance by working managers?' They defined competency as 'an underlying characteristic of a manager causally related to superior performance in a management position'. This suggests that it is more than a set of skills; it is a mix of aptitudes, attitudes/behaviours and personal attributes possessed by effective managers. In a useful discussion of the competency–competence debate, Woodruffe (1992) stresses that a competency is 'a dimension of overt manifest behaviour that allows the person to perform competently'. He explains that the reference to behaviour is important to the definition. A job analysis should isolate the behaviours that distinguish high performance.

The 'outcomes' model (NVQs)

Here we have a different methodology. 'Input' models are concerned with what it is that effective employees bring to the job – 'outcomes' models focus on what high performers achieve.

This method of analysis used for NVQs is dominated by two factors. They are outcome-led, and are based on national standards of competences ideally assessed in the workplace. Competence is defined as 'being able to perform "whole" work roles to the standards expected in employment in real working environments' (NCVQ 1991). The suggestion here is that 'whole work roles' involve more than just specific skills and tasks. As we mentioned in Chapter 2, identifying these competences is in part the remit of the SSCs, and the technique used tends to be functional analysis. The approach assumes that the competence will be used at the workplace both to define training needs and to assess 'qualified' status, because standards are set in the form of performance criteria.

In this book we have used the term 'competence' in relation to the 'outcomes' approach and the term 'competency' with reference to the 'input' approach, although it has to be said that the two terms tend to be used inconsistently by writers.

FUNCTIONAL ANALYSIS

This is the established process to decide on the standards aimed at approval for NVQ use. The statements of competence are derived by analysing employment functions of the job-holder. We describe it as specified for NVQs, but of course organisations can alter and adapt the methodology to make analyses for their own internal purposes. The CIPD, for example, has a slightly different methodology using the operational and knowledge indicators (see page 131), and smaller companies might feel a simpler format is more useful. The SSCs have drawn up competence statements for most of the jobs within their remit, which can be used as a basis. They will, however, require careful adaptation. In some organisations, the analysis will be carried out by the immediate supervisor together with the job-holder; in others by the HRD practitioner. Sources of information may include:

- The job-holder herself;
- The job-holder's manager, who can explain the job purpose and standards of performance;
- Customers or clients: information can be gained from records of customer complaints, or questionnaires about performance;
- Organisational records, such as job descriptions/specifications, organisation charts, policies, plans, procedures, sales and production records;
- Suppliers' manuals, which may be an essential source of information for HRD purposes, for example when new equipment is first used.

Briefly, the first requirement is a statement of the key purpose of the overall area of competence followed by the question 'What needs to happen for this to be achieved?' This leads to a breakdown into the key roles. The question is then repeated, generating a further breakdown into units of competence which are then divided further into elements (see figure 8.1, where an example of one of the key roles together with a constituent unit and element of competence are shown in the right hand column). The NCVQ definition of a unit of competence is:

'A coherent group of elements of competence ... which form a discrete area of activity or sub-area of competence which has meaning and independent value in the area to which the NVQ relates.' (NCVQ, 1989)

You will also see that the element of competence is accompanied by performance criteria, knowledge and evidence requirements, as well as examples of evidence. These should:

- be described with sufficient precision to allow unambiguous interpretation by different users, such as awarding bodies, assessors, trainers and candidates
- not be so detailed that they relate only to a specific task or job, employer or organisation location or equipment location or equipment.

Whilst it would be relatively straightforward to define performance criteria, knowledge and evidence requirements for one specific job or organisation, the concept of national qualifications raises questions of learning transfer to varying sets of circumstances. It is necessary to ensure that learners understand the principles involved, which will enable them to respond to different situations. Arguably, this is 'deep learning' as described by Entwistle (1988).

Used in producing occupational standards	Key purpose	The overall purpose of the occupational area	To achieve the organisation's objectives and to continuously improve its performance
	Key Roles	The different areas in which people in the occupation operate	Manage people
NVQ and SVQ	Units of competence	Broad descriptions of the different functions the people perform	Lead the work of teams and individuals
	Elements of competence	Detailed descriptions of the standard of performance expected	Plan the work of teams and individuals
	Performance criteria (selection only)	Criteria to assess if the candidate's performance meet the National Standard	You must ensure that • your plans are consistent with your team's objectives • your plans and schedules are realistic and achievable • your plans and the way you allocate work take full account of team members' abilities and development needs
	Knowledge requirements (selection only)	What the candidates need to know in order to perform to the National Standard	You need to know and understand • the importance of regularly reviewing work • the importance of planning work activities to organisational effectiveness and your role and responsibilities in relation to this
	Evidence requirements (selection only)	The evidence candidates must show to prove to an NVQ or SVQ assessor that they are competent	You must show evidence that you develop both of the following types of plans • short-term • medium term

Occupational standard

	Examples of evidence	Examples of the sorts of evidence which can be used to show that candidates are competent	Products or outcomes
Helpful for assessment			• your plans and schedules for the work of your team • minutes of planning meetings in which you have been involved • briefing notes you have developed • your revised and updated plans

Figure 8.1 An example of an NVQ. From NVQ level 3 in management, taken from the Department of Education and Skills, NVQ website: www.dfes.gov.uk/nvq/example.shtml

Although there are critics of NVQs, there is no doubt that the identification of transferable competences could be a most useful concept, particularly when in place in a national framework. This would be of use not only to employers, but also to trainees, who need to learn skills that will stand them in good stead in entirely different types of employment. A national 'scheme' of competences that can be accessed by anyone and provide certification for units that can be accumulated for qualifications is highly desirable. NVQ specifications are also suitable for comparison with European awards and so assist in mutual recognition of qualifications.

For a fuller discussion of NVQs see Jessup (1991), from which many of the ideas of this section have been taken, or Stewart (1999).

KEY RESULTS ANALYSIS

As not all parts of a job are of the same importance to the achievement of organisational objectives, it may be helpful sometimes to take a short cut and concentrate on the key areas. In rapidly changing situations, jobs cannot be predetermined or prescribed accurately, and the most important task facing the job-holder is to decide exactly what he or she should be doing to meet new circumstances. This can involve a difficult balance of priorities. There may not be time for a complete analysis, and in any case this might obscure the key tasks of the job. In particular, at management level, jobs are expressed in more general terms, concentrating on objectives, targets and key areas. Definitions of key responsibilities common to a number of supervisors and managers may be useful as a basis for standard in-house courses.

Key results analysis is appropriate for any type of task where the both following conditions apply:

- the job is made up of many different tasks, not all of which are critical for effective performance, and,
- the job is changing in emphasis or content, requiring establishment of priority tasks, standards of performance and the skills and knowledge required. This technique can be used as an alternative to full analysis, or to complement it.

PROBLEM-CENTRED ANALYSIS

This approach differs from those we have described up to now, as no attempt is made to analyse either a whole job or all of its key tasks. Analysis is limited to a difficulty believed to have an HRD solution, such as a chief chemist asking the HRD department to organise a report-writing course for her technical staff because their reports are unclear and poorly structured. The analysis is concentrated on this particular aspect of the technical staff's work and excludes others unless they are directly relevant to the problem.

METHODS OF CLOSER ANALYSIS

Having identified the competences or key aspects of a job, it is sometimes helpful to look more closely at some of the specific tasks or elements of competence, or the interface relationships. There are a number of techniques for doing this, including:

- Critical incident analysis
- Stages and key points analysis
- Manual skills analysis
- Faults analysis
- Learning analysis
- Role analysis.

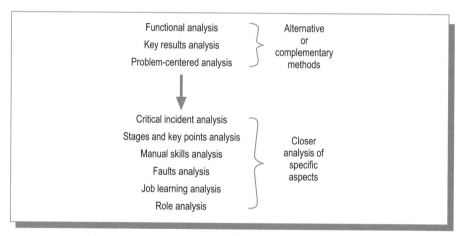

Figure 8.2 *Methods of broad analysis followed by more detailed breakdowns*

Critical incident analysis

One way of defining the areas of a job with which the incumbent is having most problems is by examining incidents that he or she sees as the most difficult to handle. This information can be gained from interview, although depending upon the status and skill of the interviewer, employees may be reluctant to reveal their real problems for fear of making themselves appear inefficient. One of the classical criticisms of the critical incident technique is that people tend to pick those incidents they think will put them in a good light. An atmosphere of complete trust and honesty is of course necessary if this difficulty is to be overcome.

Another way of establishing the information is to ask the job-holder for a short written account at the end of each day of the one incident of the day that has been the most difficult to manage, and to estimate how frequently he or she has to deal with a similar difficulty. The exercise is repeated for several days, or for several weeks on days chosen at random. The process is simplified if a special form is designed for the purpose. The forms can be returned anonymously and an overall picture can be established as a basis for general training programmes. The reported incidents can be camouflaged to make useful case studies. It is, however, very informative if the respondents are willing to identify themselves so that individualised training can be devised and, in addition, particular problems can be localised, perhaps to one department or to newly promoted supervisors. Assistance can then be given exactly where it is required.

As well as pinpointing trouble spots, this technique is useful in involving the employee. In a turbulent environment, change can be so rapid that management may be unaware of the problems and consequent stress suffered by individuals, and a simple technique such as this can often help to alleviate the situation. Of course, not all problems will have an HRD solution, and some will expose learning needs for people other than the job-holder. Before beginning this type of exercise management commitment needs to be assured, at least to a consideration of possible ways of overcoming problems that cannot be solved by training. Having asked for employees' co-operation in writing daily reports, something must be seen to happen! It is disappointing how often HRD practitioners fail to appreciate this very important point.

Stages and key points analysis

Imagine you are Eleanor Brown, an assistant supervisor of an office in a branch of an international company. You have a very busy day ahead of you and a pile of queries to sort out. Your manager asks you to look after Bill, a trainee who started yesterday, and show him the work of the office – in particular, how to use the fax machine. There are messages going out all the time, so there is plenty of opportunity; the only problem is that you have very little time this morning. You take him to the machine and let him watch you transmitting several messages. You ask Bill if he has any questions and are assured that he can manage, so you leave the last message for him to send to the United States, and just as he is starting you are called away to the telephone. When you come back you find Bill upset because, although the letter has gone through the machine, and cost three minutes of telephone time, the concluding report indicates that transmission was not OK. One of the staff sitting nearby tells you that Bill had difficulty in putting the paper in straight at the beginning, causing the alarm bell to ring. Several people had come to help him, and eventually the fax went through. However, because there was now a queue at the machine, he had pulled the paper to hurry it as it came through, interfering with the transmission. There were a number of key points that you should have made plain when you demonstrated to Bill, but because you were busy and your mind was on your own work, they did not come readily to your mind. The result was wasting money in useless telephone time, some disruption to others in the department, as well as Bill and yourself feeling inadequate. When discussing this with friends over lunch, you discover that other departments have previously prepared analysis sheets stating very simply the main stages in routine tasks and the key points associated with them. Anyone demonstrating to new recruits can use these sheets to check that they have not omitted any important part of the instruction.

This technique can be applied to relatively simple tasks that are part of a more difficult job, but it is unsuitable for complex work or tasks that require the frequent use of judgemental skills. A stages and key points analysis is normally undertaken by a trained instructor, supervisor or senior operator.

JOB TITLE: How to make a job breakdown		
Stage (what to do in stages to advance the job)	**Instructions (how to perform each stage)**	**Key points (items to be emphasised)**
1 Draw up table	Rule three columns. Allow space for column headings and job title	Use this sheet as example
2 Head the columns	On top line insert the title of job Insert: Column 1 (Stage) Column 2 (Instructions) Column 3 (Key Points)	Headings – summarise what worker needs to know to perform each job Watch for steps which are performed from habit
3 Follow through the job to be analysed	After each step, ask yourself – 'What did I just do?' Note places where the worker could go astray. Note items to be emphasised. Note hazards. Stress safety points	Write notes clearly and concisely Keep stages in order Ensure directions are complete – never assume they are
4 Fill in Columns 1, 2 and 3 as stage 3 above is performed	Make brief and to-the-point notes	Review and emphasise these 'Key Points' decisively
5 Number the stages	Follow the sequence a worker must follow when learning the job	
6 Follow the job through using directions in Columns 1 and 2	Follow the instructions exactly	
7 Check that all 'Key Points' are included	Record in Column 3 all points where the worker may be confused	
(Reproduced with acknowledgement to the former Ceramics, Glass and Mineral Products Industry Training Board.)		

Figure 8.3 *A stages and key points breakdown sheet*

DEPARTMENT: Fish-filleting		TASK: Fillet\trim small plaice		DATE:	
Section or Element	*Left hand*	*Right hand*	*Vision*	*Other Senses*	*Comments*
Select fish	Reach to trough – grasp fish with T and 1 2 3 4 around belly, p/u and bring forward to board	P/u knife with T and 1 2 3 4 around handle. With sharp edge of blade to right of filleter Knife hold:	Glance ahead for knife position on board Glance ahead for fish position on trough	Tough LH on fish	
Position fish	Place fish on board so that the dorsal fins fall to the edge of the board and the head lies to the right hand side of the filleter.	Hold knife handle against first and third joints of the fingers. Place upper part of T (1st joint) against lower blunt edge of knife and the lower part of T against upper edge of handle. Do not grasp knife tightly. Do not curl tip of fingers into palm of hand.	Check position of fish	Touch LH on fish	Knife is held in the RH during the complete filleting cycle. If knife is held correctly it should be possible to move the knife to the left and right by 'opening' and 'closing' the knuckles (when T is removed from handle).
Key. LH = left hand, RH = right hand, p/u = pick up, T = thumb, 1 = first finger, 2 = second finger, 3 = third finger, 4 = fourth finger. Synchronous movements are recorded on the same line. Successive movements are recorded on succeeding lines.					
(Reproduced with acknowledgement to the former Food, Drink and Tobacco Industry Training Board.)					

Figure 8.4 *Manual skills analysis*

Discussion question: Can you think of any jobs that could benefit from this technique? How do you think it might impact on health and safety issues?

The analyst watches and questions an operator at work and using a stages and key points breakdown sheet (see Figure 8.3) records in the 'stage' column the different steps in the job. Most semi-skilled jobs are easily broken down into their constituent parts and a brief summary is made of what the operator does in carrying out each part. The analyst then examines the stages separately and for each one describes in the 'instructions' column, against the appropriate stage, how the operator performs each task. The description of the operator's skill and knowledge is expressed in a few words. At the same time, the analyst notes in the 'key points' column of the breakdown sheet any special points such as quality standards or safety requirements, which should be emphasised to a trainee learning the job. A stages and key points breakdown sheet serves two purposes. It provides the formal underpinning which aids the analysis and, when completed, it is used as the instruction schedule. This is an efficient method of analysing relatively simple jobs. It is long established and has been used widely since its introduction from the USA as part of the TWI (Training Within Industry) Job Instruction programme during and after the Second World War.

Manual skills analysis (MSA)

This is used to isolate the skills and knowledge employed by experienced workers performing tasks requiring a high degree of manual dexterity. It can be used to analyse any task in which precision, manual dexterity, hand–eye co-ordination and perception are important features.

The hand, finger and other body movements of an experienced operative are observed and recorded in great detail as she carries out her work. This is a highly specialised technique and will be used selectively, especially since automation has had a significant impact on the numbers of jobs where manual skills are vital. Relatively easy-to-learn parts of the job are analysed in much less depth (a stages and key points approach may often be adequate) and an MSA is limited to those tasks (or parts of tasks) involving unusual skills. These are the 'tricky' parts of a job, which, while presenting no difficulty to the experienced operative, have to be analysed in depth before they can be taught to trainees. In Figure 8.4 we give an example of a typical form used in an MSA illustrating the breakdown of the task of filleting raw fish in a food-processing factory. It will be seen from this example that an experienced operative's hand movements are recorded in minute detail, together with the cues (vision and other senses) that the operative uses in performing the task. Explanatory comments are added, where necessary, in the 'comments' column. Special training is needed to apply this type and level of analysis and, in particular, to identify the cues on which the operators depend in both normal and abnormal work conditions, and the senses by which they receive them.

Faults analysis

When analysing a job, information is collected about the faults that occur, especially the expensive ones – 'the process of analysing the faults occurring in a procedure, product or service, specifying the symptoms, causes and remedies of each ...' (MSC 1981) – is termed a faults analysis. The result of this analysis – a faults specification – provides trainees with details of faults they are likely to come across in their work, how they can be recognised, what causes them, what effects they have, who is responsible for them, what action the trainees should take when a particular fault occurs, and how a fault can be prevented from recurring. A faults specification is usually drawn up either in a tabular or 'logic tree' form and is useful both for instruction purposes and as a memory aid for an employee after completion of training.

Job learning analysis

The types of analysis we have described so far have been concerned with the content of jobs and tasks. In contrast, job learning analysis focuses on processes, and in particular upon the learning skills that are required. This technique is described in detail by Pearn and Kandola (1993), who give the definition of a learning skill as 'one that is used to increase other skills or knowledge … The learning skills represent broad categories of behaviour which need to be learnt.' They identify nine learning skills:

- physical skills
- complex procedures, which have to be remembered or followed with the aid of written material
- checking/assessing/discriminating
- memorising facts/information
- ordering/prioritising/planning
- looking ahead
- diagnosing/analysing/solving
- interpreting or using written/pictorial/diagrammatic material
- adapting to new ideas/systems.

The analysis is carried out by interviewing the job-holder, starting with a description of the main aim of the job, followed by the principal activities. Using nine question cards, each relating to a particular area of learning (see Figure 8.5), the interviewer probes each main

---

CARD 1

Q1   PHYSICAL SKILLS

Are there physical skills involved in this activity which it took you a long time to get right or become proficient in? What are they?

Probes
How much time did it take before you got it right?
What would the consequences be if you did not perform the physical skills correctly?

CARD 2

Q2   COMPLEX PROCEDURES

In this activity, do you have to carry out a procedure or a complex sequence of activities either (a) relying solely on memory, and/or (b) using written materials, manuals, etc?

Probes
(a) What happens if you forget the sequence or procedure?
    What are the consequences of forgetting the sequence or procedure?
(b) What written materials, manuals, etc do you use?
    How do you use them?
    When do you use them?
    How accessible are they?
    What are the consequences of not following the procedure correctly?

CARD 3

Q3   CHECKING/ASSESSING/DISCRIMINATING

In this activity, do you make adjustments/judgements based on information from your senses (sight, sound, smell, touch, taste)? Give me some examples.

Probes
What senses, ie sight, sound, smell, touch, taste, do you use?
What adjustments/judgements do you make?
How do you make these adjustments/judgements?
What would the consequences be if you did not make the adjustments/judgements correctly?

Source: Pearn M. and Kandola R. *Job Analysis: A practical guide for managers* (2nd edn, IPD, 1993)

Figure 8.5 *Job learning analysis question cards*

activity in more depth, and the resulting analysis enables trainers to design learning approaches and appropriate material to the required type of learning. The aim is not only to ensure that trainees can learn the content of the job but that they have the skills to manage work of a similar type. For instance, in a job where considerable memory work is involved, the trainee should not only learn the items he or she needs to know, but also be aware of ways of assisting the memory, such as visual association, mnemonics etc. In this way, he or she is learning to learn.

This method can be used together with other techniques. It is particularly suitable for jobs where content cannot be analysed by observation alone. This means jobs involving planning ahead, diagnosing or analysing. It also has the advantage of making the job-holders aware of their own learning processes. It could usefully be employed by a project group, to determine their own training needs, redefining the nine 'learning skills', if necessary, to suit their own purpose. For further information about the method, see Pearn and Kandola (1993).

Role analysis

Where the job-holder has to 'liaise' with a number of people in the organisation (which should be given a specific context to be a helpful word – 'liaison' for what purpose?), it can often be illuminating to make an interactive diagram: see Figure 8.6, which depicts a 'role set'. Kahn et al (1964) demonstrated that the conflicting expectations of the same person by various members of staff can be a potent source of stress and difficulty. For instance, a production manager may have to maintain a difficult balance between the requirements of the sales manager, quality control, subordinates, the shop steward and the production director.

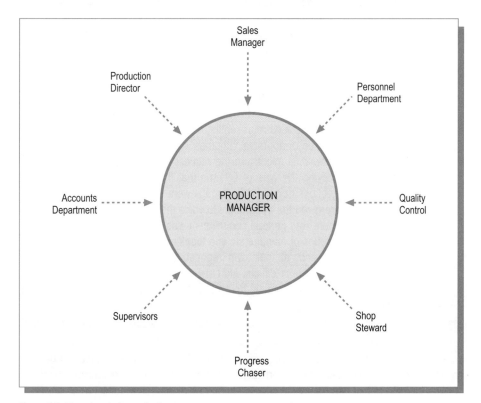

Figure 8.6 *The role set of a production manager*

Developing strategies to cope with this situation is likely to be a key area of the job, and yet might easily lack emphasis in a traditional job description.

ASSESSING THE PERFORMANCE OF OTHERS

Assessing the new employee

A new employee, selected against a personnel specification, may already have, in broad terms, the necessary ability, achievement and experience to do the job, so may only require limited training. It may be sensible to check this, either by discussion with the person concerned, or, if appropriate, by administering a test. The new job may be very familiar in many respects but differ in one or two important aspects in which previous experience can hinder effective performance. Where safety controls are involved, it is imperative to be aware of the dangers of negative transfer (see pages 78–79). Possibly the only training that might be required would be to discuss the important areas of difference and provide practice in them.

A small chemical company in the UK received instructions from its parent in the USA to install a performance appraisal scheme as standardised by the parent company. The UK HR manager protested that it would not suit the culture of the UK company, but his objections were overruled and the scheme was set in motion. The managers were called together and given some preliminary training in the operation of the scheme and in appraisal interviewing. Three years later, the scheme was deemed a dismal failure, because managers merely went through the motions of conducting the interviews with no real enthusiasm, if they did them at all. The appraisal report forms contained noncommittal comments, which were no use for any purpose. The parent company still insisted that there should be an appraisal scheme operating in the UK, but reluctantly agreed that the standard scheme could be altered or modified to suit.

Knowing that introducing a new scheme would now be a tricky operation because of the attitudes that had already been created, the HR manager enlisted the help of consultants. They set up task groups representing all grades of management, with a brief to discuss the difficulties of appraisal schemes, what the objectives of such a scheme might be, and how they might turn the request from headquarters to their own advantage by identifying the type of scheme that they felt would bring them some benefit. The suggestions from the task groups were modified at a conference where all managers were given the opportunity to voice their opinions. Only when it became apparent that there was general commitment was a new scheme drawn up on the proposed lines; groups of managers came together to clarify how they would operate the new system and, at their own request, to have further practice in conducting the interviews. After a difficult start (because the first task groups still carried over negative views of appraisal from the former scheme) the new system ran smoothly.

A trainability test is 'a validated test designed to assess whether a job applicant has the potential to reach a satisfactory standard after training'. 'The applicant is required to perform an appropriate, carefully designed, short task after being given prior instruction ...' (MSC 1981). This type of test can be used for a variety of jobs ranging from forklift truck driving to bricklaying and bottling, as well as social skills such as interviewing a client for a mortgage with a building society. It is also suitable for all ages of recruit and is regarded as more appropriate for older applicants than traditional selection tests, especially as it can build a prior knowledge of skills.

Appraisal of existing employees

The two most usual methods of assessing the performance of existing staff are performance appraisal and assessment centres (for comprehensive coverage of a wide variety of assessment methods, including unconventional techniques, see Davey and Harris 1982).

Performance appraisal

Lack of commitment and unclear aims are the main reasons why appraisal schemes fail to realise the hopes of their instigators. Some of us may feel that performance appraisal is not always an effective substitute for constructive feedback over time by a manager who also exhibits leadership behaviours. It must be said, though, that not all organisations provide such a positive managerial environment, and sometimes appraisal may be at least a beginning in developing effective performance feedback. It makes sense to use group discussions and participative approaches to draw up the scheme, so making the design of the system and the assessment criteria the first stage of training. A further cause of failure for appraisal is lack of ability and confidence to conduct the interview. Accepting criticism is painful, particularly if it is given in a tactless manner by a manager who can't accept criticism in turn! Managers are understandably reluctant to create resentment in subordinates with whom they are going to have to continue to work, and are often tempted to 'duck' important issues. Appraiser training, therefore, is an essential part of the process. In fact it is often said that appraisal can indicate more about the appraiser than the appraisee – another reason to treat it with some caution.

Discussion question: What have your own experiences been as an appraiser/ appraisee? In either case, was it a positive experience? If you have not been the subject of appraisal, comment on feedback from teachers or tutors.

Some appraisal schemes emphasise joint assessment, with the final report signed and therefore 'owned' by both parties. In cases of disagreement a two-part report may be submitted, or someone further up the hierarchy may be designated to discuss any points that either party wishes to raise. Again, this can be a very difficult process, and organisations introducing appraisal have to be very effective in practising what they preach about honesty and openness. Performance appraisal needs to be complemented by regular review meetings and informal feedback. It is quite wrong, at an annual appraisal, to begin discussion of an issue that arose several months previously, especially if that issue was difficult or challenging for the appraisee.

Findings from the Price Waterhouse Cranfield Project on trends in Europe indicate that performance appraisal is one of the major tools of management development in the UK as well as in Sweden, Switzerland and Holland, whereas it is less used in France, Spain and Germany, and rarely in Denmark. In all countries, including the UK, figures indicating the incidence of management training in appraisal are considerably lower than those relating to the regular use of the technique (Holden and Livian 1992) – a feature of concern in view of the discussion above.

The purpose of appraisal may be to assess and improve current performance usually by defining training needs, or future potential, as well as salary review. It is not advisable to attempt all three objectives at one time. Fear of losing a pay rise or promotion does not encourage an open discussion of HRD needs. It is also possible that one appraiser may not be appropriate for all three. For example, an immediate superior may be the most suitable person with whom to discuss current performance, but potential and promotion prospects may be better dealt with by someone further up the hierarchy. Some organisations make a practice of using more than one appraiser. For instance, the superior's superior may be present at the interview, and we know of one organisation where a colleague of the appraisee is also present.

A relatively new development is that of upward appraisal, whereby subordinates are given a formal role in assessing their superiors. To avoid embarrassment, this normally takes the form of anonymous questionnaires. Sometimes the questionnaires are collected and collated by independent consultants who feed back the results individually and in strict confidence, and where required, give assistance in compiling action plans. It usually complements, rather than replaces, more traditional forms of appraisal. Its supporters claim that it facilitates employee empowerment and makes for a more participative management style. It certainly has the potential to provide a new and useful perspective on training needs, but a number of studies suggest that it can be a highly political process (see Redman and Mathews 1995). Another variation is appraisal by colleagues. There is also increasing evidence of '360 degree' appraisal to include the aspects of line manager, peer, team, supervisee and self-appraisal. Kaplan and Norton (1992) have developed the 'balanced scorecard' approach, which requires managers to look at the business from customer, internal, innovation and learning, and financial perspectives, and which has been adapted as an appraisal tool.

It is normally good practice to give advance notice of an appraisal interview, then ask the appraisee to write a report of his or her own performance, and use this to start off the discussion. Some of the first appraisal schemes were designed on the basis of personal qualities such as enthusiasm, commitment, loyalty, keenness and such like, which are of course very subjective concepts especially if examples of the quality are absent. One person's commitment is another's laissez-faire – but schemes like this still operate in some organisations, even to select people for redundancy. There are some situations like this where it is not appropriate to use appraisal records. Most current schemes are usually output-based, reviewing performance against targets during the period under review, and developing new targets for the forthcoming period. Towards the end of the interview, the appraiser should identify suitable developmental steps, action plans and targets, with dates.

Objective-setting and formal appraisal are at the centre of performance management systems (PMS), where individual goals and responsibilities are linked to the objectives of the work unit and key corporate objectives as a whole. A survey commissioned some time ago by the former Institute of Personnel Management found that organisations that operate PMS normally have a mission statement, which is communicated to all employees, and express performance targets in terms of measurable outputs, accountabilities and training or learning targets. They use formal appraisal to communicate performance requirements and produce personal improvement plans, and they also have a tendency to link performance requirements to pay, particularly for senior managers (Bevan and Thompson 1991). Although the majority of companies in the survey had set up PMS to improve organisational effectiveness, the researchers found no evidence to indicate that this link existed, which is interesting to say the least. Some PMS systems make use of computer programs to subject data to statistical procedures, producing results that are as objective as possible. For a more detailed account of such a scheme, see Moorby (1991). Despite the survey findings, the incidence of PMS has increased over recent years (Armstrong and Baron 1998) and it does link up very conveniently with NVQ competences.

> Discussion question: Is it possible for all employees to 'buy in' to an organisation's mission? How can the process of engaging them with the organisation's purpose be made more effective?

ASSESSMENT/DEVELOPMENT CENTRES

These have a history based in selection procedures and are still used for this purpose today. You may have already come across them in your studies of selection tools. Many companies, however, have extended their usage to assessment for promotion and/or development centres to indicate strengths and weaknesses. Dulewicz (1989) claims that assessment centres were designed primarily as a predictor of potential, not as a method for appraising current performance, and that their record for doing this is far better than that of any other technique. When used to assess development potential development centres mean that individuals who take part are not competing for a particular job, but seeking to discover more about their own strengths and weaknesses. Consequently they are likely to be more focused on understanding themselves than outdoing the competition.

The first step in devising an assessment/development centre is to identify what strengths or characteristics are to be tested. As we have seen in considering competences, two approaches are possible: the input approach, in which case personal attributes such as leadership might be tested, or the outcomes approach, in which discrete units of the job might be given as assessed tasks. In practice, most companies seem to employ input approaches, testing competencies such as basic reasoning, strategic visioning, confidence, control, flexibility and interpersonal skills. Of course, the same caveats about subjectivity apply. With the advent of NVQs there has been a trend towards testing 'output' defined competences.

There are a number of important questions to ask:

- What are the essential competences/(ies) the organisation/job requires?
- How can we monitor the competences/(ies) required in a changing environment?
- Can we devise tasks that really do assess these competences/(ies)?
- Does performance on the task actually transfer to the working situation?
- How can we evaluate the scheme as a whole?

Ways of arriving at answers to the first of these questions include: the use of the Repertory Grid technique, which we mention on page 235, to generate a list of the critical competences/(ies) exhibited by effective managers; surveys among staff; comparing results with those of similar organisations and interpreting any differences; considering the findings of other researchers; or adapting national standards such as those established within NVQs.

Whatever methods are used it is necessary to check that the dimensions being assessed are actually relevant to work aims and objectives, otherwise there is a danger that managers and assessors will subconsciously select in their own image and that this process of 'cloning' may hinder organisational development, let alone potentially give rise to indirect discrimination. Some organisations attempt to answer the last three questions by careful performance appraisal of staff who have previously been through the centre, to compare their marks with actual performance. This, of course, is open to the criticism that since being assessed some development should have taken place. A more rigorous approach would be to rate managers in their current jobs, put them through the assessment centre and compare their scores with the ratings. Few organisations do this, because of the inconvenience, or possibly embarrassment it would cause. It may be thought ironic that standard selection tests are not marketed unless they have been thoroughly validated, and yet important career decisions may be made in many companies on the strength of procedures that have not been subjected to this rigour.

The training of assessors is obviously a crucial factor. Not only must they be capable of assessing the dimensions in question, but fairness also demands inter-assessor reliability. Continuous training and updating is therefore required. Assessors may be senior managers who have themselves been through the centre and possibly assisted in its design. The full support of top management is vital in order to gain the commitment of managers at all levels, as the following quotation from L. Jackson (1989) shows:

> If anything, we underestimated the level of inertia and opposition which faced us ... It was fortunate we had the full support of the directors ... it was noticeable that the psychological barriers were more daunting than the administrative and technical ones.

Now imagine that you are Jane Anderson and have just returned to work on Monday, having spent the end of last week going through your organisation's assessment centre. Attainment of certain standards is a prerequisite for being considered for promotion, and you have just been informed that unfortunately you did not make the grade, although after a suitable period you can apply for reassessment. You have been provided with a profile and asked to produce an action plan, to be discussed with your superior and development officer if required. You feel resentful about the whole business. You did not understand what one of the tests was getting at, and do not agree with the comments on your assessment sheet. You have just been to see your boss, who said he did not understand them either. You wonder whether it is worth trying to make an action plan and apply for reassessment or whether to start looking for another job, because you do not seem to be getting very far in this one. You wonder whether your assessment centre scores will feature in an employer's reference.

A number of organisations (see, for example, Jackson 1989), have found that merely feeding back the profile of strengths and weaknesses does not necessarily equip those assessed to take the required action. Short off-the-job follow-up courses may be necessary to give a fuller understanding of the meaning of the profile and to assist the employee to come to terms with it. Such a course is also a convenient occasion for drafting and discussing personal action plans, making learning contracts and enabling managers to begin to take charge of their own learning. This will not necessarily be related to weaknesses because, although 'development needs' are usually associated with limitations, one of the features of an assessment centre is that it also brings out strengths. Perhaps in the past we have dwelt too much on 'training gaps' and paid too little attention to helping people to learn how to understand and build upon their strengths.

Griffiths and Goodge (1994) have described 'third-generation' development centres where participants are actively involved in generating their own assessments.

For further accounts of assessment centres see Cockerill (1989), Dulewicz (1989) and Woodruffe (1990).

Discussion question: Is it possible to justify the expense of development centres for other than management jobs? If so, what types of participants/job-holders are appropriate to invite?

SELF-ASSESSMENT – CREATING EXPERIENTIAL LEARNING OPPORTUNITIES

As the rate of change accelerates rapidly, detailed job analyses become quickly outdated, placing increasing emphasis on self-analysis, self-development and situations where employees take charge of their own learning. This trend is likely to continue in the foreseeable future, so that situations where an HRD professional produces a job analysis and prescribes the necessary training are likely to become confined to lower-level routine jobs. In Chapter 12 we ask the question, 'How can we help people to develop themselves?', and one way in which we can do this is by helping them to learn from experience.

In Chapter 3 we explained the cyclical process of experiential learning (see Figure 3.2), and implicit in the reflection and conceptualisation stages of that cycle is the recognition of one's own shortcomings. Mumford (1989) has pointed out that managers tend to think in terms of managerial activities and problems first, whereas recognition of learning/training needs is a secondary stage in their thought processes. The requirement, therefore, is to accelerate this procedure and 'trigger' an acceptance of these needs and an awareness of remedial opportunities, many of which already exist in the working environment. There are numerous ways of encouraging this recognition; for instance, Mumford suggests a review based on the learning opportunities, which can encourage managers to realise how they can create learning events for themselves, often without the word 'need' being mentioned at all. (For a comprehensive treatment of this topic see Mumford 1989, and Honey and Mumford 1989.) It is possible, as we have discovered, to enhance the process by 'co-reflection, which one of us has tested out by working with a colleague in another discipline. Comparing notes in this way, if the colleague or friend is constructive, can be a powerful learning tool.

Action learning 'sets' can provide a similar kind of 'trigger', particularly when the discussion centres on what is needed to overcome a particular problem. Regular entries in a personal logbook help towards the gradual identification of needs and opportunities. This type of activity is at the heart of the process of continuous development and the concept of learning organisations, where reality is the vehicle for learning. External help can be obtained through discussion with other people, but the process itself is internal and essentially self-developmental because the assessment is an intrinsic part of the learning. It is a skill, the most vital of the 'competences' that has to be acquired and gradually cultivated as a prerequisite of 'learning to learn'. A recognition of one's own learning style is a helpful step forward, and the Honey and Mumford Learning Styles Questionnaire (see Chapter 3) is a useful diagnostic instrument. Advice on how to practise and improve styles other than that originally preferred helps the learner to become more versatile in completing all four stages of the experiential learning cycle.

Various kinds of planned interventions can be used as stimulators for experiential learning, such as courses consisting of 'contrived' experiences (group task assignments, or in their extreme form, outdoor training). The debriefing and review that follows such activities can afford significant insights into strengths and weaknesses, and into the role each participant has played in the group.

Programmes can also be structured around questionnaires to identify preferred team roles, the two most notable being the Belbin Team Roles (see Woods and Thomas 1992), and the Margerison McCann Team Roles (see Margerison 1992). Both of these feed information from a self-perception questionnaire into a computer and produce individual print-outs relating to the way participants see their roles as team members. The Belbin programme has an added dimension in that it incorporates information provided by colleagues or other course participants, thereby providing a more objective profile. The analysis into identifiable 'roles' assists an individual in making the most of opportunities for practice that arise in the course of his or her work. These programmes and the learning needs they diagnose are particularly important in view of the increasing use of teamwork in organisations. They are also useful tools to help in the diagnosis of group HRD needs.

Other ways of helping people identify their own development needs are individual action plans. Sometimes it is useful to start these with a blank sheet. Otherwise, a little helpful structure can be provided in the form of such questions as:

- Where am I now?
- Where do I want to be?
- What is stopping me from getting there?
- What do I need to know?
- What do I need to do?
- Where can I get help?

Dave is an assistant editor in a local newspaper, which is developing 'learning organisation' practices. He is fortunate in that his manager, Linda, realising that developing her staff is an important part of her responsibilities, has herself undertaken an open learning programme on coaching. She helps Dave to assess his strengths and weaknesses and take a critical look at his performance. Together they make an assessment of his learning and development needs and consider the best ways of meeting them. They make a learning/action plan and, wherever possible, they try to identify suitable learning opportunities in the working situation. For instance, Dave is praised for always producing the latest 'hot news' but, on the other hand, is sometimes criticised for holding up all his copy until the very last minute. This has caused great difficulties in the production department and has occasionally cost money in the form of overtime for production staff and loss of sales due to late delivery to retail outlets. Linda suggests that Dave might spend two afternoons in the production department, shadowing the assistant production manager and discussing problems with him. As a result he is to produce a report on better handling of last-minute 'hot items'. (This might also provide a training opportunity for the assistant production manager, as well as for the supervisor who is to deputise for Dave on the two afternoons.) Linda and Dave agree to meet on a regular basis to reassess Dave's skills, and set new targets and action plans. In this way the coaching became a continuous cycle and gradually Dave learns to manage the process for himself.

- What targets am I going to achieve by … (dates)?
- How am I going to monitor and evaluate my performance?

When completing action plans, it is important that the targets are sufficiently specific to be recognised. For instance, to plan to 'delegate more next year' is not a meaningful target, because it can be very loosely interpreted. A more specific target would be 'By 13th March I will have reviewed all my work activities and found a suitable way of delegating 20 per cent of them.'

The role of the coach in self-assessment

A coach can also help the trainee (or sometimes group of trainees) to assess performance, realise shortcomings and identify learning needs, develop and carry out a learning/action plan, reassess competence and constantly review progress. The essence of coaching is to help the learner recognise and take advantage of the learning opportunities that occur in her working situation.

We describe in a little more detail in Chapter 11 the role of coaching in management development.

BEYOND THE JOB DESCRIPTION – DEVELOPING THE 'THINKING PERFORMER'

You have probably now realised that there has been historical development of methodologies to determine learning and training needs, influenced by the dominant job characteristics at different periods, as well as the philosophies propounded by national institutions.

The analytical methods we have described so far are effective in a stable environment, but will not suffice alone against a background of fierce competition and rapidly developing technology, where successful organisations need to be able not only to grab every opportunity, but to create new openings for themselves. In such circumstances employees need to deliver in ways that go beyond the job description, by engaging in *discretionary* behaviour.

Discretionary behaviour

> Discretionary behaviour means making the sort of choices that often define a job, such as the way the job is done – the speed, care, innovation and style of the job delivery. This behaviour is at the heart of the employment relationship, because it is hard for the employer to define and then monitor and control the amount of effort, innovation and productive behaviour required (Sloman 2003).

This quotation is from the University of Bath's Work and Employment Research Centre. Sloman continues that encouraging employees to use their own initiative and try *themselves* to develop the knowledge and skills for their current and *future* jobs creates powerful business advantages. It is claimed that this is the new approach to competition. In fact, we would maintain that the concept of continuing development, which we have advocated for many years (see Chapter 2) is closely related to this philosophy. It means that while job analysis can provide useful guidelines, it is often unlikely to be the whole story. Rigid job guidelines belong to more bureaucratic and mechanistic types of structure, which are only suitable for certain organisations and for static conditions. In a rapidly changing environment, it is not possible to train everyone to do everything, particularly where time is

171

important – business can be lost while analyses are being made! We have always maintained that an organisation is a learning environment, and people need to learn within that environment, and use their knowledge and skills to see what needs to be done and to adapt rapidly. That is not to say that job analysis does not have a purpose. As well as thinking of their own jobs, employees need to understand how anything they do might impact on someone else's jobs, and to the rest of the organisation, so they need a much wider understanding of the whole picture and what other peoples' jobs entail. For this reason there must be much greater emphasis on uninhibited problem-solving discussion and teamwork. It is also necessary to have 'ground rules' for some jobs – for example, in the Health Service, specifying the boundaries of discretion. Within those boundaries, however, it is not possible to train for every eventuality – people have to be spontaneous and respond to situations. (For further information see the CIPD study *Change Agenda, Focus on the Learner.*)

This type of situation can place more focus on the interface *between* jobs, and this is where role analysis can come into play. We know of one organisation that requires all its supervisory and managerial staff to undertake a 'Written analysis of interface relationships', and to discuss this with their immediate superior, and often with all those concerned. This can be a very salutary and revealing learning experience! In some jobs, discretionary behaviour may also necessitate knowledge and understanding of the interfaces between the organisation and its environment. In this case a 'Written analysis of corporate interface relationships' may be useful. (For more information see Reid 1995.)

The 'thinking performer' also needs up-to-date knowledge, which cannot always be specified in a job analysis because it is often rapidly changing and circumstantial. This can sometimes be provided as required by the Internet/intranets, but management, project and team meetings can be valuable trigger points for transmitting knowledge and converting 'tacit' knowledge into 'explicit' (see page 275).

Figure 8.7 *Flow of information, data and knowledge within the organisation*

Analysis of sources of knowledge, information and data

Because it is not possible nowadays to specify all future knowledge requirements of a job, an analysis of sources of knowledge, information and data may be useful as an accompaniment to a role analysis. A framework for an internal analysis is given in Figure 8.7.

But how are employees to be *encouraged* and *empowered* to become 'thinking performers'?

Organisational architecture

Quoting research from the University of Birmingham/Development Partnership and the University of Bath, Philpott (2003) stresses the importance of

> a clear statement of direction and purpose that engages people at an emotional level

– hence the necessity of a vision or mission statement and information about current objectives (see Chapter 5). Senior management must play an important part in injecting and maintaining enthusiasm, but this is not sufficient unless the elements of what Philpott terms the 'organisation architecture' (people management practices, employment relationships and organisation structures), which set the framework for management and employee behaviour, are mutually reinforcing. In Chapter 12 we refer to some of these ongoing operational systems, which if set up and carried out in an appropriate way help to support HRD activities, by providing opportunities for discussion and helpful feedback. We have already discussed those, such as appraisal, mentoring, formal assessment centres and benchmarking, which obviously relate to HRD, but we would maintain that the same applies to *all* management practices, whether or not they appear to be obviously related to human resources.

It seems obvious that in an efficient and competitive organisation, these systems and relationships should give the same message and reward effectively, but this is difficult to achieve and does not always happen in practice. This is partly because many different people may be involved in the management of these systems. For instance, managers who make decisions about career development schemes may not be present at team meetings and review discussions taking place at a lower hierarchy in the organisation, and may not be aware of the actual contribution made by each team member. Trying to ensure that congruence is achieved among all systems should be an important part of the learning facilitator's remit, although for a variety of reasons (many of them historical) this is not always the case.

Feedback from some of these systems, such as benchmarking, can provide not only invaluable information on what individual learning and development needs to take place, but give the organisation an opportunity for review and 'double-loop learning'. In other words, as well as attempting to overcome any shortcomings found, to ask the questions 'Are all the systems working?' and 'Are they set up correctly for current needs?'

All management meetings, project discussions and review sessions are learning experiences. The difficulty is that this kind of learning is often imperceptible and difficult to evaluate in a formal way. It does not follow the 'traditional' pattern (analysing, assessing need, planning and providing training followed by evaluation). The realisation of need becomes part of the learning. It is unlikely to be evaluated because people do not realise it is happening, and if they did, they would not call it learning. They would probably say they 'had had a useful meeting'. It is part of what happens in carrying out a job in an appropriate environment, and it is the most potent influence. The difficulty is that there are no 'quick fixes' and, as the case study below shows, it can take considerable courage by management. It requires a recognition that mistakes are an opportunity for people and organisations to learn, the absence of a 'blame culture' where people try to shift responsibility, and an openness to reflect and discuss. People need to be encouraged to use their initiative and when necessary act beyond the confines of a rigid job description. A good system of management development can help to create the right climate.

Teamwork is essential, and although various forms of team training can help, by far the best development takes place in the real situation, where a manager or team leader has the skills

A publishing enterprise was threatened with massive changes among its suppliers, in the formulation of its products and in its channels of distribution. The company was owned by a team of partners whose skill and expertise had built it from nothing to its current state of prosperity, who could see enormous future expansion possibilities, but who were not keen to spend a further decade trying to cope with new pressures. They had explored the possibility of selling out, but both they and their employees knew that would possibly bring to an end the culture they had nurtured over the previous 27 years. The alternative was to find some other way of running the business. They decided to give all their employees who wished to do so, the opportunity to develop into managerial roles. Very fortunately the company had always thrived on an atmosphere of trust and co-operation and so the initial culture was mainly favourable.

The plan was to encourage the participants to 'action learn' their way into the key issues that would affect their future, and discuss them right across the enterprise. This was to be followed with focused education on the knowledge and skills requirements that had been exposed, and later by encouragement to attend high-level action learning groups discussing organisation-relevant research projects.

The first stage was the inauguration of a Senior Management Action Programme (SEMAP 1), which required each manager to choose an issue important for the future development of his or her role in the organisation, and to attend a nine-month in-company action learning programme. An eminent outsider, already known to the company, was brought in to act as a facilitator or set adviser, but did not in any way influence any views or decisions taken. Feedback from the participants indicated that they saw themselves as broadening their understanding of what each other did, by completing projects that would be implemented to change the way the organisation dealt with issues for which they felt responsible. The action learning process made them turn to each other rather than to the owners.

The second stage was an in-house Action Learning advanced programme, which as well as projects provided the focused education and training for the main functions and skills areas highlighted by the first programme. The education and training that had been provided gave rise to requests for professional skills development in several areas. This was encouraged, not instead of action learning, but as well. The second programme was followed by actively encouraging the emerging senior managers to follow more advanced action learning and research programmes.

of setting an informal agenda, bringing people into the discussion, and is prepared to listen to suggestions. The learning facilitator could have a useful role to play in helping to run such meetings, but this would depend upon the overall culture in the organisation and upon his or her own credibility and standing. Meetings where the team leader or manager has already decided upon a solution and attempts to 'sell' it without modification are generally counterproductive.

The next stage was SEMAP 2, when virtually every manager and supervisor in the enterprise took part either in the senior set, or on two other levels known as A-MAP and B-MAP; projects were chosen by the staff concerned, dealing with topics across the enterprise. Some of these were of great significance and retrieved the cost of the programme within a year, and led to non-owner initiatives, and a situation where the employees were leading the owners. In the words of the participants, 'spontaneous combustion' had occurred!

Important to the success of the programmes was the fact that everyone in the senior management team had an owner, partner or director as a mentor and the way in which this responsibility was carried out was a very influential feature. This case highlights some of the important factors in the success of action learning programmes, and at the same time demonstrates why in-company action learning programmes are not very common. First of all there had been a climate of trust built up over the years. There was a clear vision of where the company wanted to be within the following 10 years, and, very importantly, it was known that the owners would be willing to listen to reasonable arguments, and that well-considered and well-researched projects had a very good chance of being implemented – nothing is more discouraging than to spend days and weeks on a project that then gathers dust on a shelf. Promotion had been promised to those who did well and this was not just seen as 'pie in the sky', as it was known that the owners wished gradually to disassociate themselves from the business. There was every incentive to the participants, the 'organisational architecture' was congruent and if any systems had not been so, the employees themselves had the opportunity to discuss and recommend amending them. From the intensity and length of the programmes, some of which required study in the participants' own time, you might assume that these were people with time on their hands. In fact the majority of them were married women, with families and homes to run – some had started work on a part-time basis.

This company has now grown enormously. During the programme the premises were extended and it now trades in many countries of the world. All but one of the owners have now retired from the business, and with one or two specialist exemptions, the original staff are running it. It has to be granted that the circumstances were unusual, as introducing action learning, resulting in 'internal combustion', was a risk that in different circumstances not many company directors would feel brave enough to take, but it demonstrates how learning can be integrated with work to powerful and profitable effect. It also indicates how analysis of need for learning may be closely aligned with organisational development and succession planning – another example of successful integration of HR policies.

ACTION LEARNING

We describe Action Learning in other parts of this book (Chapters 11 and 12). It is an important way of gaining competitive advantage and coping with a rapidly changing environment by combining learning with work, but is not used as widely as it merits. Revans' original pattern involving the use of people outside the enterprise can be adapted to suit different organisational contexts. A 'set' can be formed from appropriate members from various levels of the organisation hierarchy, or several sets can be convened to represent each level – senior management, middle management, junior management and so on. The following case illustrates the point.

Further details of this case can be found in Gore (1997) and Reid (1997).

This chapter has introduced you to a portfolio of techniques that HRD practitioners might use to analyse individual learning needs. We have suggested that the 'thinking performer' is an individual who will take more responsibility for developing his or her own learning for both current and future posts. In your own situation, how would you propose to develop as a thinking performer? What assistance will be beneficial for you?

The next chapter looks at how the HRD practitioner might begin to meet learning needs and evaluate the success of his or her programmes.

Meeting Needs: Designing HRD Interventions and Measuring Their Success

CHAPTER 9

In Chapter 9, we will consider:

■ **The need for well thought-out learning/training objectives;**

■ **The range of operational strategies open to the HRD specialist to meet learning needs;**

■ **The fact that learning is not just about training courses, although even with the rapid development of online learning, the training course is still popular – and has its benefits;**

■ **The need for appropriate learning objectives, and ways to measure outcomes to ensure effective evaluation;**

■ **That evaluation of the impact of learning and training interventions is vitally important, not just for trainers and that the emphasis should be on learners to evaluate their learning experiences.**

Some time further on in your HR career, you might imagine yourself as Director of HRD for a large retail group with a significant number of outlets situated throughout the UK. You have just attended a board meeting, at which worrying figures were produced showing that in the past quarter retail shrinkage has increased dramatically. The situation is regarded as very serious and was discussed as a matter of major concern and priority. Some of the comments made by your fellow directors were as follows:

'Our branch managers need training – they don't seem to understand their responsibilities! They need to be made to see that shrinkage in their own branch is their responsibility. We should call them all in for a compulsory conference, and tell them it's not good enough.'

'That would be expensive. After the amount we have lost in shrinkage, we can't afford it. Perhaps the regional managers could hold their own conferences – make them realise *their* responsibilities as well.'

'I disagree. We don't need more training, but better security equipment and alarms.'

'I agree. It will cost the earth to run a conference, and anyway it isn't the managers who need training: it's the counter staff who let it all happen, and there is quite a high turnover there. We would be training people for the opposition to employ!'

It was finally agreed, however, that you should produce a report to be discussed at a special meeting of the board in two weeks' time. What are you going to say?

This chapter, we hope, will help to provide you with some criteria to use in deciding upon your recommendations. You will also see, however, that getting your recommended course of

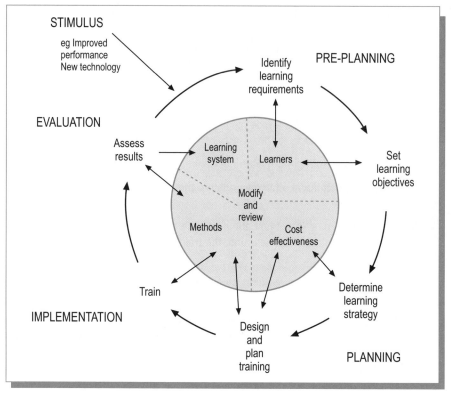

Figure 9.1 *The training process system*

action approved by your colleagues could also be a political matter, which you will have to take into consideration.

In Chapter 7 (page 144), we gave an example of a wrongly identified training need, and therefore before attempting to determine any HRD plan, it is first sensible to check that learning and training really can contribute to the situation. Once you are sure this is the case, the main stages in devising a planned learning/training intervention are illustrated in Figure 9.1:

- identifying the learning/training requirements; what do you want to achieve in terms of outcomes?
- setting learning/training objectives
- selecting the appropriate strategy
- designing and planning the programme
- implementing the programme
- evaluating the programme's impact.

We considered the first of these stages in Chapter 8, when we investigated methods of deciding on individual learning/training needs. We now consider the formulation of specific objectives, the choice of strategy, and the planning, implementation and evaluation stages of training and development.

Discussion question: Critically review a course, conference or other learning event that you have recently attended as organiser or participant.

LEARNING/TRAINING INTERVENTIONS

We use the term 'intervention' to include any event that is deliberately undertaken to assist learning to take place. It includes a wide range of activities from formal courses to structured work experiences, and we refer to these activities as strategies. As we pointed out in the introduction, by entitling the new edition of this book *Human Resource Development –Training Interventions and beyond*, we are acknowledging that in the world of learning, training and development, the emphasis has changed from the trainer as expert and centre of attention to the learner as custodian of his or her own destiny. The training 'expert' is now more usually manager of the learning environment, or facilitator of learning. This represents the change from 'pedagogic' learning to 'andragogic' – centred on the learner not the learned. Having said this, though, there is still a place for teaching and instruction as interventions designed to fill specific learning needs. The terms are fluid, as is often the case with new 'paradigm shifts', but we do not mean to suggest that trainer-led decisions and activities are no longer relevant as learning methods.

The logical first stage is to determine exactly what it is hoped to achieve by a learning intervention, ie formulate the objectives. The HRD specialist can then decide the best means of achieving these objectives, select tactics, plan the intervention accordingly, and implement and evaluate it.

It is convenient to consider these stages in logical progression. But in fact they are not entirely discrete. For instance, well-defined objectives or competences should provide criteria that can be used as a basis for evaluation. It is sometimes necessary to employ training techniques, such as structured exercises, which will provide feedback of the learning taking place and which will thus form part of the evaluation. The final evaluation serves a number of useful purposes. It provides feedback or knowledge of results, and draws attention to aspects of the objectives that have not yet been achieved. This involves a reconsideration of the remaining objectives and a return to the beginning of the cycle. Self-evaluation involves consideration of mistakes and errors made, and is a valuable part of the learning process. Let's look at each of these activities in turn.

STAGE 1 – DETERMINATION OF LEARNING/TRAINING OBJECTIVES

A behavioural objective may be regarded as an intent, expressed in the form of a statement, describing a proposed behaviour change in the learner. The term 'criterion behaviour' is used to define what the learner is expected to do at the end. It specifies the tasks, procedures and techniques that he or she should be able to carry out, the standards of performance required and the circumstances in which the work will be undertaken (see Mager 1984). There are three stages in determining a behavioural objective:

- Specify the behaviour the learner is required to demonstrate for the objective to be achieved.
- Determine the important conditions in which the behaviour must be demonstrated, for example, the type or range of equipment to be used or the environmental constraints.

■ Determine the standard to which the learner must perform. This can vary from a precise production specification to criteria such as absence of customer complaints. It is frequently the most difficult aspect to define, but it is usually possible to find a way of describing what would be regarded as acceptable performance. Sometimes it has to be no more objective than 'to the satisfaction of the supervisor', but this is rather a bland example.

An example of a behavioural objective is 'On completion of the training, the word processor operator should be capable of typing "x" words per minute with no errors, using "y" system, under normal office conditions'.

Of course, some words in the English language, such as 'understand', 'know', 'appreciate', are open to many interpretations. For instance, if a person 'knows' how a refrigerator works, he or she might be able to design one, to assemble one, to repair one, or merely to describe its operation. Words such as these are not very helpful in compiling behavioural objectives. It is better to use more precise terms such as 'identify', 'differentiate', 'construct' or 'solve', which are more capable of describing specific behaviour.

There is also a difference between 'learner' objectives and 'trainer' objectives. Examples of the latter might be 'to give an appreciation of ...' or 'to provide an adequate foundation for ...'. These do not specify what the learner is expected to **do** at the end of the training and should not be listed as behavioural objectives.

It is not always easy to structure an unambiguous learning objective in a training context, but the clearer the objective that results, the more likelihood there is of successful training. A learner cannot be expected to know what he or she should be learning if the trainer's own objectives are uncertain, and sadly this may sometimes happen – trainers are as imperfect as their learners! In some areas, such as management development, as we have seen, it is much more difficult to describe learning or development objectives in strict behavioural terms, because the specific behaviour required may not be known at the time, or the number of possible learning outcomes may be too big to list. In such circumstances, one solution proposed by Gronlund (1978) is to state the general objective first, and then clarify it by listing a sample of the specific behaviour that would be acceptable as evidence of the attainment of the objective. For example:

At the end of the programme the manager will be able to take greater responsibility for the development of her own staff. Indicative activities will include:
■ carrying out satisfactory appraisal interviews
■ enabling her subordinates to recognise and accept their own training needs
■ conducting effective coaching and counselling sessions
■ delegating successfully to her subordinates.

Objectives can also be described in this way without necessarily predicting the precise outcome. Many learning experiences raise open-ended questions, the answers to which have to be worked out when back on the job. It is clearly unrealistic to set as a behavioural objective for a course on management styles 'participants will change styles immediately on returning to work', but it is possible to determine indicative activities, such as showing an interest in developing new interpersonal skills, or initiating discussion on management styles with colleagues.

Discussion question: Now have a go at suggesting behavioural objectives for a course in presentation skills for sales staff.

Effective training can often act as a catalyst for change, and it may be useful to make a distinction between learning objectives and the ultimate outcome of an intervention. For example, a management conference might be organised with the objective of arriving at some common agreement on the solution of a problem. A subobjective might be that each manager would be able to identify the implications of the problem for his or her own department, and contribute to the solutions by putting forward practical suggestions. A second subobjective might be attitudinal: that although possibly not in entire agreement with the ultimate solution, each manager would have recognised the many facets of the problem and display commitment to the final recommendations. In other words, the learning experience of discussion with colleagues holding varied viewpoints would give each manager a broader perspective and an understanding of the reasons for the decisions, rather than an opinion based on her own narrow experience.

A record of conference proceedings including the contribution of each manager, and a subsequent follow-up of the implementation of the proposals, would be methods of checking whether the objectives had been met. What could not be specified beforehand, however, would be the nature of the conclusions reached, ie the ultimate outcome. Top management may well have had some preferred solution in mind and the conference may have approved it. If, though, in the course of debate, sound reasons emerged for adopting a different approach, top management's credibility would be lost if these findings were totally disregarded and the predetermined solution imposed from above. In these circumstances, such a conference may well have done more harm than good! In the same way, an intervention such as a series of courses using team roles exercises may have as its purpose an examination and evaluation of the work of a team, but the precise outcome of that programme cannot be predicted. As we move further towards self-development and experiential learning for the individual and the group, the outcome may be to trigger change in a variety of ways that could not have been predicted, as in the case study in the previous chapter (pages 174–6). Maybe the 'team' could decide it preferred to operate as a collection of individuals!

The learning facilitator, trainer or coach alone should not necessarily be formulating the objectives. The concept of continuous development requires employees to be able to take increasing responsibility for their own learning. Consequently they must be capable of drawing up their own objectives, although there may be some conflict between the desired objectives of the employee and those of her employer. Assisting in the judgement of learning/training objectives can be an important motivator, and indeed part of the learning process itself for any learner, particularly for young people undertaking a general basic training. The same principle applies to students from schools, colleges or universities who are undertaking work experience placements.

Objectives and NVQs

In earlier chapters we described how NVQs are based on the concept of competences, and both the learning required and its assessment are governed by statements of competence. The elements of competence bear some relationship to behavioural objectives in that they are defined by means of an active verb and also include a statement of the conditions. In addition, each element has performance criteria setting out what must be achieved for successful performance. The performance criteria must always contain a critical outcome and an evaluative statement. The critical outcome stipulates what has to be done for the element to be successfully accomplished, and the evaluative statement qualifies it in a quantitative or qualitative way. The performance criteria must relate to outcomes, and not processes or procedures. They are concerned with what the learner can do rather than how she has acquired the competence. The terminology of 'behavioural' objectives is not used, and Jessup (1991) suggests that a major difference between the two methodologies is that in the NVQ approach the statement of outcomes is not limited by considerations of assessment. Some of the earlier attempts at defining behavioural objectives were focused on educational programmes with conventional assessment schemes.

Discussion question: How would you refute the idea that the very specific behavioural objectives required by NVQs are restrictive?

STAGE 2 – DETERMINING APPROPRIATE OPERATIONAL LEARNING/TRAINING STRATEGIES

We have attempted to make clear the link between job analysis and behavioural objectives. At this stage it becomes obvious whether the necessary knowledge and skills, or in the case of NVQs the 'competences' have been investigated and described in sufficient detail. For instance, 'communication skills' is too broad a description to be of much assistance. It could give rise to a wide variety of objectives, for which appropriate training could range from report writing to learning how to chair a meeting. On the other hand, 'ability to give accurate and speedy information about train times to all telephone inquirers' gives a very clear indication of what is needed. Precise details are therefore essential to the design of a programme that requires specified outcomes. Putting these into objective writing can be surprisingly challenging!

At this point there may be a range of choices for what will constitute the actual learning activity, and selection of the most suitable ones can be critical. We have classified the possibilities under six main headings:

1   instruction and coaching on-the-job
2   planned in-house attachments
3   in-house programmes
4   planned experiences outside the organisation
5   external courses
6   self-managed learning.

We shall explain each of these in more detail, but first, the four 'decision criteria' to use in determining the appropriate training strategy are:

- compatibility with objectives
- estimated likelihood of transfer of learning to the work situation
- available resources (including money, time and staff)
- trainee-related factors.

It is not possible to give specific rules applying in every situation. In reality, most cases are likely to result in a compromise between what is desirable and what is possible. The decision-making process is likely to be one of 'best fit', as the following example illustrates:

An HRD manager was requested, as a matter of urgency, to arrange teambuilding training for a group of managers about to embark on a new project, the success of which depended crucially upon group effort. There was little time to undertake the training. Using the four criteria, the deciding factors were:

- the objectives included knowledge of skills of group membership (for example of group interaction), as well as of attitude formation.
- learning transfer to the work situation was essential. The organisation climate was influenced by a pragmatic 'down to earth' management style, which was likely to be supportive of training based on real, rather than theoretical, issues.
- resources were very limited: time was short and there was little money left in the budget.
- learner-related factors. The managers had family commitments and would not have welcomed being asked to stay away from home, although they might ultimately have been persuaded to do so. Also, they could not be spared from their departments for long periods.

The HRD manager considered the possible tactics and methods. She rejected on-the-job training as being unlikely to achieve the objectives because each manager was isolated in his or her own department. Planned activity inside the company satisfied the criteria of good learning transfer, acceptability and credibility to the managers concerned. She wondered how it could be arranged. She considered external courses and re-read a brochure for an outdoor training course she had previously thought looked useful. She knew this type of training was often effective in creating a team spirit, and if all the managers were to go together there was a good chance the learning would transfer to the work situation. The timing was suitable, but the course lasted a full week. It would be difficult to arrange for all the managers to be absent from their departments so near to the start of the project, and the cost would use all that was left of the HRD budget. She remembered that one of the managers had a visual disability, which might cause difficulties with some of the projects. She considered other external courses and rejected them for similar reasons.

She then thought about the possibility of an internal course. She decided that, because the objectives included attitudes and skill requirements, a course involving discussion sessions and group activities would be appropriate. There would be a better chance of learning transfer if it were possible to base sessions on real problems the managers would face in carrying out the project. From a resource perspective, the cost would be less than an outside course, and the timing could be arranged to suit the managers' availability. Although evening sessions might be included, they would not have to stay away from home, which would save money. That could not be considered an advantage in achieving the objectives, but she decided that in the circumstances it was the best compromise she could reach. A conference room and syndicate rooms were available.

The main difficulty was that time was short for her to prepare the programmes (a frequent complaint from all HR people!), but having considered her own commitments and those of her staff, she decided that it would be possible, especially as it might be beneficial to arrange certain problem-discussion sessions after the project had actually started. This would enable the course to be based partly on 'real' material, which would help to ensure learning transfer similar to that provided by on-the-job training. She decided to consult senior management about the possibility of building some of the later sessions into the conduct of the project itself, and also to investigate what assistance she could obtain from her local university. In this way, she would be able to combine two strategies: an in-company course consolidated and made relevant by structured in-house activity. Training would therefore be playing a direct and integrated role in implementing organisational plans.

Discussion question: Would you have made the same decision? If not, what other options would you have considered?

This example is not intended to show that an in-house course is necessarily superior to outdoor training, which on another occasion might have been more effective. Neither does it suggest that courses are always the answer. What it should show is that each decision as to the most appropriate operational learning/training strategy is contingent on the circumstances, and the resultant decision will reflect the 'best fit'.

Now we will look at each of the six main forms of operational strategies for delivering learning and training and the four 'decision criteria' in more detail, giving examples of how they relate to each other.

Instruction and coaching on-the-job

On-the-job training accounts for about half of all training, and a survey carried out for the (former) IPD in 1996 in manufacturing companies indicated that it worked 'tolerably well' particularly for simple tasks, but that improvements could be made (CIPD – formerly IPD 1998). Jobs vary from the very simple to the highly complex, and it is therefore difficult to generalise, but knowledge of the analytical techniques discussed in Chapter 8 is equally appropriate for on-the-job and off-the-job trainers or learning facilitators. In general, the success of on-the-job learning depends upon:

- well-trained trainers/facilitators. These should not only be competent at the job, but also have skills in coaching and giving feedback, and be knowledgeable about appropriate learning processes (such as those discussed in Chapters 3 and 8).
- adequate recognition of the on-the-job trainer/facilitator role. Many of them have other responsibilities and if, for instance, they are supervisors or fellow workers, they may well not regard training or coaching as their main concern. They need to be given sufficient time allowance from their other work, kept up to date with new developments and, where possible, should be given regular opportunities to act as trainers.
- adequate preparation. For an operator's task this includes not only the necessary

materials, and learning aids but a competent job training analysis (see Chapter 8). For simple tasks, the stages and key points analysis illustrated in Figure 8.3 is extremely useful. For a feedback or coaching session for any type of job (see pages 72–3 and 170) preparation would include careful study of all relevant details of the learner's progress to date.

■ safety considerations (see Chapter 3). These should be paramount, and potential dangers should always be key points on a training analysis. Training on dangerous equipment should be preceded where possible by experience on a simulator, and should at all times be monitored with extreme care.

■ appropriate target setting, performance testing and monitoring procedures. These will help assess progress and provide knowledge of results for trainer and learner.

In the case of management development, on-the-job learning/training may take the form of coaching and advice from immediate superiors or, in some instances, merely seeing the example of a good superior's work practices, and trying to perform according to appropriate standards (ie modelling) may be enough. The whole process of agreeing key areas and targets, whether as part of a formal performance management scheme or by individual agreement between manager and subordinate, may also be viewed as invaluable on-the-job training in such aspects as prioritisation, work organisation and planning.

On-the-job learning/training is obviously likely to take place in small companies where there is no HRD specialist, but it can also be an appropriate option for larger organisations, where the specialist's role may be in developing the management and supervisors as trainers. An important additional advantage of on-the-job training is that can be a useful developmental experience not just for the learner, but also for the trainer or coach.

Considered against the four 'decision criteria', the advantages of on-the-job training are that it is likely to be high in learning transfer to the specific job and to appear inexpensive in terms of resources (but see examples of learning costs in Chapter 5). The learner may take longer to reach the learning objectives, because the environmental conditions may be unfavourable, but there can be some compensation in the fact that she may well be performing some part of the job during the training period. However, the planned training may be narrow and job-specific, without the necessary underpinning knowledge, and may not transfer to other environments. For many jobs a mixture of on- and off-the job training might well be the best strategy – a view that can be reinforced by the suggestion that those who have just completed off-the-job training cannot usually be considered 'completely trained' until they have had the benefit of consolidating what they have learned by on-the-job experience, and may still require careful monitoring and coaching for some time.

See Cannell (1997) for useful case studies and tips on on-the-job training. See also *Key Facts: On-the-job Training* (IPD 1998) for an informative but concise summary, including how to implement an OJT programme, two short case studies and further reading list.

Planned in-house learning experiences

These can be designed within existing organisational processes and wherever possible as an integral part of mainstream developments (see Table 3.1). They can include planned experience in other departments or within the same department, or the assignment of special responsibilities, problem-solving discussion groups, quality circles, special projects, developing fresh aspects of activity such as a new sales promotion, or a record system.

These are likely to provide positive transfer of learning provided there is organisational support. It is counterproductive to ask someone to undertake projects and special assignments when there is little hope of eventual implementation. Action Learning to which we refer throughout the book, involving 'learning by doing', provides a means for managers to learn on the job as well as acquiring awareness of the way in which they learn.

Opportunities for planned in-house activities are sometimes deliberately created or may be planned to assist day-to-day running of departments.

> One organisation arranges for its graduate trainees to take over a production section for four weeks while the supervisor is on holiday. The graduate prepares for this by spending some time beforehand in the section, and actually takes over the week before the supervisor leaves, continuing for a week after her return. This provides a challenging work experience for the graduate, while allowing the supervisor to take her annual leave at a busy time.

Another example in this category, which is growing in popularity, is the use of coaches and mentors, discussed in page 170 and chapter 11 as a management development strategy. A mentor can be described as a 'role model ... a guide, a tutor, a coach and a confidant' (Clutterbuck 1991). As well as helping junior managers to understand organisational values and cultures, mentoring has the advantage of inducting newcomers at all levels efficiently to the organisation and of assisting them with organisational problems and personal development, so increasing motivation and job satisfaction. A properly organised scheme of mentoring is an inexpensive and efficient method of employee development. (For an example of a framework for a training course on coaching and mentoring see Moorby 1994.)

In-house programmes

Many large organisations have a regular programme of in-house courses for what might be regarded as 'maintenance' training and development. These can include updating courses in specific topics or they may be general courses, such as those for junior, middle or senior managers, and attendance by people eligible for promotion is a routine practice. Other courses and conferences may be organised for specific needs, such as changes in legislation, company policy or industrial relations practice. Some internal courses may be consultative in nature, for instance conferences to discuss future organisational development, or changes in structure or management style. Some organisations run their own part-time qualification courses. The NVQ standards, adapted to the workplace and offering certificates for the successful completion of units, which can be accumulated to qualify for awards, can usefully underpin this arrangement. For instance, 'retail skills' apprentices in a well-known supermarket chain undergo in-company programmes for the National Retail Certificates. Because these must be assessed to a national standard, they should be recognised by other employers, and can be used as a basis on which to build during later career development. Staff from local colleges are usually very happy to assist and help to plan in-house courses.

There is likely to be better learning transfer from internal, compared with external, courses, particularly if senior management are involved in some of the sessions. The presence of a senior person at a course designed to increase understanding of a cultural change initiative can be a powerful indicator of support. One of us attended a workshop on telephone training which the Chief Executive of the organisation attended – a message that he regarded the issue as most significant. Learning interventions can be directed at real organisational problems, which is likely to increase face validity and chances of effectiveness. Courses are useful when many employees require similar training at one time. A variation is open access in-house training. This can include the provision of computer-based training and the use of interactive video. For example a large motor vehicle manufacturer had the problem of training 600 engineers, within a six-week time-span, in a new specification system for vehicle components. With the help of a grant from one of the national schemes, the target was achieved on time by the use of interactive multimedia computer-based methods at half the cost of the traditional method.

Computer-based and 'online' learning has a number of advantages. It can be undertaken at or very near the learner's place of work, and progress can be at his or her own pace and convenience. Training times can be reduced by the use of pretests, which enable trainees to leave out any items with which they are already familiar. Intermediate and final tests aim to ensure that the material has really been understood. This type of intensive plan is now being used by many other large organisations. For instance, a large building society, which was in the process of altering its operational systems, was able to train all the staff very effectively by means of online computerised packages. Although the initial outlay was considerable, the overall cost per head was much lower than the estimated expenditure on 'traditional' hotel-based courses entailing travelling and residential expenses. Furthermore, the programme is always ready and available for new members of staff.

As IT systems become both cheaper and more reliable, more and more in-house training is being delivered over company intranets. At present the majority concentrate on IT/technical skills and corporate issues, but the intranet can also be used for training in personal skills (presentation skills, time management and assertiveness) and customer-care training (telephone skills, handling complaints). Although IT skills remain the most frequent type of intranet training, with corporate skills following closely, over recent years there has been a considerable increase in the use of this medium for the delivery of personal and management skills, customer care and finance skills.

Once the equipment is installed and used for other purposes as well, this is a convenient and inexpensive medium, with the possible added advantage that, where appropriate, it allows 'just-in-time' delivery. It can allow self-paced and flexible learning, can be delivered to many people on different sites, is particularly useful in global organisations and, where appropriate, can offer instant contact with a facilitator or tutor. A number of imaginative uses are in process of development such as 'virtual classrooms' where people from geographically spread sites can exchange knowledge, or individual tuition from a 'trainer' who may be located miles away. There may, though, be a number of difficulties to overcome. As with any other form of training, management support is paramount, and pilot studies suggest that a culture change may be required, so that HRD is valued. For instance, managers need to understand that staff using online programs on a PC are 'working' and arrangements need to be made so that they are not disturbed. Time management is likely to become of increasing importance as staff assess their priorities and possibly struggle with information overload. A frequent complaint from both online learners and tutors is the '24/7' culture, which allows no respite from the task unless both make a conscious decision to turn off the computer!

There is likely to be a time-lag as HRD specialists assess the results of pilot studies, but there are already steep learning curves for those responsible for online learning, and the initiative itself is continually developing. Although this method of delivery appears to have great potential, it is worth pointing out that there is often a social aspect to learning, and taking part in 'virtual classrooms' and 'group discussions' over an intranet demands new skills from the participants. For instance, during a 'traditional' discussion, participants interpret each other's 'body language' and voice intonation. They rely not just on what is said – how it is said conveys the complete meaning. The absence of these additional modes of communication puts a greater emphasis on the exact wording of contributions to avoid misunderstanding. Video-clips and videoconferencing can help to overcome this difficulty. In addition, consideration has to be given to differences in learning styles, and it is possible that not everyone can happily learn from the type of material that can be presented over an intranet. There have been suggestions that individuals who have been 'conventionally' educated do better in exams than online learners. It is unlikely to be suitable for all types of learning, either. For instance, social skills require practice and constructive feedback, although as technology develops and interactive programmes become more readily available, this difficulty may partly be overcome. The advent of voice control to eliminate the use of a keyboard would also help to make the process more widely accessible. It would be fair to say that, even after 10 years' or so development, more pilot studies and experimentation are still needed. As it becomes widespread, this medium obviously influences the role and required skills of the HRD specialist, as the accent is likely to be on selecting, designing, scriptwriting, and editing self-learning programmes or materials for virtual classrooms; and providing support and counselling rather than on direct training.

> Discussion question: What have been your experiences of online- or intranet-based learning? How do you feel the absence of a tutor's personal attention affects virtual learning?

'Blended learning'

Blended learning is a relatively new term but in fact the concept has been current for a good while. Definitions of the term vary, but it may be best described as a method of distance learning that uses a range of technologies (such as TV, Internet, intranet, voice mail, teleconferencing) and traditional lectures and seminars. Examples might be:

- traditional training sessions with teleconference back-up
- traditional courses with e-mail or bulletin boards to support discussion
- online learning supported by regular workshop sessions.

The idea is to provide a range of opportunities for the learner to access the training, and also to develop an effective learning community, somewhat like a virtual action learning set. A survey conducted by Training Magazine and Balance Learning (November 2003), which consulted a wide range of organisations, suggested that 55% of the 173 respondents were already using it and 27% were planning to. A key reason for using it was said to be the importance of matching an individual's preferred learning style with appropriate training delivery. There is little here to surprise most HRD professionals – blended learning makes sense in terms of maximising opportunities for learning for all staff.

Planned experiences outside the organisation

Secondments and visits to suppliers or to the premises of important customers to obtain external views of the organisation's products and services can provide valuable insights. Visits are sometimes arranged to competitors or suppliers abroad, although these may be expensive. These experiences can, however, fulfil a number of objectives because, as well as passing on information, they often result in attitudinal change and can be used to provide a tangible reward for a recent job well done.

Although learning objectives should be developed from organisational needs, there can be circumstances when management is justified in encouraging employees to undertake self-developmental activities to advance their own careers, such as when promotion prospects are minimised and when current jobs provide few opportunities for challenge or development. Examples of such developmental activities include undertaking a role within a relevant professional body (resulting in contact and discussion with colleagues in other organisations), experience in chairing or addressing meetings, or assisting in external projects for the local community or with local educational institutions.

Learning transfer will depend upon the particular experience, but some attitudinal change is likely to result, which will enable the incumbent to view her job in a different light. There can be dangers in arranging learning activities of this kind. Employees may gain useful experience, which could enable them to move to other organisations, although, of course, this could be a two-way process, and some organisations could attract these talented people. Also, the importance of mental activity and stimulation is a central feature of the process of continuing development. Consequently, there is a case for making allowance for this factor when setting learning objectives. It is necessary to balance the likely costs involved against the possibility of disillusioned employees who, having loyally carried out unchallenging tasks for the organisation over a number of years, discover that they are unable to adjust to change and find it difficult and threatening to learn new techniques and methods. This is one of the problems in developing a 'learning UK', as we saw in Chapter 1.

> Discussion question: Should employee learning have an immediate organisational payoff? How would you measure this?

External courses

Leaflets and brochures advertising external events constantly arrive on the desk of every HRD practitioner. To send someone on a course appears an easy, although frequently expensive, option. External courses are broadly of two kinds: the short full-time variety, run by consultants, colleges and universities, and longer (usually part-time) courses often leading to a qualification. Educational institutions are usually very happy to co-operate and organise part-time programmes specially tailored to the needs of individual organisations or, by agreement, of a consortium of organisations. Because there can be dangers in an organisation becoming too inbred, it is useful for employees to find out what happens 'outside'. Discussing the problems of others can often throw new light upon one's own situation. Where only one or two people require specialised knowledge, a course at the Open University or Open College or at one of the many distance learning programmes on offer is likely to be the best alternative.

Learning transfer is not likely to be high unless the organisation climate is supportive and the immediate manager has an important role to play. If external courses are to be effective, they must be chosen with care. Having decided whether it is policy to cater for the particular need by an external course, and whether the trainee would be prepared to attend, the main factors to be considered are the precise objectives:

- What are the course objectives? Do they match the particular learning need?

- Do the learning/training methods and length of the course accord with its declared objectives? For instance, if the intention is to improve an employee's communication skills, what aspects of communication are covered, and do they match the employee's requirements? Is there any opportunity for supervised practice and feedback? The acquisition of skill does not come through knowledge alone.
- Is there any indication of the level of the course?
- Who are the organisers?
- What experience have they had in the field?
- Is there any information to indicate their competence?
- What other organisations have supported the course?
- Is it possible to get feedback from them?
- Is the cost related to the expected benefits? There is a temptation to judge the merits of a course by its price, but that can be misleading.
- A considerable proportion of the price of a residential course is the cost of the accommodation. Does the venue appear to be suitable? This may seem to be unimportant but if, for instance, a senior manager is asked to attend a course held in surroundings that she considers uncongenial, she may approach the learning material with negative attitudes. A 'rough and ready' venue without 'ensuite' facilities may be a mere 'hygiene factor' to some, but off-putting to more sensitive souls!

HRD specialists should satisfy themselves on these points before committing their organisations to the expenditure and opportunity cost of sending their staff on external courses.

> Discussion question: Obtain a set of training course brochures and compare and contrast what they are offering.

Briefing and debriefing sessions, preferably by the participant's manager, really are a prerequisite to gaining maximum advantage from an external course. Although they are very obvious and inexpensive steps to take, managers frequently fail in this respect, with the result that participants may not have a clear idea of the objectives in sending them on the course, and on return may fail to implement any new ideas through lack of opportunity or because they feel that no interest has been taken. To overcome this problem, some courses for supervisors and junior managers are preceded by short preliminary courses for participants' managers.

Part-time courses, particularly those leading to a qualification, constitute a relatively long-term commitment and a considerable amount of personal study time. For instance, an MBA programme is likely to have broadly based objectives, be extremely demanding, and might be difficult to manage at times of work crisis and overload. It is important for prospective students to be aware that the process will never be easy and the positives of personal development and learning must be set against time pressures and loss of social life. In spite of the difficulties, requests to attend such courses often come from the employee, and are sometimes negotiated on a joint payment basis. From the company perspective it is very important that such a programme is integrated with the career development programme for the employee, and that at least one person from senior management takes an active interest in progress. Without this type of support it is likely that if, on successful completion of the programme, the employee sees no immediate prospect of promotion or recognition, he or she will seek better opportunities elsewhere. There are now many types of MBA programmes, and the Association of MBAs (AMBA) accredits the best-established ones. Some have become specialised for particular categories of participant, such as staff from the Health Service, from engineering or for personnel staff or even, in rare examples, church ministers. Some are 'executive programmes' for relatively senior managers who must be sponsored by their organisations. Such programmes will normally have a steering committee composed of representatives of sponsoring organisations as well as staff from the university to advise on the programme and monitor its development. It is useful for HRD managers from the sponsoring organisations to find out about this committee, because it is a vehicle through which they can exert influence on the conduct of the programme. Some MBAs are designed entirely for one organisation, or for a consortium. These and other part-time courses, such as those leading to professional qualifications, for instance those of the Chartered Institute of Personnel and Development, are normally regarded as a stage in career development rather than an answer to an immediate training need.

> Discussion question: Consider what information you would seek for evaluation purposes from external course attendees in an organisation.

Self-managed learning

In Chapters 4 and 12 we suggest that any organisation is a learning environment, but the efficient self-management of that learning requires particular skills and will only come about in special circumstances. Self-managed learning is not an option that an HRD manager can suddenly decide to implement, but should be regarded as an ultimate aim that may be fulfilled to a greater or lesser extent. People cannot be ordered to manage their own learning! For this to be a sustained organisational strategy a number of conditions must exist. Most importantly, learning must be seen to be valued by the organisation; in other words, there must be a learning culture in which people will be given help to learn both regularly and rigorously from their work. They should be able to identify their own needs, draw up and prioritise a plan of action and evaluate the results. Self-evaluation and the realisation of new ability and competence inspire confidence and act as a spur for further learning (see the continuous development spiral in Figure 3.3). Help will come from managers, coaches, mentors and colleagues, reinforced by organisational systems and processes such as regular discussion of needs and individual appraisal, as well as assistance in finding appropriate training, development and education. Logbooks and records of progress provide a focus, as well as stimulus to further development. Some organisations have instigated voluntary systems of 'personal development files' in which individual employees agree with their line managers to create a personal development plan based on a two-way commitment but emphasising personal responsibility. The file is owned by the individual and can hold certificates or portfolio documents belonging to the employee, and for young people it provides a follow-up to their 'Progress File'.

Self-managed learning can be experiential through recognising and making full use of learning opportunities at work (see Table 3.1), but it can also develop from courses and programmes, possibly using company open learning centres and/or educational schemes. An increasing number of organisations have recognised this and provide open learning facilities, many on site, where employees can book their own access times and embark upon programmes of their choice. There is sometimes no requirement that the programmes they choose are directly related to their current job. However, as we pointed out in Chapter 8, the perceived needs of an individual may relate to self-development and may not necessarily coincide with the immediate requirements of the organisation. Open learning centres are very expensive. The evaluation of benefit to the organisation can be difficult to calculate and quantify, particularly in the short term, and important debates may take place relating to responsibility for the choice of programme, and who should pay. The culture and ethos of a learning organisation would suggest that any learning is beneficial to the development of the whole person, and that the gain would ultimately be fed back to the organisation in the form of increased maturity and learning capacity of its personnel. But this requires a long-term focus, which realistically many organisations do not yet have.

Some organisations have gone a stage further and have set up education schemes offering employees a wide choice of programmes for their own development. The well-known Ford Employee Development and Assistance Programme (EDAP) courses started in July 1989 with the stated objectives of offering employees 'a wide range of personal and career development education and training, retraining and development activities and to make available a variety of employee assistance services to encourage a healthier life style'. A national tripartite committee comprising representatives from the staff and hourly unions and Ford management is responsible for establishing and reviewing the programme's goals and objectives and monitoring progress. Budgets, based on numbers of employees on site, are controlled by local tripartite committees at each of the 19 British locations. As well as approving individual applications for assistance, up to a predetermined limit per annum, these committees can also undertake larger projects such as establishing their own training and learning centres in order to cut down costs and make facilities available for shiftworkers.

Courses under EDAP are not job-related and take place in employees' own time; 32 per cent of courses are held on site and employees are also allowed to take non-work-related courses at local authority skill centres and evening classes, including NVQs and degree programmes. Traditionally, over 50 per cent of employees have applied for assistance each year and they receive advice on the most suitable courses from local education advisers funded by the programme. Approximately one-third of applications are for educational courses and one-third for new skills courses such as bricklaying, car maintenance and decorating. The remainder are for courses in health, leisure and hobbies. Although the direct benefits of the scheme accrue to the participants, it is felt that the scheme helps in various ways: to break down barriers within the workforce; to provide a foundation for further joint initiatives between unions and managers; and to make for a healthier and more adaptable workforce (Willoughby 1996). It is still (2004) going strong and research has shown a plethora of benefits.

As we noted in Chapter 8, from an employee's standpoint a new perspective may be beginning to emerge. The pace of change and economic circumstances are gradually bringing the realisation that instead of relying totally on an organisation for their career progression, employees need to manage their own learning in order to gain flexibility and their own portfolios of qualifications, experience and marketable skills.

Paradoxically, whereas a learning culture is necessary for self-managed learning to flourish as a recognised organisational strategy, enthusiasm for learning can become infectious and help to bring about that very culture. Enthusiasm may be generated by a number of individuals or stimulated by organisational interventions.

The decision criteria for determining a learning strategy

Objectives

Although we have argued that objectives should be formulated in terms as precise as possible, it does not necessarily follow that each can be fulfilled by matching it exactly with a particular strategy. Indeed, more than one strategy may be necessary to achieve a single objective. For instance, a junior manager may be unskilled in presenting a persuasive case at committee meetings. One way of bridging this 'gap' might be for him or her to attend an appropriate course that incorporates suitable skills demonstration and practice sessions; another method might be for a more senior member of management to give him or her appropriate coaching, followed by on-the-job experience including making presentations at specific meetings. In practice, probably a combination of all three would be useful.

Questions such as these may assist in determining an appropriate strategy:

- Is the strategy consistent with the organisation's HRD policy and/or culture?

- Is the objective mainly concerned with long-term career development, or a shorter-term need? For instance, seconding a manager to a long-term part-time course is not likely to be suitable for overcoming his or her immediate problem of time management, and might even exacerbate it!

- Is the main requirement theoretical knowledge, or is the real need that of a thorough understanding of the organisation's policies and procedures? It has not been uncommon for managers to be sent on external courses covering, for example, principles and practices of marketing, when what is really required is a better understanding of company marketing policies, procedures and objectives. Of course, a familiarity with general principles helps to set company practices in perspective (and possibly bring about an improvement in them). What is often required is a mixture of both theory and company practice.

- Is the main need really knowledge or practical skill? A course on computing that does not give 'hands on' experience may help to change attitudes and arouse interest for further training, but is unlikely to help the participants with operational skills or overcome possible anxieties about interacting with computers.

- Is part of the learning/training requirement a general understanding and discussion of common problems? An important aspect of learning can be an awareness of and sensitivity to the total situation, and although this need might be partially met by dissemination of information, it will almost certainly require some kind of relevant experience – either a problem-solving discussion or possibly brief secondments to other departments. HRD can sometimes assume the form of consultation. An example might be when a conference is called with a dual purpose of consultation about the introduction of total quality management, and possibly modifying the original plans as a result, as well as defining the knowledge and skill required to take part in the new style of management. It may be necessary to include general and theoretical material, but the organisational objective would not be met by sending staff individually on external courses.

- Does the objective involve introducing fresh ideas and new perspectives? Would it be best served by contact with people from other organisations, either by external course or visits or secondments?

- Is the objective associated with a need for reinforcement, reward or prestige? Managers have sometimes claimed that they have been offered the chance to attend a course as a reward. In the right circumstances this can be a valid strategy. It is likely that the manager will approach the training with a favourable mental set and, if impressed, he or she may give more encouragement to subordinates to attend courses.

Likelihood of learning transfer

In Chapters 4 and 12 we demonstrate that learning is an inevitable feature of organisational life. The provision of planned training could be described as an intervention into an informal, continuous and powerful learning process, which affects the transfer of learning to the workplace in a way that should not be underestimated. It is not uncommon for staff returning from a course to be greeted with 'You've had your holiday, now get on with your work.' A backlog of problems awaits, and often there is not even an inquiry into whether anything useful was learned, let alone a follow-up session about the implementation of new ideas. Sometimes there might even be direct opposition.

> Discussion question: How might you prevent such negative experiences for returning course delegates?

On page 63 we refer to barriers to learning, and it is certainly necessary to be aware of the many forms these barriers can assume, including inertia, autocratic opposition, bureaucratic procedures, work overload, interpersonal relationships, vested interests, fear of change and insecurity. Such barriers must be taken into consideration when devising an HRD strategy, as must the overall climate, dominant management culture and style, and sophistication and previous training experience of the organisation. For example, where there has been no previous planned training it might be unwise to start with a sophisticated form of interpersonal skills development for middle-aged supervisors who have been employed in the organisation since leaving school. A short, practical course where the job relevance is easy to determine would probably make a better beginning. They might then be encouraged to ask for further provision. In Chapter 3 we suggest that learning might be regarded as the process of opening a door: when it is pushed ajar, it opens up vistas of other rooms with more doors. The view often generates a desire to penetrate further, but before this first door was opened, it was not possible to realise that there was anything beyond. A sensible HRD manager will help to facilitate this process.

As a general rule, the more the HRD manager can take part in the mainstream organisational activity and can involve the sources of power in the actual training, the greater the likelihood of learning transfer. Examples might be:

- organising learning sessions as an integral part of mainstream events (see example on pages 183–4)
- emphasising the personal responsibility of managers in training their subordinates (see Chapters 6, 10 and 11), and assisting them to do this
- assisting managers to coach their subordinates
- ensuring that managers are directly involved in briefing and debriefing sessions for staff undergoing learning/training
- if the occasion is right, arranging for top management to attend a course first
- developing managers and supervisors as trainers in their own departments
- asking senior managers to lecture or lead sessions on in-house courses
- the use of mentors.

Some of these suggestions may involve development for superiors and achieving a particular objective may initially require an indirect approach.

Available resources
These include such items as:

- accommodation for running internal courses, or environmental constraints such as noise and space, for on-the-job learning/training
- equipment, or availability of money to purchase the hardware and software required for the use of new technology. Many organisations have a PC on every desk, providing a ready-made facility for the reception of in-house programmes
- staff expertise in learning/training techniques (eg coaching, writing programmes, delegating, acting as mentor)
- time span: how much time is available, and must the training be completed to particular deadlines?
- finance: is there an HRD budget? If so, is each item already allowed for at its expected cost? If not, is contingency money included and available? If not, can money be 'moved' from another use? If not, will the proposal have to wait for the next budget? Or can new finance be specially arranged? If yes, will there be an added cost (eg interest)? The existence or otherwise of a budget is of considerable importance. (See also budgets on page 107, and the section on costs and benefits of learning interventions on pages 106–8.)
- available external help: are there good facilities and staff in local universities or colleges? Is suitable help available from other organisations such as suppliers or professional bodies?
- availability of relevant external courses: some expertise is specific to organisations and is therefore unlikely to be found externally
- availability of external funding (eg in the shape of grants from the local LSC/LEC or the European Social Fund).

Learner-related factors
These include the following:

- the experience and current expertise of the learner. Superfluous training in aspects already well known can result in deteriorating performance through annoyance and boredom. Most computer-managed programmes incorporate pretests, which enable learners to 'skip' aspects with which they are already familiar.
- learning style: the ultimate aim may well be to encourage employees to use a variety of different learning styles, but in the early stages of a programme, particularly if the content may be difficult for the learner, it is better to use a mode that appears to accord with his or her preferred or natural learning style. When attempting to convince learners of the value of using different learning styles, it is advisable to start with content that is likely to be acceptable. For instance, many managers are interested in finding practical solutions to industrial relations problems. If training is required in this field, it might be useful to start with concrete examples and exercises that aim to find solutions, and subsequently progress to conceptual and theoretical aspects of the role of trade unions. On the other hand, a group of graduates with little or no experience of management might well prefer the sequence reversed. An overall objective should

be to improve learning potential; an understanding of learning styles is one way of achieving this.

■ age factor (see also page 75): older people should not be made to feel inadequate in front of younger people, particularly if they are feeling insecure because they are being retrained in entirely new skills. If, for instance, they have a knowledge deficiency in arithmetic, they may find it more acceptable to undertake a computer-assisted program or a distance learning course where they can work in private at their own speed and convenience. (Recent research, it is interesting to note, suggests that younger people's arithmetical skills may not always be highly developed because of the use of calculators!)

■ size of group: this has an obvious influence on the technique to be used. It is not practicable to organise a discussion for one person! Closely associated with group size is the availability of trainees because, although the number may be considerable, if they are separated by geographical location, or shiftworking, the effect may be to reduce numbers available at any one time, and computer-assisted learning or distance learning packages may be suitable. These have the additional advantage of standardising instructions throughout a large organisation. For instance, British Airways uses computer-based sales training, which is fully integrated with the training of booking clerks and includes such tasks as reservations, fare quotation and departure control.

■ motivation: the likely attitude towards different styles of learning is relevant here, but other practical factors such as the necessity to be away from home on a residential course should be taken into consideration.

> Discussion question: How might you build in individual and group activities for a workshop on managing diversity to be attended by 100 people?

STAGE 3 – PLANNING AND IMPLEMENTATION OF THE TRAINING

Where practicable, it is always advantageous to consult those concerned about the design of their programme. In all circumstances, careful briefing of learners and their managers is essential if learning is not to be inhibited by conjectures as to why the training is taking place. Exactly what is involved in planning and implementing will depend upon the form of programme that has been chosen. Because the most comprehensive preparation is likely to be required in planning an in-house course, we have selected this method for fuller discussion. The steps in the design of a structured in-house course are shown in Figure 9.2.

Designing and planning a structured internal training course

Step 1: Review the learning/training objectives

The objectives, and the knowledge, skill and attitudes required to achieve them, might be regarded as constituting the 'syllabus'. It is necessary to decide which objectives are the most important and therefore where the emphasis of the programme should lie, and then to arrange the material into a suitable sequence. This may be done purely by logic but attempts should be made at the outset to create interest and utilise the participant's natural curiosity (see Chapter 3). It is important to arrange the material in steps of suitable size for the learner to master. Unless structured discovery learning is intended, it is important to ensure that the programme moves methodically from the known to the unknown and that, where appropriate, each session serves as preparation for and introduction to those that follow.

Step 1
Review the training objectives

Step 2
Determine appropriate learning activities

Step 3
Assess training times

Step 4
Construct the timetable

Step 5
Brief the trainers

Step 6
Organise the preparation of material and equipment

Figure 9.2 *Stages in the design of a structured training programme*

Although Figure 9.2 does not include any reference to monitoring and evaluating, these activities are intrinsically related to the objectives. At the stage of reviewing the training objectives, therefore, professional trainers are already thinking about how they will monitor and evaluate. The more specific the objectives the easier these tasks will be.

Step 2: Determine appropriate learning activities

Decide what sessions will be necessary and set subobjectives for each, anticipating how the attainment of each objective might be evaluated. Settle on the most suitable technique (or method), bearing in mind that a particularly important objective might require several sessions using a variety of techniques. For example, during a course on organisational change, one of the objectives might be that the participants should be able to identify the barriers to change. This could be introduced by syndicate discussion sessions, where each participant describes some change they have experienced and indicates areas of concern. Syndicates could then discuss the origin and alleviation of those worries and whether they could have been avoided. A case study might then follow, allowing participants to apply and reinforce some of their findings and, after discussion of the case, the session might conclude with a short summary of the whole topic, accompanied by a 'handout' of the salient points. The trainer/facilitator would receive some evaluation of the learning that had taken place by listening to the contributions to the case study (although there may be dangers in evaluating group performance). It might also be possible to use a self-administered test before the final summary session.

The criteria for deciding on the most suitable technique for each session are similar to the decision criteria for the method (see page 193).

The following example helps to explain the need for care in the structuring of precise learning objectives.

A group of craft trainees had to learn an electrical coding comprising nine colours, and the job required instant association of a number (one to nine) with a particular colour. The objective would not be met if they learned the sequence of colours by rote, because each time they wanted to pair a colour and a number they would have to repeat the sequence, causing delay and allowing the possibility of error, which could have serious effects on safety. The training technique that was devised consisted of a visual presentation of well-known objects associated with each colour, such as one brown penny or five green fingers. The use of vision and the association with previous knowledge quickly enabled the trainees to learn the information in the exact form in which it was required, a green wire immediately bringing to mind the number five.

The age of the learners can also influence the suitability of a technique. Belbin and Belbin (1972) discovered that certain methods were more effective than others with older learners. Discovery learning or forms of 'deductive' learning (where the requirement is to reason out the answer) show the best results. Techniques that rely upon memory are not likely to be successful. Unlike older people, younger people can often enjoy a competitive approach, such as a quiz, and prefer frequent changes of topic. The former learn more effectively by concentrating on the same subject matter for longer periods; variety can be introduced by changing the training method. (For a more detailed investigation into methods of training older employees, see Plett and Lester 1991.)

If course participants are at different levels of ability and have differing degrees of practical experience, then flexible methods, such as computer-assisted learning, or sometimes discussion groups and case studies, can be useful. Those with experience can be encouraged to assist but not dominate.

Step 3: Assess training times

The time available for each session must be determined. Participative methods may be the most effective in enabling learning transfer but they can be time-consuming, so it is practical to employ them for the most important aspects of the programme. A further consideration is the time of day of each session; for instance, it may be considered wise to arrange a participative session straight after lunch, or after dinner in the evening of a residential course. Estimating the exact time required for each session is to some extent a matter of trial and error, and the requirements for the same programme can vary for different groups. An experienced course organiser can usually gauge the timing reasonably accurately by consulting with those responsible for the various parts of the training, using the duration of similar programmes as a guide and taking into account the age, experience and motivation of those to be trained.

Step 4: Construct the timetable

The course organiser should ensure that the timetable is flexible enough to be modified if required without affecting the whole programme, and decide on the trainers/facilitators for each session.

Step 5: Brief the trainers/facilitators

This is an important, and frequently neglected, step in the design process, and misunderstandings can easily arise if the objectives for every section of the programme are not fully discussed and understood. The technique to be used may well be discussed with the trainer but the final choice cannot be left to her entirely because of the need to obtain an overall balance. It is the course organiser who has to take this overall view. Otherwise, to quote the extreme case, it would be possible for each of several trainers to decide to show a video on the same day. Variety has to be planned: it cannot be left to chance. After briefing, the trainers/facilitators then prepare the detailed material for their sessions. Information about the use of different techniques will be found in Appendix 4.

Step 6: Organise the preparation of material and equipment
Professionally prepared programmes, course manuals, logbooks and other references create a professional image. Unprepared or inadequate equipment can suggest that the training is regarded as of secondary importance, and this can quickly affect the attitude of learners.

> Discussion question: Choose an aspect of managerial behaviour you would like to promote or eradicate and draft a suitable training programme.

STAGE 4 – EVALUATION OF INTERVENTIONS

Although it is generally accepted that there is a strong case for attempting to evaluate learning and training, particularly in view of the very large sums of money spent on it, HRD specialists have often been less than enthusiastic about doing it, and the attendant problems often appear too difficult. It is true that evaluation is one of the more difficult of the HRD manager's tasks, but it need not be impossible. Although we are considering it last, it must not be considered as a discrete 'add on' activity. As we pointed out at the beginning of this chapter, consideration must be given to evaluation when originally formulating objectives. Of course, people who do not know where they are going can never know when they have reached their destination; on the other hand, precise and well-defined objectives are the key indicators in recognising when one has arrived. Evaluation therefore begins at *Step 1*.

The first difficulty is that it is necessary to know the exact knowledge and skill of each learner before the start of the training. Without this information it would be impossible to assess what they have learned at the end. This would necessitate a pretest, which is practicable in programmed or computer-assisted learning. It becomes more difficult when we consider an in-house course for managers. The first objective of every trainer/facilitator in that situation is to establish rapport with the course members.

Presenting delegates with a pretest, especially if they are unlikely to be able to complete it, is hardly in accord with this aim, nor is it likely to inspire them with confidence and a favourable mental set. Many of them will have negative 'baggage' about tests and exams. Even if a pretest were arranged, it could be argued that participants had learned from the pretest not the training, and it would therefore really be necessary to set up a number of control groups. This is unlikely to be practicable, so the HRD manager will realise from the outset that he or she can only do the best that circumstances permit.

A second difficulty is that an ongoing review tends to result in changes to the detail of the programme (and even to some of the objectives) before it can be evaluated.

Here are the questions that need to be answered in evaluating a particular programme:

1   Why is the evaluation required?

2   Who should do it?

3   What aspects should be evaluated and when should this be done?

4   What kinds of measurement will be used?

Why is the evaluation required?

The answer to this question will affect the appropriate response to the other four. Five main reasons can be given:

1   The evaluation enables the effectiveness of an investment in learning and development to be appraised in general terms and provides data that can justify its expenditure. One of the difficulties in obtaining money for an HRD budget is that the results are often regarded as intangible, and the training as an act of faith.

2   It provides feedback to the trainer or facilitator about her performance and methods, and is therefore a part of her learning experience.

3   It enables improvements to be made, either on the next occasion, or if the evaluation is ongoing, as the training develops.

4   Reviewing and evaluating her achievement to date is an intrinsic part of the learner's progression round the experiential learning cycle, and therefore should be a part of the learning process itself.

5   The evaluation indicates to what extent the objectives have been met, and whether any further learning/training needs remain.

Who should carry out the evaluation?

This is a most important decision, as any suspicion of bias can invalidate the results, and also because receiving feedback can be a sensitive issue and may therefore need to be handled with extreme care. As, however, the process is itself a learning experience, it is obviously advantageous to involve those who could learn the most from it.

Tracey (1968) makes the point that:

> Evaluation must be co-operative. A one-man evaluation is little better than no evaluation, regardless of who does it, how competently he does the job, or how valid his findings may be. All who are a part of the process of appraisal, or who are affected by it, must participate in the process.

Obviously the HRD manager, relevant line managers and the learners need to co-operate in the process. However, each will bring a different perspective, and it may well be that the overall responsibility is best vested in a neutral party. This may be difficult, because even external consultants can have their own bias. Whoever takes overall responsibility, it is important that they are seen as impartial, having credible expertise and knowledge of the relevant processes, as well as possessing tact to deal with sensitive issues.

> Discussion question: Would it be feasible to use a postgraduate student to evaluate an internal training course?

What aspects of training should be evaluated and when?

A number of different models have been suggested. The structure we describe below is after Whitelaw (1972) and Hamblin (1974), but for alternatives see Warr et al (1970) or Jones

(1970); see also Bramley (1996). Hamblin and Whitelaw suggest that training can usefully be evaluated at different levels, each of which requires different techniques. An example of this type of model is given below.

Level 1: Reactions of learners to the content and methods of training, to the trainer and to any other factors perceived as relevant. What did the learner think about the training?

Level 2: Learning attained during the training period. Did the learners learn what was intended?

Level 3: Job behaviour in the work environment at the end of the training period. Did the learning transfer to the job?

Level 4: Effect on the learner's department. Has the training helped departmental performance?

Level 5: The ultimate level. Has the training affected the ultimate well-being of the organisation, for example, in terms of profitability or survival?

These are sequential stages in the process: if it is found that behaviour on the job has not changed after the programme, unless evaluation has been carried out at Level 2 it will not be possible to ascertain whether the failure was owing to lack of learning transfer or to the fact that the learning never took place at all. If the evaluation is to perform any of the functions we have outlined then this type of detail is essential.

To help the evaluation process, it is possible to set objectives at each of these levels. For instance, the objectives of a course providing an introduction to the organisation's networked computing facility might be:

- that participants would recommend the course to their friends and wish to attend a further course themselves. This would involve a favourable 'reactions level' evaluation (Level 1).

- that participants should be competent in the use of a variety of software. This would involve objectives at Level 2.

- that participants should request terminals on their desks and suggest how they could be used to make daily work practices more efficient (Level 3).

- that the introduction of desk terminals for the course participants should result in increased output in the department (Level 4).

- that this increased productivity in the department should contribute to the profitability of the organisation (Level 5).

Clearly, the easiest levels to evaluate are 1 and 2. The process becomes increasingly difficult as Level 5 is approached. This is partly because of difficulties of measurement, but also because the problem of establishing cause and effect. Organisational changes are multicausal: for example, it is usually impossible to determine how much of an increase in profitability is the result of a specific training intervention. There is also likely to be a time-lag between the completion of the training and its effect on the organisation, and the relevant learning may have arisen from a later source. It can be said, however, that the more successful the evaluation at the earlier stages, the more likely is the training to affect overall departmental or organisational performance.

What kind of measurement will be used?

Different techniques and yardsticks are appropriate for each level of evaluation.

At Level 1, where an attempt is being made to assess the recipients' reactions to their training, techniques such as questionnaires, interviews, group discussion, individual interview or asking trainees to write a report can be used. Care must be taken with the timing of these methods. For example, if participants have enjoyed a course, they may finish in a mood of euphoria, which may not last after they return to work, and therefore a misleading impression might be conveyed if they are asked to complete a questionnaire at the end of the course (see Easterby-Smith and Tanton 1985).

Similarly, learners may not be in a position to know immediately whether what they have learned will be useful. It may be necessary to wait a while before being able to obtain informed opinion. Although learning should ideally be a helpful experience, it can at times be painful, and learners may encounter difficulty or criticism and attempt to divert this to the training activities. If such people happen to be the most vociferous during an evaluation discussion, the trainer may obtain a completely false impression. Experienced trainers learn to interpret this type of feedback and to use a series of techniques to obtain their information. For instance, they might use a short questionnaire and/or hold a general discussion, or interview the participants separately after an appropriate length of time. Another method is to issue a questionnaire, ask the delegates to complete it, hold their own discussion session and present what they consider to be the most important points to the trainer.

A number of other indicators can also be used to provide evaluation at this level, including requests from participants for further training, their recommendation to others to follow the same programme, or the return of past delegates for further help and advice. No single one of these can be taken out of context, but they can all assist to confirm or contradict an apparent trend.

At Level 2, the following techniques might be used:

- Phased tests, as in craft training: These are useful in monitoring progress and providing feedback, which can be used to modify the training as it develops. In addition, they provide intermediate targets and knowledge of results to learners.
- Final test: Workplace-based tests of competence, such as those required for NVQs, are relevant here, and their incidence is likely to increase as more and more organisations become involved in these qualifications. Because jobs and the contexts in which they are performed are very varied, they can take a number of forms, such as the situation described on page 257, where the learner sends a claim form, and her performance is tested by a visiting assessor.
- Final examination: This is still the most common type of evaluation in academic, and some professional, circles, although other types of continuous assessment have gradually been introduced. Final examinations have a number of disadvantages. They are influenced by the learner's ability to perform on a few chosen days and may therefore be affected by short-term memory, domestic circumstances or health. It is important that they are designed to incorporate a representative sample of the activities to be evaluated.
- Projects: As well as being useful learning methods, these can provide valuable

feedback on the ability to apply what has been learned to an organisational problem or issue.

■ Structured exercises and case studies: Performance on these can give the trainer indications as to how well people are learning. Structured exercises, such as interviews using closed-circuit television, are particularly helpful because it is possible to watch performance improving as the training progresses, and a record remains for comparison. Many of these activities, however, take place in groups, and the trainer must beware of assuming that because a group has performed well, every member of that group has learned what was intended. One or two members can lead or inspire a group to the extent that it is difficult to realise that some people have contributed little.

■ Participation in discussion during training: This can be another indicator but requires skilled interpretation, because there can be a variety of reasons delegates remain silent. They may feel overawed by prominent members of the group, or the entire group atmosphere may be alien to them. It is also possible that they have a different preferred learning style. An experienced trainer tries to interpret the meaning of such a situation and manage it.

Level 3 requires assessment of improved performance on the job. This is easiest in the area of operator training, where before-and-after measures can often be made. It becomes more difficult to evaluate performance further up the organisational hierarchy, where jobs are less prescribed and measurement imprecise. There is also likely to be a time-lag between training and the appearance of indicators of performance improvement. For instance, on returning to work after attending a course on sales techniques, a salesperson may immediately practise the new learning and sow the seeds of extra future orders. These may not materialise for some time, after which other factors in the situation may have changed – there may have been some alterations to the product – and it is difficult, if not impossible, to attribute cause and effect. Attempts have been made to identify any change of behaviour on the job after the completion of training by questioning supervisors and colleagues. These have yielded some positive results. They must always, though, be open to the criticism that if colleagues are asked to look for behavioural change, they may be more focused in seeing things that were there all along. Alternatively they may lack the objectivity to interpret information effectively.

In general, the more care that has been taken in the assessment of needs and the more precise the objective, the greater will be the possibility of effective evaluation. In the case of the salesperson above, rather than an overall objective of increasing sales it might be possible to be more precise by using subobjectives such as increasing second sales, or reducing customer complaints directed at staff.

Levels 4 and 5 are the most difficult to evaluate, for the reasons we have already mentioned. Also, departmental and organisational results depend upon many people, and it is difficult to apportion improvements to the efforts of specific individuals. Evaluation can often be related in a more general way to the health of the organisation. Evidence might be found in: overall profitability; lack of customer complaints; a favourable attitude to training; the standing of the HRD manager and the nature of requests made to him or her (is he or she, for example, included in discussion of matters that are central to the organisation?); a system of performance appraisal that works; the availability of suitable people to promote from within; and a labour force that not only accepts change, but initiates it proactively.

The majority of learning/training in the private and public sectors takes place in a busy working environment. A rigorous scientific approach to evaluation, involving pre- and post-training tests, control and experimental groups etc., although very desirable, is often not practicable. However, if adequate resources are not made available for evaluation purposes, the effectiveness will remain unchecked.

This dilemma can be resolved to some extent by adopting the following pragmatic approach:

- Set clear learning/training objectives, expressed as far as possible in behavioural terms, or in competences, specifying the performance evidence required and the range (see Table 8.1).
- Include objectives for each level of evaluation.
- Evaluate systematically at as many levels as practicable to obtain the total picture.

Together, these three steps will go a long way towards helping an organisation maximise its benefit from investment in training.

Richard Hale of the International Management Centres Association was quoted recently on the ITOL members' site describing the 'myths' surrounding evaluation (Hale 2002). He believes overreliance on structured models may have caused trainers and trainees to assume:

1 Learning is the responsibility of the trainer.
2 Courses *prove* learning.
3 Good course evaluation sheets mean learning has occurred.
4 Real learning is classroom-based, not on the job.
5 There is clear correlation between management education and business improvement.

He believes the reality is more subtle, and to counter the myths he recommends that:

- Participants should be responsible for identifying and consulting the 'stakeholders' in their learning process.
- Training departments should be transformed from a 'team of officers and administrators to a team of consultants and facilitators to "oil the wheels of learning" '.

Hale's 'call to action' for HRD specialists wishing to take evaluation seriously can be found on http://www.itol.co.uk /cgi-local/dcforum/.

Let's now return to our case study at the beginning of the chapter. You should now have a good idea of the kind of decisions that would have to be made and of the alternatives available. The HRD director's report was accepted and the recommendations successfully implemented as follows:

It was realised from the outset that the support of district and regional managers was vital, and a working party of representatives from these groups and from security staff was appointed. A form of 'cascade' training was agreed upon and the store managers therefore had a key role to play. In reality, this was a very large project and it is not possible to give all the details here. In summary, however, it was agreed that the first requirement was to raise managers' awareness of the problem. Secondly, managers needed to define their own key role in decreasing shrinkage, and identify the specific actions and procedures required to bring about an improvement. They then needed to raise awareness in their staff and encourage and give guidance on good practices. As the managers had little experience in training, they also required some assistance in this direction, and it was decided to produce a special training package for them, as well as material that could be used either as a guide for training their staff or as self-instruction material.

The actual package produced consisted of: a video giving practical tips and portraying models of appropriate behaviour; posters made from stills of the video, as a constant reinforcement of the message; a booklet to assist managers to identify problems in the store and draw up appropriate preventative procedures; guidance for managers on introducing the staff package to store assistants; and an individual booklet for staff, including a checklist for regular use.

The training programme consisted of four team-briefing sessions in each store. These took place over a four-week period with store and departmental work and discussions during the intervals. The sessions were carried out by HRD department staff and store managers. The booklets and training materials were made by desktop publishing in-house, so could be updated when needed. The investment was therefore not for a 'one-off' training event, but for material that could be used and modified for a significant period.

In this particular case the evaluation could be carried out on all of the levels above. A questionnaire at the end of the team-briefings gave the reactions of the participants, and a question-and-answer sheet gave an indication of the learning that had taken place. The shrinkage statistics provided evidence for evaluation at departmental and store level, and the overall improvement in shrinkage costs was reflected in company profitability – Level 5.

(This case is based upon, although does not exactly replicate, an assignment undertaken and written up in full detail by Bailey, 1991.)

This chapter has introduced you to a sample of operational training strategies and has stressed the need for effective evaluation of the impact of these on learners. We have also pointed out the need for learners to evaluate their own learning, which complements the thinking performer concept discussed in the previous chapter. With this in mind, how might you encourage learners to review the impact of a six-month graduate management trainee programme that involved delegates in both formal courses and work placements?

Developing New Employees and Future Managers

Part 3 examines learning needs of two important and discrete groups of people in the organisation. New workers are arguably the key to our future national prosperity, whereas managers are key to the effective achievement of organisational objectives, and through this, again, economic prosperity. You will see that, in spite of a generation of management writers' warnings, the UK still appears to have too many managers lacking the skills and competences to do the job. What can HRD specialists do to improve development of leadership and management skills?

Chapter 10 describes the way that new employees are **incorporated into organisations**, and proposes ways in which the process may be improved. It also examines the contribution of 'vocational' education to preparing new workers for employment.

Chapter 11 looks at the complex process of **developing managers**, a process that, as you will see, has proved very difficult, for many reasons, for UK organisations to get right.

Educating and Developing the New Workers

CHAPTER 10

In Chapter 10, we consider:

- **The role of formal education in the UK and its vocational impact;**

- **The new demographics of work and the consequently diverse workforce profiles of the 'new workers';**

- **The concept of delivering education, and whether it needs to be academic, vocational or a mix of both;**

- **The interaction between employers and education providers;**

- **The need for suitable workplace induction to welcome new employees and to assist them to achieve their full potential;**

- **The effective introduction of new employees to working practices and cultures.**

The primary purpose of national targets for education and training should be to make Britain more competitive internationally. But they will also play a vital role in promoting social cohesion. (NACETT Fast Forward for Skills 1998)

We have looked at the reality of learning and training provision in Part 1. A national system of vocational courses has been introduced with the aim of providing better preparation for work, and employers and educational institutions are liaising in many ways to help to bridge the gap between education and work. The students who were asked to think about a strategy for improving the skills base of 'UK Plc' (see Chapter 2) suggested a number of proposals for developing the workforce of the future in order to maintain and develop UK prosperity. Now we will look at the various ways in which entrants to the world of work are introduced to the reality of the work environment. Three main themes emerge in this chapter:

- The first relates to the revision and restructuring of educational provision to make it more vocational. However, we suggest that altering the structure and content of courses cannot alone achieve the desired result. What is needed is increased understanding, leading to a degree of cultural change in educational institutions, and better preparation of newcomers by employing organisations.

- The second theme, then, relates to collaboration between employers and educational institutions. This can help not only to provide students with experience of the working environment, but also opportunities at staff level to help to bring the two cultures of education and work closer together.

- The final theme considers the induction of newcomers, including young people starting National Traineeships and Modern Apprenticeships. Induction is effective not only in helping young people in their transition to work, but for all new starters, and sometimes for established employees who are promoted, or move to different departments or sites in the course of their career development.

WORKFORCE PROFILES

The structure of employment is changing quickly, in directions that make increasing demands on the labour force. Demand for unskilled manual jobs is declining, in favour of nonmanual jobs that require higher qualifications (see Figure 10.1).

There has been a significant decline in the UK's production industries, mainly manufacturing, but also agriculture, mining and utilities (although there is still a need to train some people in these sectors to replace those who leave), and a major increase in the service sector. In addition the skill requirement within all jobs is rising and there is a move away from manual skills to communication and understanding and monitoring systems. De-layering in many companies has meant that more junior staff have to show greater initiative and take part in more decisions, and may sometimes have to learn routine quality control tasks. There is now a need for flexibility and rapid adaptation to change. The labour force required to cope with these developments is changing in structure and has the following characteristics:

- The labour force is growing, but the growth rate is greater for women than for men. Projections vary, but it is generally agreed that during the first decade of the new millennium the number of women in employment is likely to have increased to around 50 per cent of the total;

- Women are more likely to want part-time work, and the number who have dependant children is increasing;

- The population is ageing. An increasing working population over the age of 35 is counterbalanced by decreasing numbers in those under that age;

- The numbers of 16-year-olds staying in education continues to increase;

- The share of employees working part time is expected to increase. In 1997, 29 per cent of employees (6.6 million) were part time, and it is estimated that by 2007 there will be an extra 600,000 part-time workers, about three-quarters of whom will be women. This is part of a wider trend towards progressively greater flexibility of employment through the use of temporary and part-time workers, variation of hours worked and greater ability to switch staff between different tasks. It can therefore be said to benefit potentially both employers and employees;

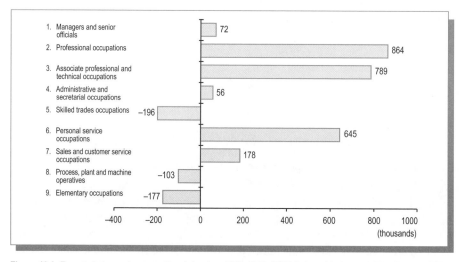

Figure 10.1 *Expected change in occupational structure 1999–2010.* DfEE 'Labour Market and Skills Trends 1997/8', Crown Copyright

■ The number of people with no significant skills still gives cause for concern. Research reported in the Employers' Skills Survey 2002 (DfES) indicated that over a third of establishments employing people aged 16–19 thought there was a skills gap among this group. The main skills that younger employees appear to lack are general communication skills, practical skills, customer handling skills and personal skills.

Discussion question: Is it possible for the UK to achieve full employment for all those who want to work? If not, what support should be available to unemployed people?

Women entrants (and re-entrants) to the employment market

Women are much more likely, although not exclusively, to want part-time work, and an increasing number have dependent children and some will be single parents. Women have traditionally been employed in a narrow range of industries, and there is often much unrealised potential. Women are significantly underrepresented in managerial positions, in many professional occupations and at technician level in a wide range of jobs. It has been suggested that the process of de-layering has resulted in fewer women in management because of a tendency to cut out the middle level where many women have tended to 'stick'.

Nowadays many women return to work after a career break to bring up a family. Some may have had little or no working experience and may be apprehensive about entering a totally different environment, and careful induction is needed. Flexible learning provision will increasingly be required so that it can be combined with family responsibilities. Courses at the Open University or Open College will be helpful in this respect, as will self-learning materials, technology-assisted learning, distance learning and open access programmes of all kinds. The telephone service 'LearnDirect', and the 'University for Industry' (see Part 1) may be very useful in helping women to find flexible learning courses most suited to their needs. If, during their previous education, the new entrants have 'learned to learn' then the task will be much easier. For this and many other reasons a 'learning to learn culture' is rapidly becoming an essential requirement of modern life.

Flexible arrangements will also be required to cope with career breaks. Some organisations already have internal schemes to enable women to return for short periods to update themselves and maintain their skills during a career break. Corresponding educational facilities will be needed, including part-time work experience. Courses that can be undertaken during the career break could assist women to remain informed about developments in their area and would assist the quickest possible return to work.

Many women will have received vocational education earlier in their lives and/or will have work experience. Although they may need refresher and updating courses in certain aspects, they will not always need to undertake a whole programme from beginning to end. Courses that have rigid entry requirements, and offer no facility for accrediting previous experience or learning, are likely to be unsuitable, prolonging the necessary education and training time, as well as running great risks of boring the participants. The national framework provided by NVQs, together with the flexibility of CATS and APL schemes (see pages 216–7), which recognise appropriate prior learning or prior experience, should go a long way towards helping vocational education meet the needs of these women. Financial assistance in the form of career and development loans, which provide an interest-free 'holiday', are available to encourage people of both sexes to invest in their own training. The government's National Childcare Strategy, under which tax credits have been available to low-income working families since April 1999, as well as increased provision of childcare places and help with childcare costs, is also of assistance. We have, of course, assumed that it is mainly women who have responsibility for dependants and look for flexible working arrangements. These days increasing numbers of men also want to enjoy being parents as well as taking responsibility for the new generation, and although still a minority, some men are becoming temporary 'houseparents' for a range of reasons, including the fact that their partners may earn a higher salary. They will also benefit from return to work incentives as their children become more independent. Both sexes, of course, will be concerned about the lack of high quality childcare, not just for very young children, but those of school age. The 'long hours culture' in the UK, which seems to be spreading to Europe, exists despite the Working Time Regulations and the increasing research into the need for a work/life balance, unfortunately making it necessary for pre- and after-school care to be in place.

> Discussion question: Given the recognised importance of good parenting in developing children to be responsible adults, should parents be financially supported for wishing to spend more time doing this than in paid employment?

Single parents

Under the New Deal for Lone Parents on income support a personal adviser contacts all lone parents whose youngest child has reached the second term of full-time education, to assist in job search and accessing appropriate training. Views as to the success of this scheme vary: it has been suggested that it is merely a ploy to remove women from benefits and that children without the support of two parents could benefit more in social and education terms from having the undivided attention of the remaining one. However, many lone parents are equally keen to earn more to increase the family standard of living and are often highly motivated to succeed, especially when they have not previously had a positive experience of education or training.

Disabled people

The main provisions of the Disability Discrimination Act 1995 are now in force and should extend the number of disabled people in the labour market. The recent strengthening of the Act requires education providers to take positive action in catering for disabled learners, arguably a helpful first step in assisting people with disabilities to obtain the qualifications needed by mainstream employment. Like single parents, many disabled people are highly motivated to succeed at work and only require some minor adjustments to their working environment to do so.

> Discussion question: Currently the Disability Discrimination Act only requires 'reasonable adjustments' from employers to assist disabled job applicants. Should some form of 'positive discrimination' operate to improve their chances of careers and career progression?

Older workers

We have in the UK an ageing workforce. There will be more over-65s than under-16s in the UK by 2014. A significant number of people over 65 remain in the labour force. Although they are a valuable source of skills and experience, some older people tend to be less qualified, their qualifications are often outdated, and overall they receive less training. Only 50% of unskilled men over 50 are working (Employment Policy Institute). 'Downsizing' during the 1990s often involved early retirements, resulting in a considerable number of people looking for 'post-first retirement' jobs. There is a need for others to create jobs for these early pensioners, a striking example being a large self-service DIY chain store that opened one branch staffed entirely by people over 50, and has found the experiment extremely successful. The new workers were found to be better at product knowledge and customer care than their younger counterparts in other stores, and there was less incidence of absenteeism and labour turnover (Hogarth and Barth 1991; Worsley 1996). Some of these 'older returnees' may reappear in the educational system (possibly to take NVQs as an addition to existing qualifications). They are also likely to require flexible programmes, which they can carry out at their own pace, and through which they can be credited for prior experience and knowledge.

It would be pleasant to believe that the government's recent proposals to make age discrimination in employment illegal come from a concern for social justice and a desire not to consign over 50s, or even younger people, to the employment scrap-heap. The reality is that the economy cannot support such large numbers of retired people, especially with larger numbers of young people remaining in full-time education. As with single parents, at times the interests of the state and the individual can usefully align: many older people would welcome the chance to remain in meaningful employment, especially as advances in healthcare have meant that the 'baby boomers' of the post Second World War era are remaining more active and assertive into the 'third age' than their predecessors did (see Chapter 4). Whatever the motive, there is no doubt that significantly more people are likely to continue working well into their 60s and sometimes beyond. Many will retire from one job to take up another, and the consequent 'stretching' of the age range for educational programmes presents some stimulating challenges for the HRD practitioner.

> Discussion question: What should the appropriate age be for compulsory retirement? Should people be obliged to retire at a set age? Is it possible to continue learning new skills indefinitely?

Young people

Young people represent an investment in the future. In these days of rapidly changing technology, they are an important source of new skills and can bring energy and ideas into an organisation and rejuvenate an ageing labour force. They represent an invaluable resource, which the nation cannot afford to underutilise, but those with no qualifications are likely to find the job market difficult. Quality education and training for young people has a critical role to play in ensuring that the skills and international competitiveness of our workforce will continue to improve, and the National Learning Targets (see page 43) provided an appropriate stimulus. Fortunately, the proportion of young people participating in education beyond the statutory school leaving age has been increasing (see Figure 10.2). The LSC focus on all aspects of young people's skill development should raise awareness of the need for continuing education and development.

Those continuing in full-time training are drawn from the entire ability range. The levels of qualification attained by those staying in compulsory education continues to rise, but the fact that two-thirds of 16-year-olds do not achieve a GCSE grade C or above in maths and English (two of the key skills stressed by employers) gives rise to considerable concern, as well as the revelation that one in 12 attains no GCSEs at all. Proposals to overcome these

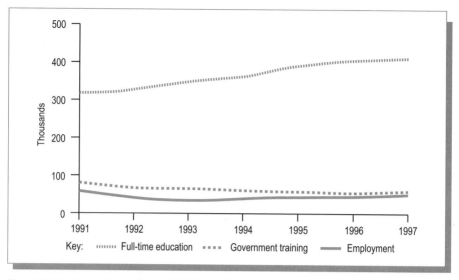

Figure 10.2 *Destination of school leavers.* DfEE 'Labour Market and Skills Trends 1997/8', Crown Copyright

problems include: taking steps to ensure that each pupil acquires the basic skills of numeracy and literacy at an early stage; improving the quality of teaching; and involving parents and local communities in education. Some new FE centres are concentrating on new methods, such as group projects and computer-based methods, for underachieving students. IT tools have been both a hindrance and a help to developing literacy. On the one hand, computers and the Internet have encouraged young people who might otherwise not have read for pleasure to research topics that interest them. On the other, e-mail and mobile phone text messaging have encouraged a casual approach to English, which has often infected formal writing style. Even postgraduate students may produce 'e-mail English' such as the lower case first person pronoun and absence of, or inappropriate use of, apostrophes. However, it seems Latin is making a comeback in some schools as an aid to understanding grammar and language, especially when spelling unfamiliar words.

> Discussion question: How can teachers and educators teach good written English skills in an imaginative way? Include your own experiences of learning to write: do you agree that it is less important today to possess such skills?

MAKING EDUCATION MORE VOCATIONAL

The National Curriculum

Under the Education Reform Act 1988 the National Curriculum for state schools in England and Wales is prescribed by the Secretary of State for Education and Employment, who consults and is advised by the Qualifications and Curriculum Authority. The aim is to give pupils adequate preparation for adult life (including working life) by providing a broad and balanced framework of study for all throughout the whole period of compulsory education, and the Curriculum sets out what children should be able to do at each key stage from age 5 to 16. (The system in Scotland is somewhat different and has its own overseeing body, the Scottish Qualifications Authority.)

In England and Wales, the curriculum is made up of Core Subjects (science, mathematics and English) and Other Foundation subjects (such as design and technology, information and communications technology, a modern foreign language, and physical education). With the addition of religious education and personal and social education, this work takes about 60 per cent of teaching time, leaving 40 per cent for options. For each subject there are:

- levels of attainment, or end of key stage descriptions, which define the knowledge expected of pupils at each level or stage
- programmes of study, which detail what pupils should be taught in order to reach the levels
- statutory assessments at the ages of 7, 11 and 14, which are based on the levels as they are defined in the National Curriculum. There were originally 10 levels, but the Dearing Reports (1993 and 1994) have resulted in changes in the way that the attainment levels and programmes of study are defined for each subject. As well as evaluating progress, it is intended that the assessments will be diagnostic in that they will pinpoint where pupils need help.

New ideas for the 14–19 curriculum should bring greater cohesion to learning opportunities within schools and colleges, as well as the workplace. Schools are encouraged to find flexible learning routes for students, particularly those unsuited or disinclined to follow a purely academic curriculum, and for those at risk of 'dropping out'.

The National Record of Achievement (NRA) and Progress File

The NRA was introduced in 1991 with the idea that it should be maintained for every pupil whose property it would be. It contained a record of main assessments and also an account of experience and attainments written by the owner. The newly named 'Progress File' will replace the NRA for all 16 year olds from 2005, although many young people have used them already. Materials are available for 16–19 year olds and adults who are encouraged to use the developmental activities to review and reflect on their progress, to set targets, analyse strengths and areas for improvement, in order to identify opportunities and make choices about which materials and means of presenting them are most appropriate in different situations. The booklets 'getting started' and 'moving on' are targeted at KS 3 and 4 students, and 'widening horizons' and 'broadening horizons' are targeted at post-16 students and adults. The Progress File concentrates on recording achievements rather than experiences.

NATIONAL DEVELOPMENTS IN FURTHER AND HIGHER EDUCATION

A few years ago it would have been possible to structure a discussion of education under neat headings such as 'Initial Full Time Education', and Further and Higher Education. The flexibility of today's system no longer allows this. For instance, the work of the QCA ranges from schools to colleges. General NVQs can be taken in schools, but it is more likely that schools will begin to offer 'Applied GCSEs', which are more vocationally based. They include traditional areas such as Art, Business, IT and Science, together with more vocational areas like Construction, Engineering, Hair and Beauty, or Health and Social Care.

Many students take advantage of part-time or distance learning facilities, which enable them to complement their employment with relevant study. The employer's support is of the utmost importance; this can include the granting of day release and the facilities to undertake a work-based project. Of equal importance (and something employers often forget) is the interest shown by management. It can be possible for an employee to take a year's work-related course, either by day release or in the employee's own time in the evenings, only for the manager to show no interest in the achievement. Some may even be hostile, because they find the idea of a better educated subordinate threatening. Attempting to integrate learning with the work environment or with general career planning is also critical, and will usually cost very little; it will not only make the educational programme more effective, but will help to retain the employee afterwards. As well as discussing progress with students, employers/managers can contact tutors, or in many cases can attend 'open days' or sponsors' evenings when they can also meet other participants on the programme. They can often offer useful visits of students to their premises to discuss aspects of particular interest.

Discussion question: Discuss your own feelings about work experience – have you participated in such schemes from either employer or student perspective, and if so, how successful was it?

The range of post-16 educational courses is broadening and much of the growth is accounted for by vocational courses. A number of common themes can be observed, which include:

- the provision of many diverse qualifications within a co-ordinated national framework within defined levels, subject to one Qualification and Curriculum Authority
- the necessity for an education system that imparts the knowledge and skills required for adult life and a competitive workforce
- desire for equality of value for academic and vocational qualifications
- increasing numbers of young people entering HE, together with government emphasis on 'widening access'
- transfer of credits from one programme to another (CATS – see below)
- accreditation of prior learning and experience (APL and APEL – see below)
- assessment based on targets and outcomes
- records of achievement
- work experience for all
- change in orientation from academic to workplace-led programmes and qualifications
- more collaboration between educationalists and employers, and greater opportunity for the latter to influence and become involved in national training and education schemes.

We will now look at the ways in which some of these requirements are being achieved.

Credit Accumulated Transfer Scheme (CATS – SCOTCATS in Scotland)

This is a national scheme to assist progression from one programme to another. Specific courses (ie qualifications or parts of qualifications) can be given a credit rating towards exemption from similar content on other programmes. These credits may be transferable from one institution to another. It is for individual institutions to decide precisely how many credits are given for any specific qualification, but the candidate may be required to 'confirm' the notional points score by undertaking a 'portfolio exercise' at the request of the institution to which the candidate is applying.

Accreditation of Previous Learning

Further and higher educational institutions are now much more willing to take account of prior learning, so avoiding situations where students have to cover the same ground twice. There are two forms of recognition, Accreditation of Prior Learning (APL) or Accreditation of Prior Experiential Learning (APEL):

- Accreditation of Prior Learning (APL) is based on evidence of successful completion of a relevant formal programme;
- Accreditation of Prior Experiential Learning (APEL) is based on evidence of learning through work experience. This evidence will normally consist of a portfolio of relevant documents and may also include written assignments relating to work experience which the educational institute requires.

Both APL and APEL enable students to gain exempting credits on many degree courses. Some professional bodies are co-operating to link APEL with second degrees and professional qualifications. Accreditation of prior learning can also apply to entrants on NVQ programmes. These schemes, as well as the provisions under CATS, are in harmony with the concepts of continuous development and continuing professional development. They can make further and higher education more accessible and attractive to adults, especially those who may not have had a positive experience of education the first time round. The CIPD has begun to develop APEL in its 'Professional Assessment Centres', which support HR professionals to put together portfolios of work-based experience matched against the CIPD standards. Although marketed as graduate membership without exams, is not an easy option by any means, and requires significant research and commentary by applicants.

Assessment based on targets and outcomes

The way in which performance on many formal courses is assessed has gradually been changing, so that rather than a pass or fail, or an overall grade, they give more detailed indication of what the student can actually do. Older traditional forms of assessment have been described as 'norm-referencing', because the results would be expected to conform more or less according to a normal curve of distribution (where the majority cluster around the average – small numbers obtaining either very high or very low marks). Although these systems enable trainees to compare their performance with each other or with a given standard, they provide a general grading rather than a clear picture of where strengths and weaknesses lie. The extreme case might be where one student obtains a first-class honours degree and another student obtains a third-class degree. An employer might judge the first student to be a better resource than the second, but it is still not clear what either student can actually do. The second student might have other attributes, such as self-presentation and communication skills, that might make him or her a better choice for an appointment in sales management than the student with first-class honours. Leading graduate recruiters have called for the existing system of degree classification to be scrapped and replaced with more detailed grades of skills and achievements. They have described the current system of rating the quality of degree as 'outmoded and discredited' and are pressing for ratings that give a clear indication of the standard of academic study, core business skills, the outcome of their work experience and what the degree means (Welch 1997).

> Discussion question: Is there any argument for abandoning grades for undergraduate degrees in favour of a postgraduate-type system of fail, pass, distinction?

In contrast to the traditional method of 'norm-referencing', 'criterion-referenced' assessment gives more detailed information. It involves assessing the performance of trainees, pupils or students on a number of specified dimensions. These may be competences (such as leadership, tolerance of stress or negotiation) or outcomes (such as ability to use a micrometer or to use a particular computer program). The assessment may consist of awarding a grade for each dimension, which can then be recorded on a 'profile'. Ideally, learners should draw up their own profiles, which should be completed with more than one tutor or workplace supervisor in more than one context (eg shopfloor, classroom, lecture room). In this way the 'profile' works both as a record and a learning tool. The ability to evaluate one's own strengths and weaknesses is one of the essentials of self-development. A useful dimension of the assessment profile is 'the ability to learn new competences quickly and effectively', which is of interest to any prospective employer.

Criterion-referenced assessment requires explicit trainee/pupil objectives. In the case of the National Curriculum, these are expressed as targets in the form of standard assessment tasks for each level, and assessment is based on one of 10 grades. For NVQs, what is assessed is stated in terms of competence, performance criteria and range statements, which give details of the conditions under which the competence is to be measured. Those conditions are designed to replicate as closely as possible those of the working environment under which the activity normally happens. Although this is a fine idea, it is not always easy to implement. The idea is that assessment will be delivered locally. As the context of the working environment can vary greatly from one organisation to another, the achievement of national standards at the workplace might be disputed, there is no guarantee that all supervisors will be impartial, and external verification is likely to be expensive. Assessment bodies require those who assess candidates to be properly trained and this can be an expensive undertaking.

How far should we go in the 'vocationalisation' of education?

There is no doubt that changes were needed within the education system to prepare young people for work in a modern environment. The quality of life in the UK depends upon competitive organisations to provide good jobs for everyone who wants them, and a well-trained and efficient labour force, where continuous learning is the norm, is a main ingredient for this success. School leavers need basic skills such as numeracy, literacy and information technology, which are necessary to hold their own in modern work and society in general. Yet, basic skills are still low in many areas, and initiatives such as Skills for Life, launched by the DfES in 2003, are attempting to develop basic literacy and numeracy. Young untrained people are particularly vulnerable to unemployment; in times of high skills shortages, the country cannot afford to waste this resource; in times of recession, the social consequences of sizeable numbers of unemployed youngsters have been seen in incidence of substance abuse, petty crime and vandalism.

Globalisation, downsizing and technological change have brought about a situation where it is not sufficient to have a well-educated élite; all young people must have adequate preparation. At the higher educational level, employers have expressed their concerns about the value of degrees and have called for a 'revamp of the system to make common competences a fundamental part of passing the test' (Welch 1997). A recent survey shows that graduates have high job and career expectations, but employers continue to complain that university leavers have little general business knowledge, and lack communication and IT skills (Prickett 1998). Sometimes their written English is poorer than nongraduates who have worked hard at the subject. The Dearing Committee into Higher Education (1997) believed that this issue should be addressed and that the four key skills of communication, numeracy, IT skills and the ability to learn should be integrated in the longer term into the higher education curriculum. We have already mentioned the very high percentage of small and medium-sized firms (SMEs), and this is where most employment growth is likely to be. Graduates entering small organisations are likely to be required to make a useful contribution straight away, and key skills are likely to be prerequisites. In addition, higher education needs to stimulate graduates to become entrepreneurs and equip them to start up a business, and an increasing number of modules and even degree courses are being offered in this field.

So far we have discussed the need for better vocational education, but the question we have not asked is what is what the overall function of education should be. It might be argued that education's prime function is to produce good citizens who, as well as being highly employable, can also use their spare time wisely; can, if necessary, stand back and indulge in healthy criticism of organisations and institutions; and can also pose challenging questions and cope with a changing environment. Reg Revans argued that in times of change when no one knows what to do, people need not only what he describes as 'programmed knowledge' (P), but questioning ability (Q) and the skills to explore the possible answers (Revans 1983). Are NVQ competences (derived from functional analysis basically of the status quo) and teaching taking place in schools that are judged and rated publicly in 'league tables' on their ability to 'get pupils through' prescribed tests, the best preparation for this creativity and initiative?

> Discussion question: What is education for? As we saw in Chapter 3, a group of first-year undergraduates unanimously stated it was to get a better job. Are there other reasons for getting an education, and if so, what are they?

Individuals today need to be able to think flexibly and across traditional disciplinary boundaries, which is an argument for a broadly based education and an increase in the range of interdisciplinary studies. This country has always been famous for its inventors and creators, and one wonders, for instance, whether NVQs would have helped the young Isaac Newton to question why the apple fell to the ground. In fact Newton, supposedly the founder of scientific rationalism, has recently emerged as a religious eccentric who spent years trying to crack the 'secret code' of the Bible and experimented with alchemical techniques (Gleick, 2003). These days he would have been considered a very eccentric student. There have been a number of significant criticisms of NVQs. Not least of these is that they emphasise the ability to perform a given task at a particular time, and tend to neglect the background knowledge and concepts that might help the learning to transfer to different times and places.

We stress in many parts of this book that the employee of the twenty-first century will have to have 'learned to learn'. This can be a function not just of content of syllabuses, but the way in which that content has been learned. The preoccupation with test results and targets does not always encourage attention to this fact. The concept of learning organisations has been debated for some time, but there are still few organisations to be found that could honestly claim to practise learning organisation precepts. One of the reasons for this is the lack of the necessary skills and methodologies to create such cultures. Such skills and thought patterns are unlikely to be encouraged by narrow vocational education.

Mistakes may have been made in the past, and some spheres of education may have tended to isolate students from the needs of industry, instead of encouraging them to take part in the creation of national wealth (on which even our educational institutions rely for their own funding). However, an ability to think for themselves, to question, to think laterally and creatively, and to research, are all requisites of tomorrow's workers, and it can be argued that a broader education would provide wider perspectives, enabling employees to look at their jobs from the outside and take a more balanced view. Academic education directed at challenging people's thinking can be an invaluable asset. We should not forget this as we attempt to make education more vocational. Tomorrow's citizens will require more than the sum of a collection of workplace competences. This debate re-emerged in 2003 when the current Minister for Education, Charles Clarke, appeared to suggest that the 'old' university courses like philosophy were irrelevant to the UK's needs. The fictional 'University of Poppleton' in *The Times Higher Education Supplement's* famous spoof column by Laurie Taylor, is always trying to get rid of its philosophy or history departments in favour of such courses as 'Semiotic Media Studies' or 'Comparative Retail Management Paradigms'. The reality is of course that we need both vocational and nonvocational study, and for graduates to work together to solve the UK's problems.

Discussion question: Do you agree with Charles Clarke? If not, why?

EMPLOYERS AND EDUCATIONALISTS WORKING TOGETHER

The recent revisions to the structure and content of courses aim to make education a better preparation for working life, but full benefit will not be obtained without a change of ethos. It is neither practicable nor desirable for the cultures of education and the working environment to be exactly the same. But one way of assisting to bridge the gap between school and work is to bring these cultures closer together. In further and higher education greater collaboration can ensure that course design keeps pace with the changing demands of employment.

However, the need is not totally one-sided; a better understanding of the educational system, the teaching/learning methods used and the objectives of tutors is helpful to employers in recruitment policies as well as in formulating realistic expectations of new entrants and providing appropriate initial training and induction programmes. At another level there is potential benefit to both parties from collaborating in research to solve organisational or industry-wide problems, particularly at the 'leading edge'. Universities and colleges can be particularly helpful to small and medium-sized businesses in terms of advice, research or use of facilities. On a local basis there are numerous examples of partnerships between educational institutions and industrial and commercial organisations, many initiated and sometimes pump-primed by local LSCs to meet the specific needs of the locality. Education business partnerships (EBPs) had been established over many years throughout the country to bring education and business closer together in ways that best meet local needs, and in 1995 the National Business Education Partnership Network was established to promote and give greater coherence to the work of the EPBs. We give below a few examples of the ways in which the gaps between educational institutions and employing organisations are being bridged.

Work-related experience

This can take a variety of forms, some examples of which are given below:

- visits to organisations by individuals or groups
- assignments, projects and research

- short-term placements
- sessions in school or college by staff from organisations acting as visiting lecturers.

These activities can be time-consuming and the benefit gained from them is likely to be in proportion to the quality of preparation beforehand by both parties. It is unlikely that a group of schoolchildren who have received no prior briefing will have a profitable experience from a 'standard' organisation visit, where no effort is made to consider their particular needs. Such visits need to be integrated with other aspects of the curriculum, with lead-in sessions beforehand, working with the host organisation to define exactly what is required from the visit, and following up with a debriefing session. Similarly, careful discussion is required as to what help or facilities will be provided when a student undertakes a project in a host organisation, and a visiting lecturer needs to be briefed very carefully about what it is hoped to gain from his or her session. There is of course also the point that the increasing links between school and work will highlight not just what is taught in schools and colleges but how – and this will consequently influence skills development.

Work experience

Work experience is different from work-related experience: the student actually carries out the job as closely as possible to the conditions in which an employee would work, although the emphasis is obviously on educational aspects. If carefully planned, supervised and debriefed there is no doubt about its value. Since 1997/98 all pupils in their final compulsory year at school have been entitled to two weeks' work experience (Labour Market and Skill Trends 1997/98) and many programmes and sandwich courses require much longer periods: year-long placements are frequent. The Dearing Report of the National Committee of Enquiry into Higher Education (July 1997) recommended that the government should work 'with representative employer and professional organisations to encourage employers to offer more work experience opportunities for students'.

Discussion question: Are short periods of work experience (eg a week) ever worth the effort? How might such a short period of experience have maximum benefit for student and employer?

In 1998 the National Centre for Work Experience was launched as a subsidiary company of the Council for Industry and Higher Education, with the aim to promote and support work experience for the benefit of students, organisations and the economy. It also attempts to bring about greater recognition in the academic world of various ways in which students can obtain experience of the working world. Its website (www.work-experience.org) is well worth visiting if you are looking for appropriate experience as a student or employer.

However, although work experience is a commendable inclusion in the educational curriculum, it is not an easy option. To be successful it demands careful planning, time and resources from the host organisation and the young person's tutor. Timescales for placements, realistic objectives, work programmes, visits by the college tutor during the placement, discussion time with the student and evaluation, all have to be agreed, and some large organisations have found it necessary to appoint a work experience tutor or co-ordinator. The Chartered Institute of Personnel and Development has urged its members to manage work experience professionally by taking the following steps:

- finding out about the programme of which the work experience will form a part

- setting learning objectives for work experience in collaboration with the young person's tutor
- bringing young people together for common briefing sessions, eg induction, which is essential – particularly the health and safety items
- reviewing the work experience against the learning objectives at the end of the placement
- producing written material to avoid duplicating instruction
- updating the work programme continuously in the light of experience.

The attitude and commitment of teaching staff is most important, and there needs to be enough time for initial discussions with the student and the host organisation, and for appropriate follow-up. Unless students have a very clear idea of what they are want to get out of the experience, there is a great danger that within the short time available they will obtain a superficial impression or will not take the opportunity seriously. Some programmes require work experience overseas, and with increasing globalisation this requirement may become more commonplace. Naturally, such placements require even more care in preparation and monitoring. Work experience is increasingly in demand for teachers and tutors, but the timing can cause particular difficulty for employers if there are only certain times of the year, such as school holidays, when they can be spared. There have been a number of imaginative developments, such as offering places on company management development schemes to teachers.

PREPARING AND WELCOMING THE NEWCOMER

Careers guidance

Careers professionals exist to provide guidance to individuals in matching their ambitions and skills to suitable occupations. The White Paper on Competitiveness: Helping business to win (HMSO 1994) specifies that young people have an 'entitlement' to careers guidance and that advice should be given at ages 13, 15 and 17 for those still in full-time education. The Green Paper, The Learning Age: A Renaissance for a New Britain (DfEE (1)), stressed the importance of careers advice for lifelong learning, and government programmes have set aside funds to improve this service by increasing the numbers of careers advisers and providing training and updating. The 'Connexions' service has been developed to provide guidance to young people on all aspects of life, including career advice (see Chapter 2). Flexible and innovative methods of delivery have also been used, including group discussions for young people, action plans and planned programmes of career education. Careers education takes place in schools and the careers libraries initiative helps schools update their careers information. In addition, the LSCs, with assistance from government, have created around 3,000 Training Access Points to provide information on learning opportunities, and the free national phone helpline, 'LearnDirect', is also available. Provision for special groups of people, such as single parents, or those under the New Deal (details of which are given in Chapter 2), also include the service of a personal adviser.

National Traineeships

Following the recommendations of the Dearing (1996) report, National Traineeships have replaced the former Youth Training. These offer work-based training up to NVQ Level 2, normally to people within the 16–24 age range. They provide a helpful route into Modern Apprenticeships (see below). The Sector Skills Councils, which have representatives from both large and small organisations, design the structured framework and standards for each industry. National Traineeship frameworks are now available in most of the main industrial and service sectors. Prospective employers work with their local LSC and training providers to determine what form the young person's training will take to meet both the standards and the needs of the business. The local LSC may provide financial support to help pay for the training provided. Where the organisation has a qualified assessor, the assessment can take place in-house, or a number of organisations can pool resources and employ or train their own assessor. Alternatively, the assessment can be made by a local college or training provider. This is a flexible system designed to suit small companies as well as large ones. Trainees under this scheme can also carry on to Modern Apprenticeships.

Modern Apprenticeships

Modern Apprenticeships are not the same as the old-style time-served schemes associated primarily with manufacturing and construction. The old schemes existed for a very limited range of jobs and many were unsatisfactory for a variety of reasons, often including inadequate supervision. The result was that overall the UK has continued to compare very badly with its competitors in the supply of skills at craft, technician and supervisory level. New technology brought the need for additional skills, and de-layering in many organisations increased the importance of this intermediate level. The new schemes were introduced nationally in September 1995 as a major initiative to remedy the situation by providing employer-based learning to NVQ Level 3 or above for young people. The schemes have been developed by LSCs throughout the UK working with SSCs and employers in a wide range of industrial and commercial sectors to develop their respective sector models based on a common framework of core criteria to ensure quality and consistency.

Discussion question: How can employers be persuaded to revitalise apprenticeships? Do you think there is still snobbery about the idea of being an apprentice rather than a university student?

Training – contents and outcomes

Training must lead to an NVQ at Level 3 or above and provide for breadth and flexibility according to sector and employer needs, drawing on units from related GNVQ or NVQs to make a modular structure. Sectors also allowed for multiskill schemes. The core content emphasises standards of literacy and numeracy as well as job-specific and technical skills and broad occupational knowledge. Problem-solving, the ability to get on with people, assuming responsibility and promoting ideas are also prominent. There is no time-serving: training outcomes are achieved in the shortest and most realistic timescales and progress is measured by target milestones.

Trainees – rights and expectations

The programme provides equal opportunities for both sexes. The normal age range is 16–24. There must be a written 'pledge' between the employer and the young person underwritten by the appropriate LSC. Apprentices normally have full-employed status, although in a small minority of industries there can be exceptions.

Progress to date

Modern Apprenticeships are currently available across a wide span of industry and commerce, as the following examples show: marine engineering, craft baking, floristry, horse riding and equine management, electricity supply, electronic systems service, banking service, insurance, and museums, gallery and heritage sector.

There are many examples from small and large organisations, from the apprentice stonemasons at the works department of a cathedral, to the apprentices at London Broncos Rugby League Football Club, or the business administration apprentices working for a chartered accountant who is prepared to support them beyond NVQ Level 3 to train as accounting technicians. The Modern Apprenticeship scheme is flexible and can be adapted to suit the needs of small and large organisations, in many types of industries, as well as the specific interests of the trainees. The DfES has set targets of 28% of 16–21 year olds entering the scheme by 2004/5, but recognises that many employers still regard the scheme as bureaucratic and inflexible (*Training Magazine*, October 2002).

INDUCTION

Although all the measures we have described help to reduce the gap between education and work, the way in which new entrants are received into an organisation remains a critical factor in forming their attitudes and ensuring that they reach the desired standard of performance as quickly as possible. The process of induction begins with the initial contact between the new employee and the organisation, as this is when first impressions are formed that can be long lasting. Induction in fact ought to include the whole recruitment process. This includes recruitment literature, which should be well-produced, attractive, but realistic and truthful, to avoid later disappointment and the creation of negative attitudes, as well as the way the interview process is managed. Our main concern here, however, is with welcoming the new employees into the organisation and department, ensuring that they understand core information about the job and its environment, and helping them into their new jobs.

Induction then is the one type of training necessary for all types and levels of newcomers, whether young or old, qualified or unqualified, whether they are recruits or have changed their work within the same organisation. Labour turnover is frequently highest among those who have recently joined an organisation, and the term 'induction crisis' is used to describe the critical period when new starters are most likely to leave. A well-planned induction programme can help to decrease labour turnover by ensuring that new starters settle quickly in their jobs and reach an efficient standard of performance as soon as possible.

> Discussion question: Is it possible to run an induction course where those attending are senior managers down to junior clerical staff? What are the pluses and minuses?

Legislation – for example in the field of health and safety – has caused employers to review the content and effectiveness of their induction arrangements. It has become clear that the traditional 'standardised' induction course, which all employees attend, often disregards the particular needs of special groups such as school leavers, national trainees, people from ethnic minority groups, disabled people, women returners, adults being trained for new jobs, managers and work-experience students. Although such staff will share some common induction needs, their programmes must also reflect the differences and, as a result, might need to vary in both content and duration from one category to another.

The wider induction objectives for young people cannot be achieved in an initial short course of training. The following quotation from the MSC (1975) study on the vocational preparation of young people is still highly relevant:

> What is needed ... is a personnel policy specifically for young entrants which recognises the special problems they face in the transition to the new environment of adult working

life, at a time when they are also experiencing the personal problems of growing up. Such a policy would reflect awareness of the teaching methods in use in schools, the common attitudes of young people towards work and the community; their ideals and expectations; the difficulties faced by young people in . . . adapting to working life, in working with older people and in understanding and accepting the discipline of the workplace. Particular attention would be given to trying to see that those close to the entrants, particularly their supervisors and workmates were able to guide them in their development, both as individuals and as capable members of the working community, and that the young people themselves know where they can go to get advice whenever they need it.

From this it follows that induction cannot be fully carried out by the HRD specialist or central HR department alone, but must be an overall managerial responsibility. Many induction needs are concerned with the immediate working environment; superiors and those working in the vicinity must play an important part. For these reasons, induction should be regarded as an integral part of the corporate training plan and its importance should be stressed in the training given to all employees, and especially to managers and supervisors.

The following list indicates the types of material that are likely to be generally relevant to newcomers:

- conditions of employment: the contract of employment, payment procedures, holiday arrangements, relevant legislation, absence and sickness procedures, meal and tea breaks, disciplinary procedures, and equality and diversity policy. Care should be taken to ensure that new employees really understand these matters, and that they sign a document verifying that they have read any relevant matter. This is important not only for the welfare of the employee, but from an organisational perspective, to avoid misunderstandings, which, in extreme cases, could lead to industrial tribunal procedures, when proof that the employee received the necessary information may be required

- welfare: pension and sickness schemes, welfare and social activities, medical services

- the organisation: vision and objectives, products, standards, market, future developments

- introduction to workplace: meeting the supervisor and fellow employees, geography of department (eg canteen, toilets), the job, who's who, any impending workplace changes

- safety: hazard areas, fire alarm procedure, fire points and exits, no-smoking areas, first aid and accident procedures, safety rules (eg safety clothing), security arrangements, safety committees, safety representatives. (Thorough instruction in safety aspects is a legal requirement. New starters, including those on short periods of work experience, are particularly at risk.)

- training and education arrangements: people responsible for training, content of training programmes, further education, including release arrangements and awards made

- organisation facilities: clubs, discount schemes

- pay and rewards system: how to read a pay slip, performance-related schemes, overtime and incentive payments, share option and pension schemes, overtime and incentive schemes, income tax and other deductions

- nonfinancial benefits: car parking, rest rooms, canteens, clothing, products
- discipline and grievance procedures: rules and regulations, how to register a grievance
- trade unions and staff associations: the role of trade unions, joint consultation.

The content, approach and methods of delivery should be planned around the needs of the learner. In some cases a few hours' induction is adequate but in others it may last for several weeks. Appropriate timing of sessions can be a decisive factor in effectiveness. It is usually preferable to split the content of longer programmes into several sections, sometimes over a number of weeks, providing the learner with the information as he or she needs it. School-leavers, for example, are unlikely to be interested in the details of the pension scheme the minute they arrive on the premises. Their first concern is likely to be 'Will I be able to do the job, and what will my supervisor and "mates" at work be like?' On the other hand, in a certain chemical company, safety conditions are so paramount that no new starter (or visitor) is allowed into the production area without satisfactorily completing an interactive computer-based programme on the safety requirements and regulations, and signing a statement to verify that they have done so!

Training methods will vary, depending upon the subject matter and the type of trainee. Self-study methods that allow self-pacing and choice of timing, such as computer-based programmes, or by means a company intranet, may be useful for giving certain types of information to employees in dispersed locations in this country or overseas or possibly for employees transferring from one department to another. This can happen even before they officially start the job. If the software contains a facility to record who has undertaken the program and how they scored, this is obviously an advantage. With the aid of computers and word processing systems, some companies with dispersed sites have standardised their induction and early training by producing templates or 'proformas' of induction and training manuals. These contain basic information and training programmes for all employees, but have blank spaces and 'prompt' points for management at different locations to add site-specific information and to adapt the programmes to their own needs. A language translation facility can be included in the software for multinational organisations.

Management trainees

Management trainees have special requirements in four main categories:

- organisational knowledge, encompassing most of the items mentioned above
- the political system, in particular the types of managerial behaviour that tend to be respected and rewarded; sensitivity to organisational culture
- management skills, such as time management, delegation
- technical and/or professional knowledge and skills. Although they should provide an excellent basis for further learning, even highly specialised degrees are unlikely to encompass the precise needs of an organisation, or be 'at the leading edge' of the company's particular interest.

Discussion question: Is it appropriate for an organisation committed to diversity to run a 'fast track' management trainee scheme where trainees are assumed to progress rapidly to senior jobs?

Care should be taken that such trainees, recruited potentially as top managers for the future, do not receive conflicting messages. If the recruitment brochure has given the impression of immediate responsibility and rapid career progression, it can be demoralising to be given a lengthy (12–18 months') 'Cook's Tour' of the organisation. It is likely that attitudes to the job are developed at an early stage and become internalised. It can be extremely beneficial to set reasonably demanding projects, which will not only help to solve problems for the company, but will require the learner to find out useful information about it. Technical graduates, whose university course has prepared them for a particular profession, such as engineering, may require considerable information about the organisation's specific technology and particular niche. General Arts graduates will, of course, require much more. One problem is that the student culture is very different from that of a business organisation, and unless they have had a significant amount of work experience, graduates are likely to require assistance in this direction. Senior managers acting as mentors and coaches can be an invaluable resource in helping the development of awareness and sensitivity to organisational culture and practices. They can also play a major role in assisting with career planning, drawing up action plans and identifying 'milestones', which are particularly important when the training is lengthy, so that the trainee can work to objectives and see what progress is being made.

THE EDUCATION/WORKPLACE INTERFACE: CHALLENGES AND CONTRADICTIONS?

There are many ambiguities and contradictions in the current scene: for example, closely defined competences for NVQs alongside a need for initiative and creativity, the requirement for people with ever deeper technological knowledge and ability who must still have generalist competences and key skills. The challenge is enormous and complex, but we cannot afford to fail. You should now be able to distinguish the main current trends in vocational education and training: if you are not already familiar with the situation, a useful exercise would be to investigate what is happening in your own local schools and colleges and see how many examples you can find of liaison between educational institutions and employers.

If you are employed, what does your own company do in this respect, and how effective is it? It is quite likely that your local university or FE college would be delighted to discuss with you ideas for mutual collaboration, for example, bringing in a student to be responsible for a specific project you might otherwise not have time to complete. It is this sort of local small-scale project that can begin to develop mutually helpful working relationships between academics and the 'real world'. (For a humorous view of this, which also touches on the decline of UK manufacturing industry in the 1980s, see David Lodge's novel *Nice Work* 1989.)

Summing up, it is clear that new workers of the future will need to be increasingly skilled, and there is still a gap between what they know and what industry needs them to know, especially in the case of young people. Demographics in the UK indicate that 'nontraditional' employees, such as women returners, people with a disability, people from minority ethnic groups and older people, are increasingly in demand, and require learning and training appropriate to their needs. 'Education' as we know it is still a very mixed bag of vocational programmes and academic achievement. There is a move away from neat academic categories like FE or HE. The trend is more to 'portable' qualifications. However, all new entrants to the work environment benefit from sensitive acclimatisation to help them make the most of their role – not only for their own benefit, but also for the organisation, and the UK as a whole.

> **In this chapter you have read about the changing profiles of new entrants to the workforce, and how effective induction can assist them to fulfil their potential to the advantage of the employer and themselves. Imagine you have just been offered a new job in HR in an organisation of your choice. Plan your own induction programme, to last two weeks. Who would you talk to, and where would you go? How would you evaluate your experiences?**
>
> In our next chapter we consider the managers of the present and future, and how to develop their ability to learn to become more effective.

Management Development in Action

In Chapter 11, we consider:

■ **The meanings we attach to management and leadership, suggesting that there are differences between management and leadership, but that effective managers need leadership skills;**

■ **Suggestions for improving management development from management writers, who maintain generally that we appear still to have much to do in the UK to improve our success in appointing and developing managers;**

■ **Strategies and methods for establishing competences and appropriate learning to develop them;**

■ **The importance, before embarking on management training and learning, of specifying the management skills and competences the organisation wishes to develop;**

■ **A case study looking at development of organisationally specific management behaviours.**

In this chapter, we would like to introduce you to some of the key theories and practices of management and leadership development. Neither concept seems to have been easy to put into practice. As you will see, after twenty-five years of UK writers' and training specialists' criticisms of management development in the UK there are still concerns about the overall competence of managers. However, as we stress throughout the book, we are not talking about skills and abilities that are easy to develop, and management is an art, not an exact science. This makes it difficult to prescribe lists of skills for a generic manager (although we will look later at some interesting attempts to do so). It also means that development for these skills is likely to be a complex matter, requiring strategic decisions from HRD specialists. At least in the early twenty-first century we do now have a better idea of what the problems are, and understanding these problems and issues will make it easier, and probably more fulfilling, for HRD practitioners to create learning environments that will make a positive difference to management behavioural competences.

You will see that there are a number of expressions around management and leadership development, which might initially appear confusing. We will look in a moment at the ongoing debate about management and leadership (which will probably never be completely resolved) but first would like to clarify what we believe are the differences between 'management development' and '*manager* development', as that is rather easier. We described management development in an earlier chapter as 'preparation for future moves, and the forward organisational planning that may be dovetailed with them' (p 122). Here we might venture a little further, and suggest that it is also about organisations making decisions about the sort of managers they are trying to grow and develop, and the role models they want to adopt. What skills do they require? What behaviours should they be demonstrating?

Manager development and training, on the other hand, involves any learning or training intervention aimed at developing specific skills and competence in their present roles for individual managers or groups of managers. It lacks the future development emphasis that management development possesses. Both are important, and manager development will usually be part of a management development strategy, but the latter can also involve a whole range of other interventions, as you will see later.

MANAGEMENT OR LEADERSHIP?

Now the difficult issue to untangle! Leadership has always been a very popular topic for writers and trainers. For years they have argued (and are still arguing) about whether leadership can be taught, or is an innate ability possessed by only a few people. Of course, cynics might argue there is a significant advantage in trainers claiming that leadership can be taught. If leaders were born, not made, there would be little point in leadership trainers charging high fees for their services, unless they refused to work with those who hadn't already demonstrated high leadership potential. Not surprisingly, most trainers seem to accept the material they are given.

Academics have also been keen to examine leadership, and particularly to separate leadership from management, usually at the expense of the latter. Much of the leadership literature appears to portray management as a rather pedestrian, 'transactional' (Burns 1978) term, which Burns contrasted with 'transformational' leadership activity. Leadership on the other hand seems to be a quality of 'charismatic', 'transformational' people who are not concerned with everyday administrative matters but take a strategic view and inspire others to get the work done.

A recent IDS study of leadership development (753, July 2003) made the point very strongly that 'management and leadership roles are quite different and demand different competencies ... good (managers and leaders) are usually quite different types of people'. This is the approach often taken by management writers. The implication is that 'management' skills like planning and administration were needed in stable environments, whereas, in the world of hyper-change, leaders are required who have a vision of the future and can inspire and influence their staff to embark on journeys of discovery to fulfil that vision. But is management really just about planning and administrative skills? Haven't successful managers always possessed leadership qualities as well as organising ability?

There is a way out of the management/leadership dilemma. We might consider leadership as one of a range of behaviours required by effective managers, like good delegation ability, skill in organising projects, motivation skills and self-management, for example. In terms of these skills and abilities, we do not say of a manager that she has innately good prioritisation skills, or that he was born with the ability to cope expertly with ambiguity. Even psychologists who suggest 'personality' is inborn would not be so prescriptive as this. We assume that people, either through nature or nurture, might possess a higher or lower level of ability. Some may be good prioritisers with no training or development at all, whereas others may need to develop the skill: but both may become equally effective. The individual who is already effective might also enhance his or her skills through suitable learning and development experiences. So why is leadership any different?

Part of our romance with leadership, and so we would argue our difficulty in developing leadership behaviour effectively, is that we seem to mix up the concept of leadership with that of heroism. When we also throw in the idea of entrepreneurship, which some people also equate with leadership behaviour, and which can certainly involve both leadership and heroism, it is clear why we are confused. Some good leaders and some good managers have also been heroes, but they are not synonymous. We once asked a well-known local entrepreneur who he would nominate as his favourite hero. He responded 'my grandmother', a lady who could scarcely read or write but had brought up a large and happy family on a tiny budget. It was inspiring that he chose a woman, and a woman who was not a 'high flyer' in contemporary terms. However, she was probably more of a leader than a hero. Heroism certainly requires bravery, but it is often a very individualistic pursuit – the hero does not often get other people to do things for him or her, and although heroes can work as part of a team (the Three Musketeers, for example) they often make very individual contributions. In the early 1980s, the cricketer Ian Botham made a poor captain of the England cricket team. He was replaced by Mike Brearley, a reasonable player but a highly effective leader and manager. Brearley's leadership and trust in him enabled Botham to become the 'hero' of the 1981 Test series.

Brearley retired from cricket captaincy to become a psychotherapist – he seems to have recognised that ability to understand other people is a key skill in the effective manager's portfolio. Brearley, as we suggested above, appears to possess skills both as a manager and leader, and presents those skills in a low-key, understated way. Another possible misconception about leadership is that it needs to be much larger than life. However, even a famous leader like Napoleon, who was in some ways a poor people manager, made use of basic management techniques to support his legend. He would, for example, ask one of his staff to research the names and family backgrounds of the soldiers he was to review, who were duly impressed when he was able to ask after their wives and children by name. Not charisma but good planning!

In assuming that leadership is the same as heroism, and that both are somehow larger than life skills, we also make a fundamental error about *where* leadership skills can be exercised. We would suggest that leadership behaviours can be demonstrated at any level in organisations, not just by senior management. Trainers and educators (the word educate comes from the Latin word 'educo' meaning to lead out) who are helping learners to achieve their full potential have to employ leadership skills to be effective. Parents are constantly exercising leadership skills because their children rightly or wrongly take them as examples. Health experts who are trying to persuade people to be more active and eat less junk food are trying to lead people into better habits.

> Discussion question: Do you agree with our view that leadership is just one part of the overall management role? Or is leadership somehow 'superior' to management?

We have discussed these concepts in some detail not least because there have been examples of the damage that 'toxic' leaders can do when their followers accept their excesses without judgement. Within living memory we have Hitler and Stalin, and recent times have shown that toxic leadership is still with us – in Zimbabwe, in the Balkans, and the Middle East. The rise of toxic leaders is determined by many different circumstances, but one may well be people's tendency to 'project' their own responsibility onto someone who will make decisions for them. Being able to access our own leadership skills in fact makes us all better followers, since we will be more likely to challenge poor or unethical leadership by others. The concept of 'servant leadership' arguably was first suggested by Jesus to his followers, but has been articulated more recently by Robert Greenleaf in the 1970s into a philosophy that 'supports people who choose to serve first, and then lead as a way of extending service to individuals and institutions. Servant leaders may or may not hold formal leadership positions. Servant leadership encourages collaboration, trust, foresight, listening and the ethical use of power and empowerment' (http://www.greenleaf.org/leadership/servant-leadership/). Leadership then becomes a role to which employees at all levels of an organisation can aspire.

So, what key points are we suggesting about management and leadership, before we go on to discuss how these behaviours may best be developed? Remember we have said that management is not an exact science and neither is leadership – so you may want to challenge and debate some of our suggestions:

- Leadership is a set of behaviours that differs from heroism in that leaders are concerned with influencing other people, whereas heroes are action people focused on achieving an objective (usually) single handed;
- It is not necessary to be a manager to be a leader – leaders can be found at every level in an organisation and not just in management jobs;
- It is (on the other hand) necessary to possess some leadership skills in order to be an effective manager. It might be helpful to think of a continuum of management skills, with transactional (administrative, organisational) skills at one end, and transformational (inspirational, motivational) at the other. No-one will be excellent at all aspects of the manager's role, but everyone, with suitable development, can improve.

With the last point in mind, we would like to focus our subsequent discussion of management and leadership development on the manager's role, as managers have a defined responsibility for others' development as well as their own, so it is particularly important that they model the behaviours their organisation wishes to promote. However, it could be argued that leadership development should be offered to all staff in an organisation, not just managers. Given that leadership is important at all levels in the organisation, it would be an interesting exercise for HRD practitioners to include some nonmanagers in their next leadership training course.

Discussion question: Have you ever been a delegate on a leadership development course? If so, how would you rate its effectiveness?

THE MANAGER'S ROLE: WHAT ARE WE DEVELOPING MANAGERS TO DO?

We have said that we believe leadership is a key management skill. But if it is at one end of a continuum of management competences, what other skills should managers possess? Many published books have attempted to answer the question of what we expect from managers and managers as leaders. Some of them may be slightly tongue in cheek, such as those self-improvement books on sale at airports promising to teach you all the 'secrets' of management in no time, but others have been more serious attempts to understand the manager's job. We will mention just a few of the best known, but you may be interested in following up others in the list of further reading in Appendix 1. Rosemary Stewart (1967) studied a hundred managers. Among other interesting discoveries, she found that in a four-week period they only had overall nine periods of half an hour without interruptions. Stewart suggested that the job was a mix of demands, choices and constraints. In essence, as she saw it, the manager's job involved 'deciding what should be done and getting other people to do it'.

Some years later, Mintzberg (1973) described an almost all-consuming role, which was difficult to escape from. It seemed that managers were most frequently reactive and controlled little of what they actually did. His suggestion was that they should attempt to control their commitments to focus on gaining information and exercising leadership. In the UK in the early 1980s, concern was raised at the gap between the UK's economic and commercial performance, and particularly the quality of its managers. A number of key consultants' reports proposed that better HRD might help. The Management Charter Initiative was set up in 1988 to review the performance of managers. Its work is continued by the Management Standards Centre, part of the Chartered Institute of Management, another institution among the many bodies referred to in Chapter 2 as influencing the UK development scene. A visit to its website shows that it is now seeking to improve 'weaknesses' that exist in the quantity and quality of managers and leaders in the UK by consulting widely to develop a new set of standards. After more than 20 years' work on improving management standards, there still appears to be a gap between what the UK needs and what it has. Of course, not every problem has an HRD solution, and other factors have a part to play, such as the selection of future managers, the increasing complexity of the management role or the need for short-term business solutions. We might suggest, though, that the emphasis in the UK has been on training and skills, while low on situational and reflective learning through exploration. The latter is important if leadership is to be more about values and behaviours and less about learned skills. Since socially acceptable values and behaviours change over time, this means that the nature of leadership changes as society's values change. That means leaders are a reflection of their time and context, and must be able to respond to societal change.

Discussion question: Why has so little successfully changed around UK management development over the last 20 years or so?

However, the work done by MCI and MSC has at least been helpful in focusing managers on what they should be doing. The key elements of the current standards focus on seven main areas:

- Manage activities
- Manage resources
- Manage people
- Manage information
- Manage energy
- Manage quality
- Manage projects.

This expanded list (which used to include self-management, but it may be surmised that this threads through the whole) has been the basis of a good deal of management development material. Leading thinkers and management writers seem to agree on the point that 'traditional' management activities have concentrated in the past more on the planning and administrative end of the 'management continuum'. So the traditional manager, operating until the late 1970s/early 1980s in a fairly stable environment, might be focusing energy on areas such as:

- planning
- organising
- forecasting
- co-ordinating and controlling.

A good traditional manager wouldn't just be expected to be an effective administrator, however. Even descriptions of the management role up to the 1970s would make reference to the need for managers to lead and motivate, but the emphasis was on the manager/leader as a command and control figure, rather than an inspirer or motivator. We have developed from a view of the leader as 'General' (such as Napoleon) to an understanding of the importance in leadership of the 'softer' skills. 'Softer' is actually not a very appropriate term, because skills like diplomacy, 'emotional intelligence' and intuition can be much harder to develop. Perhaps 'subtle skills' would be better. Certainly, the activities in which modern managers have to succeed suggest a much more complex organisational environment requiring more subtle and sophisticated competences:

- tolerance of ambiguity (no pat answers) and ability to manage in organisational turbulence;
- management of change, and (often as a result of change) management of pressure and stress;
- political awareness – suggesting a need for diplomacy and persuasion skills;
- problem-solving, especially with complex ethical dilemmas;
- management of diverse, and sometimes challenging, people.

Discussion question: What would you add to the list above?

The role of the modern manager appears to be comparable with finding one's way across a quicksand with a group of inexperienced explorers following. There is a need not only to avoid the boggy spots and maintain a course through them, but also to change course when unexpected obstacles are presented.

We have mentioned 'emotional intelligence' above: an ability to perceive correctly your own and others' emotions (Persaud 1997), supposedly possessed by more women than men. There are more women coming through as managers, but it is still open to question how far the successful ones are actually modelling 'masculine' behaviours. As the majority of very senior managers are still men, there is a tendency perhaps for them to appoint women with whom they can 'do business' and it remains to be seen whether these women have any more of the 'soft' skills than their male counterparts.

Many organisations have considered the complexities of the management role and sensibly decided to develop organisation-specific competencies. In the case study at the end of this chapter (p 241) we will explain a little of what Robert Gordon University did to develop such role definitions for managers. Many organisations have established these; the IDS study gives an example of the Inland Revenue, which developed its list from a senior civil service competence framework. This was helpful in giving examples of effective and noneffective behaviour for a competence area, for example 'gives and expects frequent constructive feedback' is contrasted with 'blames others'!

Put in this way it is clear which behaviours are to make a positive difference, but organisations must ensure that managers practise what the organisation preaches, otherwise people at junior levels in the organisation will be cynical and switch off their involvement. One of us worked in an organisation that developed a 'preferred management style': the problem was that none of the senior managers who developed this and signed up to it actually practised the 'preferred' behaviours. Organisations need to be aware that it is dangerous to commit such competence lists to public scrutiny without a real intention to live the values. If, for example, my organisation expresses effective management behaviour in terms of 'is comfortable working with colleagues from a diverse range of backgrounds', what will I think as a junior female employee if my manager expresses a view that women take more sick leave to look after their children?

It would be sensible at least to consider this issue when drafting competence lists. While stopping short of encouraging 'whistleblowing' along Stalinist lines, staff need to feel confident that challenging inappropriate behaviour will not be used against them by management.

Of course, many writers have sensibly pointed out that even before establishing management competences, let alone prioritising them, it is important to get commitment at the most senior levels in the organisation to introduce a management development programme in any formal sense. The decision to do so might well result in a review of organisational structures and resources overall. Management development initiatives may become very resource intensive. Firmly anchoring what needs to be done in the overall business plan and business goals makes obvious good sense. Why, for example, seek managers who exhibit collaborative and team oriented behaviours when the organisation is firmly focused on rewarding individual achievement?

STRATEGIES AND METHODS OF DETERMINING MANAGEMENT COMPETENCE

Deciding on the management competences that the organisation wishes to nurture is never easy, but it would appear to be helpful to involve the managers themselves in defining preferred behaviours. As long ago as 1976, Andrew and Valerie Stewart were considering the issue of management development in a groundbreaking book called *Tomorrow's Men Today*. Nowadays it would be 'tomorrow's people', but the concept of equality and diversity was in its infancy then. The book is still extremely useful for managers trying to introduce management development professionally. One of the techniques used by the Stewarts to focus on management competence was the Repertory Grid (Kelly 1955). Developed as a psychotherapeutic tool to assist people with emotional problems to understand themselves better, the Repertory Grid has helped psychologists and subsequently management trainers to assist individuals to describe their thought processes and attitudes with minimal input from the investigator. In the context of this book we don't have time to describe all its features and uses, but its adoption by management consultants and researchers has enabled them to probe the views of managers in organisations in developing generic management competences. By asking interviewees to compare and contrast the activities of managers they know, and who are either effective or less effective, a series of 'constructs' may be teased out. These can be as simple as 'always speaks to people when she comes into the office in the morning', to 'does not trust his subordinates to achieve goals'. These behavioural statements can then be adapted for use in assessment or development centres to rate candidates on a performance questionnaire. Frequently a 1–5 scoring system is used, with polarities such as, for example, 'he always breaks his promises' to 'he always keeps his promises'.

The Stewarts' procedure is extremely detailed and well thought through, but there is no reason why the technique cannot be used in a slightly more succinct way. The important issue is that the constructs are developed initially by the managers themselves. This firmly anchors management competence in the organisation, and requires managers to 'own' the behaviours in a way that would not be possible with a generic, theoretical list. This commitment to understanding and accepting the behaviours requires analysis and discussion, which avoids simplistic 'cloning' of managers. For researchers there is endless fascination in seeing how the 'real-life' constructs compare with the management literature.

Other tools to elicit management competences may be focus groups (see the Robert Gordon University case study), questionnaires, observation, diaries and journals ... even job descriptions if well produced. In the IDS study, Cliff Allen, Head of Corporate Development and Learning at Portsmouth City Council, developed a fascinating list of behaviours to select 'high flyers'. These included:

- challenging everything with 'why', and appearing at times confrontational;
- wanting to change things even if they appear to be working well;
- learning quickly and with impatience;
- exhibiting creativity and innovation;
- focusing concern for the future rather than the past;
- enthusing about the big picture and outcomes;
- experimenting and risk taking;
- demonstrating courage, and ability to move out of 'comfort zones';
- showing special insight and ability to solve complex problems;
- tending to clash with, irritate and annoy (traditional) high achievers.

(IDS study, 753, July 2003, reproduced with permission of Cliff Allen of Portsmouth City Council)

The study does not say how these behaviours were derived, but one wonders how many organisations would ensure such people got nowhere near a management development programme. For some organisations, a few of the list of behaviours above would be a reason to fire someone! Clearly Portsmouth City Council thought otherwise, recognising that people with high potential are not always easy to manage. They may also exert strong informal leadership in the organisation, and if they do this from a position of being 'against the government' they can have a very destructive influence. Developing their leadership potential constructively therefore doubly makes sense.

> Discussion question: What do you think? Are awkward people like this good managers and leaders, or are they too individualistic?

Assuming that somehow an organisation has committed to a management development programme and has managed to decide on the management behaviours it wishes to promote and develop, what happens next?

APPROACHES TO MANAGEMENT DEVELOPMENT

First of all, of course, before trying to develop a manager you need to catch him or her. This is not as frivolous as it sounds, because it is our contention that many organisations have been in the past casual about appointing managers, and this may well have something to do with the UK's poor record in the area. We don't propose to go into much detail about recruitment and selection of managers, because there are excellent CIPD published textbooks on this topic (see, for example, Taylor 2002; Armstrong 2003). But we would stress that to select for a complex and sophisticated role requires complex and sophisticated techniques, not just the ubiquitous interview.

Most organisations are not quite as casual as to rely on interview alone to select managers, but few invest in high-quality assessment centres or contract them out to professional consultants. This is in spite of the excellent advice from writers like the Stewarts, which has been available for over twenty-five years. Many organisations unfortunately retain the old-fashioned belief that:

- managers should be promoted from within (not always a bad idea, but they do need to show potential for the job);
- managers who are professionally or technically competent will also be, or become, good people managers without any systematic development for the role.

So, assuming your managers are properly selected, what next? Mumford (1997) suggested that most organisations develop their managers in one of the following ways:

1. *Informally*. Managers in this type of organisation develop accidentally, purely by serendipitous learning;
2. *Integrated methods*. Managers are developed in an opportunist sense: there is some planning of learning experiences; on the whole learning is on the job with possibly some formal material;
3. *Formalised*. Managers are developed in a planned and organised way, often away from the workplace, through complex organisation-wide programmes.

Discussion question: What are the pluses and minuses of these approaches?

There is no doubt that many managers still learn their jobs accidentally, but all the available evidence suggests that the first method is haphazard and depends very much on the self-motivation of the individual. However much we might value on-the-job learning (as Reg Revans developed Action Learning to build on the practical aspects of learning for managers), there is no doubt that some formal structures are required for management development programmes to be regarded with any respect in organisations, not least because their effectiveness can be more effectively evaluated. There is also the vexed question of performance appraisal in the process. It is possible to be sceptical of formal appraisal systems, but still accept that frequent and constructive feedback of subordinates is necessary, and should be an integral part of the manager's role. Appraisal systems of themselves rarely fulfil the needs of effective constructive feedback, since they often tend to focus on 'how are you performing?', rather than 'how can you perform more effectively?'

Techniques to try?

It used to be far more common for organisations to use *succession planning* as a management development tool; that is, deciding how a manager's subsequent career moves might assist development of potential. This process tended to be questioned with the emphasis in the 1970s and 1980s on equal opportunity and diversity. Why should job opportunities be restricted to certain individuals in an organisation? But even bearing fairness in mind, a form of succession planning can still be used. Effective performance feedback can also encompass discussion of future career moves, and focusing on skills to be developed can help the aspiring manager to apply for more senior positions. Judicious use of placements can also assist the development of a range of specific skills.

> Discussion question: Is it possible to combine commitment to diversity with a succession planning process?

Formal education and training

Formal management education as a management development tool has long been a feature in the USA with its trend for business schools, and the UK swiftly followed. Many universities and colleges are now responding to the needs of people who want to study part time, and part-time programmes as well as continuing professional development (CPD) are becoming increasingly popular with busy managers, aided by online learning programmes. Some organisations have developed company-specific academic programmes, customised to meet their specific needs. There are both potential advantages and problems with this approach. Organisational norms and policies may be reflected; but one of the advantages of working with a heterogeneous group is that it is possible to explore new ways of doing things that are not organisationally specific.

From the beginning there has been general criticism of academic management qualifications like MBAs – see, for example, Revans below – for being too general, too academic, and not based in the 'real world' – wherever that might be. Have MBA courses embraced the concept of continuous learning throughout careers, for example? Probably market forces will ultimately decide which MBA programmes survive – hopefully those which focus on the need for effective 'subtle' skills as well as technical competence.

Formal training courses

There is of course a proliferation of training providers, and organisations need to be very focused to get best from them. HRD specialists in organisations who invest in external providers (and 'invest' is probably an appropriate word for what can be very high fees), need to be focused on what delegates need to achieve. We discuss the concept of evaluation of learning interventions exhaustively in Chapter 9, but arguably it is especially important to evaluate the impact of high profile, high cost courses. The question also arises of whether is it better to have in-company training or to send aspiring managers on 'open' courses, which give them a chance to network and exchange ideas with others. Many organisations have considered outdoor development in this context, which as we will see has had a mixed reception in the UK.

Outdoor management development (OMD)

The ITOL website recently produced a flurry of e-mails about what was termed 'team building madness'. Many of the so-called 'outdoor development programmes' that were critiqued involved bizarre activities such as firewalking, which was introduced as part of a corporate development programme in a large American company and caused some delegates to suffer second-degree burns with the aim of 'achieving things they never thought possible'. In his book *Outdoor Management Development: A critical introduction for the intelligent practitioner*, Bill Krouwel (2002) mentions other equally grotesque activities passed off as outdoor development, such as lawnmower racing or fake kidnapping. Krouwel rightly refers to the producers of such activities as 'chancers, exploiters of trends, and downright fools'. It is unfortunate that the potential of OMD is often undermined by such quick-fix solutions, for done well it has rich potential as a learning tool. HRD specialists considering its use as a management development tool need to ensure that the following caveats are observed:

- OMD should not be just for the superfit. Activities can be designed to be appropriate for all levels and achievable by people with disabilities.

- OMD should not be physically or emotionally dangerous. Requiring people to swim in icy seas or to confront other delegates aggressively is bullying and should be treated as such.

- OMD should not emphasise activities or competition. The emphasis should be on sophisticated group review techniques by the trainer, which help delegates to reflect on their individual learning process.

If OMD is used as a problem solving exercise with constructive feedback, it can be extremely beneficial in helping managers to understand their individual strengths and weaknesses. But group facilitation skills and individual coaching ability of a high level are a prerequisite of those providing the experience.

> Discussion question: What are your views about the OMD controversy? Is it possible, for example, to transfer insights learned from OMD to the work environment?

Action Learning: problem-solving in the 'real world'?

Reg Revans (1983) is probably the antidote to academic approaches to management development. Indeed, he referred to MBA as 'Moral Bankruptcy Assured'. Unless your ideas are ridiculed by experts, Revans claimed, they are worth nothing: and Revans was certainly at times a prophet without honour in his own country.

Revans' contribution to management development was the concept of Action Learning (AL), to which we refer at several points in this book. It is a deceptively simple approach (and perhaps this partly explains the experts' ridicule). It proposes that small groups learn from each others' successes and failures rather than from experts (another explanation for their ridicule). Revans had observed this approach when working with the Nobel Prize physicist Rutherford in Cambridge. Like many great minds, Rutherford and his team were not egocentric: they were realistic about their individual limitations and found team problem-solving helpful. Revans saw no reason why less brilliant minds could not emulate their approach, and proposed that managers should work in action learning 'sets' to problem solve. He talked of $L = P + Q$: learning is programmed knowledge and the ability to ask good questions. Like Socrates, he had also realised the difference between the 'cleverness' encouraged by our education system and genuine wisdom. Action Learning may seem simple but it presents a fearful challenge to organisational thinking. Revans loved questioners and asking questions, and this ignores any assumption that 'managers know best'. But it is also a prerequisite of the Learning Organisation. Cliff Allen at Portsmouth City Council was prepared to accept that high potential people will constantly challenge the status quo, but many organisations will not accept this to their own loss. So Revans' ideas, as we will discuss in the *Afterword*, are frequently still looking for followers.

Coaching and mentoring

As we suggest in Chapter 8, coaching and mentoring have taken place informally throughout history between senior managers and their subordinates. Indeed, as you may be aware, Mentor was the older warrior who guided Odysseus' son Telemachus in his father's absence in the Trojan wars, so the concept has a pretty long history. As with management and leadership, there is some blurring of boundaries. A mentor can also coach, and a coach does not necessarily have to be a mentor. Coaching is usually more specific and may involve a junior manager's supervisor or an external mentor in working with the junior person to help him or her develop a specific skill or set of skills. It is usually more interventionist, in that the coach will work closely with the individual to help him or her practise, and may involve specific agreements for action on both sides. Most effective managers will include an element of coaching in their management repertoire, especially when dealing with junior staff. A mentor on the other hand is usually not the junior manager's line superior, but a relatively senior manager who is slightly removed from the mentee's work area.

The plan is that the junior will be able to talk through problems, queries and aspirations with the mentor, who will be able to advise on issues such as organisational culture and etiquette, getting ideas into practical application, or suggesting who might be able to assist the mentee with specific projects. Of course, there will also be occasions when the mentor might have to assist the mentee to put right things which have gone wrong (we are assuming here that most organisations have moved a little beyond the blame culture). See page 170 for an example of mentoring in action.

There are differing views as to whether mentoring should be an informal process – probably most of us in a new organisation have sought out a more experienced person to get a feel for the culture and values of the place. For some organisational HRD specialists, this could have some drawbacks: first, the informal mentor may not be positive about the organisation (we have all come across the department cynic who will ridicule and criticise any new idea), and secondly, even if the mentor is positive, they may not have the time or ability to deal with some of the complex issues the mentee wants to discuss. Organisations reporting success with mentoring tend not to do it cheaply by simply bringing together experienced and new managers, but ensure that the right people are selected as mentors, that they are matched effectively with mentees, and that both undergo some training to understand their roles fully and get the most from them.

The ideal mentor is clearly not always to be found, but a formal mentoring scheme can at least deal with any disasters that might happen from mismatches. There will also be questions for the individual(s) managing the programme: should gender or age be a factor; how far should couples have a formal agenda with defined learning outcomes; can an individual's line manager also be their mentor? These questions of course do not have 'right' answers, but depend very much on the nature of the scheme and the organisational setting. But they do need to be asked, in order for a scheme to have value and for its effectiveness to be assessed. Evaluation of effectiveness, as we suggested above, is particularly important when any element of a management development programme is introduced, because it can have a positive or negative impact on the whole organisation. Organisations that have introduced mentoring as part of a management development programme generally report favourable outcomes.

> Discussion question: What do you think would be the essential requirements for a formal mentoring scheme to be successful? Consider this question either from the viewpoint of an organisation with which you are familiar, or in general terms.

Self-development and continuing professional development (CPD)

If managers are operating in an environment with any aspirations to develop Learning Organisation practice, there is no doubt that they should be focused on their own development. The CIPD, like many professional bodies, requires its members to keep records of their development activities, and very frequently members grumble about the need to update these records when, like all managers, they are busy performing myriad other tasks. But to be effective, self-development and CPD do not need to be tremendously complicated. All of us keep some sort of diary and usually a brief diary entry of a particularly helpful experience or project will be sufficient to record the learning. These can also be useful if the diarist has a mentor with whom to discuss the outcomes and further aims. Self-development should not be seen as a substitute for the involvement of the manager's supervisor, in the same way as self-motivation should not mean that the individual does not need constructive feedback and encouragement from higher management. It is particularly important in an organisation that wishes to encourage learning, or has aspirations to develop Learning Organisation practices, that managers, especially the senior and hence more visible ones, 'model' learning behaviours by showing their own staff that they take time to maintain and develop their own skills and competences. If responsibility for self-development and CPD is seen to be important to the trend-setters, other staff will follow suit. If managers accept their role as staff developers, they will ensure that their staff regard CPD not as a chore but a benefit.

An example of a management development strategy in action: Identifying key leadership behaviours at Robert Gordon University

We suggested earlier that educators can and should be leaders – the very word 'educate' means to lead. However, like other sectors, Higher Education has had to reconsider many of its views about developing managers and leaders. Early in 2003, the then Minister of State for Higher Education announced the development of a new leadership college for the learning and skills sector, to be run by a consortium of providers including the Open University, Lancaster University Management School, Ashridge Management College and the Learning and Skills Development Agency. The fanfare greeting the initiative included phrases such as 'transformation in the leadership and management of post-compulsory education and training'…'drive change in leadership and management skills across the sector'…'help to raise the standard of education and training in the UK'…'determined and committed to improving dramatically [the split infinitive has become educationally acceptable!] the quality and importance of leadership and management across the sector'. These are slightly flowery phrases, but they give a flavour of the concern that insufficient attention may have been paid by government to these issues. We saw in Chapter 1 how governments have periodically intervened in training and education provision in the UK, and it could be argued that a focus on 'educating the educators' as leaders might pay dividends in their impact on future leaders of industry and commerce.

Like many 'new' universities, which achieved university status in 1992, Robert Gordon University (RGU) has concentrated on vocational professional degree programmes and has built up a significant reputation as a teaching establishment. Today, however, it is also competing with other Higher Education institutions for the best students, and the development of many online programmes has meant that competition may come from a wider geographical area. The concentration on teaching and commercial activity in the past has meant that research, a key area in terms of achieving educational excellence, has not always received the same attention. All of these issues have meant significant cultural and organisational change, and the Principal and Senior Management Team gave considerable thought to developing a leadership programme for senior managers that would assist them not only to manage change but positively promote it.

The Director of HR, David Briggs, and his colleagues looked at the implications of contemporary organisational life for the role of manager/leader. They concluded that it was necessary to develop leaders as well as managers, because leaders could engage in 'over the horizon' thinking. The university's reputation, and hence its chances of attracting excellent staff and students, would be determined by the way that people were treated, and would affect its chances of recruiting and retaining good quality people. The behaviour of leaders and managers would therefore determine future success, so behavioural expectations, together with review of behaviour and performance, were imperative.

The impact on the leadership role would require that leaders at every level would need to be able to lead effective 'smart' change very quickly, and to support people through that change with empathy and compassion. The emphasis would be on coaching rather than command and control, requiring leaders with the necessary degree of humility who could grow and develop others. This is of particular interest, of course, to the HRD specialist, especially as it is one of the key underpinning principles of Learning Organisation theory that managers should be accountable for their employees' development.

The Robert Gordon University Leadership Strategy was based on work with individuals and teams at all organisational levels, and was underpinned by consensus around the organisation's mission, vision, values and behaviours.

Key to the programme was research with groups and individuals at all levels in the organisation, to identify the behaviours managers and leaders should be modelling in order to be effective as change agents as well as accountable decision-makers. Perhaps not surprisingly, senior managers and staff identified very similar competence areas. After initial research with employee focus groups and senior management brainstorming sessions, the following were identified as 'emerging behaviours' of effective leaders:

Table 11.1 Emerging behaviours of effective leaders

▪ act with integrity and honesty	▪ inspire and sell our vision with a passion	▪ facilitate others and instil self-belief
▪ keep confidences	▪ are visible and known	▪ manage expectations
▪ value the individual as well as the team	▪ treat colleagues with respect	▪ play to strengths
▪ communicate regularly, consistently and with care	▪ display humility	▪ have clear priorities and convey these to others
▪ deal with difficult situations	▪ value and recognise the contributions of others	▪ praise and celebrate success
▪ tackle internal conflict decisively	▪ promote fun	▪ promote a blame-free culture
▪ show passion and belief	▪ are compassionate and caring	▪ learn from others
▪ actively encourage	▪ see the 'big picture' and articulate that effectively to others	▪ build bridges
▪ provide effective feedback	▪ communicate positively and with a sense of conviction	▪ tackle underperformance effectively
▪ shape the future	▪ take well-informed risks	▪ develop clear strategies
▪ set realistic targets and standards	▪ have confidence in others	▪ deliver
▪ build effective teams	▪ develop people through effective feedback and a supportive environment	▪ are influential and persuasive
▪ give responsibility	▪ reflect on mistakes and learn from them	▪ give recognition
▪ act consistently	▪ challenge convention, tradition and assumptions	▪ make time
▪ are fair and nonpartisan	▪ show enthusiasm	▪ delegate effectively
▪ actively listen and ask questions		▪ take difficult decisions
▪ believe in and articulate our vision and sense of purpose clearly, consistently and regularly		▪ are motivational
		▪ plan

Further work was done with the external consultants retained, Penna Consulting, to develop these 'wish lists' into specific leadership themes:

Table 11.2 Leadership themes

1. Sets the context and direction

Brings ideas to life for others	Brings ideas to life for others, seeking to engage them and gain their buy-in
Seeks to create debate	Embraces different viewpoints, seeking to create positive debate
Identifies underlying reasons	Challenges issues to find underlying reasons
Is decisive	Is decisive, taking action at the right time
Understands political agendas	Understands political agenda but does not seek to 'play games'
Interest and belief in institution	Displays a genuine interest and belief in the institution and in education
Makes decisions based on 'big picture'	Uses own understanding of the 'big picture' to support decision making
Commitment and passion	Communicates with commitment and passion
Communicates a clear vision	Communicates with a clear and consistent vision
Understands wider context	Understands the wider context of decisions, explaining them to others

2. Engages people

Celebrates success	Celebrates achievements and successes
Is able to persuade	Is able to persuade without resort to authority and power
Asks questions	Asks questions rather than giving instructions
Treats others with respect	Treats others with respect, giving credit and recognition
Shows appreciation	Shows appreciation of others
Puts the fun back into work	Puts the fun back into work/has a sense of humour
Self-aware	Demonstrates self-awareness and humility
Encourages commitment	Encourages personal enthusiasm and commitment
Encourages contributions	Encourages others to contribute
Listens to others	Listens to others, demonstrating interest in their perspective

3. Sets expectations/delivers results

Keeps others informed	Keeps customers and colleagues informed on progress
Takes ownership	Takes ownership of issues, ensuring they are resolved
Sets high standards	Sets and adheres to high standards of delivery
Encourages progression	Encourages others to aspire to progress
Tackles issues	Tackles issues/underperformance
Negotiates effectively	Negotiates with others, seeking to deliver a solution acceptable to all
Knows how to say 'no'	Says 'no' when required
Encourages calculated risks	Encourages calculated risks
Delegates effectively	Gives responsibility to others, providing the support and resources required
Delivers on time	Delivers what he/she says they will deliver on time

4. Encourages development

Keeps confidences	Keeps confidences
Practical approach	Combines forward/lateral thinking with practicality
Manages risk	Encourages and manages calculated risk-taking
Adapts to opportunities	Is focused but able to adapt and take opportunities
Not bound by convention	Is not bound by convention
Builds high performing teams	Builds high performing teams
Learns from mistakes	Adapts and learns from own and others' mistakes
Gives constructive feedback	Gives constructive feedback
Encourages development	Encourages individual development, instilling belief in others
Provides developmental opportunities	Provides others with developmental opportunities

(Derived from Penna Consultants' research.)

This has formed the basis of early 360-degree feedback activity and one-to-one coaching with members of the university's most senior Executive Group in phase 1 of the leadership programme.

As we suggested earlier, it is rare to find a managerial paragon who exhibits all these behaviours, but one of the strengths of the RGU programme has been to identify preferred behaviours with managers and employees, and to begin to work towards developing them. Any management development programme is by its nature a long-term strategy and results will not be immediate. Tools and techniques to assist will vary but it is important to anchor them in the behaviours the organisation wishes to encourage to fulfil its vision.

For the RGU programme, as well as leadership development, there has been emphasis on leaders also as team members, using instruments such as Belbin's team roles and team competences to help members understand themselves and others in the team environment. Action learning sets have been set up in the

Revans style to get leaders working in unfamiliar territory and in project settings of strategic importance. They have presented challenges that have still to be overcome. External consultants have worked with key individuals in the HR team to ensure creativity, innovation and relevance in the development tools selected. We have seen in Chapter 9 the variety of learning strategies available to the HRD specialist to develop management competences like the RGU leadership themes. In the case of a leadership development programme, which will of necessity take shape over a significant period, the emphasis must not be on short-term training interventions but on long-term coaching and support. Also key to the RGU programme is an emphasis on self-understanding by managers, together with an understanding of the impact their actions have on their subordinates.

In 2002 a report on management and leadership by the organisation OPP (Optimising People Performance, previously Oxford Psychologists' Press) revealed that lack of trust in their managers and leaders was most employees' biggest area of concern. The underlying theme of the leadership competences developed at RGU is one of managerial integrity. A manager who practised an appropriate range of behaviours set out in the tables above would be well on the way to confirming the perception of his or her subordinates that integrity and authenticity were his or her true values. These values, as we suggested, can be practised by leaders at all levels in the organisation, not just at the top.

The RGU programme has several important objectives but the ultimate aim is to be certain about the behaviours to be practised by managers and leaders, and to encourage and positively reward those behaviours, as RGU believes these are the behaviours that will deliver long-term business success. This links with the need to evaluate the success of the programme with constructive feedback both downward and upwards. This can be challenging, especially if individual managers are unable or unwilling to commit to the required behaviours, and RGU, like any other organisation that commits its leadership policies to the public domain, will be aware that employees will be measuring the gaps between rhetoric and reality. There will of course always be a gap, just as Learning Organisations can never be fully realised, but the size of the credibility gap and the pace of closure of that gap will determine overall employee commitment. Perhaps the next edition of this book will be able to present an evaluation of the programme's overall success. (With thanks to David Briggs, Director of HR at RGU, for contributions to the above.)

Putting it all together

We have described a range of management development tools and techniques. A good programme may use a section of these, but more is not necessarily better. In Chapter 9 and Appendix 4 we look at a variety of different learning and training methods, and many of these can also play a part in an effective management development programme. We also looked in Chapter 9 at the importance for HRD specialists of evaluating the impact of their work, and as we have suggested, management development is particularly important to get right.

THE LAST WORD?

The management writer Alistair Mant wrote a book on leadership and management called *Leaders We Deserve* (1983). The emphasis is clear to us; that if we project all responsibility for developing ideas and making decisions on to very senior managers, we abdicate our own accountability. Not everyone can be a manager in an organisation, but all of us can develop our skills of leadership to become more effective in our own area, and the responsibility for ensuring this happens rests with both individual employees and their organisational managers working as a team. Perhaps Reg Revans would also approve!

Discussion question: Is it possible for you to evaluate the success of management development in your organisation? How would you set about doing so?

We see this seventh edition of our book as something of a transitional text. There are so many potential new tools and strategies open to the HRD specialist to achieve his or her aims that we have only just begun to understand their impact; but there is no doubt that online and blended learning, team-learning strategies, and the whole field of knowledge management are opening up all sorts of new possibilities for management development. We hope that in the next edition, as well as being able to share with you some of the ways in which these learning tools have been used to develop managers, we will be able to report that more organisations are producing managers who are really making a difference to their organisations and to UK prosperity.

This chapter has introduced you to some recent thinking about management development, although you will have gathered that many writers believe we still have some way to go before we make significant progress. Should management and leadership development begin at the formal education stage, when young people are school students? Draft a proposal for the Secretary of State for Education suggesting how this might be done.

From Training Interventions to Learning Environments – Has the 'Learning Age' Delivered its Promise?

Part 4 of the book consists of two chapters that look towards the future. We have emphasised throughout this edition of the book that HRD specialists are having to adapt to new paradigms of learning, which emphasise the need to focus on developing learning environments rather than training solutions. But how far has this happened in organisations as opposed to in the academic community?

Chapter 12 examines the **cultural differences which influence organisational learning** and looks at ways in which HRD practitioners can maximise their opportunities to create effective environments for learning.

Chapter 13 examines further the impact of the 'knowledge economy' on the world of work, and suggests ways in which organisations are **moving 'beyond training interventions' to Learning Organisation paradigms**. How much has really changed since the last edition of this book? We ask a number of questions, but the answers will probably have to wait until the next edition. In the meantime, HRD practitioners can expect exciting challenges to their roles and remits.

Analysing Organisational Cultures to Develop Effective Learning Environments

In Chapter 12, we will consider:

- **Conceptual models of cultural differences in organisations, which can affect the learning process;**

- **How organisations can assist the development of learning environments by being aware of, and developing, appropriate systems that support employees to learn;**

- **Organisational learning systems that provide frameworks for learning interventions;**

- **The significant number of variables that affect decisions on HRD in organisations, ranging from the type of learner involved to the resources available.**

Earlier in the book (Chapters 3 and 4) we introduced you to some key concepts about individuals' learning behaviour. In the last analysis, of course, all learning is performed by individuals. Only individuals can truly 'learn'. A machine may be programmed to collect and store data, and to adjust its future responses to newly received messages, but its programme will still be based upon assumptions and decisions made by its human programmer. 'Garbage in, garbage out', as the saying puts it. But individual learning is itself to some extent influenced, conditioned and moulded by the environment in which the individual moves.

We would like here to remind you of some of our key themes:

- Each organisation is a learning environment;
- Learning, development and training interventions are made within that environment to promote learning, or to direct learning to specific purposes, or to make learning processes more efficient.

In much the same way that a machine's behaviour reflects programming assumptions made by humans, so learning and training interventions often reflect human assumptions built into the organisations in which people work.

This chapter will introduce you to some of the 'conceptual models' researchers have drawn to describe key cultural differences between organisations, and key differences between organisational learning systems. It will then explore a variety of specific learning systems – such as 'sitting by Nellie', 'competence-based' and 'problem-centred' systems, the 'training process' and 'knowledge management' – which reflect these differences.

Throughout the chapter, the word 'system' is used flexibly to cover a wide variety of formal and informal groups of activity norms, with widely differing degrees of explicitness and sophistication. Do not assume that we are at any time equating the concept of a learning system with that of a formal and systematic management control system that has clear-cut inputs and outputs; in many ways, our notion is that of an ongoing, organic process with characteristics that are observable on a regular basis.

Think again about your own environments – your family, their workplaces, your school, college, university, the local supermarket, the local football club, place of worship, and so on. These are all organisations in which people live and work. Are they 'organised' to promote learning – or does it just 'happen'?

> Discussion question: What 'organisational variables' do you think might dominate an organisation's approach to learning?

THE DIMENSIONS OF ORGANISATIONAL LEARNING SYSTEMS

Unlike research into the psychology of individual learning, and despite sociologists' interest in organisational models, specific research into organisations' learning systems has not been widespread. More usually, sociologists have addressed problems in the structuring of work tasks or procedures, or explored relationships between people and their work, or analysed political systems. Perhaps because of the wide differences between organisations, alternative 'theories' of organisational learning have not appeared; instead, a variety of complementary ideas or perspectives have emerged to describe specific organisational models. Many of them, though, differ quite widely in their basic assumptions.

In a lengthy typology of organisations, which extends even to the consideration of organisations as 'psychic prisons' and 'instruments of domination', Morgan (1997) includes chapters on organisations as 'machines', as 'organisms' and as 'brains'.

'Machine' organisations are of course mechanistic in nature, and operate as bureaucracies, tending to 'scientifically' manage via prescribed rules and procedures. Even if there were no overt rules or procedures relating to learning in this type of organisation, one would expect individuals to conform to a relatively standard approach to learning, which would be that adopted by the key decision-makers; their decisions would naturally include decisions on whether formal training arrangements should exist or not. We shall see later that in 'machine' organisations of any size, decisions in favour of such arrangements usually include well-defined training routines and who carries responsibility for them, and teaching processes predominate. You may think these are slightly old-fashioned concepts for modern organisations, but some still operate in this way (and some otherwise modern organisations contain pockets of the 'machine age'). Gabriel, in his *Organisations in Depth* (1999), which uses psychoanalytic theory to analyse organisational behaviour, confirms this point in his discussion of what he calls obsessive organisations, where the key norms are control, conformism and detail consciousness, with little concern for emotion or innovation.

'Organisms' are much more open to their environments, and accept that there is no one best way of managing, encouraging a flexible and even enquiring outlook on the part of all. Contingency theory ideas ensure that authority is likely to be informal and to change through time. In such organisations, training activities and methods are also likely to vary through time, with new techniques being encouraged, especially during periods when substantial operational problems are experienced.

'Brains' take flexibility to a higher level, prompting innovation on the back of superior information processing. In an organisation like this, individuals endlessly question and challenge their operating norms, and aim to create a trouble-free future by anticipating problems and creating solutions. Learning is not geared to any specific type of training approach, but 'learning to learn' is an endless aim, and indeed the organisation is reasonably described as a 'learning organisation'. Formal training activity tends to give way to creative dialogue between open minds, development being continuously integrated with work itself.

Morgan (1997) also describes organisations as 'cultures' and 'political systems' – generalised terms that overlap the three organisation types we have just noted, and which encapsulate first the ethical and social philosophies, and second the distribution of power, within organisations. (If this sounds fascinating – and Morgan's book is a fascinating analysis by a very original writer – further material on organisations as cultures or political systems is available in Morgan's extensive bibliographical commentary.) Within each of these new types, variations abound, deciding for example whether individual or group learning predominates, and again the extent to which learning is short term or strategic. Cultural and political factors can in fact dominate learning systems, and may indeed be the determinants of how strong any given learning system itself may be.

> Discussion question: How far is HRD influenced by organisational politics in an organisation with which you are familiar or have read about?

Shrivastava (1983) studied organisations' learning systems before the brain metaphor had emerged. He first conducted a literature search, and concluded that research in this area had developed through four distinct and contrasting perspectives. In sequence, organisational learning was viewed as:

- First, organisational learning was viewed as the gathering of experience, repetition ensuring improved future performance;
- Second, it was viewed as the development of a knowledge base, more and more sophisticated knowledge allowing superior decision-making;
- Next, it was viewed as the sharing and meshing of assumptions via 'cognitive maps', allowing the correction of naive thinking and concerted action;
- And finally, it was viewed as adaptation, allowing resources to be directed to new aims or new problems as they arise.

Shrivastava's synthesis of these perspectives brought him to conclude that, although contrasting, they are not mutually exclusive. (We might ourselves now suggest that the first two seem naturally to serve 'machine' organisations, and the last two naturally to serve 'organisms'. All four might be employed within 'brains'.) All involve individual learning, contributing to the organisation's collective knowledge, skills and attitudes base. This in turn serves wider decision-making, becoming a part of an organisational learning process rather than merely an individual one. This organisational learning process is itself influenced by a broader set of physical, social and political variables, but in a given decision area the developing knowledge, skills and attitudes base allows the organisation to adopt new aims, to pose new solutions for problems, and even to innovate in terms of new products, services or working methods.

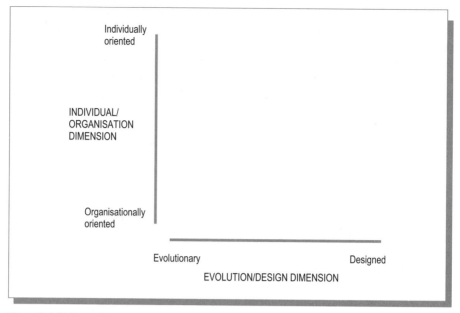

Figure 12.1 *Shrivastava's 'key dimensions'*

Shrivastava identified two 'critical dimensions' that allowed him to generate a typology of organisational learning systems (see Figure 12.1). The first critical dimension is the 'Individual–Organisation' dimension. At the one extreme, learning is 'single person-dependent': the individual learns in isolation, serving his or her own needs, without any clear shared use in prospect. Bearing in mind our loose definition of the word 'system', and despite the fact that most large organisations have in recent times tried to use learning interventions to improve operational performance, a bias towards this extreme unfortunately still remains the norm. We might speculate that this relates somehow to the UK's fairly individualistic national culture (see Hofstede 1980, and Trompenaars 1994). 'Learning by exposure' is the prevailing system in most organisations, even where learning interventions are frequent and sophisticated. Most learning happens randomly, and is self-centred, self-determined, self-controlled. Attendance at external courses is usually arranged individually, without pre-course briefing to establish how the eventual learning might be used at work, or shared with colleagues. Manuals and textbooks (like this one) are usually compiled with the individual learner in mind, not any particular organisation.

> Discussion question: How far do you believe it is possible for books like this to reflect readers' individual experiences?

Of course, there will always be the possibility of some organisational benefit. It simply means that the link between what is learned and operational performance is assumed as an act of faith, the learner being trusted to put the learning into practice at the workplace and indeed to 'spread the gospel' through normal, unplanned social contact. A common practice among small organisations is for the chief executive regularly to arrange attendance at external management conferences or trade association meetings, essentially to keep contact with equals; many such people, enjoying substantial decision-making power in their home organisations, can then impose their personal learning output on their return as 'organisationally worthwhile' – or they can simply reject its operational value.

At the other extreme, the system overtly and directly serves the organisation independently of any one person's input. The expressed aims are here described not in terms of what the individual learns, but in product attributes, or operating procedures, or statistics – overall results concerning safety, perhaps, or productivity, or even worker loyalty. Such a system may still involve individual learning, but the content or area of study is prescribed – as for example in a research laboratory engaged on a defined programme of product development. Another example might be integrated with the organisation's safety procedures: after fire drills, safety stewards might be required to meet en masse to review their responsibilities collectively and agree amendments. We shall see later how most bureaucratic learning activity is aimed in this direction, requiring employees to experience standard learning processes or routines, usually in the cause of explicit work goals.

The second of Shrivastava's critical dimensions describes the degree to which learning is designed or not. At the latter extreme, with literally no planning whatsoever, the learning processes simply evolve as accepted traditions, valued not as the result of any formalised review of results but because they have stood the test of time, appear to be generally respected, and are easily recognised. Many old-style 'time serving' engineering apprenticeships were like this so far as workplace learning was concerned (although the mandatory educational element – for many the key training element – was of course planned). Some large private-sector companies mount annual top management strategic 'away-days', which are planned in terms of a time programme but not as learning experiences, and hence might be said to fall into the evolutionary category.

The opposite is the scientifically designed planning and information system, dedicated to serving specific information and learning needs identified in equally consistent ways. Perhaps less sophisticated, but still similar in type, is any standardised skills development system that takes newcomers through a series of prepared, supervised exercises with tests establishing the extent to which the skills have been mastered.

In recent years those UK organisations with substantial HRD activities have tried to develop organisational learning systems as a way of improving upon individual learning systems, simultaneously increasing the planned, and decreasing the evolutionary, elements. Smaller organisations such as SMEs, without the resources to mount substantial learning and training activities of their own, have either left management to decide what to communicate and how, or have relied on using external facilities – which effectively means the perpetuation of an individual and evolutionary approach, although this is now affected by published national standards.

SPECIFIC LEARNING SYSTEMS

We have already suggested that Shrivastava's typology might be updated. We offer here our own set of contrasting systems, using Shrivastava's key dimensions to distinguish differences between them. It is perhaps necessary to repeat that (a) our use of the term 'system' can be taken only to imply regular, consistent use, (b) an organisation can exhibit more than one system at any one time, and (c) our list of systems is not exhaustive.

The 'sitting by Nellie' system

XYZ Limited is a manufacturing organisation, the managing director of which believes 'we cannot afford to train' (IiP consultants frequently tell us that they usually hear this complaint from owner/managers of small businesses). The firm recruits 'readymade' workers, paying them higher wages than local competitors. Learning happens solely 'on the job', supervisors and established workers giving new recruits whatever information they (the 'trainers') think is needed, the recruits picking up routines and standards as they go along.

Strictly speaking, this is not a learning system (it could be called an 'anti-system', since it relies on chance), but, because learning still happens, it is in its way a management option, and it is of course widely preferred, if perhaps by default. If it can be said to reflect any of the values that we have set out above, it assumes an individual and essentially undesigned, ie evolutionary, set of norms.

In this example, the learner is assumed to be able to gather knowledge and to use it without any real help other than that randomly offered by colleagues, who may set other tasks as priorities as they think fit. There are no obvious incentives to train, or disincentives not to do so – indeed, the managing director might be expected to criticise anyone who made training itself a priority ('We haven't time to train – we're too busy meeting production targets'). The 'trainers' are not themselves trained, nor are they prepared in any way for their training roles.

The last two sentences suggest ways whereby this approach might be made less haphazard and operationally more useful. As we saw in the last chapter, experiential learning can be improved if learner motivation is increased. In the SME above, this may involve little more than offering to remove probationary status once competence is demonstrated. Another incentive might involve the creation of explicit learning objectives against which the learner can measure progress. Second, 'Nellie' can be trained to train. This is likely to change the way Nellie talks, and to introduce learning plans, making it easier to appreciate and copy what Nellie does. It will also identify an 'authority' to whom the learner can direct questions without feeling embarrassed. It might also motivate Nellie herself, especially if she is a 'plateaued manager' who sees no opportunity for career progression. Such moves would have the effect of developing a more definable (and properly termed) system.

Discussion question: How far can an HRD specialist in an organisation turn 'Nellie' into a professionally competent trainer? Should he or she, for example, need to obtain an academic qualification?

Competences and other analytical systems

A small bus company has paid a fee to engage in the Vehicle Engineering Competence Assessment scheme developed by its Sector Skills Council. The fee entitles the company to receive literature explaining the scheme, the forms on which its administration is based, plus the training of its own staff as trainers and assessors. The central aid is a manual setting out in detail 'standard' elements of vehicle fitter jobs in the industry, including performance criteria. The elements are collected under a number of generic headings; a requirement of the scheme is that each fitter (the scheme applies to all ages) must be trained to master all the essentials of an actual site job, which must include some elements from each generic heading. When learners thinks they are 'competent', a claim form must be completed, an assessor then visits the workplace and tests the learner, using real-life materials and processes. Satisfactory results allow the award of national qualifications.

Our example, which represents one of the many in-company systems based on the existing National Vocational Qualifications system, aims to develop the individual to prescribed and carefully designed competence standards, which are set outside the organisation. These standards are described (with quotations from NCVQ January 1995) in terms of:

- elements of competence, which are evidence of 'what the competent performer can do' – that is, 'an action, behaviour or outcome which a person should be able to demonstrate' (the approach to learning has been labelled by some the 'outcomes' approach, ie as opposed to 'inputs' such as examination knowledge);

- performance criteria, which are 'statements which describe the quality of outcomes of successful performance', and 'the basis against which an assessor can judge whether an individual can achieve the outcome specified in the element';

- knowledge requirements which indicate what learners need to know, and evidence requirements detailing what evidence learners need to show to prove they are competent.

These three components collectively form the 'standard'. They must, however, be backed by evidence requirements, which detail both performance and knowledge essentials that the assessor must check.

This is a heavily prescriptive system, but has considerable appeal to employers who simply do not have the resources to complete time-consuming analytical work. Similar systems that are geared more specifically to individual organisations can be seen where an employer has produced a unique, organisation-specific manual that is used as the basis for a standardised recruit training programme, and for regular refresher course activities (eg sales training systems); but, even here, unless there is provision for regular review and updating of the manual, the learning system still cannot be said to be developing the organisation itself.

Critics have challenged the emphasis on 'outcomes' to the exclusion of learning processes – that is, the lack of interest in learning processes. NVQ enthusiasts have responded (eg Stewart and Hamlin 1993) by proposing a hierarchy of competence levels, and possibly (Stewart 1999) a theoretical underpinning to include some form of certificated vocational education. It is difficult to argue, though, that an outcome can be affected by the learning route. For example, a fitter who has memorised a sequential procedure will operate differently from one who has acquired diagnostic skills. Proponents of the idea that learning can be 'surface', ie memorising sets of procedures, or 'deep', understanding concepts and their application (Entwistle, 1996) might claim that the diagnostic fitter would probably perform better. This suggests that the 'competences' system might be most appropriate where the actual job need, the prescribed standards and the training methods can be consciously matched – as indeed might be the case in our example, where the trainers and the assessors are employed by the same employer.

Discussion question: What experience do you have of NVQ/SVQ qualifications? Is it possible to develop a 'pick and mix' approach to them by combining with more 'academic' type modules? What would be the advantages and disadvantages of this approach?

Problem-centred systems

An advertising agency includes in its organisation a part-time 'trouble-shooting' team comprising five senior managers, who attend the monthly board meetings as observers and meet immediately after to draft corporate plans stemming from problems identified by the board. Because agency performance levels are often criticised, it is usual for plans to include learning or training interventions. The company does not employ its own learning/training unit, nor has it a dedicated learning budget. Hence training has usually taken the form of formal in-house departmental 'teach-ins' conducted by external consultants.

Predominantly short-term, pragmatic and ad hoc in nature, this system is dominated by operational problems, senior management deciding on change and what this means in learning terms – and dredging their own operational budgets for whatever has to happen. Systems of this kind are often highly acceptable to subordinates: they attack real work problems, produce quick, visible action, and are usually believed to produce cost-effective results. However, their success depends on diagnostic skills rather than the instant panacea of expert knowledge in named spheres. As the example implies, they can tend to adopt 'quick-fix' teaching solutions, which do not serve real organisational learning needs. A useful example comes from an office in a finance company where the output from the word-processing team was criticised, the diagnosed need being little more than 'sort that team out'. In the hastily mounted ensuing course, the external trainers quickly became convinced of operational faults, line managers lacking the skills to use the word-processors effectively. These managers never became the subject of a training plan, and a number of word-processing staff went to work elsewhere. The main point is that the gearing of training to operational problems often requires careful diagnostic activity.

The Action Learning (AL) system

Alison Smith is currently halfway through a six-month attachment to a large computer software establishment; under normal circumstances she is a shift manager at a power station. Together with three other secondees, she has been asked to look into the methods of distribution of software packages to a variety of types of outlet; the company is concerned at delays in delivery, which have been reported by too many clients. Alison's team has gathered data from several sources, and has set up several more 'action sets', incorporating selected line managers from the host firm and a transport manager from a mail-order house. They are being tutored in their search for solutions by staff from a local business school.

Action Learning (AL) is, as we have seen in Chapter 11, basically the study of real-life problems and their resolution within the real-life environment. Its justification as a learning system that at the same time develops individuals (usually managers) and organisations rests on the mix of a motivating challenge for fresh, sharp minds and the transformation of problems into opportunities for flexible organisations. The combination of motivated self-study and high quality tutorial resources is a strong developing force. Action Learning has been used in a variety of forms. The approach was pioneered by Reg Revans (see Revans 1980 and 1983), and involved setting up and maintaining 'task cultures'. The experiences involved in achieving this are claimed to develop superior understanding of organisation, leadership and team skills, which advocates of the system see as the prime managerial competences. We examine AL in more detail in chapter 11 and the *Afterword*.

The 'training process' system

A local authority has recently appointed a learning and development manager to work within its HR department. The manager's job is first and foremost the establishment of annual learning and training plans for all departments; the new manager has already set about the task of systematising the identification of needs, and has linked up with department heads to allow draft plans to be discussed and, it is hoped, agreed. A central budget has been allocated and all major learning expenses except salaries will be charged to it. Once agreed, the HRD manager is empowered to make implementation arrangements direct with learners and their superiors, both concerning individuals and groups. The manager is also committed to producing in the future an annual review document, which will summarise learning achievements during the past year and suggest improvements to the system in the future.

This system owes its origins to Fayol's ('plan-organise-do-review') classical process theory of management, and was strongly advocated by most Industrial Training Boards during the 1960s and 1970s, when it became synonymous with the 'systematic training' ideal widely preached by them. As we saw in Chapter 9 as a model for planning, implementing and evaluating training interventions. Here it is applied to an organisational context.

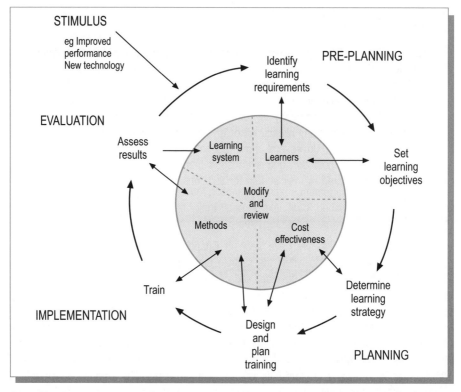

Figure 12.2 *The training process system*

Many organisations are increasing their adherence to what have come to be known as 'basic system requirements' – accepting that HRD interventions will be a regular phenomenon throughout an organisation's life, with posts explicitly named as carrying responsibility for seeing that appropriate processes exist and are followed. Typically, those processes are seen as including:

- the promulgation of HRD policy
- the inclusion of learning and training responsibilities in job descriptions
- the regular, periodic definition of learning/training needs
- the creation of learning/training plans
- the provision of resources
- the training of trainers
- implementation of learning plans
- the assessment of results.

There is a fundamental difference between this system and the next system we are about to describe. In the training process system, the extent to which HRD serves the organisation and its employees, and the extent to which development evolves or is designed, are determined essentially by a few key people, notably professional trainers and their leading line contacts, who naturally manage the system in what they consider to be its preferred direction. In our next system, a strong central design has its own evolutionary characteristics, and seeks to maximise both individual and organisational learning.

The 'knowledge management' system

ICL's 'Project Vik' developed an intranet (an internal computerised network) covering many countries.

An initial series of forums was run in which key employees were asked about information needed to do their jobs more effectively. They said they needed information about the company, its customers, its services and products, and most importantly about internal ICL services. They also asked for improved communication aids, even down to copies of site directories. 'Café Vik', a unit with six PCs, plus discussion and meeting facilities, opened 11 weeks later with company-wide management briefings; a mobile roadshow took the message all over Europe, and established 'Café Viks' in most major outlets. A year later, the rapidly developing system was said to be used by about 10,000 of 19,000 employees. A central focusing and development department included positions with titles such as 'knowledge officer', 'information service provider' and 'web master', while selected operating managers are designated part-time 'knowledge sponsors'.

The concept of knowledge management is a recent innovation, but interest in it has grown rapidly with the development of information technology. In its simplest organisational form, a knowledge management system requires carefully prepared, structured management information systems in which information is recorded, stored and made available to those who are encouraged to retrieve it – 'systems for capturing knowledge and moving it to where it is wanted' (Garratt 2000). Designated 'knowledge developers' design the computer programs that control the database, and 'Learning Options' guides help employees to find, at any given time, information that serves their personal development and/or work needs. Access to 'classified' information is automatically confined to those whose responsibilities allow it, but the system allows all levels to share unclassified knowledge without the problems that geography or hierarchy normally produce. And there is a much more sophisticated, ambitious version of knowledge management, aimed at not just the sharing of formal data but extending to the sharing and meshing of assumptions and beliefs. We noted this earlier as one of Shrivastava's researched ways in which the organisation learns; proponents of knowledge management now suggest ways in which what is called 'tacit' knowledge (meaning expertise that is stored not in formal management databases but in peoples' heads) can be clarified and shared with others, eventually combining to become 'newly created knowledge', understood and accepted throughout an organisation. Depending on one's viewpoint and position within the organisation, encouraging a team approach to sharing knowledge and skills may be a benefit to all employees, or a strategy for senior management to extract peoples' key knowledge in order to 'deskill' them. In an organisation that is aggressively competitive and rewards individual achievement rather than teamwork, I am unlikely to share my idea for a new service with my manager if she presents the idea to the Board of Directors and gains a performance bonus, while I get nothing. In organisations that practise a 'hire and fire' approach in volatile markets, staff are likely to guard their expertise jealously as a bargaining tool. An organisational climate of trust and mutual respect would seem essential in developing effective knowledge management systems.

Discussion question: What do you think about the knowledge management issue? Is it ever possible in an organisation to develop a climate of trust and openness to the extent that all knowledge is shared?

Other systems

We have described systems that are visible in present-day UK organisations, omitting several that you may believe are more usual, important or interesting – for example, the 'political system' (in which learning activity follows the political aims of the key opinion moulders); the 'organisation development' system (in which behavioural science techniques are applied to organisational change); and the 'self-development' system (in which employees with a strong commitment to learning regularly allocate time to exploring things of their own choosing, using their own preferred methods). We suggest that concepts such as the Learning Organisation and Knowledge Management are still for many managers no more than concepts they might study or that students might debate and discuss. The chances of making them work in real-life organisations very much depend, as we suggested above, on developing a supportive organisational culture – one supportive of the learning of ALL employees.

OTHER ORGANISATIONAL VARIABLES

HR managers and HRD professionals sometimes complain that defining and categorising learning systems is unrealistic and of little value. They argue (and our case examples perhaps confirm) that each organisation develops its own unique system without a particular model in view, that a variety of learning systems coexist side by side at any one time, and indeed that decisions about learning and training are always influenced by matters that are operationally, rather than organisationally, important. They suggest a large number of important variables, including:

- *The learners themselves* Some learning systems are specifically geared (in terms of both resources and methods) to employee types – eg graduate management trainees, or technical specialists, or people with disabilities (eg the Royal National Institute for the Blind's centres).

- *Learning/training methods* During the 1960s, many large companies bought or built residential training centres, which became the focal centre of their (formal) learning activities. More recently, self-study has become a new focus for some, especially after the advances in online learning that have occurred in recent years.

- *The size of the 'learning unit'* Some organisations define needs in terms of individuals; others group people in departmental units or occupational groupings (eg managers, drivers). The larger the organisation, the more likely it is that group activities will at least have a place in the system.

- *HRD resources* Many organisations feel they cannot afford their own learning/training resources, preferring to use local providers (eg local colleges or universities, which often provide expertise at a reasonable cost).

- *Lead times* Plans can be 'long-term general' or 'short-term specific'. The former are most usually seen in organisations that are internally stable. Even such organisations like this may, of course, abandon long lead times in periods of recession.

- *Status and power* The status and power of those pressing for the learning to take place.

- *Operational purposes* Whether mainstream operational priorities are served or not.

- *Management commitment* Whether or not the prime responsibility for ensuring that HRD interventions are made is seen throughout the organisation as resting with line management, and whether or not line management actively support this idea.

- *The HRD function* Whether or not learning, development and training roles are defined and built into the organisation as specialised responsibilities.

In this example, top management may not have consciously reviewed their organisational learning system, but they did show their trust in it. They also judged that, as potential recruits

A long-established medium-sized food manufacturing company maintained for many years a strategy of recruiting school-leavers and graduates, 'growing its future management', and promoting from within to fill all management vacancies. The HR department handled recruitment, but no formalised induction training was given. Line management were responsible for any workplace training. No specialised HRD unit or management was employed. When local competition for labour increased with the arrival in the area of three major new employers, all of whom had more formal training programmes and training departments, traditional recruitment sources tended to dry up, and top management were forced to review their strategy. They decided generally to continue with the established management approach, believing it still had significant operational strengths, but that some improvements should be introduced. Recruitment staff were asked to improve their links with local schools, colleges and universities; a recently recruited graduate was given the task of planning a two-hour induction course, and a team of five supervisors were later briefed on how to present the course. Attendance at the induction course was given priority over workplace needs. First, line management were asked to give priority to initial job training, and to incorporate new training estimates into their budgets.

value training facilities, and competitors are offering it, management must commit themselves more strongly to training, and – most important – new entrants must be able to see the commitment. This is important: it is not enough to have a good system if it is not appreciated by those for whom it is intended.

In this example, a small organisation uses its own established strengths to buy in

A fast-growing commercial photography business was originally formed by the current director with the aid of two enthusiastic assistants. The firm now employs 35 in premises created from three side-by-side shops. The Managing Director recently introduced new equipment, including high quality colour reprographic machines; he talked the suppliers into providing training in the use of these last machines on his premises without charge. A further commercial success is a contract with the Defence Ministry for a new type of aerial map, which combines real-life photographs with three-dimensional map layouts. This has been enabled by part-time secondment arrangements for one of the assistants to the cartography department of a local college, and similar arrangements for the other assistant to a printing college. Both assistants help their respective colleges by handling practical sessions with students, and providing advice on photography for the staff. Neither arrangement has to be paid for. The director knows that he cannot yet justify internal trainers, nor can he employ technical experts in these new fields. He has therefore searched for them elsewhere, and found them in local colleges. The 'cost' to the business is negligible (ignoring the nonavailability of the assistant while away from the business), because the secondment arrangement has allowed him to barter some of the firm's own expertise for new technological knowledge – and the assistants have had some useful personal development in the process.

technological and training expertise that it does not possess. They do not already have an organisational learning system – but their commercial growth, which is based in technology, is beginning to make one commercially desirable. The decision-maker may not understand this clearly: he thinks operationally, and 'finds' externally the learning the organisation needs, then works out how to import it. In the process, the organisation grows further – technologically, commercially and in human terms.

> In a London office of a large commercial organisation, much discontent developed from a sequence of what were seen by clerical and administrative staff as 'unfair' decisions on further education facilities. Some workers were given paid release to attend classes that they, the workers, had chosen. Others were refused similar requests. Some refunds of travelling expenses and book expenses were authorised while other, similar, requests were turned down. Most employees' complaints implied that they wanted equal treatment. The HRD manager believed in equality, but any idea of establishing rights on a collective basis had always been strongly challenged by top management as 'uncommercial', and the manager had himself insisted in the past that he must be consulted before release was granted to any employee. He talked with various line managers and with several day-release students; virtually all wanted a tighter set of rules. The manager drafted new 'rules' governing release decisions and these rules were quickly approved by the board. In future, support would be given only for classes that were appropriate to the work that staff were undertaking or expected to undertake in the near future; approval required both the line manager's and the HRD manager's signatures on a newly designed form. Support would follow prescribed rules concerning paid time away from work, payment of fees, refund of travel and book expenses, payment coming out of the HRD manager's budget.

In this example the HRD manager reviewed and re-established his operating policies and procedures. First, he decided that learning must be in both the company's and the employee's interests as expressed in work arrangements; second, decisions on facilities would be individual, not group; third, the power to decide would rest jointly with the line superior and the HRD manager; and fourth, resources would be provided from a central budget, which the manager would control. Other variables (eg the nature of the learners, lead times) were not considered important enough to influence the new system, which, once agreed, was imposed on and quickly accepted by all. Discontent disappeared overnight. The 'singles versus groups' issue was treated as an important one and resolved in favour of an individualised system; but it was subordinated to the issue of company need and again made subject to the twin issues of management control and available resources.

More fundamentally, the 'educational system' was here the cause of workplace problems, primarily because different line managements were interpreting and developing the system in varying ways. Luckily the organisation had a specialist who was able to re-establish a common approach. He knew the detail of the learning arrangements, had access to the various parties, and could draft a solution to the problem without damaging the system. The solution was a bureaucratic one, involving new rules that must be observed by all, and it put him in a critical position to ensure that future arrangements honour those new rules.

> Discussion question: Do you agree with the relatively bureaucratic solution above? What other solutions might have been tried?

The essential points to remember from these three case examples are that:

1 each specific learning, development or training intervention is an 'operational' one, not to be dominated by philosophy or theory, although both may influence it. It is also a 'political' one, in the sense that it affects the balance of power and authorities in the organisation.

2 unless a major new strategic plan is involved, HRD interventions will usually be taken within the framework of the (usually undefined) learning system that exists; and – perhaps the key point in this chapter –

3 just as management is a situation-specific art, so, as we have seen in Chapter 6, the structure and identity of the HRD function is invariably determined in an organisation-specific way.

> We have seen in this chapter how HRD specialists might develop systems to assist the process of organisational learning by understanding the organisation's cultural norms and values. How might you advise an HRD manager in a traditional bureaucracy (say in the NHS or some local government departments) to begin to create an environment where commitment to learning was regarded as a key competence for all staff? What problems might she come across, and how might she address these?

Chapter 13: From Training Interventions to Learning Environments – Towards Theories of 'Learning to Learn'

In Chapter 13 we will consider:

- **Key HRD concepts and their varied impact on organisational practice;**

- **The changing world of work and the impact of the knowledge economy;**

- **The importance of continuous development to secure individual and national prosperity;**

- **The practices recommended by advocates of the Learning Organisation and Knowledge Creation approaches, and their relative successes in influencing the work environment;**

- **The creation of continuous learning cultures at work, with recommendations on how these cultures may be helped to evolve.**

The current Labour Government, elected in 1997, put what it called 'education' at the heart of its political agenda. Involvement in the 'knowledge society' was to be key in creating improved social inclusion, as well as securing UK prosperity. Improved learning for managers was supposed to create a world-class commercial impetus, with employees inspired to model positive behaviours that would spread learning throughout organisations. The Learning Organisation was to be reality, not just aspiration. Such were the messages of New Labour.

However, the transformation has not quite succeeded. Although there has been increased resourcing of NVQs, continuous development policies have not significantly evolved, and while there has been EU-led promotion of lifelong learning, it does not appear as though politicians and bureaucrats really understand these processes well enough to apply them effectively. The same headlines appear in HR practitioner journals: skills shortages damage UK economy; staff changes at the Department for Education and Skills fail to change attitudes to learning; UK school-leavers lack basic skills; UK managers cannot manage; employees do not trust their managers. Journalists of course tend to report bad news, but even positive HRD practitioners can sometimes feel discouraged. So what should they believe? Have we made any progress to creating learning environments which can encourage employees to be responsible for their learning, in such a way that the organisation also learns?

We now want to discuss some ideas that, although they have been in circulation for some time, have not always had the impact on workplace practice that they might have had. They may, we believe, still have the potential to influence tomorrow's 'standard practice' to make moves towards genuine organisational learning. These ideas are (a) socio-technical and contingency theory, (b) action learning, (c) continuous development, (d) learning organisations, and (e) knowledge creation. We end with our predictions for learning interventions for the future – for individual learners, for teams and groups, for middle management, and finally for top management.

NEW HORIZONS

If we compare UK life in the early years of the twenty-first century with a hundred years ago, we have no difficulty in noting widespread and substantial differences affecting how and what we learn. To begin with, there is much more knowledge available: a high proportion of what is now known was not known in the early 1900s. By far the greatest part of today's knowledge is accessible to anyone who wants to use it if they have, or can acquire, some basic accessing skills. Most of this growing mountain of knowledge is needed by a steadily expanding number of potential users. New knowledge has usually emerged in response to a 'practical' purpose, and the pace at which it has emerged has escalated, directly mirroring the increasing frequency with which innovations have developed.

It is now 50 years since Drucker (1954) predicted a forthcoming 'knowledge society', and over 30 since Toffler (1970) alerted us to the notion that any idea in general circulation might already reasonably be considered redundant in terms of its practical value. This notion has changed the way in which some people think of knowledge. Knowledge now no longer consists only of reliable, stable, finite data, but extends to cover opinions, preferences, values, likes, dislikes and so on – and many more 'knowledge-based intangibles' (Nonaka and Takeuchi 1995).

We do not seem to have made much progress towards the concept of 'Learning Organisations' over the last fifty years. You should have a better idea of why this is the case after you have read this chapter, and may even have thought of your own strategies for responding to these theories in your current or future employment.

 Drucker and Toffler were two early examples of writers who suggest that organisations' health will in future rest upon intellectual assets rather than land or machinery, or even money. The concept of 'intellectual capital' (described comprehensively in Armstrong 2003) can be positive – employees are of significant value to the organisation, as their knowledge can be the key to success in hostile environments – or negative – that employees are assets to be bought and sold or replaced, the corollary being of course that that they will have no loyalty towards the organisation. Whichever view prevails, there is little doubt that the greatest asset for modern organisations seems to be the 'knowledge worker', meaning a person who continuously updates his or her knowledge, continuously questions what has traditionally been accepted, continuously redefines old and senses new problems, and continuously searches for new solutions. Competitive advantage will rest with organisations that employ or create and retain such people: the successful organisations will develop new-style 'learning cultures' in which employees are naturally helped to learn on a continuing basis.

We are now going to look at the historical origins of some of the more complex theories of organisational learning originated, and how organisational theorists have sparked new concepts, which imaginative practitioners have in some cases applied to their own areas. The ideas we are going to discuss are not brand new, but have not always attracted significant numbers of organisational advocates – perhaps after reading this chapter you might see ways of developing them that the 'experts' have failed to see.

Learning cultures reflect new philosophical assumptions. Table 13 offers a comparison between traditional assumptions, which accepted the possibility of stability and order at the workplace, and assumptions that accept change.

Table 13.1 *Assumptions underlying learning systems and cultures*

Traditional	Future
Stability	Transience
Bureaucracy	Contingency
Homogeneity	Heterogeneity
Dependency	Confidence
Hierarchy	Heterarchy
Division of labour	Teamwork
Quality control	Social accountability
Problems defined academically	Problems defined operationally
'Disciplinary' knowledge	Transdisciplinary knowledge
Teaching	Learning

The assumptions in the right-hand column of Table 13.1 simply reflect society's realisation that workplace certainty is a rare phenomenon – a realisation that has sprung from experience. But they also spring from real-life technological developments that have served organisations' motivation to meet more efficiently its needs for new, superior products and services. These technological developments are real, and have bred confidence among writers and managers alike. Where once the 'modern' approach was to set and manage by objectives, the more confident 'post-modern' view is proactively to create products, methods and systems – which are themselves capable of further development. Learning systems both exemplify and serve this post-modern ideal.

IT systems are well-established throughout the commercial world, and are involved in most workplace communications. The Internet is available to anyone with a computer, a modem and a telephone line. In the UK, virtually everyone can now link directly to servers which transfer knowledge at will throughout the entire world. Already there are many examples of large organisations having established internal 'intranets', allowing groups of employees to have access to their own endlessly increasing internal data banks. The use of intranet systems has transformed education, training and learning procedures. Soon also we shall have voice-activated computers, reducing the need to sit at a keyboard to communicate. Prototypes already exist, and may be especially useful to people with specific disabilities. The science fiction idea of the computer that answers back is no longer merely fiction. Fast-flowing electronic mail discussions will often replace meetings, and 'attendance' at conferences is possible without leaving home. 'New' knowledge will be available more quickly at the specific workplace than in purpose-built learning sites.

Young people who enter the world of work will be used to new learning norms. We might even speculate that children could have a 'smart card' at birth, giving them access to individual learning guides to, in collaboration with parents, help them continuously to plan their formal learning paths. Formal learning achievements could be centrally logged as they happen, and not be tied to age. Indeed, although educational qualifications are still likely to be the prime aim of full-time education experience, later learning will be assumed to follow. Schools, colleges and universities as we have known them may no longer be needed: the need for lecturers, for example, seems likely to decline, although such people may well exist in different capacities working with new learning processes essentially aimed at facilitating self-development. Future workers may therefore be more likely to practise self-development, to expect managers to have 'facilitator' roles and to commit themselves to group learning activities.

It is these processes, roles and activities that we will explore in this chapter. Let's now look at some concepts that support them.

We will be looking at how organisations as well as individuals can learn – and how both can 'learn to learn'. Also, in an age of rapid transition, we need to consider how to encourage 'unlearning' of redundant ideas and methods. Organisations and their members might endlessly learn to learn into the future. This is the ultimate learning and training intervention: one that ensures that future learning interventions happen naturally.

CONCEPTS AND THEORIES TO SUPPORT 'NEW LEARNING'

There have been several relevant approaches by the previous generation of writers, to which we would like to introduce you.

'Socio-technical' and 'Contingency' theory

The first suggestion that learning specialists might recognise stability as unnatural, and might instead aim at creating work units that sought to manage change on a continuing basis, came from the Tavistock Institute's researchers, and their support of socio-technical theory, during the 1960s. These researchers were mainly psychologists and sociologists, who spent much time investigating the relationships between employees and their employing organisations (and indeed between employees and their work) at a time when automated processes were increasing.

Socio-technical (ST) theory offered a model for flexible organisation and change management. Its basic model suggested four key contingent (ie interdependent) organisational elements – 'tasks', 'technology', 'structure' and 'people' – which must be collectively managed in the service of the organisation's goals. Morgan (1997) has proposed 'management' as a fifth and co-ordinating element. The key message was that as each of these elements varies through time, the relationships between them must be continuously monitored and frequently adjusted to maintain a 'healthy' operation.

For example, if new technology or bureaucracy subordinates creative workers to routine, low-discretion jobs, an abrasive interaction is likely, calling for conscious changes to either or both. The lack of such changes might lead to absenteeism, job turnover and a variety of behaviours that 'interrupt the main work task'. This was not an explicit 'learning to learn' message, but it suggested that each unique organisation should promote among all its employees an endless acceptance of change, an endless need to see or feel the need to change, and an endless attempt to create unique situation-specific answers to relationship problems.

Discussion question: How far do you think employees at junior level need to be able to manage change?

There are several other messages. First, adjusting the relationships between any two elements might of course demand the adjustment of either or both. New technology might demand employee learning, and trained employees might justify changed tasks, and new tasks might lead to new management systems, which might again demand new employee learning. But second, each element's internal stability might be expected to fluctuate – a phenomenon that certainly applies to the 'people' element (for example, people do not all learn at the same pace), and justifies time spent away from the mainstream work tasks on 'process review' discussions, which means unscripted interpersonal learning activities. Taken together, these messages confirm that 'managing the process' is as important as 'managing the task'. They also lead to a third message: group or team learning must itself be continuously reviewed and influenced 'as it happens'. These three messages suggest that a healthy work team will learn, and must manage its own learning without waiting for an external training imposition. (The latter, as we have seen, has been the UK norm.)

ST theory influenced a wide body of consultancy-oriented researchers in the field of organisation development (OD), who conducted OD seminars, study groups and projects in many of the UK's larger firms during the 1970s. These interventions usually accepted the basic 'contingency' view, adopting the whole organisation as the basic unit to be researched or studied. The human element was usually studied as part of the organisation's culture, but learning methods and processes were often ignored – except perhaps during discussions on specific options for forward cultural change. Perhaps the learning concept was seen as too practical for some of these theorists. OD activity did nevertheless involve much open discussion, especially at senior management levels, and undoubtedly improved awareness throughout management that the various socio-technical elements need to be both internally consistent and adapted to outside environmental conditions. There was much internal talk with HRD management about training needs and options in organisations where senior management found OD useful; in a few firms, it led to the training of staff specialising in process consultancy. It is unfortunate that so little of contingency theory and process consultancy was retained during the expansion years of the 1980s, when focus switched to competition and efficiency savings.

'Action learning'

The philosophy behind Action Learning (AL), which we also discussed on pages 239 and 259, makes it much more than a set of procedures. AL's creator Reg Revans was a great example of the ability of human beings to continue to develop. He considered and preached his ideas relating to management learning from as early as 1945, yet they have never been widely understood, despite being wholly relevant to the task of improving performance in a changing environment.

As we have seen, AL starts with the assumption that any change means uncertainty. Managing uncertainty demands more than drawing on stored memory: decisions must also be based on ideas about the future and the probability of the decision being correct. When a problem occurs, it is risky to assume that the way a similar problem was dealt with in the past must also now be the 'best solution'. In such a situation, managers need to update their view of what must be taken into account – aims, constraints, options and likely outcomes – and then need to create a new view of what should be done. In the process of doing this, the manager may need to do some research – that is, to 'understand' the implications of the problem more deeply by gathering new information. This is what Revans meant by 'action learning': finding things out while getting on with the real management job. The process is essentially question-based, ignoring established answers unless they satisfy whatever questions are being asked.

Some questions are likely to be useful in all, or at least most, situations. Revans listed a few: for example, 'What am I trying to do?', 'What is stopping me from doing it?', 'Who can contribute to a solution?' Real problems usually need tailor-made questions, which must be specially created – and Revans judged that the most useful questions are often posed by people who are not familiar with the problem. He suggested the best vehicle for AL is a group or 'set' of several members from different backgrounds, disciplines and cultures. It can be as simple as a group of colleagues who are joined by one or more 'outsiders' to work on a given problem. The AL set is typically a group that is meeting for the first time. It is introduced to the problem by the manager who 'owns' the problem (and who remains part of the set); it has the help of a 'co-ordinator', who essentially acts as secretary, arranging meetings, writing up findings, collecting material and so on.

AL philosophy holds that the best opportunities for management learning lie in everyday management jobs. A few organisations (notably within the large multinationals, where trans-national and intercompany sets still appear, and in the Health Service) continue to support the approach, and at least one university degree course is based upon it; but industry as a whole rarely saw it as a major alternative to sending managers on external courses.

> Discussion question: The ITOL website, which brings together trainers and developers to discuss new learning approaches, reports a resurgence of interest in AL recently (2003). Why do you think this might be?

The continuous development approach

Continuous development (CD) originated in the late 1970s with a group of training practitioners who formed the then Institute of Personnel Management's national committee on training and development. They had become concerned that much government-inspired research seemed to propose bureaucratic solutions to the nation's overall economic problems. Most of them had acquired an understanding of the main socio-technical principles. They had also adopted Kolb's experiential learning ideas (see page 56). They had doubts about the 'total organisation' approach of the OD consultants; in their pragmatic view, training specific to any given work unit could dramatically improve both the organisation's and the nation's economic health, and its absence was often the result of the need for it never being appreciated by top management. They believed that the relationships between people and work should be adjusted to allow the people who were closest to the work significantly to influence decisions on their own training, and again to allow time for that training to happen.

CD emerged in the form of a five-year Institute-led 'ABCD' ('A Boost for Continuous Development') campaign. It was preached not as a theory, and not primarily even as a group of work practices, but as an attitude – justifying and explaining the term 'continuous'. Two mainstream ideas were preached as front campaign runners: first, self-development, and second, the integration of learning within work. If managers, and especially HR/HRD managers, could adopt the CD attitude, both these ideals could be realised in myriad unique, situation-specific ways – national prescription would be redundant – with organisations coming to value, to create where necessary, and to use enthusiastically (a) already-known systems for appraisal of weaknesses and identification of training needs in line with forward operational plans, and (b) process review. To stimulate cultural change in this direction, the Institute launched a Code of Practice, which stressed the importance of:

- clear organisation-wide CD policies (eg corporate commitment to CD, interdependence of technical and social systems, self-development as a responsibility of every employee, all employees to learn as much as possible about learning processes, facilities for learning during work time etc)

- CD responsibilities and roles (eg senior management to promote CD policy, and to demand adherence to the CD concept from management; management to spend a substantial amount of their time on CD activity; PM/HRM professionals to take the lead in arranging discussions wherever they felt learning activity is inadequate to operational results; all learners to clarify their own learning goals with their superiors and colleagues, and without waiting for directives endlessly to propose ways of learning that minimise operational disruption etc)

- several CD practices (eg learner involvement in appraisal processes; mandatory CD agenda items for standing committee (including board) meetings; explicit reference in contracts for the introduction of new plant or equipment to the early involvement of staff during commissioning processes; regular process review discussions, wherever possible aided by facilitators, for all work teams)

- CD training (of managers, and especially HRD specialists, as facilitators).

The ABCD campaign drew sustained interest from a number of professional bodies, and from the academic world. Along with the CIPD, some of the former have since developed 'continuing professional development' systems for their membership, which promote CD's self-development aim. The academic world's interest was also sustained, but (as we shall shortly explain) soon tended to follow more ambitious theories covering the integration of learning with work. Most training specialists and line management viewed the campaign with caution, however, searching for hidden motives that did not exist. Government's training advisers flirted with CD briefly, then quickly abandoned their involvement in the campaign in favour of the employer-led Management Charter Group development (which included the CD ideal in its Charter but did nothing to promote it) and the introduction of the qualifications-based NVQ system (which initially claimed to ensure competence at the workplace, but which explicitly avoided the issue of how to integrate learning and work).

> Discussion question: How far do you think managers today are engaging with the CD concept? Is it accepted that managers should give more time to CD practices than they currently do?

The learning organisation approach

In a society where knowledge is power, organisations have become very interested, for pragmatic reasons, in managing knowledge. Here we will look at the theoretical underpinning of the learning organisation approach.

'Learning organisation' (LO) theory came from academic sources at roughly the same time as training practitioners were promoting CD. This concept develops the ST and contingency approaches. LO theory makes an important distinction between the 'adaptive' organisation (in which change is managed by 'reading' opportunities and constraints, and training plans are created to produce improvement), and a higher level of 'generative' organisation that aims to take the lead in controlling its environment. LO enthusiasts argue that people's ideas and behaviour do not have to be subordinated to corporate strategy and centrally defined working procedures; policy, operations, ideas and action are all viewed as being in the ideal evenly balanced and linked (see Figure 13).

In this ideal 'learning organisation', learning is seen as the process element that links the

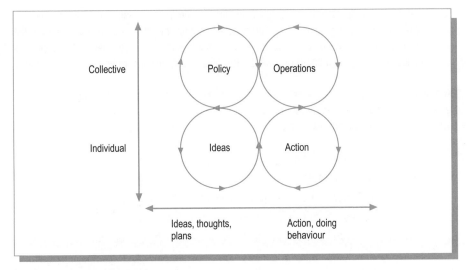

Figure 13.1 *The learning organisation*

other four essentials – but the process is two-way, with people and practices continuously influencing each other, with learning and change management following naturally.

Garratt (2000, 1995) has described the historical flow of management thinking that has led to this concept. He thinks it dates back as early as 1947. A convergence of disciplines (eg psychology, sociology, cybernetics, economics) established basic ideas about:

- the key role of people as the only source of organisational learning
- learning having both an intrinsic (personal development) and extrinsic (organisational asset-creating) value
- the necessity for multiple feedback loops of learning to create continuous organisational learning.

Garratt (2000, 1995) also credits the Tavistock Institute's research on socio-technical systems in the 1950s and 1960s with demonstrating the critical nature of learning processes in healthy workgroups. He finds it surprising that these ideas have taken so long to become accepted within the world of work, more especially because a host of management thinkers (Weber, Revans, Lewin, Emery, Argyris, Hodgson, Schumacher, Mintzberg, Handy, Pedler, Burgoyne and, latterly, Senge are among many that are named) have built upon ST ideas.

Discussion question: Why do you think the 'world of work' has for the most part rejected the psychologists' ideas?

Senge (1990) calls the learning organisation 'an organisation that is continually expanding its capacity to create its future'. His four basic management disciplines are:

- personal mastery
- mental models
- building shared vision
- team learning.

273

His fifth discipline is systems thinking, which is for him the discipline that integrates the others, the payoffs of integration being immense – creating the integrated whole prevents the individual disciplines from being gimmicks or fads. According to Senge, these five disciplines allow the 'learning organisation' to be built systematically and not just to happen.

Burgoyne (1995) is less ambitious than Senge. He proposes the following practices as necessary to ensure the 'balanced' corporate learning process that is inherent in Figure 13 (which we reproduced from his article):

- a learning approach to strategy
- participative policy-making
- 'informating' (internal openness, plus dialogue/communication via IT)
- internal exchange (mutual adaptation between people and work units)
- reward flexibility (reward systems that incentivise learning and openness)
- enabling structures (simple enough to allow learning and to accommodate its consequences)
- interorganisation learning (learning with, learning from, benchmarking for development as well as imitation)
- a learning climate (cultural norms that support shared learning from experience)
- processes that support self-development.

All these practices are almost impossible to prescribe, even within a theoretical ideal. Burgoyne concedes that the learning organisation is 'not a standard formula, or a proven winning formula to be benchmarked and imitated'. He calls it a 'proposal, an invention and a broad concept – the best suggestion about how work and organisations proceed in this period of history'. It remains a powerful set of ideas to challenge and condition the thoughts of anyone whose responsibilities extend to managing the relationship between learner and organisation.

Carling and Heller (1995) provide forceful practical arguments to support the academic ones in favour of learning organisations as a foundation for success. They point out that a learning climate is by no means new in the field of sport: great champions act as both master and pupil, giving lessons to others and learning themselves both from experience and from other coaches. They quote Drucker's maxim that information is replacing physical assets as the backbone of business, and add that as information constantly becomes obsolete those who would be winners must update continuously, which involves learning. The adaptive learner and organisation react to changing circumstances, but victory will go to the leaders in creativity. Carling and Heller quote from Alan Kay: 'The best way to predict the future is to invent it.' The learning organisation seeks to generate the future it wants. It is vital to know and to reinforce one's strengths, and recognise and eradicate one's weaknesses; this involves learning, and applies to winners who want to stay ahead, just as much as to losers. In the learning organisation everybody learns, which means everyone is taught – an idea with which many senior managers feel uncomfortable.

Discussion question: What vested interests in an organisation might be threatened by the LO concept?

The knowledge creation approach

During the 1980s, at roughly the same time that the LO approach was becoming well known, academic journals in the USA carried a number of articles by one or both of two Japanese business experts, putting forward the elements of a new theory of 'organisational knowledge creation', which they were constructing from research into successful Japanese organisations. The full theory was published in 1995 (see Nonaka and Takeuchi 1995).

Here we attempt to summarise a complex set of ideas.

Knowledge creation (KC) theory defines knowledge broadly, to include not merely factual information but also attitudes and skills. If knowledge is 'justified belief', at individual level it incorporates every assumption, preference and even intention. Knowledge is said by Nonaka and Takeuchi to be either 'tacit' or 'explicit'. The former is personal and 'context-specific', which means that it has been experientially acquired by the individual, is subjective, and cannot easily be formalised or communicated to others. The latter is objective, 'situation-free', removed from the individual's personal bias, and can be transmitted in formal, generally recognised language. The first need in knowledge creation is to stimulate the conversion of tacit knowledge to explicit knowledge. Four modes of knowledge conversion are defined at length. These are sequentially required in a 'learning spiral' that moves knowledge from the individual outwards to an ever-widening group and eventually to an entire organisation. (A key stage in the conversion is 'triggered by dialogue or collective reflection'.) The learning spiral is said to function only when several supportive conditions exist, such as clear strategy and significant autonomy.

Dixon (2000) lists five different types of knowledge transfer, but like Nonaka and Takeuchi distinguishes between tacit and explicit knowledge, and suggests organisational requirements yielding corporate results that promote cohesion. Since these results are greater than the sum of individual contributions, she sees this as newly creating what she terms 'common knowledge'. Her design guidelines, based on research in several of the USA's major companies, include discussions, meetings and inputs by 'knowledge specialists' – but they vary dependent on the type of transfer attempted. This is a new world with new responsibilities for HRD specialists, who constantly visit workplace teams, collect documents, videos and tools of all kinds, synthesising outcomes in the cause of blending new operational forms with operational goals elsewhere.

'Knowledge management' (KM) is not, as has often been suggested, a set of concepts that naturally stem from KC. The recognition and growth of KM has come with the development of IT systems, which has dominated technological progress across the entire world since the mid-1980s. We included an example of a 'knowledge management system' in the previous chapter (page 261) when we described organisational learning systems. It is important to point out that while KC has a lot to say about learning, and acknowledges that people are the essential agents of learning at all levels, KM says little or nothing about the human dimension; human resource issues that follow the establishment of new information networks are treated as 'hygiene factors'. Most writers on KM are communications experts or information scientists: their ideas relate essentially to ensuring that information flows widely and smoothly, the assumption being that 'more people with more information means more learning' – a conclusion that is not necessarily shared by those influenced by any of the previous approaches.

Discussion question: How might HRD practitioners 'add value' to the concept of KM, when the latter may sometimes ignore the human dimension?

The increased availability of computer-based information, and the increased speed at which it can be accessed, plus the opportunity to establish forum-type electronic discussions on a worldwide basis, offers significant incentives and new levels of motivation for individual learners and organisations alike. Several large UK companies are now committed to extensive KM activity, HRD practitioners are working with IT specialists, and view KM as an in-house resource that will continue to grow in importance alongside further developments in learning.

Knowledge creation overturns many of the traditional assumptions in our approach to HRD. It assumes that work people, especially managers, actually 'know' more and better than the textbook, even though they cannot easily articulate the solutions to problems and the requirements of 'best practice'. Through endless discussion of tacit knowledge, new insight is obtained and innovation occurs, it is claimed. We doubt that KC is strong enough to replace traditional HRD norms, but its assumptions seem to rest on firm foundations, and hence it seems reasonable to expect systemic training interventions appearing within work alongside systemic interventions devised and implemented alongside it. This in turn means the offer of new, exciting horizons for HRD practitioners and managers at all levels.

LEARNING TO LEARN

During 1998/9, the Institute of Personnel and Development commissioned research into KM and LO, aiming to determine the importance of each for short-term operational success and long-term organisational renewal, the contribution employees must make to each, and the implications for the PM/HRM function. The first stage, a literature search (see Scarborough, Swan and Preston 1999), yielded disappointing conclusions. KM and LO were reported as representing 'new approaches to the problems of competitiveness and innovation', but judged as approaches that 'will eventually be blown away'. According to the researchers, the literature confirms 'an alarming gap in the treatment of people management issues' – a remark that perhaps sprang from the fact that in recent years KM articles have ignored KC and severely outnumbered articles on LO. Moreover, academic studies on LO were seen as 'failing to generate useful implications for practitioners'. Knowledge was criticised as an 'over-theorised and under-specified concept that admits of too many interpretations to be useful'.

These judgements appear harsh, to say the least. There is no doubt that LO writers such as Burgoyne, Garratt and Senge have shown as large an interest in people, and again in operational practice, as in systems. Senge et al's *Fifth Discipline Fieldbook* (1998) is a good example of an attempt to be operationally specific. Nonaka and Takeuchi's KC theory is similarly accompanied by a very practice-ordered set of recommendations, although these assume large-scale cultural change. And if articles in *People Management* vary in their views on the practical value of KM, they still quote actual organisations that are experimenting with the KM concept.

Our own attempts to reflect constructively on all the approaches that we have described in this chapter, within the wider context of attempting to predict the likely future for HRD, lead us to believe that they collectively suggest a number of key messages that will or should influence the future practice of people management, and that they individually highlight important HRD interventions for the future. First, a few 'general' messages:

- Change will continue to be *a*, and quite possibly *the*, major influence upon life, and especially life at work.

- The most important requirement for the ongoing management of change is that of 'learning to learn'.

- Within the changing environment, competitiveness and efficiency needs will demand that management roles are, where necessary, extended to incorporate the management of learning.

- While information technology will make more information more accessible more quickly, learning will remain essentially a human activity.

- 'Learning to learn' has varied implications for the individual, the manager and the organisation, and involves the development of experiential learning alongside, and not instead of, more formal traditional learning processes.

- Both managers and employees who have a positive impact on the organisation need to cope with ambiguity – there are no pat solutions.

Now, some messages that are geared more to operational practice, and are inevitably in the form of recommendations:

- Operational management must continue to be based on 'top-down' decision flows.

- Organisational learning requires a 'middle-up-down' flow of new ideas.

- New-style HRD interventions should address new learning processes and activities alongside their traditional teacher-led predecessors.

- The concept and practice of self-development should be adjusted to become 'assisted self-development'.

- Team development should incorporate team learning activity.

- New learning processes demand new roles, and some old roles should decline for (a) senior management, (b) management generally, (c) individual learners and (d) HRD specialists.

- Learning and Training interventions – which may often ignore the use of the word 'training' – should be managed primarily to serve performance at three levels – those of the individual, the work team and the organisation.

> Discussion question: Do you agree with the proposals above? Do they apply to your organisation or one with which you are familiar? Which of them do you believe will have most impact over the next five years and why?

We now make our own suggestions on how the more important of these developments might be helped to happen.

Individual learners

Changes in society's attitudes toward learning will continue to develop slowly – not as quickly as many learning specialists would like! These changes will increasingly tend to acknowledge and promote ideas about thought processes involved in **learning** rather than **teaching**, facilitating **development** beyond **instruction**, and **creativity** instead of **dependence**. All levels within the organisation need to appreciate that this cultural change is taking place, and that the term 'individual learners' extends to all levels, without exception. The new thought processes are important for both short-term operational performance and for long-term organisation renewal. Senior management need to appreciate this and set about devising strategic plans explicitly aimed at stimulating their use.

The new thought processes all centre on 'reflective' behaviour. It has been clear since Kolb's research (see page 56) that experiential learning requires the learner to reflect; Argyris' work pointed to ways whereby reflection can be helped to happen; and LO writers have more recently redefined its nature in detail. Nonaka and Takeuchi quote Schön (1983, p68) as follows:

> When someone reflects in action, he becomes a researcher in the practice context. He is not dependent on the categories of established theory and technique, but constructs a new theory of the new case.

We will briefly explain the concept here. Basically, the 'researcher' practises 'double-loop learning' (see page 84), which involves an endless attempt to find a use for new information, an answer to a problem, a modification to an assumption, and so on. The key to this is the introduction of questions into the thought process, which in turn helps build new or 'polished' ideas that can be communicated to others. Learners must be helped – possibly by traditional methods – to develop the habit of using questions, and again to devise or accept questions relevant to their jobs and appropriate to varying situations. Table 13 offers a few generally relevant options for questions.

While 'generally relevant' questions can be the subject of collective learning interventions, each job – and especially each management job – should have its own list of questions that are specifically relevant to its ongoing operational management. A 'prompt list' should ideally be created for each, containing essentially questions that inevitably command 'opinioned' answers, ie answers that the job-holder is expected to own but which are liable to change or

Table 13.2 *Examples of questions to promote 'Reflection in Action'*

Situation	'REFLECTION IN ACTION' Questions
New experience	Is this likely to happen again? If so, should I behave differently? Do I need to be better informed for a repeat?
New information	Will I need this information in the future? If so, how can I ensure access to it then?
New problem	Has anyone else experienced this? Is this problem analogous to . . .? How can I share the problem with others?
Clash of opinions	What are the assumptions underlying each? How fundamental is the difference?
Request for advice	Am I the best adviser? How can I advise without creating dependency?
All situations	Do I need to communicate this to others?

are far from finite. Marketing people are used to this type of question. To manage a brand, one must take decisions about consumer needs and preferences, which change through time: hence the existence of continuing market research programmes, which provide regular data on which up-to-date decisions can be taken. If such questions are formally established, and the job-holder is committed to always having the 'best available' answer, a 'research in action' attitude exists, and the attempt to stay abreast of new knowledge is naturally prompted.

Accessing the Internet and/or intranets will probably become a standard method of updating knowledge in future, although traditional methods will probably not disappear. Where new knowledge is directly relevant to the learner's prompt list, the general question is 'In what ways will, can or should this new knowledge influence my work in the future?' But where knowledge does not seem to be immediately relevant, there is another, more complex thought process, that ideally will be brought into play – that of looking for parallels between the new knowledge and the prompt list, or searching for 'analogies'. LO writers stress the value of this type of thinking, and claim that it lies at the heart of most creative learning. Learners, and especially management learners, should be helped to practise it by traditionally mounted sessions on lateral thinking, and practice in brainstorming.

If the job-holder is known to be the custodian of clear, informed, up-to-date views, plus a range of creative suggestions, other job-holders tend to contact that person as an 'authority' when searching for answers to their own related 'prompt list' questions. This is perhaps the main incentive for the job-holder to practise self-development: it generates prestige and builds confidence, providing the overall culture does not give superior recognition to other values.

Discussion question: Does self-development bring its own rewards to those who practise it in their organisations? If so, what are they?

Teams and groups

As we have just suggested, a key reason why organisations as a whole should promote self-development is the generation of a strong internal source of up-to-date information and opinion held by confident, articulate employees. We also saw that self-development can be 'helped to happen'. Three key factors encourage this:

- First, 'reflection in action' is easier and more likely to happen when two or more people work on it together.
- Second, if an 'openness' culture exists, group learning helps individual learning to happen at a faster rate than simple self-development.
- Group learning tends to be more creative than individual learning.

These are not new conclusions. They were in general circulation over 20 years ago among those who led study group activities based on the earlier Tavistock Institute's socio-technical research. The fact that they have not been adopted by industry in general suggests that the culture inside most organisations has favoured defensive routines that have acted as a deterrent to learning about learning. So we have to report them as suggestions of what should, rather than predictions of what will, happen in the future.

> Discussion question: Do you agree with our analysis of organisational culture? Is it true of any organisation with which you are familiar, and if not, in what way does this organisation differ?

We mentioned the 'prompt list' as an aid to self-development. If the job-holder's manager understands the value of these open-ended questions, he or she can use them as an aid to face-to-face, one-to-one, operational discussions with the job-holder. The job-holder's views are then tested against further operational realities, and against the boss's own problems, and are likely to be stretched. If they remain strong, learning is being reinforced; if they have to give way, new learning is happening. Senge (1990) and others describe this joint activity as 'dialoguing' – having adopted the idea from the work of the quantum theorist, David Bohm. 'Dialoguing' is 'open' discussion in which assumptions are suspended, and the participants regard each other as equals in a process that allows incoherent thinkers to become 'open to the flow of a larger intelligence … in dialogue, people become observers of their own thinking'. Nonaka and Takeuchi (1995) use the term 'collective reflection'.

The process becomes even more useful in terms of operational learning if the group is more than a pair – although it simultaneously becomes more difficult to manage, especially if the group is a real-life operational team. As we have said, the necessary stimulus for 'reflection in action' is the introduction of questions, and 'dialoguing' requires a culture of openness. But the operational grouping incorporates differing operational roles, and unless the meeting is explicitly named as a learning session, these roles inevitably intrude on the 'open' dialogue, transforming the process into a traditional operational discussion. Senge maintains that the prime role of the team leader (usually the most senior person present, or the person who has convened the meeting) involves balancing the process between learning dialogue and operational discussion: in the former, complex issues are presented as questions, while in the latter, different answers are presented and defended, consensus views emerge, and authoritative judgements are made. What this means is that the team leader must be able to pose the questions, listen to members' contributions, sum up alternative views, judge when to shift the process into operational mode, extract or expose the operational implications, call on those with operational responsibility (including him or herself) to declare their own commitment or otherwise – and then return the meeting to dialogue mode.

This is not just about chairing a meeting. It is a formidable task that only few currently perform with any real confidence, and calls for formal training in what we shall call 'modern' chairing techniques. To maximise the learning opportunity, the natural tendency to move forward into operational decision-making must be resisted, more questions being fed into the discussion. Senge quotes Bohm again in insisting that a 'facilitator' is needed alongside the team leader, at least in the early phases of developing a true 'learning team'. Here is a new role for the HRD professional – although anyone who values the role and commits time to learning what it involves can perform it. The facilitator is required to 'hold the context' of the dialogue – that is, he or she must monitor the flow of ideas and inject new questions aimed at ensuring that understanding is widespread and contributions are not ignored. The role demands skill – in listening, watching, interpreting, intervening to pose new questions – and judging when to encourage operational discussion, which is effectively returning the reins to the team leader. A strong mutual respect is needed between the team leader and the facilitator, who ideally will meet before the meeting and share views on who the members are, how the dialogue might be helped to happen and so on. In some circumstances, and especially in the early phase of a team's development, they might agree to split the meeting into two, three or four meetings – covering sequentially team briefing (traditional style, incorporating some explanation of their own roles), the 'learning dialogue', the 'operational discussion' and feedback on the process.

But there is even more on which the team leader and facilitator must co-operate. In addition to the learning process, and the operational process, there is also an interpersonal process to be continuously monitored, understood and managed. Individual learning is at its strongest when ideas are being accepted and further developed in a way that confirms the assumptions behind those ideas. In practice, confidence is dissipated if colleagues seem to ignore or reject those assumptions, or prefer alternative ones of their own making. Loss of confidence shows up as silence, or attempts to 'pair' with another member, or aggressiveness – or a host of other behavioural symptoms, the most dangerous of which was described well over 40 years ago by Bion (1961) as 'the basic assumption' – in which the individual behaves 'as if' believing in the majority or strongest view, while showing a lack of commitment to or enthusiasm for it. Such behaviour usually goes unnoticed, and draws no comment, although the person/s concerned is/are actually building defensive behaviour – they are 'learning how to avoid learning'. Such behaviour needs to be recognised and to form the basis for further work – this is how 'learning to learn' acquires a collective meaning. A 'healthy' team will be prepared to suspend its knowledge-creating process and work on any such process issues if and when the situation is clear to them, but such clarity does not normally emerge naturally. Here is the justification for formal training in process consultancy as well as the skill of chairing a meeting, on the part of team leaders and facilitators alike.

'Reflection in action' and 'learning teams' are the twin bases of the continuously developing learning organisation. Together, they form the means whereby – in Senge's terms – 'personal mastery' can flourish as a discipline (ie a series of practices and principles that should be applied and can be taught) and 'team learning' can be forged via a system of situation-specific ground rules that evolve to promote both dialogue and operational decisions. In our opinion, a culture of this type will ideally be developed by any organisation that aims to stand out in its changing environment as flexible, confident and determined to manage its own future.

Middle management

Middle managers are the main generators of knowledge creation and distribution. As team leaders they can help team members to extend and articulate what they know about workplace reality, collecting *en route* ideas for future improvement, and judging when and if operational changes should be made within their own areas of responsibility. Organisation-wide HRD needs the new knowledge to be spread among others, both laterally and vertically. Middle management must carry information and ideas from their own team meetings as contributions for others they attend. Where once they may have created minutes for a named distribution circle, in future they will increasingly place the record on an intranet (voice-operated computing will help enormously with this task) for a wider audience who can access it in their own time. While security matters may dictate some sophistication in the way the material is presented and made available, the main point to remember is that keeping information to oneself is NOT efficient management within the context of the learning organisation. Not least among their responsibilities is that of quickly alerting their superiors to matters with significant strategic or organisational implications.

The overall learning process is modelled in a simple form in Figure 13 It shows how important

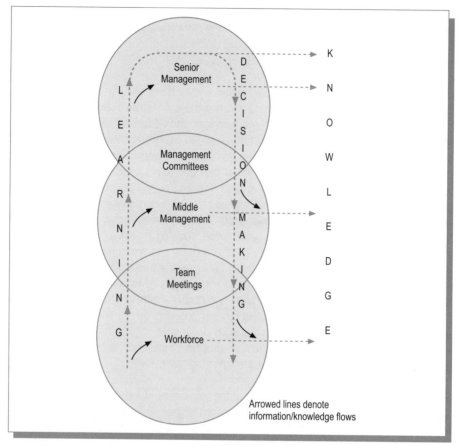

Figure 13.2 *The organisational learning process*

are middle management's roles, and calls into question the current tendency to 're-engineer' in medium-sized organisations by reducing the number of middle management. Of course, in unhealthy organisations the middle management layer can effectively stifle innovation and creativity, or claim it all for itself.

> Discussion question: Critically analyse the competences needed by middle management to become managers of learning.

Top management

All that we have written about individual and team learning applies at the 'top' of organisations as well as elsewhere. But top management have their own extra responsibilities and roles. Leadership is still needed, but in a different form from the past, to install and maintain the learning culture.

UK organisations traditionally manage their operations from the top downwards, and authoritarian top managers have tended either to avoid consulting others or to listen only to their immediate subordinates before taking their decisions. In the ideal learning organisation, a more complex process is needed, with top management spending very much less time in operational management decisions, and more on managing the overall learning/decision-making process – while retaining their traditional roles in determining and maintaining

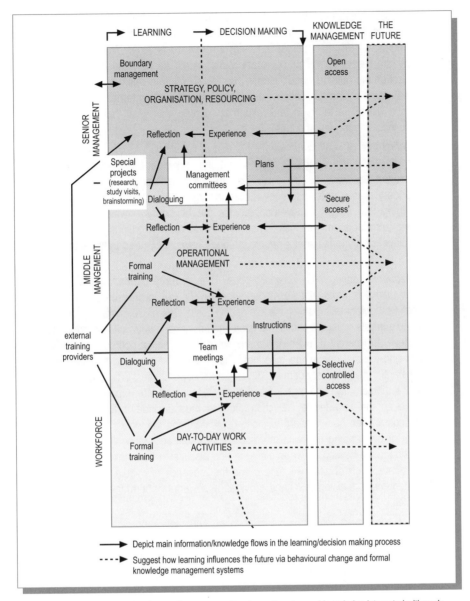

Figure 13.3 *The 'continuous development' management system – learning and knowledge integrated with work*

strategic, political, organisational and resourcing control. Figure 13 attempts to chart a continuously developing management system in more complex schematic detail than Figure 13 although it remains, of course, no more than a simplistic and contrived attempt to consolidate the ideas we have learned from the many sources quoted.

Several principles must be stressed:

- *Top management does not 'know better' than subordinates about everything*, and must be prepared to collect up-to-date information (including ideas and opinions) before using their decision-making powers. Middle managers will ideally become used to being asked for advice or information, with their requests for time (and even new resources) being treated sympathetically. But just as middle management are being trusted to know and understand the reality of the workplace and its operating problems, so top management's frame of reference is wider. They must continue to carry the responsibility for boundary management (ie how the organisation should impact on the outside world), strategy (ie the direction in which the organisation must head), policy (the philosophy underlying operations), internal organisation (how people will relate to work) and resources (people, and what they will have to work with, including money and time).

■ *The first role of senior management is that of questioner.* As in the ideal prompt list, the questions will deal with issues that are not clear-cut, and therefore require opinioned answers. As we have just implied, they should carry implications for boundary management, strategy, policy or organisation (the first of these includes anything that involves movement across the boundary – which therefore covers money, products and services). There is a tendency known as 'ingratiation theory' for employees only to tell senior people the good news; they need to know the bad news too.

■ *A sequential dialogue/discussion process is even more dramatically relevant at this level than it is within middle management levels.* But in pressured times it may be useful to delegate much of the dialoguing task. One-off research projects, ad hoc value analysis groups, special brainstorming sessions, study visits, literature searches – these are merely a few of the many ways (including, of course, agenda items on standing internal committee meetings) that it might be made to happen, all offering substantial middle management development opportunities if the work is managed and led internally, and not least if external sources are tapped. In every case, however, the knowledge collection process must include a final stage in which findings are fed back upward to those commissioning the work. There is much to be said for overlapping this with the discussion stage: separating the two prevents the important see-sawing between dialogue and discussion that makes for decisions that anticipate much of what will follow, and the presence of middle management at top management decision meetings provides a powerful opportunity for developing the former.

■ *Top management must commit itself to trusting their subordinates* – which means finding and developing people whom they can trust, if the feeling of trust is not already there. This need has considerable implications: for recruitment (top management must be part of the process of recruiting direct into management or management trainee positions), for appointments (top management must identify with each and every management appointment), for appraisal (top management must personally confirm promotability ratings), and even for counselling (top management must learn to understand middle management 'problem behaviour' in much the same way that team leaders manage process review activity).

What these four key points add up to is a system in which top management promote the learning culture while retaining their responsibility for managing the entire organisation. Mayo and Lank (1994) quote Garratt as offering five key conditions that top management 'need to consider' (which we would suggest might read 'must promote'):

■ clear formulation of strategy and policy
■ taking time and space to think and learn themselves
■ demonstrating their own willingness to learn from each other

- delegating problem-solving operational issues to others
- setting a climate that encourages continuous learning.

We should perhaps add one more important condition:

- ensuring that staff in general, and especially middle management, similarly have time and space to think, engage in dialoguing, communicate, develop knowledge management facilities and make endless HRD interventions.

Time spent on learning must be accepted not as an alternative to work, but as work, without question. HRD interventions must be based on the firm belief that they are part of work, and wherever possible they must be integrated, and not merely dovetailed, with work. Middle management must be assessed on their ability to manage both learning and operational decision-making processes concurrently; top management must become used to asking for information and advice from their subordinates before imposing plans. Staffing levels must recognise all this – the very existence of widespread computer terminals and expanding data banks itself demands the rethinking of levels upwards, but the opportunities provided for creative learning disappear if there is not time for additional dialoguing and team learning. Once top management grasp this, they will find that their own lives become more creative, and indeed more interesting as a result.

Whatever the future, learning must surely grow in importance in the eyes of the community. If this is the case, greater interest in continuous development and learning organisations seems more rather than less likely. Strategies that seek short-term financial reward by reducing the time and space available for learning work in the opposite direction, and delay, if not prevent, the operational success that can only come from encouraging the learning, development and training interventions that a changing world requires. If the nation reaches a point where the majority of its workforce believes in continuous development, and a larger majority of its management strives to maintain a learning culture, the ultimate move will have been made, endlessly generating its own infinite number of interventions into the nation's ongoing learning organisation.

> We look forward to the next edition of our book, to see how far these ideas continue to influence practice. Meanwhile, we can perhaps develop the argument on the website to accompany this edition, and if you feel this is an area where you would like to contribute, please visit it, and help to develop the community of readers into a learning organisation.

For further reading

We have listed here some useful additional books and websites that you may like to follow up to investigate specific topics. The website accompanying this book has some helpful web links, so for web addresses please visit it. It also includes some advice about developing your reading skills, which some students may find useful. The books and articles we mention are not exhaustive, of course, and you may also find it helpful to consult some of the practitioner journals, such as the CIPD's *People Management*, or the broadsheet *Personnel Today*, together with its occasional *Training Magazine* insert, which are helpful for discussion of the latest practical applications of many of the topics we cover. Lastly, if you want to improve your literacy skills generally, make sure you read a quality newspaper such as *The Times*, *Telegraph* or *Guardian* regularly. They may be using 'journalistic' English, and there may be the odd spelling error, but generally you will widen your vocabulary and achieve more succinct English.

CHAPTER 1

There appear to be no standard texts covering all this material, although some of the organisational behaviour aspects are explored by:

Gabriel, Y. *Organisations in Depth.* Sage Publications, London, 1999. A fascinating psychoanalytic view of organisational behaviour.

Gabriel, Y. Fineman, S. and Sims, D. *Organising and Organisations.* 2nd edn. Sage Publications, London, 2000.

Jackson, N. and Carter, P. *Rethinking Organisational Behaviour.* Financial Times Prentice-Hall, Harlow, 2000.

Morgan, G. *Images of Organisation.* Sage Publications, London, 1997. The text discusses organisational learning since the 1970s.

Watson, T. *Organising and Managing Work.* Financial Times Prentice-Hall, Harlow, 2002.

Websites for the well-known government inspired initiatives are bookmarked on the website for this text.

CHAPTER 2

All the main bodies mentioned in this chapter have dedicated websites, and the website for this book has links to them. Of course, they are unlikely to be critical of themselves, and tend to focus on the 'good news', especially government departments like the DfES (although their site is one of the more informative with links to other useful sites). A more critical approach to the government-inspired initiatives is taken by academic journals or commentators in the practitioner journals mentioned above.

CHAPTER 3

The organisational behaviour texts referred to for Chapter 1 may be relevant, together with:

Atkinson, R.L. et al. Hilgard's *Introduction to Psychology*. Thomson Learning, Stamford, Ct, 1999. A good general introduction.

Bander, R. et al. *Neuro-Linguistic Programming, Vol. 1: The Study of the Structure of Subject Experience*. Meta Publications, California, 1980.

Dobson, C.B. and Hardy, M. et al. *Understanding Psychology*. Weidenfeld & Nicolson, London, 1990. Chapter 3, 'Learning and conditioning'; Chapter 4, 'Remembering and forgetting'.

Honey, P. and Mumford, A. *Manual of Learning Styles*. 3rd edn. Honey, Maidenhead, 1992.

Patrick, J. *Training: Research and practice*. Academic Press, London, 1992. Covers many aspects and relates them in a practical way.

Routledge, C. 'Brains, learners and trainers – a three-part series'. *Training and Management Development Methods*, Vol. 13, section 7, 1999. Examines the structure and processes of the brain, and the strategies and methods that trainers use to facilitate learning.

CHAPTER 4

Atkinson, R.L. et al. *Hilgard's Introduction to Psychology*. Thomson Learning, Stamford, Ct, 1999.

Belenky, M.F. et al. *Women's Ways of Knowing*. Basic Books, New York, 1997. Although the focus is on women learners, there are some very interesting insights into the process of learning generally, especially relating to disadvantaged learners. Useful also in the context of Chapter 10 on the 'new' workers.

Bromley, D.B. *Behavioural Gerontology: Central issues in the psychology of ageing*. Wiley, Chichester, 1990.

Dobson, C.B. and Hardy, M. et al. *Understanding Psychology*. Weidenfeld & Nicolson, London, 1990. Chapter 13, 'Attitude change'.

Downs, S. *Learning at Work*. Kogan Page, London, 1995.

Moon, J. (1999) *Reflection in Learning and Professional Development*. London, Kogan Page.

Patrick, J. *Training: Research and practice*. Academic Press, London, 1992. Useful all-round text. With reference to the content of this chapter, see learning transfer, retention of skill and knowledge of results.

Pedler, M. and Aspinwall, K. *Learning in Company*. McGraw-Hill, Maidenhead, 1995.

CHAPTER 5

Friedman, B. and Hatch, J. et al. *Delivering on the Promise: How to attract, manage and retain human capital*. Free Press, New York, 1998. A useful practical approach.

Harrison, R. *Employee Development*. 3rd edn. CIPD, London, 2002.

Moorby, E. *How to Succeed in Employee Development*. McGraw-Hill, Maidenhead, 1991. Particularly Chapter 6 and its Appendix, for an illustrative case of an employee development plan.

Richards-Carpenter, C. *Relating Manpower to an Organisation's Objectives*. IMS, Report No. 56, 1982.

Sloman, M. 'Coming in from the cold: a new role for trainers'. *Personnel Management*, January 1994. Pages 24–27.

CHAPTER 6

Texts that specialise in the organisation of the training and development function are rare, but here are some you may find useful.

Child, J. *Organisation: A guide to problems and practice*. Harper and Row, London, 1982. A comprehensive outline of the many choices that must be made when attempting to organise *any* function.

Handy, C. *Understanding Organisations*. Penguin, Harmondsworth, 1985. Another comprehensive general text on organisation, including cultural characteristics and their implications for organisational design.

Sloman, M. *Training in the Age of the Learner*. CIPD, London, 2003. A recently published text that is succinct and stylish. It is worth reading not only for the author's views on the HRD function, but also for its discussion of the change of emphasis from training to learning, to which we return throughout this book.

Walkin, L. *Training and Development NVQs*. Stanley Thorne, Cheltenham, 1996. Explores in detail the content of the Training and Development NVQ Level 3 Further and Adult Education Teachers' Certificate; it offers lengthy descriptions of each unit of competence (and even activity within each unit) and incorporates many self-assessment questions.

CHAPTER 7

Boydell, T.H. and Leary, M. *Identifying Training Needs*. IPD, London, 1996.

Bramham, J. *Human Resource Planning*. IPD, London, 1994.

Fowler, A. 'Benchmarking'. *People Management*, 12 June 1997.

Hirsh, W. and Reilly, P. 'Cycling proficiency'. *People Management*, 9 July 1998. Pages 36–41.

CHAPTER 8

Fransella, F. and Bannister, D. *A Manual for Repertory Grid Technique*. Academic Press, London, 1977.

Jessup, G. *Outcomes: NVQs and the emerging model of education and training*. The Falmer Press, London, 1991. Particularly Chapters 5, 18 and 19.

Megginson, D. and Whitaker, V. *Cultivating Self-Development*. IPD, London, 1996. Gives comprehensive and practical guidance on a variety of methods to diagnose one's own needs and to formulate a self-development action plan.

Moorby, E. 'Mentoring and Coaching', in J. Prior (ed.) *Handbook of Training and Management Development*. 2nd edn. Gower, London, 1994.

Mumford, A. *Management Development: Strategies for action*. 2nd edn. IPM, London, 1993.

Patrick, J. *Training: Research and practice*. Academic Press, London, 1992.

Pearn, M. and Kandola, R. *Job Analysis: A practical guide for managers*. 2nd edn. IPD, London, 1993.

CHAPTER 9

Appendix 4 of this book.

Bramley, P. *Evaluating Training*. IPD, London, 1996.

Easterby-Smith, M. and Mackness, J. 'Completing the cycle of evaluation'. *Personnel Management*, May 1992.

Fowler, A. 'How to decide on training methods'. *Personnel Management*, 21 December 1995. Pages 36–37.

Hardingham, A. *Designing Training*. IPD, London, 1996.

Megginson, D. and Whitaker, V. *Cultivating Self-Development*. IPD, London, 1996.

Plett, P. and Lester, B. *Training for Older People*. International Labour Office, Geneva, 1991.

Reid, M.A. 'Approaches and strategies', in J. Prior (ed.) *Handbook of Training and Development*. 2nd edn, Gower, Aldershot, 1994.

Sloman, M. *Training in the Age of the Learner*. CIPD, London, 2003. Also helpful for advice on technology-related learning.

CHAPTER 10

Vocational education and development is changing rapidly. The website for this book links to the main websites such as the DfES and LSC, which are updated regularly with new initiatives. *The Times Educational Supplement* and *The Times Higher Education Supplement* are also useful sources of information.

People Management is also an excellent source of updating material and critical commentary. The latest issue can be read on www.peoplemangement.co.uk.

Burke, J. *Outcomes, Learning and the Curriculum*. Taylor and Francis, Basingstoke, 1995.

Fowler, A. *Employee Induction: A good start*. IPD, London, 1996.

CHAPTER 11

There are numerous texts about management development and leadership and a number of websites of interest, to which the website for this book directs you. Some particularly interesting texts, together with those listed in the bibliography are:

Bass, B.M. *Bass and Stodgill's Handbook of Leadership*. 3rd edn. Free Press, New York, 1985

Drucker, P. 'On the profession of management'. *Harvard Business Review*, Boston, Mass., 1998

Greenleaf, R.F. *Servant Leadership*. Paulist Press, New York, 1977

Mant, A. *Leaders We Deserve*. Martin Robertson, Oxford, 1983

Mant, A. *Intelligent Leadership*. Allen and Unwin, St Leonards, 1997. Alistair Mant is a most stimulating and entertaining writer better known in the USA and Australia, and is the antithesis of dry academic textbooks. His writing is full of insight and humour.

CHAPTER 12

Jessup, G. *Outcomes: NVQs and the emerging model of education and training*. The Falmer

Press, London, 1991. Although outdated by more recent developments, this gives the basic philosophy underlying 'competences' systems.

Morgan, G. *Images of Organisation*. Sage, Thousand Oaks, California and London, 1997.

Shrivastava, P. 'A typology of organisational learning systems', *Journal of Management Studies*, Vol. 20, No. 1, Jan. 1983.

Chapter 13

Apart from the major titles named in the text (especially those by Garratt, Senge, and Nonaka and Takeuchi – see Bibliography), the 1999 'literature search' report by Scarborough et al, commissioned by the (then) IPD, provides an in-depth commentary on the key ideas in this chapter.

For a more comprehensive overall guide to organisational learning, see Mayo and Lank (1994), who incorporate an appendix entitled 'a complete learning organisation benchmark'. This provides the reader with over 20 pages of prompt-list questions aimed at helping identify which components a given organisation (ie 'yours') might need to establish a continuous learning culture, and how to plan moves towards the new ideal.

Senge deals well with minutiae of dialoguing and team learning. Schein (1969, 1970) is still the best source for facilitator skills and process review. Hardingham (1996) has two chapters on training options to develop process review skills. Barrington (1998) deals with prompt lists and their application.

To review learning organisation within a much wider conceptual study of organisation into the future, see Gareth Morgan's *Images of Organisation* (1997).

List of abbreviations

ACAS	Advisory, Conciliation and Arbitration Service
ACCAC	Qualifications, Curriculum and Assessment Authority for Wales/CYMRU
AI	Artificial Intelligence
AL	Action Learning
APEL	Accreditation of Prior Experiential Learning
APL	Accreditation of Prior Learning
BIM	British Institute of Management
BTEC	Business and Technology Education Council (formerly Business and Technician Education Council) (now retitled EDEXCEL)
CATS	Credit Accumulation and Transfer Scheme
CBI	Confederation of British Industry
CBT	Computer Based Training
CD	Continuous Development
CG	City and Guilds
CIPD	Chartered Institute of Personnel and Development
CPD	Continuing Professional Development
CRE	Commission for Racial Equality
DfEE	Department for Education and Employment (now replaced by DfES q.v.)
DfES	Department for Education and Skills
DVD	Digital Versatile Disc
DV-I	Digital Video-Interactive
EDEXCEL	Current title of the Business and Technology Education Council (abbreviation for 'educational excellence' – used since 1997)
ENTO	Employment National Training Organisation
EU	European Union (superseded the European Community 1993)
FA	Functional Analysis
FE	Further Education
FEFC	Further Education Funding Council (now subsumed into LSC q.v.)
GCSE	General Certificate of Secondary Education
GNVQ	General National Vocational Qualification
HE	Higher Education
HRD	Human Resource Development
HRM	Human Resource Management
ICT	Information and Communications Technology
IES	Institute of Employment Studies (formerly Institute of Manpower Studies – IMS)

IiP	Investors in People
ILTHE	Institute of Learning and Teaching in Higher Education
IPD	Institute of Personnel and Development
IPM	Institute of Personnel Management
IT	Information Technology
ITB	Industrial Training Board
ITD	Institute of Training and Development
ITOL	Institute of Training and Occupational Learning (now incorporated into CIPD q.v.)
KC	Knowledge Creation
KM	Knowledge Management
LEC	Local Enterprise Company (Scotland)
LEN	Local Employer Network
LO	Learning Organisation
LSC	Learning and Skills Council
MA	Modern Apprenticeships
MBA	Master of Business Administration
MCG	Management Charter Group
MCI	Management Charter Initiative
MSA	Manual Skills Analysis
MSC	Manpower Services Commission (no longer in existence)
NACETT	National Advisory Council for Education and Training Targets
NCVQ	National Council for Vocational Qualifications (now replaced by QCA)
NGL	National Grid for Learning
NIACE	National Institute for Adult and Continuing Education
NLP	Neuro-Linguistic Programming
NRA	National Record of Achievement (now replaced by Progress File)
NT	National Traineeships
NTA	National Training Awards
NTO	National Training Organisation (replaced by SSC)
NTT	National Training Targets
NVQ	National Vocational Qualification
OC	Open College
OMD	Outdoor Management Development
OU	Open University
PMS	Performance Management System
QCA	Qualifications and Curriculum Authority
ROI	Return on Investment
RSA	Royal Society for the Encouragement of Arts, Manufacturers and Commerce
SQA	Scottish Qualifications Authority
SSC	Sector Skills Council

SSDA	Sector Skills Development Agency
ST	Socio-Technical
SVQ	Scottish Vocational Qualification
TEC	Training and Enterprise Council (replaced by LSC)
TQM	Total Quality Management
TUC	Trades Union Congress
TWI	Training Within Industry
Ufl	University for Industry
VR	Virtual Reality
YC	Youth Credits
YOP	Youth Opportunities Programme (now YT)
YT	Youth Training (National Traineeship – NT – replaced YT in 1997)
YTS	Youth Training Scheme (replaced first by YT, and more recently by NT)

A 'quick guide' to national and European training schemes, institutions, programmes and initiatives

Accreditation of prior experiential learning (APEL)

A national methodology by which, in some circumstances, educational institutions may accept evidence of learning through work experience, normally in the form of a portfolio of documents and relevant written assignments, to enable students to claim exemption credits from national and university awards.

Accreditation of prior learning (APL)

A national methodology which in some circumstances enables students to claim exemption from examinations or exemption credits from college/university awards on the basis of evidence of successful completion of a different but relevant and similarly rated formal programme. This avoids a situation where students have to cover the same ground twice.

Awarding bodies

Independent bodies who design course curricula and administer examinations leading to recognised qualifications. Were jointly responsible with national training organisations (NTOs, which are being replaced by Sector Skills Councils, or SSCs q.v.) for the design of national vocational qualifications (NVQs q.v.), and individually for the implementation of specific NVQs. Issue qualification certificates to successful examination candidates.

CEDEFOP

EC-established (but independent) training agency with UK wing at the CIPD. Source of reliable information on all aspects of vocational training in Europe.

Chartered Institute of Personnel and Development (CIPD)

The CIPD came into existence on 1 July 2000, having formerly been the IPD (Institute of Personnel and Development), itself formed in 1994 from the Institute of Personnel Management (IPM) and the Institute of Training and Development (ITD). Substantial membership (ca 100,000), more than half being trainers. Professional qualification scheme incorporates Certificate in Training Practice plus a variety of standalone Employee Development modules.

City and Guilds (CG)

An independent examining body which for over 100 years has set nationally recognised standards for operatives, craftspersons and technicians through its wide range of certificates. Individual subject exams are usually classified into three performance levels. Many CG awards are now also approved as National Vocational Qualifications (NVQs) q.v.

Compacts

Partnerships between specific employing organisations and specific educational institutions, offering to students training opportunities, to educationists updating in changing techniques and processes, and to employers a flow of potential recruits. A key service is the provision of Work Experience for students and staff alike.

'Connexions'
A one-stop service for young people in England and Wales that has replaced the specific Careers Service, and which advises on education and training choices, health, housing, personal relationships and sport. It aims to help young people make an effective transition into the adult world.

Continuing Professional Development (CPD)
An unco-ordinated series of initiatives designed to promote the ongoing development of professional people. Most initiatives emphasise formalised learning.

Continuous Development (CD)
An approach to learning, pioneered by the former Institute of Personnel Management (now CIPD), which emphasises self-development and the integration of learning with work.

Department for Education and Skills (DfES)
Government department responsible for all aspects of education and skills development in the UK. The current Secretary of State (2004) is Charles Clarke. Replaced the previous Department of Education and Employment (DfEE).

Duke of Edinburgh's Award Scheme
To achieve these awards, young people must successfully participate in some type of service to the community, develop practical and social skills relevant to their own particular interests and participate in some form of organised physical recreational activity.

EDEXCEL
Major UK awarding and examining body, based in London. Formed from the amalgamation of two earlier bodies – the Business and Technology Education Council (BTEC) – a leading provider of vocational qualifications – and London Examinations – one of the main GCSE and GCE q.v. examining boards. The name 'Edexcel' stands for 'educational excellence'. Closely associated with the University of London. Continues to use the term 'BTEC' for its professional development certificate/diploma, higher national certificate/diploma, national certificate/diploma, first certificate/diploma, and key skills awards; also offers Foundation, Intermediate and Advanced GNVQs q.v., and NVQs q.v. at Levels 1 to 4.

Education and Business Partnerships
EBPs are set up across the UK to co-ordinate education and business links and strengthen liaison between educational institutions and the world of work. They do not conform to one model but have developed their own structures, financial arrangements and specific activities in line with local needs. There is a national EPB with representatives from local partnerships, which provides support and a national voice for the network.

Employment National Training Organisation (Employment NTO)
Formed from the amalgamation of three previous lead bodies – the Training and Development Lead Body (TDLB), the Personnel Standards Lead Body (PSLB) and the Trades Union Sector Development Body (TUSDB). Now (2004) being replaced by Sector Skills Development Agency and its network of Sector Skills Councils (q.v.).

Further Education Funding Council (FEFC)
Created by the Further and Higher Education Act of 1992, the FEFC was set up to 'ensure that all reasonable needs for further education in England are met'. Now subsumed into the Learning and Skills Council (q.v.).

General Certificate of Education (GCE)

General Certificate of Secondary Education (GCSE)
UK's single system of examining at 16+, introduced in 1986/8, and designed to cater for all abilities. Emphasis is on using knowledge and skills, not just memory. The exam is taken on a 'subject by subject' basis: grades are awarded against performance in each, grades A to G being considered 'Pass' grades, with work below grade G remaining unclassified.

General National Vocational Qualifications (GNVQs)
Qualifications approved by QCA, available to full-time students in schools and FE colleges. GNVQs are 'broader-based' than NVQs, and are grouped under 14 occupational headings.

Institute of Learning and Teaching in Higher Education (ILTHE)
Organisation set up in 2000 to set and develop standards of excellence in teaching in HE. Accredits training for new lecturers. Currently (2004) merging with other bodies including Learning and Teaching Support Network (LTSN) to form new Academy of Higher Education.

Institute of Training and Occupational Learning
Organisation set up in 2000 to represent HRD practitioners and trainers. Aims to raise the profile of HRD and training in organisations and to maintain and develop standards. Produces *British Journal of Occupational Learning*.

The Internet and Intranets
The 'Internet' is a worldwide network of sites offering computerised information accessible to computer users who are themselves linked into it telephonically and electronically via computer hardware and an external server's software. Each site has its own Internet address; 'home pages' (each of which may be many pages long, and lead to a vast range of subsidiary sites or pages) ensure that information is automatically available to anyone who makes contact. Messages can be sent to and from sites, thus allowing 'forum dialoguing' as well as simple information retrieval. 'Intranets' are networks that group together a number of Internet sites usually, but not necessarily, within a given organisation, managing the flow (and availability) of information to the various users.

Investors in People (IiP)
An initiative aimed at increasing employers' commitment to training 'activities and attitudes' throughout the UK.

'LearnDirect'
Free telephone helpline (managed as part of the UK government's University for Industry (UfI, q.v.) arrangements) offering nationwide information and confidential advice to adults and employers on courses and qualifications available.

Learning and Skills Council/Councils(Local Enterprise Councils in Scotland)
Replaced TECS in England in 2000. Responsible for funding and planning education and

training for over-16 year olds in England. Local Enterprise Companies in Scotland provide a similar function.

Leonardo
Major, multi-stranded EU vocational training action programme, offering both a policy framework and operational support, including funds, for projects and exchanges under three headings: Vocational Training Systems (including the development of common training modules, the promotion of continuous learning, trainer training, the networking of guidance centres, and measures to help the unqualified become qualified); Vocational Training Measures; and Language Training. Leonardo subsumes and builds on earlier EU programmes named Petra, Force, Comett and Eurotecnet, together with part of the Lingua programme and the Iris initiative. These are the types of measures supported:

- pilot projects to design new training approaches, content and materials
- placement and exchange programmes
- analyses and surveys examining training problems
- networks and dissemination projects
- open and distance learning.

A call for proposals is made annually. Funding does not fully match costs; approval demands a transnational element, which in practice means operational arrangements with one or more organisations in at least one other EU state; research-type activities must also provide for dissemination of results.

Management Charter Group (MCG)
An independent network of UK employers who put their names to a new charter promoting management education and training, and a linked 'management charter initiative' (MCI q.v.).

Management Charter Initiative (MCI)
A UK initiative in which employers combine to promote higher standards of management practice by sharing resources, exchanging information, devising new management qualifications and observing a Code of Practice. MCI have issued lists of management competences, which they recommend as the bases for future management qualifications. MCI-defined competences are accepted by NCVQ (q.v.) as meeting their criteria for national standards as defined within NVQs.

Modern Apprenticeships
Initiative launched 1994 with target of 150,000 'apprenticed' young people following new-style programmes (developed by National Training Organisations (NTOs) q.v.). A key element in each programme is training and education to NVQ/SVQ Level 3. Learning and Skills Councils (TECs) q.v. co-ordinate arrangements involving employer commitment to 'start-to-finish' training, and similar pledges from the trainees.

National Council for Vocational Qualifications (NCVQ) and Scottish Vocational Education Council (SCOTVEC)
See Qualifications and Curriculum Authority (QCA).

National Curriculum

Prescribed parts of UK's secondary education curriculum – introduced via the 1989 Education Reform Act and implemented via a timetable over the following six years. The prescription comprises 'Core Subjects' – Science, Mathematics and English – and 'Other Foundation Subjects' – Design and Technology, Information Technology, a Modern Foreign Language, and Physical Education.

National Grid for Learning

A UK government initiative launched in January 1998 to harness technology to raise educational standards, and to provide up-to-date teaching and learning materials for teachers of all kinds and at all levels. Provides excellent range of web links.

National Learning Targets (NLTs)

Targets originally devised and launched in 1990 by the Confederation of British Industry as 'World Class Targets' for the UK; adopted and renamed by government as 'national' targets in 1991. Monitored, reviewed and revised by a National Advisory Council (NACETT wound up in 2001 to become part of LSC). Specific goals relate to NVQ/SVQ attainments by young people and employees generally, and the attainment of 'Investors in People' (IiP) status by employers.

National Record of Achievement (NRA)

A sequential portfolio system of collecting and collating qualifications and reports on vocational studies and training. Replaced by a dedicated 'Progress File'.

National Traineeships

Introduced in September 1997, national traineeships are the UK government's attempt to offer 'a job with training' to young people who are not able to match the requirements of Modern Apprenticeships (q.v.). Replacing earlier youth training programmes, they focus on a combination of workplace skills training and the educational achievement of Level 2 NVQs. Structured 'frameworks' and standards have been devised by a large number of National Training Organisations and Sector Skills Councils; it is usually possible for a successful trainee to proceed to a Modern Apprenticeship.

National Training Awards

A national awards scheme, giving public recognition to organisations and training providers who claim to have demonstrated 'excellence in the training field'. Award-winners are selected from an annual batch of entrants.

National Training Organisations (NTOs)

Network of UK industry-wide or occupation-wide bodies (often technically 'employer-owned', but since 1998 funded from the Treasury) recognised by government as the strategic bodies responsible for defining the needs of their respective industries or groups, and ensuring that these needs are addressed. Replaced by Sector Skills Councils (q.v.).

National Vocational Qualifications (NVQ)

A term used to describe any qualification that has been approved by the National Council for Vocational Qualifications (NCVQ). Over 600 subject headings exist, most fronting qualifications at more than one level, and overall applying to well over 500 occupations. Over 4 million NVQ awards had been made by summer 2003. Qualifications are initially awarded by independent organisations (eg CG, BTEC), but the 'NVQ' kitemark appears alongside that of the awarding body. NVQs are arranged in a hierarchy of five levels, from 1 (the most basic) to 5 (management and professional level). 'General' NVQs (GNVQs) are available for those young people still in full-time education. The Scottish Vocational Qualification (SVQ) is the Scottish equivalent of NVQs.

New Deal
UK government initiative aimed at helping specific groups of people who have been unemployed for over six months to find work and improve their prospects of employment. Consists of (a) 'Gateway' provision (help with job searches, careers advice) and preparation for (b) a range of four education, training, and/or work options together with (c) a follow-through strategy. Delivery is Department of Work and Pensions' responsibility, achieved via local partnerships of LSCs, employers, local authorities and voluntary associations.

Open College (OC)
A 'distance-learning' organisation, established 1987 on lines similar to those of the Open University (OU) q.v. – but primarily addressing vocational skills training needs.

Open University (OU)
A 'distance-learning' organisation, offering degree-level and other courses on a national basis through flexible learning methods including online delivery. Apart from receiving learning material by post, internet and email, students study by watching prepared TV or computer programmes, completing planned assignments and attending residential workshops.

Qualifications and Curriculum Authority (QCA)
Established in 1997, the QCA brings together the work of the earlier National Council for Vocational Qualifications (NCVQ) with that of the Schools Curriculum and Assessment Authority (SCAA). London based. Keeps under permanent review all aspects of the UK's statutory and nonstatutory curricula, including the National Curriculum. Accredits proposals for National Vocational Qualifications (NVQs q.v.) developed by National Training Organisations (NTOs) and awarded by awarding bodies q.v. QCA also itself develops and accredits GNVQs. q.v.

Sandwich training
Arrangements whereby degree and diploma students from UK universities and polytechnics spend periods of time working in industry or commerce (eg in a laboratory or a marketing department) – essentially as part of their course. Sandwich students usually receive special rates of pay and are given 'real' jobs of work.

Scottish Vocational Education Council (SCOTVEC)
See National Council of Vocational Qualifications (NCVQ) and Scottish Vocational Education Council (SCOTVEC).
The Scottish equivalent of National Vocational Qualifications (NVQs) q.v.

Sector Skills Councils/Sector Skills Development Agency
SSCs are a network of employers, trade unions and professional bodies set up to lead skills and productivity drive. SSDA was established to underpin the network and promote effective intersector working. Replaced NTOs – in 2004 the changeover is still in progress.

Socrates
Major, multi-stranded EU programme for transnational co-operation in the field of education,

covering learners of all ages, types and social groups. Sister programme to Leonardo, with which it shares responsibility for language training. Encourages open and distance learning.

Teaching Companies
An arrangement whereby an employing organisation and a college join together on a project (at the instigation of the former). The college provides a tutor/supervisor and associates to work on the project. The associates may be registered with the college for a research degree, but are paid by the employing organisation.

Training and Enterprise Councils (TECs) and (Scotland) Local Enterprise Companies (LECs)
See Learning and Skills Councils.

University for Industry
A UK government initiative, which aims to create a 'national learning network'. Six core functions are stressed: marketing to stimulate mass demand for lifelong learning, in-depth guidance services, brokerage (connecting people with learning programmes), commissioning new materials, 'kitemarking' (to assure users of quality), and market analysis + strategy. This is currently the main national initiative supporting the EU's campaign to promote lifelong learning for all.

Work Experience
Arrangements made between employers and educational institutions whereby students spend periods of time within industry and commerce experiencing the world of work. Schemes vary, sometimes involving projects and group work; some schemes are integral with courses such as TVEI or Business Studies GCSE. q.v. Wages are not normally paid.

Work and Pensions (Department of)
Government department responsible for social security benefits and initiatives designed to help unemployed people back into work, such as New Deal. q.v.

Work Shadowing
An arrangement whereby a trainee gains an insight into a job by 'shadowing' the incumbent as he or goes about his or herwork.

Youth Training (YT)
Government-led programmes for young people – discontinued in 1997. Replaced by Modern Apprenticeships (q.v.) and National Traineeships (q.v.) together with New Deal (q.v.).

A 'quick guide' to training methods and techniques

METHOD: WHAT IT IS	WHAT IT CAN ACHIEVE	POINTS TO WATCH
BLENDED LEARNING (BL) A relatively recent concept, although the principle has a long history. There are consequently a number of different definitions, although all stress that it has its origins in online learning methods. It is essentially a method of distance learning that uses technological tools such as e-mail, the Internet, intranets, teleconferencing and so on, together with traditional (usually 'stand-up') education or training.	The key advantage claimed by enthusiasts for BL is that it focuses on the learner's best style. There are as many opportunities as possible given to allow the learner to absorb the content. It's also convenient and, if done properly, is user friendly.	As for all online methods, there is a need for expertise by the learning facilitator to make the most of a number of different methods. Technology needs to be reliable and not all programmes will be suitable for online delivery. Also, the trainer/learning facilitator will require specific new online skills to be effective, including understanding of all learners' skills in the different methods. As with any learning method, good evaluation of the process is necessary.
LECTURE Structured, planned talk. Usually accompanied by visual aids, eg slides, OHP foils, flipchart.	Suitable for large audiences where participation is not wanted. Content and timing can be planned in detail.	Lively style needed. Communication of material may be limited if no provision for feedback to lecturer.
FILMS/VIDEOTAPES 'Visual lectures' – but often presented in dramatised form.	As 'Lectures' – but addition of moving images and drama can significantly aid motivation. Useful as precursor to discussion; can be 'stopped' at key points for discussion.	Tailor-made products are expensive. Care needed to ensure material (not just title) is relevant.
CASE-STUDY Examination of events or situation – often real life – usually aimed at learning by analysing the detailed material or defining, and posing solutions for, problems.	Opportunities exist for both exchange of views on 'what matters' and problem-solving. Especially useful for analysis of financial/statistical data. Can incorporate exercises.	Simple cases may give wrong impression of reality. Difficult to reproduce the 'political climate'.

METHOD: WHAT IT IS	WHAT IT CAN ACHIEVE	POINTS TO WATCH
PROMPT LIST List of 'questions to which a person should have answers'.	Useful basis for self-study or discussion in cases where opinions are important but no clear 'correct' answer exists.	Can highlight inter-personal differences in terms of values – and hence stimulate conflict.
DISCUSSION Free exchange of information, opinions, etc. A 'controlled' discussion may follow a planned path, the leader controlling the agenda; an 'open' discussion may mirror members' priorities.	Especially suitable for development or adjustment of attitudes and opinions. Promotes group cohesion. Also offers feedback to trainer on learning achievement.	May be time-consuming – especially if discussion wanders or 'process problems' emerge. Attitudes may harden rather than adjust. Individual participation may be affected by group composition.
DIALOGUE 'Collective reflection' – two way discussion (or group – often with 'facilitator'). Participants suspend assumptions and work as colleagues.	Shared mental models, and shared understanding of problems/situations; team coherence and discipline.	Facilitator must be skilled; careful line is needed between comment/help and 'expert/intrusion' roles.
INSTRUCTION Formula-based 'teaching' session: 1 Tell – how to do 2 Show – how to do 3 Do (supervised practice) 4 Review process and results.	For introducing skills, usually in line with a planned breakdown of small sequential practice stages. Confidence is built by mastery and link-up of stages. Typically must follow input of knowledge, the skills to be learned being those of application.	Skill may be best addressed as a whole rather than in parts – but lengthy stages 1 and 2 yield memory problems. Design/balance of session important.
LANGUAGE LABORATORY Individual booths equipped with audio programmes and linked to a central tutor.	Allows learner-paced language tuition and practice without 'speaking in public'. Machine management seems to promote motivation.	Good for early stage but cannot replace eventual need to practise in public.
DISCOVERY LEARNING 'Learning without a teacher' – but usually in a controlled (ie pre-designed) set-up, and under supervision.	Offers challenge and builds confidence as learner masters new skills. Best suited to tasks involving dismantling, checking, adjusting, rebuilding. Helps understanding of principles.	Considerable design work needed. Safety paramount – may need special adjustments, and so be unrealistic.

METHOD: WHAT IT IS	WHAT IT CAN ACHIEVE	POINTS TO WATCH
EXERCISE Carrying out a particular task along prescribed lines. Often a test of knowledge communicated earlier.	Highly active form of learning; satisfies need for practice to apply knowledge or develop skill. Often linked with test to judge extent of learning.	Exercise must be realistic, objectives attainable.
PROJECT 'Large-scale exercise', but leaving most of the process within learner discretion. Frequently involves collecting and reporting data, then offering conclusions and recommendations for improvement.	Like exercises, offers practice and simultaneously 'tests'. Stimulates analysis + creativity; also reporting skill.	Like exercises, needs realism and attainability. If 'real life', must have support of those responsible for reality. Ideally will be 'actioned'.
ROLE-PLAY Enactment of role(s) in protected training environment.	Mainly used to practise face-to-face skills (eg selling) combined with review critiques from trainers and/or other learners.	Unless disciplined, can cause embarrassment. Realism of set-up important.
ROLE-REVERSAL Enactment of reversed roles by two or more learners in simulated situation.	Mainly used to help those who operate in face-to-face situations to appreciate their contacts' needs and feelings.	As with role-play, needs discipline and realism.
SIMULATIONS/BUSINESS GAMES Dynamic exercises or case-studies – usually involving 'coming to terms with' a situation, then managing it via a set of imposed decisions. Computerised models offer complex data, and often decisions that interact.	Offers practice in management – observation, analysis, judgement, decision-making, etc. Interactive element generates enthusiasm, notably when teams are in simulated competition. Can be linked with team development.	Model can be challenged as unrealistic.
STUDY GROUPS Task-briefed groups which also practise process review, aided by a process consultant, who does *not* operate outside this role.	Offers appreciation of need for both task and process management; also group learning processes.	Some learners dislike lack of structure. May generate stress.

METHOD: WHAT IT IS	WHAT IT CAN ACHIEVE	POINTS TO WATCH
OUTDOOR TRAINING/OUTDOOR MANAGEMENT DEVELOPMENT Dynamic open-air exercises, usually carried out in teams.	Offers practice in management, in challenging or problematic circumstances; also leadership and teamwork opportunities, as well as self-analysis.	Physical challenge can be tough. Some learners may not accept relevance of unusual environment.
VIDEO-CONFERENCING AND TELE-CONFERENCING Two-way audio and two-way visual link-up (see Hogan 1993).	Participative training sessions: trainers in different locations. Can interact with each other and with a tutor.	Special training needed for tutor. Careful preplanning essential.
ELECTRONIC BRAINSTORMING Participants sit in a laboratory at individual PCs connected through a local area network. One computer acts as a file server (see El-Sherif and Tang, 1994).	By using special packages eg Meeting Ware, each participant can contribute anonymously by computer to a brainstorming session. The results are analysed by computer.	Careful preparation needed. Experienced team guide required.
SELF-MANAGED LEARNING: READING Learner-paced coverage of printed material, with or without basic learning plan.	Knowledge retention can be good if learner motivation is high. Learning packages are often augmented by audio- and/or videotapes.	Motivation often declines if reading is difficult/'dull'. Tutorial help can be important.
RADIO + TV BROADCASTS	Large potential audiences permit costly programmes. Often linked with national (eg Open University) courses and qualifications. Satellite TV is likely to offer new and wider subjects. Can be linked with tutorial assistance by phone.	Viewing times often unsocial.

METHOD: WHAT IT IS	WHAT IT CAN ACHIEVE	POINTS TO WATCH
SELF-MANAGED LEARNING: TECHNOLOGY-ASSISTED Learner-managed coverage of programmed material, usually involving keyboard and screen.	Many varied uses. Computer-based training (CBT) can offer workplace simulations and link with videotape to provide still or moving pictures. Compact Disks offer huge information storage, with visual additions. Moves to introduce artificial intelligence (AI) yield prospect of using machine as a tutor and managing one's own learning process.	Hardware may be expensive. Present state of technology makes logic-based programs most reliable.
Computer-based Training (CBT) (Learner uses keyboard in line with screen instructions, calling forth information and responding to questions.)	Screen material can be complex and include animation. Good for presenting statistics. With addition of 'artificial intelligence' (CBT – AI) learner responds to computer question, computer interprets response and adjusts own program.	Compatible hardware and software needed; perhaps also tutorial help.
The Internet, and intranets Worldwide computerised information network, and grouped user sites.	Allows worldwide information gathering, including planned programmes of learning, plus worldwide forums. Useful data source for projects of all kinds. Intranets offer flows of information to specific workplace sites. Some organisations are developing intranet systems in which members continuously input data for central storage which all can access as needed.	Need for discipline in 'surfing' the Net and coping with vast amounts of available material. Security systems may be required to manage 'classified' intranet data.

METHOD: WHAT IT IS	WHAT IT CAN ACHIEVE	POINTS TO WATCH
Compact Disc Training (CDT) and Video Disc Training (VDT) (Used in conjunction with TV or personal computers)	Compact Disc and Digital Versatile Disc 'Read-Only Memory' (CD-ROM and DVD-ROM) offer high-capacity data-storage facilities. Retrieval can include text, pictures and sound.	Special hardware needed. Limited to retrieval of stored data.
	CD and DVD 'Read-Only Memory – Extended Architecture' (CD-ROM-XA and DVD-ROM-XA) allow learners to 'play with material', practising analysis and synthesis. (DVD allows complex simulations.) Particularly suitable for assembling, dismantling, diagnosis and decision-making.	Learner needs some basic awareness of data in order to manipulate it.
	CD 'Interactive' (CD-I) is similar to CBT-AI (see page 352) in allowing learner much greater control of the learning process, the programme adjusting to learner questions and responses.	May not reproduce realistic workplace language; hence tutor may also be needed.
	'Digital Video' Interactive (DV-I) offers CD-I together with the facility to videotape the learner's own actions, and replay the results. Ideal where the learner must perfect a *physical* movement (eg golf swing, or sign language), and needs to see the result.	Hardware and software are likely to be costly.

NB: VDT are increasingly available as CBT, CDT and 'multi-media programs', which can offer both information and practice in using the information to specific ends eg problem-solving. Program-making equipment, though expensive, can now also be purchased. The DVD's superior data-compression is likely to make it a standard learner-centred aid of the future, employing new style disc-playing equipment linked to the PC.

METHOD: WHAT IT IS	WHAT IT CAN ACHIEVE	POINTS TO WATCH
Virtual Reality (VR) A method of constructing, visualising and interacting with computer-generated three-dimensional worlds. It differs from conventional playback technology, which depends upon previously recorded images. A VR system must rapidly recalculate a fresh image in response to the participant's every move. To appear realistic each new image must be recalculated in under 100 milliseconds.	By using specialist equipment or by viewing the virtual model on the computer screen, users move through the simulated world and interact with it. In use worldwide by Motorola for teaching employees how to run assembly lines. Also in use by British Nuclear Fuels in the design of a control room, the model then to be kept for training purposes.	Currently very expensive to create. Only to be used with large numbers or for reasons of health and safety. A Virtual Reality Simulation Project launched in the UK in 1993 now has 14 members, including British Nuclear Fuels.

Bibliography

ADAIR J. *Training for Leadership*. Gower, Farnborough, 1978.

ALLEN C. 'Best Value – a job for high fliers or high achievers'. M J *Best Value News*, 28 February 2000.

ALLINSON C.W. and HAYES J. 'The Learning Styles Questionnaire: an alternative to Kolb's'. *Inventory Journal of Management Studies*, 25, 3 May 1998.

ALLINSON C.W. and HAYES J. 'Validity of the Learning Styles Questionnaire.' *Psychological Reports.* 1990 67 859–866.

ANNETT J. in *Psychology at Work*. Warr P. (ed.), Penguin Education, Harmondsworth, 1974.

ARGYRIS C. *Personality and Organisation*. Harper and Row, New York, 1957.

ARGYRIS C. 'Double loop learning in organisations'. *Harvard Business Review,* Sept./Oct. 1977. Pages 115–125.

ARGYRIS C. *Reasoning, Learning and Action: Individual and organisational.* Jossey-Bass, San Francisco, 1982.

AGRGYRIS C. *Overcoming Organizational Defenses.* Prentice-Hall, New York, 1990.

ARGYRIS C. and SCHON D. *Organisational Learning: A theory of action perspective.* Addison Wesley, New York, 1978.

ARGYRIS C. and SCHON D.A. *Organisational Learning II: Theory, method and practice.* Addison Wesley, Wokingham, 1996.

ARMSTRONG M. *A Handbook of Human Resource Management*. Kogan Page, London, 2003.

ARMSTRONG A. and BARON A. *Performance Management*. CIPD, London 1998

ATKINSON R.L., ATKINSON R.C., SMITH E., BENN D. and NOLEN-HOEKSEMA S. *Hilgard's Introduction to Psychology*. Thomson Learning, Stamford, CT, 1999.

BAILEY D. 'Training to reduce retail shrinkage'. *Training and Management Development Methods*, Vol. 5, 1991.

BANDLER R. and GRINDER J. *The Structure of Magic: Parts 1 and 2*. Science and Behaviour Books, California, 1976.

BANDLER R., GRINDER J., DILTS R. and DELOZIER J. *Neuro-Linguistic Programming*, Vol. 1: *The Study of the Structure of Subject Experience*. Meta Publications, California, 1980.

BARNETT S. and RICHERT A. 'Trustworthy'. *People Management*, 28 May 1998. Pages 46–57.

BARON B. in *Managing Human Resources*. Cowling A.G. and Mailer C.J.B. (eds) Edward Arnold, London, 1981.

BARRINGTON H. *Learning about Management*. McGraw-Hill, London, 1984.

BARRINGTON H. 'The prompt list'. *Training and Management Development Methods,* Vol. 12, 1998.

BASS B.M. *Bass and Stodgill's Handbook of Leadership*. 3rd edn. Free Press, New York, 1985.

BASS B.M. and VAUGHAN J.A. *Training in Industry – The management of learning.* Tavistock Publications, London, 1966.

BELBIN E. and BELBIN R.M. *Problems in Adult Retraining.* Heinemann, London, 1972.

BELBIN R.M. *Employment of Older Workers.* No. 2, *Training Methods.* OECD, Paris, 1969.

BELENKY M.F. et al. *Women's Ways of Knowing: The development of self, voice and mind.* Basic Books, New York, 1997.

BENNISON M. and CARSON J. *The Manpower Planning Handbook.* McGraw-Hill, Maidenhead, 1984.

BEVAN S. and THOMPSON M. 'Performance management at the crossroads'. *Personnel Management,* November 1991.

BION W.R. *Experiences in Groups.* Tavistock, London, 1961.

BOHM D. *Unfolding Meaning.* Foundation House, Loveland, California, 1985.

BOYATZIS R. *The Competent Manager.* John Wiley, Chichester, 1982.

BOYDELL T.H. *A Guide to Job Analysis.* British Association for Commercial and Industrial Education, London, 1977.

BOYDELL T.H. and LEARY M. *Identifying Training Needs.* IPD, London, 1996.

BOYDELL T.H. and PEDLER M. (eds) *Management Self Development.* Gower, Aldershot, 1981.

BRAMHAM J. *Human Resource Planning.* CIPD, London, 1994.

BRAMLEY P. *Evaluating Training.* IPD, London, 1996.

BROMLEY D.B. *The Psychology of Human Ageing.* Pelican, Harmondsworth, 1975.

BROMLEY D.B. *Behavioural Gerontology: Central issues in the psychology of ageing.* Wiley, Chichester, 1990.

BROOKES J. *Training and Development Competence: A practical guide.* Kogan Page, London, 1995.

BROWN J.A.C. *The Social Psychology of Industry.* Pelican, London, 1954.

BURGOYNE J. 'Feeding minds to grow the business'. *People Management,* 21 September 1995.

BURGOYNE J., PEDLER M. and BOYDELL T. *The Learning Company – A strategy for sustainable development.* McGraw-Hill, Maidenhead, 1991.

BURKE J. *Outcomes, Learning and the Curriculum.* Taylor and Francis, Basingstoke, 1995.

BURNS T. *Leadership.* Harper and Row, New York, 1978.

BURNS T. and STALKER G.M. *The Management of Innovation.* Tavistock, London, 1961.

BUS AND COACH TRAINING LIMITED. *Vehicle Engineering Competence Assessment Scheme.* Bus & Coach Training Ltd, Rickmansworth, 1990.

CABLE & WIRELESS. *Annual Review.* 1998.

CAMPBELL C.P. 'A primer on determining the cost effectiveness of training, Part 1'. *Industrial and Commercial Training,* Vol. 26, No. 11, 1994. Pages 32–38.

CAMPBELL C.P. 'A primer on determining the cost effectiveness of training, Part 2'. *Industrial and Commercial Training,* Vol. 27, No. 1, 1995. Pages 17–25.

CANNELL M. 'Practice makes perfect'. *People Management*, Vol. 3, No. 5, March 1997. Pages 26–30, 33.

CARLING W. and HELLER R. *The Way to Win: Strategies for success in business and sport.* Little, Brown and Co., London, 1995.

CARRINGTON L. 'Apprenticeship Schemes Can Work'. *Training Magazine.* Oct 2002.

CASSELLS J. 'Education and training must be geared to match the demand for more skills in British industry today'. *The Times*, 18 June 1985.

CHAPPLE F. 'A report on the Electrical, Electronic, Telecommunication and Plumbing Union's retraining programme'. *The Times*, 13 March 1984.

CHARTERED INSTITUTE OF PERSONNEL AND DEVELOPMENT. *The Changing Role of the Trainer.* CIPD, London, 1999.

CHARTERED INSTITUTE OF PERSONNEL AND DEVELOPMENT. *The CIPD Code of Professional Conduct and Disciplinary Procedures.* CIPD, London, 2000.

CHILD J. *Organisation: A guide to problems and practice.* Harper and Row, London, 1982.

CLUTTERBUCK D. *Everyone Needs a Mentor.* IPM, London, 1991.

COCKERILL T. 'The kind of competence for rapid change'. *Personnel Management,* Sept. 1989.

COLLARD R. *Total Quality: Success through people.* IPM, London, 1989.

CONFEDERATION OF BRITISH INDUSTRY. *World Class Targets.* CBI, London, 1991.

COSH A.D., DUNCAN J. and HUGHES A. 'Investments in training and small firm growth and survival?' GB Department for Education and Employment Research Briefs. Report 36 (DfEE 1998).

COULSON-THOMAS C. and COE T. *The Flat Organization.* BIM Foundation, Management House, Cottingham Road, Corby, Northants NN17 1TT, 1991. Also cited in *Skills and Enterprise Briefing,* Issue 3/92, Feb. 1992, Skills and Enterprise Network, PO Box 12, West PDO, Leen Gate, Lenton, Nottingham NG7 2GB.

CROSS M. *Towards the Flexible Craftsman.* The Technical Change Centre, London, 1985.

CULLEN W.D. 'Report into the Piper Alpha Disaster' *Scots Law Times* 1123 32/2000, 13 October 2000.

CUMING M. *A Manager's Guide to Quantitative Methods.* Elm Publications, Kings Repton, Cambridge, 1984.

DAVEY MACKENZIE D. and HARRIS M. *Judging People: a guide to Orthodox and Unorthodox Methods of Assessment.* McGraw-Hill, Maidenhead, 1982.

DEARING Sir R. *The National Curriculum and its Assessment.* School Curriculum and Assessment Authority Publications, Dec. 1993. Ref. D/F.

DEARING Sir R. *Review of National Curriculum: Report on the 1994 consultation.* School Curriculum and Assessment Authority Publications, 1994. Ref. COM/94/118.

DEARING Sir R. *Review of Qualifications for 16- to 19-year-olds.* School Curriculum and Assessment Authority Publications, PO Box 235, Hayes, Middlesex UB3 1HF, 1996.

DEARING Sir R. 'Committee of enquiry'. *Higher Education in the Learning Society*, July 1997.

DEPARTMENT FOR EDUCATION AND EMPLOYMENT (1). *The Learning Age: A renaissance for a new Britain* (Green Paper). Stationery Office, Cmnd 3790, London (Crown Copyright), 25 February 1998.

DEPARTMENT FOR EDUCATION AND EMPLOYMENT (2). *Investment in Training and the Growth and Survival of Small Firms: an empirical analysis for the UK.* Centre for Business Research, Cambridge, DfEE, Sudbury, Suffolk 1998

DEPARTMENT FOR EDUCATION AND EMPLOYMENT (3). *University for Industry: Engaging people in learning for life.* (Pathfinder Prospectus). DfEE, Sudbury (Crown Copyright), 1998.

DEPARTMENT FOR EDUCATION AND EMPLOYMENT (4). *New Start*, Issue 4. DfEE, Sudbury (Crown Copyright), 1998.

DEPARTMENT FOR EDUCATION AND EMPLOYMENT (5). *Modern Apprenticeships. Employer Case Studies.* Vol. 3, 1998.

DEPARTMENT FOR EDUCATION AND SKILLS (1) *Learning and Training at Work Survey 2002* (Crown Copyright) available online at www.dfes.gov.uk/rsgateway/DB/SFR/s000378/index.shtm/

DEPARTMENT FOR EDUCATION AND SKILLS (2) *The Future of Higher Education* (White Paper), 2003, (Crown Copyright). Available online at www.dfes.gov.uk/highereducation/hestrategy

DEPARTMENT OF TRADE AND INDUSTRY. *Competitiveness: helping businesses to win.* (White Paper) Stationery Office (Crown Copyright), 1994.

DILTS R.B., EPSTEIN T. and DILTS R.W. *Tools for Dreamers.* Meta Publications, California, 1991.

DIXON NANCY M. *Common Knowledge: How companies thrive by sharing what they know.* Harvard Business School Press, Boston, Mass., 2000.

DOBSON C.B., HARDY M. et al. *Understanding Psychology.* Weidenfeld and Nicolson, London, 1990.

DONNELLY E.L. *Training as a Specialist Function – An historical perspective.* Working Paper No. 9, Faculty of Business Studies & Management, Middlesex Polytechnic, London, 1984.

DONNELLY E.L. 'The need to market training', in *Gower Handbook of Training and Development.* Prior J. (ed.) Gower, Aldershot, 1991.

DORE R.P. and SAKO M. *How the Japanese Learn to Work* (Nissan Institute/Routledge Japanese Studies Series). Routledge, London, 1989.

DOWNS S. *Learning at Work: Effective strategies for making things happen.* Kogan Page, London, 1995.

DOWNS S. 'Designing training for competence'. *Competence and Assessment.* Issue 31, February 1996.

DRUCKER P.F. *The Practice of Management.* Harper and Row, New York, 1954.

DRUCKER P.F. *Managing for Results.* Heinemann, London, 1964.

DRUCKER P.F. 'On the profession of management'. *Harvard Business Review.* Boston, Mass., 1998.

DULEWICZ V. 'Assessment centres as the route to competence'. *Personnel Management,* Nov. 1989.

DUNCAN K.D. and KELLY C.J. *Task Analysis, Learning and the Nature of Transfer.* Manpower Services Commission, Sheffield, 1983.

EASTERBY-SMITH M. and MACKNESS J. 'Completing the cycle of evaluation'. *Personnel Management*, May 1992.

EASTERBY-SMITH M. and TANTON M. 'Turning course evaluation from an end to a means'. *Personnel Management*, April 1985.

EL-SHERIF H.H. and TANG V. 'Team focus electronic brain storming'. *Training and Management Development Methods*, Vol. 8, 1994.

ELMS A. 'Investors in People accreditation: One large organisation's journey to IiP status'. *Training and Management Development Methods*, Vol. 12, 1998. Pages 2.15–2.24.

EMERY F.E. (ed.) *Systems Thinking.* Penguin, London, 1981.

EMI Group. *Annual Report*, 1998.

ENTWHISTLE N. *Styles of Learning.* D Fulton, Edinburgh, 1998.

ESTES W.K. *Learning Theory and Mental Development.* Academic Press, New York, 1970.

ETZIONI A.A. *Comparative Analysis of Complex Organisations.* Free Press, Glencoe, Illinois, 1961.

EUROPEAN COMMISSION. *White Paper: Growth, Competitiveness, Employment: The challenges and ways forward into the 21st century.* European Commission, Brussels, 1993.

EUROPEAN COMMISSION. Leonardo Da Vinci Programme: Vademecum. EC, Directorate General XXII – Education, Training and Youth, Brussels, 1995. (a)

EUROPEAN COMMISSION. Socrates: Vademecum. EC, Directorate General XXII– Education, Training and Youth, Brussels, 1995. (b)

EUROPEAN COMMISSION. White Paper: Education and Training. European Commission, Brussels, 1995. (c)

EUROPEAN UNION, see EUROPEAN COMMISSION.

EUROPEAN UNION. 'Memorandum on lifelong learning', 2000. available online at http://europa.eu.int/scadphs/legle/cha/cll047.htm

FAIRBAIRNS J. 'Plugging the gap in training needs analysis'. *Personnel Management*, Feb. 1991.

FARNHAM D. 'Corporate policy and personnel management', in *Personnel Management Handbook.* Harper S. (ed.) Gower, Aldershot, 1987.

FAYOL H. *General and Industrial Administration.* Durod, Paris, 1915.

FEFC see Further Education Funding Council.

FESTINGER L. A. *Theory of Cognitive Dissonance.* Row Peterson, Evanston, Illinois, 1957.

FLEISHMAN E. A. and HEMPEL W. E. 'The relationship between abilities and improvement with practice in a visual discrimination task'. *Journal of Experimental Psychology*, 49, 1955.

FLEMING D. 'The concept of meta-competence'. *Competence and Assessment*, Issue 16. Employment Department Group, Sheffield, 1991.

FOWLER A. 'How to decide on training methods'. *People Management*, 21 December 1995. Pages 36–37.

FOWLER A. *Employee Induction: A good start.* IPD, London, 1996.

FOWLER A. 'Benchmarking'. *People Management*, 12 June 1997.

FOX M. *Original Blessings: a primer in creation spirituality*. Bear and Co., 1996.

FRANSELLA F. and BANNISTER D. *A Manual for Repertory Grid Technique*. Academic Press, London, 1977.

FRIEDMAN B., HATCH J. et al. *Delivering on the Promise: How to attract, manage and retain human capital*. Free Press, New York, 1998.

FURTHER EDUCATION FUNDING COUNCIL. *General National Vocational Qualifications in the Further Education Sector in England*. FEFC, London, 1995.

FURTHER EDUCATION FUNDING COUNCIL. *Post-16 Vocational Education and Training in France*. FEFC, Coventry, 1995.

FURTHER EDUCATION FUNDING COUNCIL. *Post-16 Vocational Education and Training in Germany*. FEFC, Coventry, 1995.

FURTHER EDUCATION FUNDING COUNCIL *Inclusive Learning* (The Tomlinson Report) FEFC, Coventry, 1996.

FURTHER EDUCATION FUNDING COUNCIL *Learning Works: Widening participation in further education* (The Kennedy Report). FEFC, Coventry, 1997.

FURTHER EDUCATION FUNDING COUNCIL. *Quality and Standards in Further Education, 1996–7*. FEFC, Coventry, 1997.

FURTHER EDUCATION STAFF COLLEGE. *A Guide to Work-based Learning Terms*. Training Agency. HMSO, London, 1989.

FURTHER EDUCATION UNIT *How Do I Learn?* 1981.

GABRIEL Y. *Organisations in Depth*. Sage Publications, London, 1999.

GABRIEL Y., FINEMAN S. and SIMS D. *Organising and Organisations*. 2nd edn. Sage Publications, London, 2000.

GARBUTT D. *Training Costs with Reference to the Industrial Training Act*. Gee and Company Limited, 1969.

GARDNER H. 'The theory of multiple intelligences'. *Annals of Dyslexia*, Vol. 37, 1987. Pages 19–35.

GARRATT B. *The Learning Organisation and the Need for Directors Who Think*. Gower, Aldershot, 1987.

GARRATT B. *Creating a Learning Organisation*. Director Books, Cambridge, 1990.

GARRATT B. *Learning to Lead*. HarperCollins, London, 1991.

GARRATT B. 'An old idea that has come of age'. *People Management*, 21 September 1995.

GARRATT B. *The Learning Organisation*. HarperCollins, London, 2000.

GIBB S. *Learning and Development: Processes, Practices and Perspectives*. Palgrave, London, 2002.

GIBBS R., GLENDENNING R. and McCARTHY J. 'Learning in the workplace through employee development: three perspectives'. *Training and Management Development Methods*, Vol. 9. 1995. Pages 1.1–1.25.

GLASER R. *Training Research and Education*. Wiley and Sons, New York, 1965.

GLEICKS J. *Isaac Newton*. Fourth Estate, London, 2003

GOLDSTEIN I.L. 'Training in work organisations', in *Annual Review of Psychology,* 31, 229–72, 1980.

GORE L. et al. 'Leading courageous managers on'. In A. Mumford (ed.) Gower Publishing, Aldershot, 1997.

GREGORY R.L. (ed.) *The Oxford Companion to the Mind*. Oxford University Press, Oxford, 1987. Pages 740–47.

GREENLEAF R.F. *Servant Leadership*. Paulist Press, New York, 1977.

GRIFFITHS P. and GOODGE P. 'Development centres: The third generation'. *Personnel Management*, June 1994. Pages 40–43.

GRONLUND N.E. *Stating Behavioural Objectives for Classroom Instruction*. Macmillan, London, 1978.

HACKETT P. *Training Practice*. CIPD, London, 2003.

HALE R. How Training Can Add Real Value to the Business. Available from ITOL members' site: http://www.itol.co.uk/cgi-local/dcforum/dcextracgi?az accessed 24/11/03.

HAMBLIN A.C. *Evaluation and Control of Training*. McGraw-Hill, Maidenhead, 1974.

HANDY C. *Understanding Organisations*. Penguin, London, 1985.

HANDY C. *The Making of Managers*. National Economic Development Office, London, 1987.

HANDY C. *The Age of Unreason*. Hutchinson, London, 1989.

HANDY C. *The Empty Raincoat*. Hutchinson, London, 1994.

HARDINGHAM A. *Designing Training*. IPD, London, 1996.

HARRISON R. *Employee Development*. 3rd edn. CIPD, London, 2002.

HAYES C., FONDA N., POPE N., STUART R. and TOWNSEND K. *Training for Skill Ownership*. Institute of Manpower Studies, Brighton, 1983.

HAYES C., et al. 'International competition and the role of competence'. *Personnel Management*, September 1984.

HAYES R.H., WHEELWRIGHT S.C. and CLARK K.B. *Dynamic Manufacturing: Creating the learning organisation*. Free Press, New York, 1988.

HERZBERG F. et al. *The Motivation to Work*. John Wiley, New York, 1959.

HEWSTONE et al. (eds) *Introduction to Social Psychology*. Blackwell, Oxford, 1990.

HIRSH W. and REILLY P. 'Cycling proficiency'. *People Management*, 9 July 1998. Pages 36–41.

HOFSTEDE G. *Culture's Consequences: international differences in work-related values*. Sage, Beverley Hills CA, 1980.

HOGAN C. 'How to get more out of videoconference meetings: a socio-technical approach: experience of CURTIN University of Technology'. *Training and Management Development Methods*, Vol. 7, 1993. Pages 5.01–5.32.

HOGARTH G. and BARTH M. *Why Employing the Over-50s Makes Good Business Sense*. Publications Department, Institute of Employment Research, University of Warwick, 1991.

HOLDEN L. and LIVIAN Y. 'Does strategic training policy exist? Some evidence from ten European countries'. *Personnel Review*, Vol. 21, Issue 1, 1992. Pages 12–23.

HONEY P. and MUMFORD A. *Using your Learning Styles*. (2nd edn), Peter Honey, Ardingly House, 10 Linden Avenue, Maidenhead, 1986.

HONEY P. and MUMFORD A. *The Manual of Learning Opportunities*. Peter Honey, Ardingly House, 10 Linden Avenue, Maidenhead, 1989.

HONEY P. and MUMFORD A. *Manual of Learning Styles*. (3rd edn), Honey, Maidenhead, 1992.

HONEY P. and MUMFORD A. The *Learning Styles Helper's Guide*. Peter Honey Publications, Maidenhead, 2000.

HONEY P., BURGOYNE J., CUNNINGHAM I. et al. 'The debate starts here'. *People Management*, 1 October 1998.

HORTON, W. and E. *E learning Tools and Techniques*. John Wiley, New York, 2003.

HUMBLE J. *Management by Objectives*. Industrial Educational and Research Foundation, London, 1967.

INCOMES DATA SERVICES. *European Management Guide: Training and development*. IDS, London, 1992.

INCOMES DATA SERVICES. *Leadership Development*. London, July 2003.

INHELDER B. and PIAGET J. *The Psychology of the Child*. Basic Books, NY, 1969.

INSTITUTE OF PERSONNEL AND DEVELOPMENT. *Continuing Professional Development (Policy Document and User Guide)*. IPD, London, 1995.

INSTITUTE OF PERSONNEL AND DEVELOPMENT. *Professional Education Scheme*. IPD, London, 1996.

INSTITUTE OF PERSONNEL AND DEVELOPMENT. *Qualification Routes*. IPD, London, 1996.

INSTITUTE OF PERSONNEL AND DEVELOPMENT. *IPD Professional Standards*. IPD, London, 1997.

INSTITUTE OF PERSONNEL AND DEVELOPMENT. *The IPD Code of Professional Conduct and Disciplinary Procedures*. IPD, London, September 1997.

INSTITUTE OF PERSONNEL AND DEVELOPMENT. *Key Facts: On-the-job-training*. 1998. Website: www.ipd.co.uk

INSTITUTE OF PERSONNEL MANAGEMENT. *The IPM Code: Continuous Development: People and work*. IPM, London, 1984 and 1986.

INSTITUTE OF PERSONNEL MANAGEMENT. *TVEI Recommendations on improved School/Work Liaison*. IPM, London, 1984.

INSTITUTE OF PERSONNEL MANAGEMENT. *Towards a National Training and Development Strategy and An Action Plan for the UK*. IPM, London, 1992.

INVESTORS IN PEOPLE UK. *Investors in People: The benefits of being an Investor in People*. IiP, London, 1995.

INVESTORS IN PEOPLE UK. *Investors in People: How to get started*. Investors in People UK, London, 1997.

JACKSON L. 'Turning airport managers into high fliers'. *Personnel Management*, October 1989.

JACKSON N. and CARTER, P. *Rethinking Organisational Behaviour*, Financial Times Prentice Hall, Harlow, 2000.

JENNINGS S. and UNDY R. 'Auditing managers' IR training needs'. *Personnel Management,* February 1984.

JENSEN E. *Brain-Based Learning and Teaching*. Turning Point Publishing, Del Mar, California, 1995.

JESSUP G. *Outcomes: NVQs and the emerging model of education and training*. Falmer Press, London, 1991.

JOHN G. 'Share Strength' (Knowledge Management). *People Management,* 13 August 1998.

JOHNSON P.R. and INDVIK J. 'Using brain hemisphericity to enhance career management'. *The International Journal of Career Management,* Vol. 3, No. 3, 1991. Pages 3–10.

JOHNSON R. (1991) 'Neuro-linguistic programming'. in *Handbook of Training and Development*. Prior J. (ed.) Gower, Aldershot, 1991.

JONES A.M. and HENDRY C. *The Learning Organisation: A review of literature and practice*. The HRD Partnership, London, 1992.

JONES J.A.G. *The Evaluation and Cost Effectiveness of Training*. Industrial Training Service, London, 1970.

KAHN R.L., WOLFE D.M. et al. *Organizational Stress Studies in Role Conflict and Ambiguity*. Wiley, London, 1964.

KAMP D. 'Neuro-linguistic programming'. *Training and Development,* October 1991. Pages 36 and 38.

KAPLAN R.S. and NORTON D.P. 'The Balanced Scorecard: measures that drive performance'. *Harvard Business Review*. Jan/Feb 1992.

KAY H. 'Accidents: Some facts and theories', in *Psychology at Work*. Warr P. (ed.) Penguin Education, Harmondsworth, 1983.

KELLY G. A. *The Psychology of Personal Constructs*, Vols 1 and 2. Norton, New York, 1955.

KENNEY J.P.J. and REID M.A. *Training Interventions*. 2nd edn revised. Institute of Personnel Management, London, 1989.

KENNEY J.P.J., DONNELLY E.L. and REID M.A. *Manpower Training and Development*. Institute of Personnel Management, London, 1979.

KOHLER W. *The Mentality of Apes*. International Library of Psychology, Routledge, 1973.

KOLB D. *Experiential Learning: Experience as the source of learning and development*. Prentice Hall, Englewood Cliffs, 1984.

KOLB D.A., RUBIN I.N. and MCINTYRE J.M. *Organizational Psychology: A book of readings*. Prentice Hall, Englewood Cliffs, 1974.

KROUWEL W.G. *Outdoor Management Development: A critical introduction for the intelligent practitioner*. ITOL, Stockport, 2002.

LANK E. 'ICL's information supercafé'. *People Management,* 19 February 1998.

LAWRENCE P.R. and LORSCH J.W. *Organisation and Environment*. Harvard Graduate School of Business Administration, Cambridge, Mass., 1967.

LEWIN, K. *Field Theory in Social Sciences*. Harper and Row, New York, 1952.

LODGE D. *Nice Work*. Penguin Books, London, 1989.

MCGREGOR D. *The Human Side of Enterprise*. McGraw-Hill, Maidenhead, 1960.

MAGER R. F. *Preparing Instructional Objectives*. Fearon, California, 1984.

MALCOLM S. 'Most training is boring, ineffective or both.' ITOL Members' Forum. www.uk/cgi-local/dcf/dcextra.

MALONE S.A. *Learning about Learning*. CIPD, London, 2003.

MANAGEMENT CHARTER GROUP. *The Management Charter Initiative*. MCI, London, 1987.

MANCHESTER UNIVERSITY. *All Our Futures*. Centre for Education and Employment Research, University of Manchester, Manchester, 1993.

MANPOWER SERVICES COMMISSION. *Vocational Preparation for Young People*. MSC, Sheffield, 1975.

MANPOWER SERVICES COMMISSION. *Training of Trainers. Two reports from the Training of Trainers Committee*. HMSO, London, 1978 and 1980.

MANPOWER SERVICES COMMISSION. *Glossary of Training Terms*. MSC, HMSO, London, 1981.

MANT A. *Leaders We Deserve*. Martin Robertson, Oxford, 1983.

MANT, A. *Intelligent Leadership*. Allen and Unwin, St Leonards, 1997.

MARCHINGTON M. and WILKINSON A. *People Management and Development*, CIPD, London, 2002.

MARGERISON C. 'Margerison and McCann discuss the team management wheel'. *Industrial and Commercial Training*, Vol. 24, No. 1, 1992.

MARKS J. 'Britain out of training for world success'. *The Sunday Times*, 2 January 1996.

MASLOW A.H. 'A theory of human motivation'. *Psychological Review*, 50, 1943.

MAYO A. 'Memory bankers' (re Knowledge Management). *People Management*, 22 January 1998.

MAYO A. and LANK E. *The Power of Learning*. IPD, London, 1994.

MAYO E. *Human Problems of an Industrial Civilisation*. Macmillan, New York, 1933.

MEGGINSON D. and WHITAKER V. *Cultivating Self-Development*. IPD, London, 1996.

MERRICK N. 'The leisure principle'. *People Management*, 11 June 1998.

MINTZBERG H. *The Nature of Managerial Work*. Harper and Row, New York, 1973.

MINTZBERG H. 'The manager's job: folklore and fact'. *Harvard Business Review*, July 1975.

MOON J. *Reflection in Learning and Professional Development*. Kogan Page, London, 1999.

MOORBY E. *How to Succeed in Employee Development*. McGraw-Hill, Maidenhead, 1991.

MOORBY E. 'Mentoring and coaching' in *Gower Handbook of Training and Management Development*. Prior J. (ed.) (2nd edn), Gower, Aldershot, 1994.

MORGAN G. *Images of Organisation*. Sage Publications, London, 1997.

MUMFORD A. *Making Experience Pay*. McGraw-Hill, Maidenhead, 1980.

MUMFORD A. *Management Development*. IPM, London, 1989.

MUMFORD A. *Management Development: Strategies for action*. 2nd edn. IPM, London, 1993.

MUMFORD A. and GOLD, J. *Management Development*. CIPD, London, 2004.

NATIONAL ADVISORY COUNCIL FOR EDUCATION AND TRAINING TARGETS. *First Annual Report* (1993) and *Reports on Progress* (1994 and 1995). NACETT, London.

NATIONAL ADVISORY COUNCIL FOR EDUCATION AND TRAINING TARGETS. *Fast Forward for Skills: A summary of NACETT's report on future National Targets for Education and Training.* October 1998.

NATIONAL COUNCIL FOR VOCATIONAL QUALIFICATIONS. *National Vocational Qualifications: Criteria and procedures.* NCVQ, London, 1989.

NATIONAL COUNCIL FOR VOCATIONAL QUALIFICATIONS. *General National Vocational Qualifications.* NCVQ, London, 1991.

NATIONAL COUNCIL FOR VOCATIONAL QUALIFICATIONS. *NVQ Criteria and Guidance.* NCVQ, London, January 1995.

NATIONAL COUNCIL FOR VOCATIONAL QUALIFICATIONS. *Your Introduction to NVQs and GNVQs.* NCVQ, London, 1995.

NATIONAL ECONOMIC DEVELOPMENT OFFICE. *Young People and the Labour Market: A challenge for the 1990s.* NEDO, London, 1988.

NATIONAL INSTITUTE FOR ADULT AND CONTINUING EDUCATION. *The Learning Divide – A study of participation in adult learning in the United Kingdom.* NIACE, Leicester, 1998.

NATIONAL INSTITUTE FOR CAREERS EDUCATION AND COUNSELLING. *Helping People to Succeed: The future of the National Record of Achievement.* NICEC, Sheraton House, Castle Park, Cambridge, CB3 0ZX, 1995.

NATIONAL STATISTICS. 'Women in the Labour Market: results from the 2001 Labour Force Survey'. www.statistics.gov.uk/cci/article/asp.

NEALE F. *The Handbook of Performance Management.* IPM, London, 1991.

NIACE see National Institute for Adult and Continuing Education.

NONAKA I. and TAKEUCHI H. *The Knowledge-Creating Company.* Oxford University Press, New York, 1995.

NORD W.R. 'Beyond the teaching machine: The neglected area of operant conditioning in the theory and practice of management'. *Organizational Behaviour and Human Performance,* Vol. 4, 1969.

OPP LTD 'Lessons in leadership'. *Opinions,* October 2002.

OTTO C.P. and GLASER R.O. *The Management of Training.* Addison-Wesley, London, 1970.

PATRICK J. *Training: Research and practice.* Academic Press, London 1992.

PEARN M. and KANDOLA R. *Job Analysis: A practical guide for managers.* 2nd edn. IPD, London, 1993.

PEDLER M. et al. *The Learning Company: a strategy for sustainable development.* McGraw-Hill, London, 1991.

PEDLER M. and ASPINWALL K. *Learning in Company.* McGraw-Hill, UK, 1995.

PEDLER M., BURGOYNE J. and BOYDELL T. *A Manager's Guide to Self Development.* McGraw-Hill, Maidenhead, 1978.

PEDLER M., BURGOYNE J. and BOYDELL T. *The Learning Company Project.* Training Agency, Sheffield, 1988.

PEDLER M., BURGOYNE J. and BOYDELL T. *The Learning Organisation.* McGraw-Hill, Maidenhead, 1992.

PEDLER M., BURGOYNE J., BOYDELL T. and WELSHMAN A. (eds), *Self-development in Organisations.* McGraw-Hill, Maidenhead, 1990.

PEPPER A.D. *Managing the Training and Development Function.* Gower, Aldershot, 1984.

PERSAUD R. (1997) *Staying Sane.* Cygnus Books, Llandeilo, 1997.

PETERS, T. *Liberation Management.* Pan Books, London, 1993.

PETTIGREW A.M., JONES G.R. and REASON P.W. *Organisational and Behavioural Aspects of the Role of the Training Officer in the UK Chemical Industry.* Chemical & Allied Products Industry Training Board, Staines, 1981.

PETTIGREW A.M., SPARROW P. and HENDRY C. 'The forces that trigger training'. *Personnel Management,* December 1988.

PHILPOTT J. (2003) 'Hit the right note'. *People Management,* 25 September 2003.

PICKARD J. 'A Yearning for learning'. *People Management,* 6 March 1997.

PLETT P. and LESTER B.T. *Training for Older People.* ILO, Vincent House, Vincent Square, London SW1P 2NB, 1991.

PRAIS S.J. 'How Europe would see the new British initiative for standardising vocational qualifications'. *National Institute for Economic Review,* May 1991. Pages 52–5.

PRASHAR U. 'Evening up the odds for black workers'. *Personnel Management,* June 1983.

PRICKETT R. 'Employers unimpressed by graduates' lofty ambitions'. *People Management,* 3 September 1998. Page 19.

QUALIFICATIONS AND CURRICULUM AUTHORITY. *Data News,* Issues 9, 10 and 11. QCA, London, 1998–9.

REDMAN T. and MATHEWS B.P. 'Do corporate turkeys vote for Christmas? Managers' attitudes towards upward appraisal'. *Personnel Review,* Vol. 24, No. 7, 1995.

REID M.A. 'Approaches and strategies', in *Gower Handbook of Training and Development.* Prior J. (ed.) 2nd edn. Gower, Aldershot, 1994.

REID M.A. 'The use of written reports in action learning programmes or more traditional management development programmes'. *Training and Management Development Methods.* Vol 9, 1995 1.01–1.09.

REID M.A. 'A set within a set'. In *Action Learning at Work.* Mumford (ed.) Gower Publishing, Aldershot, 1997.

REVANS R. *Action Learning.* Blond & Briggs, London, 1980.

REVANS R. *The ABC of Action Learning.* Chartwell-Bratt, London, 1983.

RICHARDS-CARPENTER C. *Relating Manpower to an Organisation's Objectives.* Institute of Manpower Studies, Report No. 56, 1982.

RICHARDSON J. and BENNETT B. 'Applying learning techniques to on-the-job development: Part 2'. *Journal of European Industrial Training,* Vol. 8, No. 3, 1984.

RODGER A., MORGAN T. and GUEST D. *A Study of the Work of Industrial Training Officers.* Air Transport and Travel Industry Training Board, Staines, 1971.

ROLLINSON D. et al. *Organisational Behaviour and Analysis.* Addison-Wesley, Harlow, 1998.

ROSE C. *Accelerated Learning*. Accelerated Learning Systems Ltd, 50 Aylesbury Road, Aston Clinton, Aylesbury, 1991.

ROUTLEDGE C. 'Strategies of effective learners on interpersonal skills courses'. *Training and Management Development Methods*, Vol. 9, 1995. Pages 4.07–4.18.

ROUTLEDGE C. 'Brains, learners and trainers – a three-part series'. *Training and Management Development Methods*, Vol. 13, Section 7, 1999.

SCARBOROUGH H., SWAN J. and PRESTON J. *Knowledge Management and the Learning Organisation*. IPD, London, 1999.

SCHEIN E. H. *Process Consultation*. Addison-Wesley, Reading, Mass., 1969.

SCHEIN E. H. *Organisational Psychology*. Prentice Hall, New Jersey, 1970.

SCHÖN D. A. *The Reflective Practitioner*. Basic Books, New York, 1983.

SCOPE KETCHUM. Q115 – *On-line Distance Learning Research*. July 1998.

SELIGMAN M.E.P. *Helplessness*. Freeman, San Francisco, 1975.

SENGE P.M. *The Fifth Discipline: The art and practice of the learning organisation*. Century Business, London, 1990.

SENGE P.M., KLEINER A., ROBERTS C., ROSS R.B. and SMITH B.J. *The Fifth Discipline Fieldbook: strategies and tools for building a Learning Organisation*. Nicholas Brearley, London, 1998.

SENGE P.M., KLEINER A., ROBERTS C., ROSS R., ROTH G., SMITH B. et al. *The Dance of Change: The challenges of sustaining momentum in Learning Organisations*. Nicholas Brearley, London, 1999.

SEYMOUR W.D. *Industrial Training for Manual Operatives*. Pitman, London, 1954.

SHACKLETON J.R. and WALSH S. 'The UK's National Vocational Qualifications: the story so far'. *Journal of European Industrial Training*, Vol. 19, No. 11, 1995. Pages 14–27.

SHRIVASTAVA P. 'A typology of organisational learning systems'. *Journal of Management Studies,* Vol. 20, No. 1, Jan. 1983. Pages 7–28.

SINGER E. *Training in Industry and Commerce*. IPM, London 1977.

SINGER E. *Effective Management Coaching*. IPM, London, 1979.

SKINNER B. F. *Science and Human Behaviour*. Free Press, New York, 1965.

SKINNER B. F. *Walden Two*. Collier Macmillan, London, 1976.

SLOMAN M. 'Coming in from the cold: A new role for trainers'. *Personnel Management*, January 1994. Pages 24–27.

SLOMAN M. Learning curve. *People Management*. 25 September 2003. Pages 28–31.

SLOMAN M. *Training in the Age of the Learner*. CIPD, London, 2003.

SLOMAN M. *Change agenda: focus on the learner*. CIPD, London, 2003.

SPARROW S. 'Blended learning spices up the training mix'. *Training Magazine,* November 2003. Pages 10–11.

STAMMERS R. and PATRICK J. *Psychology of Training*. Methuen, London, 1975.

STEEDMAN H. and HAWKINS J. 'Shifting foundations: the impact of NVQs on youth training for the building trades'. *National Institute Economic Review,* Aug. 1994. Pages 93–102.

STEWART A. and STEWART V. *Tomorrow's Men Today*. IPM, London, 1976.

STEWART J. *Employee Development Practice*. Financial Times Prentice Hall, Harlow, 1999.

STEWART R. *Managers and their Jobs*. Macmillan, London, 1967/1988.

STEWART J. and HAMLIN R.G. 'Competence based qualifications: a way forward'. *Journal of European Industrial Training*. Vol. 17, 6, 1993.

STOREY J. (ed.) *Human Resource Management: a critical text*. Routledge, London, 1995.

TALBOT J.P. and ELLIS C.D. *Analysis and Costing of Company Training*. Gower, Aldershot, 1969.

TANNEHILL R.E. *Motivation and Management Development*. Butterworths, London, 1970.

TAVERNIER G. *Industrial Training Systems and Records*. Gower, Aldershot, 1971.

TAYLOR B. and LIPPITT G. (eds) *Management Development and Training Handbook*. 2nd edn. McGraw-Hill, Maidenhead, 1983.

TAYLOR M. *Coverdale on Management*. Heinemann, London, 1979.

TAYLOR S. *People Resourcing*. CIPD, London, 2002.

THATCHER M. '"Campus fugit" (BAe's Virtual University – British Aerospace Case Study)', *People Management*, 3 September 1998.

TOFFLER A. *Future Shock*. Bantam, New York, 1970.

TRACEY W.R. *Evaluating Training and Development Systems*. American Management Association, 1968.

TRIST E. *The Evolution of Socio-Technical Systems*. Ontario Ministry of Labour/Ontario Quality of Working Life Centre, Ontario, 1981.

TRIST E. et al. *Organisational Choice*. Tavistock, London, 1963.

TROMPENAARS F. *Riding the Waves of Culture*. Nicholas Brearley, London, 1994

VERNON P. E. *Intelligence and Attainment Tests*. London University Press, London, 1960.

VOGT O. 'Study of the ageing of nerve cells'. *Journal of Gerontology*, No. 6, 1951.

WALKER I. and REECE S. *Teaching, Training and Learning*. Business Education Publishers, 2003.

WALKIN L. *Training and Development NVQs*. Stanley Thorne, Cheltenham, 1996.

WALSH J. 'No stamp for passport to EU training'. People Management, June 1998. Page 15.

WANLESS D. (NACETT). 'Time for new targets: an open letter to David Blunkett.' www.tmag.co.uk, archive 14, 2001

WARR P.B., BIRD M. and RACKHAM N. *Evaluation of Management Training*. Gower Press, Aldershot, 1970.

WARWICK UNIVERSITY, Centre for Corporate Strategy and Change. Study for Department of Employment, 1991. Reported in *Skills and Enterprise Briefing*, February 1992. Employment Department, Moorfoot, Sheffield.

WATSON T. *Organising and Managing Work*. Financial Times, Prentice Hall, Harlow, 2000.

WEBER M. *The Theory of Social and Economic Organisation*. Oxford University Press, Oxford, 1947.

WELCH J. 'Stress ruling ups the stakes for employers'. *People Management*, 16 May 1996. Pages 13–14.

WELCH J. '"Discredited" degree grades under attack'. *People Management*. 24 July 1997.

WELCH J. 'HR blamed for employers' single-currency ignorance'. *People Management,* 30 April 1998. Page 10.

WELCH J. 'Police admit that £100m of training is misdirected'. *People Managemen*t, 3 September 1998. Page 9.

WELFORD A. T. 'On changes in performance with age'. *Lancet*, Part 1, 1962.

WELLENS J. 'The Exploitation of Human Resources', *The Times*, 16 August 1968.

WELLENS J. 'An approach to management training'. *Industrial and Commercial Training*, Vol. 8, No. 7, July 1970.

WHITELAW M. *The Evaluation of Management Training – A review.* IPM, London, 1972.

WHITTAKER J. 'Three Challenges for IPD Standards'. *People Management*, 16 November 1995.

WILLOUGBY B., SPENCE C. and GORMAN D. Conference paper presented at 'Geared Up for Learning', organised by the International Consortium for Employee Development, University of Salford, January 1996.

WILSON J. (ed) *Human Resource Development: learning and training for individuals and organisations.* Kogan Page, London, 1999.

WOLF A. 'Measuring competence: the experience of the United Kingdom'. *European Vocational Training*, Vol. 1, 1994.

WOOD S. (ed.). *Continuous Development: The path to improved performance.* IPM, London, 1988.

WOODRUFFE C. *Assessment Centres: Identifying and developing competence.* IPM, London, 1990.

WOODRUFFE C. 'What is meant by a competency?' in *Designing and Achieving Competency.* Sparrow P. and Boam R. (eds) McGraw-Hill, Maidenhead, 1992.

WOODS M. and THOMAS E. 'The Belbin Interface 111 – an expert system to assist personnel and trainers in personal and team development'. *Training and Management Development Methods,* Vol. 6, Section 2.01, 1992.

WOODWARD J. *Industrial Organisation, Theory and Practice.* Oxford University Press, Oxford, 1965.

WORSLEY R. 'Only prejudices are old and tired'. *People Management*, 11 January 1996. Pages 18–23.

XEBEC Intranet Technology and Training. *Is the marketplace ready for training on demand?* A Joint Survey between IT Training (Journal) and Xebec. McGraw-Hill, June 1998.

YOUNG R. 'The wide-awake Club' (re virtual teams). *People Management*, 5 February 1998.

INDEX